The Life of Allan Bennett,
Bhikkhu Ananda Metteyya

Allan Bennett, Bhikkhu Ananda Metteyya: Biography and Collected Writings

Elizabeth J. Harris
University of Birmingham

John L. Crow
Florida State University

This two volume work is devoted to the life and work of Allan Bennett, one of the first British men to gain higher ordination as a Buddhist monk and one of the seminal figures in the development of Buddhism in the UK.

Bennett rejected Christianity early in his life and turned to late-nineteenth-century occultism and esoteric new religious movements, namely Theosophy and the Hermetic Order of the Golden Dawn. His involvement in the latter led to a friendship with Alistair Crowley. After he travelled to Ceylon (Sri Lanka) around 1900, he was attracted to Buddhism. Believing that Buddhism in Burma (Myanmar) was purer than in Sri Lanka, he opted for ordination there in 1902.

From Burma, he created an international Buddhist network, founding the International Buddhist Society, the *Buddhasāsana Samāgama* and starting a journal, *Buddhism—An Illustrated Quarterly Review*. In 1908, he led a Buddhist mission to England. Convinced that the West needed Buddhism as an antidote to growing materialism, he became a prolific writer. Two volumes of his writings were published. The first, *The Wisdom of the Aryas*, which recorded a series of talks he gave in London in 1919–1920, was published just two months before he died. The second, *The Religion of Burma and Other Papers*, was published posthumously. Controversy has surrounded his life, particularly in Western Buddhist circles, because of his early involvement with occultism.

The Life of Allan Bennett, Bhikkhu Ananda Metteyya
(Volume 1)

Selected Writings of Allan Bennett, Bhikkhu Ananda Metteyya
(Volume 2)

The Life of Allan Bennett, Bhikkhu Ananda Metteyya

ELIZABETH J. HARRIS AND
JOHN L. CROW

SHEFFIELD UK   BRISTOL CT

Published by Equinox Publishing Ltd.

UK: Office 415, The Workstation, 15 Paternoster Row, Sheffield, South Yorkshire S1 2BX

USA: ISD, 70 Enterprise Drive, Bristol, CT 06010

www.equinoxpub.com

First published 2025

© Elizabeth J. Harris and John L. Crow 2025

All rights reserved. No part of this publication may be reproduced or transmitted in any form or by any means, electronic or mechanical, including photocopying, recording or any information storage or retrieval system, without prior permission in writing from the publishers.

British Library Cataloguing-in-Publication Data

A catalogue record for this book is available from the British Library.

ISBN-13 978 1 78179 798 3 (hardback)
         978 1 80050 651 0 (paperback)
         978 1 78179 799 0 (ePDF)
         978 1 80050 661 9 (ePub)

Library of Congress Cataloging-in-Publication Data

Names: Harris, Elizabeth J. (Elizabeth June), 1950- author. | Crow, John L., author.
Title: The life of Allan Bennett, Bhikkhu Ananda Metteyya / Elizabeth J. Harris and John L. Crow.
Description: Sheffield, South Yorkshire ; Bristol, CT : Equinox Publishing Ltd, 2025. | Series: Allan Bennett, Bhikkhu Ananda Metteyya | Includes bibliographical references and index. | Summary: "Biography of Allan Bennett, one of the first British men to gain higher ordination as a Buddhist monk and one of the seminal figures in the development of Buddhism in the UK"-- Provided by publisher.
Identifiers: LCCN 2025013181 (print) | LCCN 2025013182 (ebook) | ISBN 9781781797983 (hardback) | ISBN 9781800506510 (paperback) | ISBN 9781781797990 (pdf) | ISBN 9781800506619 (epub)
Subjects: LCSH: Ānanda Mettēyya, bhikkhu, 1872-1923. | Buddhist monks--Great Britain--Biography. | Buddhism--Great Britain--History.
Classification: LCC BQ942.A63 H37 2025 (print) | LCC BQ942.A63 (ebook) | DDC 294.3/657092 [B]--dc23/eng/20250527
LC record available at https://lccn.loc.gov/2025013181
LC ebook record available at https://lccn.loc.gov/2025013182

Typeset by Scribe Inc.

Contents

Acknowledgements	vii
Introduction: Ananda Metteyya and Liminality	1
1 The Formative Years	13
2 Allan Bennett in Ceylon	48
3 Ananda Metteyya in Burma	72
4 Ananda M's Mission to Britain and Return to Burma	130
5 In Britain: 1914–1923	168
6 Ananda Metteyya's Legacy	197
Concluding Thoughts	227
Selective Glossary	229
Notes	235
Bibliography	283
Index	309

Acknowledgements

During the six years that this research has taken, both Elizabeth and John have worked with many people that they would like to thank.

Elizabeth Harris would particularly like to thank those in Sri Lanka and Myanmar who facilitated her research. In Sri Lanka, Professor Asanga Tilakaratne found a wonderful research assistant for her, Ms. Sewwandi Marasinghe. Sewwandi was able to locate invaluable sources in Sinhala in the National Archives of Sri Lanka, and facilitated research visits to Kamburugamuwa and Vajirārāma Vihāraya. Grateful thanks must also go to the staff of the following libraries and archives: University of Peradeniya Library (Special Collections); the Museum Library; Mr. Amarasinghe and Ven. Banagala Upatissa of the Maha-Bodhi Society; the Young Men's Buddhist Association (YMBA) library and archives; the Theosophical Society library; and the libraries at Tulana Research Centre, Kelaniya. Among those who pointed her to valuable sources are Bindu Urugodawatta of the SAARC Cultural Centre, Professor Sunanda Mahendra and Professor Manouri Senanayaka. When she visited Kamburugamuwa, she was indebted to the Head Monk of the Divigalahēna Dēvāgiri Purāna Vihāraya, Malandeniye Vipassi Thera, and to Hewadiddenige Mahindaratne, the son of Peter Singho, who had been principal lay devotee at the temple and an expert in its history. Venerable Succitha of Vajirārāma Vihāraya in Bambalapitiya kindly helped her with the biographical background to the life of Cassius Pereira, a close friend of Ananda Metteyya, who was eventually ordained at the Vihāraya as Venerable Kassapa. This, in turn, led to contact with Dilkushi Pereira, niece of Cassius Pereira, who was able to give Elizabeth invaluable insights into the life and involvements of her uncle.

For Elizabeth's research in Myanmar, Alicia Turner and Francois Tainturier gave her invaluable assistance about whom to contact for permission to use the different archival sources in the country. One of these was U Thaw Kaung, former librarian at Yangon University Central Library, who gave unstintingly of his time, arranging a letter of recommendation for the National Archives, and meetings with the Head Librarians of the Universities' Central Library, and the National Library of Myanmar. His son, Thant Thaw Kaung, of the Myanmar Book Centre, also helped in this. Dr. Pyi Phyo Kyaw of Shan State Buddhist University recommended the person who became Elizabeth's research assistant, Ms. Swe Swe Mon. Swe became a rock of strength for Elizabeth, discovering numerous Burmese sources and answering questions right up to the point the manuscript was submitted. Elizabeth is very grateful to her. She is also grateful to the following librarians and archivists: U Ntin and Ms. Ni Ni Naing of the Universities' Central Library; Dr. Latt Latt Soe, Assistant Director of the National Archives Department; and Daw Yi Yi Htwe and Dr. Kong Thi Aye of the National Library of Myanmar. Ni Ni Naing helpfully introduced her to Ms. Aye Ohnmar Aung at the Kaba Aye Tipitaka Library, which also had some useful resources. In Mandalay, she is indebted to Dr. Than Yin Mar and Aung Myint Oo of Ludu U Hla Library. Aung Myint Oo helpfully accompanied her to the pagoda and monasteries that Ananda Metteyya had been linked with when he lived in Mandalay. She was also graciously hosted by the Theosophical Society in Yangon, and would particularly like to thank its then General Secretary U Htay Myint and its Vice President, Professor Dr. Thein Kyu.

Elizabeth is also grateful for conversations with and help in Myanmar from Ven. Professor Kammai Dhammasami; Ven. Dr. Dhammacara of Mandalay Sitagu International Buddhist Academy; Ven. Gandhamalabhivamsa of the Cluster of Middle Tawya Monasteries; Arvind D. Ram, who helped her through some Burmese material at the university library; Professor Hla Myint of the International Theravada Buddhist University; Aung Soe Min of Pansodan Gallery; Dr. Kerstin Duell; Professor Dr. Thein Hlyne, who helpfully took her to the Buddhist temple founded by Ven. Adiccavamsa; Professor Samuel Ngun Ling; Ms. Khin Khin Lwin; and Ko Pyay of Nawaday Tharlar Gallery, Yangon. Alicia Turner also answered questions throughout Elizabeth's research into Ananda Metteyya's time in colonial Burma.

Through Dr. Anna Allott, Elizabeth was put in touch with descendants of Daw Mya May (Mrs Hla Oung), Ananda Metteyya's primary sponsor in colonial Rangoon. This began with Maung Bo Bo (Bo Bo Lansin), then a student at the School of African and Oriental Studies, who introduced her to Khai or Sao Khaimong, who, in turn, put her in touch with Myadali, the great-granddaughter of May Oung, Daw Mya May's nephew. These family contacts gave her incredibly rich insights into the family that cared for and funded Ananda Metteyya in colonial Burma. It brought the biography of Ananda Metteyya alive.

In Britain, both Elizabeth and John are grateful to Ven. Galayaye Piyadassi Thera and Ven. Handupelpola Mahinda Nayake Thera of the Sri Saddhatissa International Buddhist Centre, and Desmond Biddulph and Odin Biddulph of The Buddhist Society, Ven. Professor Mahinda Deegalle and David Evans. Elizabeth is also grateful to Ven. Bogoda Seelawimala of the London Buddhist Vihara, Professor Kate Crosby, Professor Hiroko Kawanami, U San, Ron Maddox (former General Secretary of The Buddhist Society), Tom Pemberton, Dorienne Pemberton, Julia Williams and Joanna Hodgkin. In searching for the school in Bath that Bennett could have attended, she is grateful for the help of Richard Meunier, Record Office Manager of the Bath Record Office; Graeme Edwards, archivist at the Somerset Heritage Centre; Zoe Parsons of Kingswood School; and Emma-Louise Goymer of Prior Park College.

Thanks and appreciation must also go to those who helped Elizabeth in her early research into Ananda Metteyya, including Balangoda Ananda Maitriya Mahāthera (1896–1998), Sr. Nyāṇasirī (Helen Wilder d. 2004) and Myo Kyo Ni (Irmgard Schlögl 1921–2007).

John is very grateful to Kristie Crow for her love, support and patience. He is also grateful to C. V. Agarwal; W. Michael Ashcraft; Egil Asprem; Phil Baker; Betty Bland and Janet Kerschner of the Theosophical Society in America; Colyn Boyce and Barry Thompson of The Theosophical Society of England; Tim Boyd of the Theosophical Society, Adyar; Steve Brachel and 100th Monkey Press; William Breeze and Ordo Templi Orientis Archives; Mick Brown; Keith Cantú; Sasha Chaitow; Andre F. Clewell; Jan Cook at Lake County Library; John Corrigan; Nicholas Culpeper; Sally Davis; Anthony DeSantis; Renger Dijkstra of the Theosofische Bibliotheek in Amsterdam; Michael Effertz; Joscelyn Godwin; Matthew Goff; Karen Hamaker-Zondag; Wouter Hanegraaff; Clive Harper; Richard Kaczynski; Daniel Kline; Darcy Kuntz and the Golden Dawn Research Trust; Kurt Leland; Maria Montgomery; Marco Pasi; Amanda Porterfield; Keith Richmond and Marilyn Rinn at Weiser Antiquarian; Ian Rons; James A. Santucci; Justin Sledge; Adam Stout; Harriet Taite; Melody Talcott; and Tabitha Tuckett and Philip Young at the Warburg Institute.

Both Elizabeth and John are grateful to those who gave permission for the use of their illustrations and photographs. Tissa Madawela gave permission for them to use his photographs of Ananda Metteyya's lodgings in London, taken on behalf of the Sri Saddhatissa International Buddhist Centre in London. The Sri Saddhatissa International Buddhist Centre also gave permission for them to use a photograph held by them of Ananda Metteyya's first teacher of Pali in colonial Ceylon. Harriet Tait allowed them to use her photograph of another of Ananda Metteyya's lodgings, 42 Dorothy Road in South London. John Randall of Books of Asia very kindly allowed them to use a portrait of Ananda Metteyya that he had bought, painted by Gerald Festus Kelly (1879–1972), when he was in Burma from 1908–1909. Both Elizabeth and John thank Philip Young and the Warburg Institute for supplying the photographs of Bennett's notebooks. The Buddhist Society in London provided high-resolution copies of three of the magic lantern slides that Ananda M brought back to Britain in 1908, and of Alexander Fisher's crayon drawing of Ananda M, with permission to use them.

Thanks also go from both authors to Janet Joyce, Valerie Hall, and Sarah Lee of Equinox Publishing, whose patience when asked for repeated extensions to the submission deadline was exemplary. Thanks also go to Daniel Gronow for his copyediting, and to Mark Lee for producing the covers of both volumes.

Introduction

Ananda Metteyya and Liminality

Allan Bennett, who became the Buddhist monk Ananda Metteyya, appears in many accounts of the transmission of Buddhism to Britain and, more widely, to the west. The information given is sketchy and sometimes misleading.[1] Bennett tends to appear as a neat cardboard cut-out, with little depth or complexity, and as far less interesting or significant than, for instance, the Irish working-class opponent of the British Empire who became a Buddhist monk with the name U Dhammaloka—a contemporary of Ananda Metteyya.

This biography and the accompanying collection of edited writings (Volume Two) narrates a different story. It presents Allan Bennett as a liminal figure, who stretched across different nineteenth- and early twentieth-century contexts.[2] He gained a good education but lived in poverty and illness for a large part of his life, neither elite nor working class. He was able to live in Ceylon and Burma because of British imperialism, but mercilessly critiqued its failings in his writings. He became a Buddhist monk and brought one of the first Buddhist missions to London, but in his early years was a Theosophist and a ceremonial magician of some repute within the Hermetic Order of the Golden Dawn, and a close friend of Aleister Crowley. In addition, he never gave up forms of yogic meditation that he learnt from a Ceylonese Hindu teacher, Ponnambalam Ramanathan. As such, he was an insider and an outsider of both the Theravada Buddhist tradition and nineteenth-century occultism. For Ceylonese and Burmese Buddhists, he became a symbol of the agency and resilience of Buddhism under imperialism and Christian missionary attack, but for some Westerners he was a dubious figure and a 'sham' monk. For yet others in the West, he remained a magician, a master of hidden esoteric practices.

Allan Bennett was a morally intense and quite solitary person. He was born within the optimism of late Victorian England, as scientific discovery opened new worlds of possibility, but died after the death of this optimism through the massacre of a generation of young people in World War I. Self-trained as a scientist, he continuously sought scientific verification for Buddhist teachings about the mind, and could have made a career for himself in science. Yet, he also bought into the racist views of his day, concerning the superiority of the Aryan 'race,' within which he counted the people of India. In this context, he can be placed within the frameworks of orientalism and Buddhist modernism. Yet, at the same time, he contested several modernist representations of Buddhism in his appeal to the lived, devotional tradition in Ceylon and Burma, moving in his writings between the textual and the anthropological, and between Buddhist practice and academic research. After his death, people connected with the different facets of his life sought to claim him for their own, placing him within their own narratives, categories and histories. In addition, academics saw new aspects to his work. Todd LeRoy Perreira, for instance, argues that he was the first person to use the term 'Theravada' to denote the entire institutional culture of those Buddhist countries held together by the Pali Canon (LeRoy Perreira 2012).

Throughout most of his life, Ananda Metteyya suffered from chronic asthma. In the late 1880s, the remedies prescribed by doctors for asthma were opium, caffeine, iodine, morphine and ether. Patients were also encouraged to adjust their diets, as well to try different types of physical therapy. Thorowgood recommended the Epsic cigarette—containing, among other ingredients, belladonna, stramonium and opium—and also cannabis and morphine, as well as less toxic drugs (Thorowgood 1894: 87). Adam advised the use of cocaine and, with restrictions, morphine (Adam 1913). Wootton affirmed the beneficial effects of laudanum, an opium-based drug, in a variety of ailments (Wootton 1910). According to Mark Jackson, a historian of medicine, 'As a number of brief histories of inhaler technologies have indicated, most ancient cultures recommended inhaling smoke from burning certain plants for both therapeutic and recreational purposes [to treat asthma].' British doctors were no different, and, as Jackson continues, 'by the end of the nineteenth century fumigations, inhalations and smoking were regularly recommended by doctors and employed by patients in order to relieve and prevent debilitating paroxysms of asthma' (Jackson 2010: 184).

We are in no doubt that Bennett was recommended this kind of drug treatment. (Crowley 1989: 180). Crowley describes the cycle of his treatment vividly:

> His cycle of life was to take opium for about a month, when the effect wore off, so that he had to inject morphine. After a month

of this he had to switch to cocaine, which he took till he began to "see things" and was then reduced to chloroform. I have seen him in bed for a week, only recovering consciousness sufficiently to reach for the bottle and sponge. Asthma being a sthenic disease, he was then too weak to have it any more, so he would gradually convalesce until, after a few weeks of freedom, the spasms would begin once more and he would be forced to renew the cycle of drugs. (Crowley 1989: 180)

The effect of these drugs on his energy, his mental state and the way he was perceived in both Asia and the West cannot be underestimated.

Our new narrative, therefore, shows that Ananda Metteyya's life did not open to one key. On the one hand, Ananda Metteyya's personal struggle with poverty, illness and disappointed hopes is important. Buddhism spoke to his deep awareness of suffering at the heart of life as no other religion, in his experience, could. His goal-centred approach to life was thwarted by friends who disappointed him, and by his own physical limitations. His mind leapt continually ahead of him, his encounters with hard reality forcing him to rein it back. On the other hand, his life offers a complex lens through which the spiritual seekership of this period of history can be viewed, and the transmission of Buddhism to the West assessed. For what was true for Ananda Metteyya was also true for the history of Buddhism in the West. Concepts such as Buddhist modernism and Protestant Buddhism have been used to model the transmission of Buddhism to the West in the context of imperialism. Emphasis has been placed, for instance, on the orientalist tendency of scholars such as T. W. Rhys Davids (1843–1922), who saw Buddhist texts as the ultimate bearer of meaning (e.g., King 1999: 143–160; Harris 2006: 125–138). Less attention has been placed on other cultural and religious streams that fed into this history, such as the role of Theosophy, esotericism and occultism.[3] The life of Ananda Metteyya demonstrates the inadequacy of accounts that ignore these elements. They were key to the early reception of Buddhism in the West, and conditioned the negotiation of boundaries within early Western Buddhist communities.

Given the importance of the Theosophical Society and the concept of occultism in Ananda Metteyya's history, it is worth saying something about them here. Founded in 1875 in New York City by Henry Steel Olcott (1832–1907) and Helena Petrovna Blavatsky (1831–1891), usually referred to as 'Madame Blavatsky,' the Theosophical Society was created at first to explore Western esoteric ideas, in opposition to Modern Spiritualism, which the founders claimed misunderstood how the spirit world operates and what happens to people when they die. At first, the orientalism of the Society's members understood 'the East' to mean Egypt. However, after a few years, the Society set its sights on Tibet and India as 'the East,' with its founders relocating to Adyar, India, which is in modern Chennai. Along the way, Olcott and Blavatsky began incorporating Hinduism and Buddhism into their esoteric teachings, both becoming the basis of what Blavatsky termed 'occultism.'

The word 'occultism' entered the English language in 1871, in Albert Pike's well-known Freemasonic text, *Morals and Dogma* (Pike 1871). The word was adopted in 1875 by Helena Blavatsky as a label for her teachings. Her initial use of the term established a contrast with Spiritualism and its claims about life after death. Later, Blavatsky expanded her definition. Occultism was a system of so-called 'Ancient Wisdom' relating to the spiritual evolution of humanity and the universe, which she claimed had begun in antiquity and had been passed down through the ages. Among her claims, which all became associated with the term 'occultism,' was that there were spiritually advanced men and women, called 'The Masters' or 'Mahatmas' (Great Ones), secretly guiding humanity's spiritual development, and that Buddhism and Hinduism were the religions that had best kept this 'Ancient Wisdom' intact. As a consequence, the Theosophical Society was responsible for educating the average person in Europe and North America about karma, reincarnation and many other Eastern religious concepts. Theosophists also performed the first cremation in the United States of America, drawing on Eastern precedents (Prothero 1996; 2001; Hammer and Rothstein 2013).

As more people learned about the Theosophical Society and its esoteric teachings, some joined hoping to learn practical occultism, to obtain magical abilities similar to those claimed by Spiritualist mediums. Blavatsky resisted this, stating that occultism required years of study and great emotional and spiritual discipline, before even the most basic of practices could be taught (Crow 2012). As a result, members of the Society began looking for other ways to learn practical occultism. One of these was through The Hermetic Order of the Golden Dawn, hereafter referred to as the Golden Dawn. This organisation, founded in London in 1888, claimed to teach practical occultism, including the arts of ceremonial magic, alchemy, astrology and much more. Many members of the Theosophical Society were also members of the Golden Dawn. Perhaps one of the most well known was the poet William Butler Yeats (1865–1939). In response to the founding of the Golden Dawn, Blavatsky created the Esoteric Section of the Theosophical Society, promising to teach practical occultism to the worthy. However, even here she resisted, continuing to favour theoretical versus practical occultism.

Occultism, the Theosophical Society, and the Golden Dawn all emerged at a time when the boundaries between religion, science and magic, as well as between the material and spiritual worlds, were porous. They all operated in liminal and complex spaces within the West, as well as in the colonised East. The liminal, as we have already stressed, is also where Ananda Metteyya lived and practised. As a result, up to now, no biographical attempt has been made to piece together the myriad facets of his life. Occultists lose interest in him once he leaves for Ceylon around 1900, because he renounced occultism. In contrast, Buddhists, especially scholars of Buddhism, have had little to no interest in Bennett prior to 1900, since what he was involved in was considered to be pseudoscience. The policing of these boundaries leaves Allan Bennett and Ananda Metteyya fragmented, prone to misrepresentation and subject to reinterpretation and appropriation.

The liminality and complexity of Ananda Metteyya's biography is reflected in the different names by which he was known. Born Charles Henry Bennett, after his mother had changed her name, 'Allan' was added when he was a teenager. Under the influence of one of his mentors in the Golden Dawn, he added 'MacGregor' to 'Allan' as a lay person and sometimes passed himself off as Allan MacGregor. When he was ordained with the name Ananda Metteya Sāsanajotika, he changed this at first to 'Maitriya,' the Sinhala pronunciation of 'Metteyya' in Ceylon, a cross between Pali and Sanskrit. Later, he was persuaded by Charles Lanman to revert to the Pali, 'Metteyya.'[4] The name he preferred to call himself in his later years in Burma, however, was Ananda M. After he disrobed and returned to England, he did not return to his lay name, at least not when he wrote for publication, but continued to use 'Ananda M.' Due to the variety of names he used during his lifetime, with the exception of this introduction, we will use the name Allan Bennett prior to his ordination in Burma and Ananda M throughout the rest of the biography.

CO-WRITING THE BIOGRAPHY

The two authors of this biography encountered the life of Ananda Metteyya in different ways, and brought different academic specialisms to the task of re-constructing the narrative of his life. Elizabeth Harris encountered the writings of Ananda Metteyya in the early 1990s in the library of the Buddhist Publication Society in Kandy, which held *The Wisdom of the Aryas* (Bennett 1923) and *The Religion of Burma and Other Papers* (Bennett 1929). She was carrying out research for a doctorate in Buddhist Studies on the encounter between the British and Buddhism in nineteenth-century Ceylon, and was impressed by the passion and poetry in Ananda Metteyya's writing. Here was a British person who contested, with the enthusiasm of the convert and the knowledge of a scholar, the negative representations of Buddhism that she had encountered in so much nineteenth-century writing, particularly from the pens of Christian missionaries. Ananda Metteyya was, therefore, brought into her doctorate as 'a convert to compassion,' who spanned the nineteenth and twentieth centuries and contested, for instance, the orientalist tendency to reduce the stature of the Buddha (Harris 1993: 351–369; 2006: 148–160). After her doctorate, she investigated the thought of Ananda Metteyya further, for a booklet published by the Buddhist Publication Society (Harris 1998). The biographical sketch included within it was based on limited sources and perpetuated a couple of misconceptions. She met John L. Crow when she was asked to supervise and examine his research MA on Allan Bennett, and a dream developed between them to write a more accurate and nuanced biography.

John L. Crow encountered Allan Bennett in 2007, while preparing for his master's degree in Religious Studies, with a focus on Western Esotericism, at the University of Amsterdam. One of the books suggested as preparation for the programme was Joscelyn Godwin's *The Theosophical Enlightenment* (Godwin 1994). As covered in more detail in Chapter Six, Godwin's book ends with a chapter on the encounter between East and West. Allan Bennett emerged in his narrative as a pivotal figure in this encounter. Having previously studied Buddhism while earning his undergraduate degree, and having spent a month at a Buddhist Monastery in Taiwan, a historical figure who combined both esotericism and Buddhism became very interesting to Crow, and potentially a topic for his MA thesis. Crow contacted Godwin, who was kind enough to send copies of the Bennett material he had. Entering the MA programme in Amsterdam, Crow studied under Marco Pasi, one of the world's authorities on Aleister Crowley, who was Bennett's magical student in the Golden Dawn. Under the direction of Marco Pasi, Wouter Hanegraaff and Elizabeth Harris, Crow completed his MA thesis on Bennett (Crow 2009). After this, Crow returned to the United States to begin a doctoral programme in Religious Studies at Florida State University, focusing on American religious history. His dissertation examined the role of the Theosophical Society and the place of the body within its teachings (Crow 2017). After completing his dissertation, Crow and Harris, hereafter 'we,' began work on the biography of Allan Bennett/Ananda Metteyya that you have before you.

RESEARCH METHODS

In working together, we divided the chapters between us, each according to our specialisms, but took joint responsibility for the whole, adding to each other's chapters and sections, and challenging each other at crucial points. Our exploration has been exciting but has had its setbacks. We have met with suspicion and non-responsiveness, for example from some individuals and organisations with a stake in the legacy of Ananda Metteyya. We have even been contacted by different individuals claiming to be the reincarnation of Ananda Metteyya. Our primary method of data collection has been archival research in Myanmar, Sri Lanka, the United Kingdom and the United States of America. This has been complemented by personal contact with descendants of Ananda Metteyya's friends and sponsors in colonial Ceylon and Burma. The names of these people, to whom we are most grateful, are given in the Acknowledgements section. Elizabeth visited Sri Lanka and Myanmar twice for data collection, particularly to access material in Sinhala and Burmese. She was helped by two wonderful research assistants, Ms. Sewwandi Marasinghe and Ms. Swe Swe Mon. She also worked closely with The Buddhist Society in London to recover the early history of Buddhism in Britain.

Finding documents relating to the early life of Bennett was especially difficult, as he lived in poverty at times, moved frequently, and then abandoned most of his possessions when he left for Ceylon. Fortunately, he gave many of his notebooks and letters to his magical student, Aleister Crowley, who retained them all his life. After Crowley's death, many have researched and collected material on Crowley and those connected to him. This material is now stored in archives located in both the United Kingdom and the United States, and these institutions and organisations have been extremely helpful, especially the Warburg Institute in the University of London, the Theosophical Society in England, and the Ordo Templi Orientis, headquartered in the United States. With their help, and the help of many others, we have been able to piece together Bennett's life prior to his departure from England. Additionally, today's genealogical archives and systems have contributed to our ability to cover much of Bennett's genealogy. While we are pleased with what we have recovered about his early life, we know there is much more to be learned. We look forward to the work of those who come after us, who will expand, deepen and possibly correct what we have discovered.

A BROAD READERSHIP

These volumes will appeal to both academic specialists and non-specialists. While written broadly for those within the academic disciplines of Buddhist Studies and Esoteric Studies, they will nevertheless appeal to anyone interested in what this introduction has termed 'spiritual seekership.' The Theosophical Society did much to popularise Buddhism in the late nineteenth and early twentieth centuries, and many in the West connected Buddhism with esotericism due to publications such as *Esoteric Buddhism* (Sinnett 1883), and to Theosophical assertions that Buddhism was a continuation of the Ancient Wisdom tradition central to occultism. By the first decades of the twentieth century, however, many Buddhists were policing the boundaries between Buddhism and esotericism. This effort was joined from the 1980s by scholars of Buddhism. For example, Philip Almond, in *The British Discovery of Buddhism*, excludes anyone associated with Theosophy from his history:

> Only at the end of the century do we have any clear cases of conversions to Buddhism, though here it is generally to the somewhat eccentric and spiritualistic Esoteric Buddhism of Madame Blavatsky and her Theosophical Movement. Not until 1907 were there sufficient persons, either Buddhists or as students of Buddhism, to form a Buddhist Society of Great Britain and Ireland. (Almond 1988: 36)

A footnote to the first sentence of the above gives an example of this kind of boundary policing. Almond writes, 'I have not dealt with the Esoteric Buddhism of Madame Blavatsky and her English disciple, Alfred Sinnett. Esoteric it may have been. Buddhism, it certainly was not, at least in the eyes of most late nineteenth-century interpreters of Buddhism' (Almond 1988: 147n10). The irony in Almond's statements, as will be shown in this biography, is that the 1907 creation of the Buddhist Society of Great Britain and Ireland mentioned in the above quote would not have taken place without Bennett and his involvement with the Theosophical Society, the group Almond so quickly dismisses.

Thomas Tweed, in his history of Buddhism's emergence in America (Tweed 1992), is an exception to this, in that he includes significant mention of 'Esoteric Buddhists,' but most scholars, when discussing Buddhism in the West, have included only a brief mention of this history, if any mention is made at all. For instance, David McMahan's excellent *The Making of Buddhist Modernism* devotes approximately four pages to 'Olcott's Theosophical Buddhism and Occult Science' (McMahan 2008: 97–101), and this is one of the longer engagements. At the time of the writing of this biography, there is no single book or monograph dedicated exclusively, or even primarily, to examining the role of esotericism/occultism/Theosophy in the spread of Buddhism in the West. Perhaps the closest is Prothero's biography of Olcott (Prothero 1996). However, a biography is not a sustained examination of the Western adoption of Buddhism. Yet, like Prothero's biography, we hope that this study will show that the distance between esotericism, especially occultism, and Buddhism, in the late nineteenth and early to mid-twentieth centuries, is not as wide as many imagine. Biographies, however, are not substitutes for comprehensive histories of a topic.

Scholars of Western Esotericism are no better, unfortunately. Buddhism rarely emerges in their historical examinations, and, when it does, it is a minor inclusion. For instance, the index of the excellent survey of Theosophical history, Brill's *Handbook of the Theosophical Current* (Hammer and Rothstein 2013), contains only 48 pages, out of 500, that make reference to Buddhism, and these are scattered throughout the volume. There is no sustained discussion of Buddhism and Theosophy.

The policing of the boundaries between Buddhism and esotericism must be challenged. This biography is only possible because the authors combined their extensive backgrounds in both Buddhist and Esoteric Studies. If scholars of Buddhism are to grasp the full history of how Buddhism emerged in the West, the interaction of Buddhism and occultism will have to be taken more seriously. If scholars of Western Esotericism are to understand the greater impact of occultism, the history of Buddhism needs to be taken into account. We hope that our biography will highlight the need for these interdisciplinary examinations.

Lastly, we hope that this volume will appeal to both practising Buddhists and occultists interested in the histories of their movements. Each will see that Allan Bennett/Ananda Metteyya had a significant influence on both movements, with a legacy that is still visible today. We hope readers interested in the life of one of Crowley's main teachers will see why Frater I.A. had To Mega Therion's, that is, Crowley's, deepest respect for his entire life. Those interested in how Buddhism became established in England will find that Ananda Metteyya played a large but forgotten role. As we understand that some of our readers may not be familiar with either the Buddhist or esoteric terminology, we have attempted to define technical terms when used for the first time to make the text as accessible to all readers as possible.

STYLISTIC POINTS

In our bibliography, we list Ananda Metteyya's works according to the name given on the publications themselves. For instance, when Ananda Metteyya lectured on the four noble truths in Colombo in 1901, before his ordination, he was calling himself Allan MacGregor, and the lecture was subsequently published under that name. It is, therefore, listed in the bibliography under 'MacGregor.' In referring to the two Asian countries that Ananda Metteyya visited in his spiritual quest, we use the names current in Ananda Metteyya's time, namely Ceylon and Burma (now Sri Lanka and Myanmar). Technical terms are italicised with the use of diacritical marks, with the exception of words that have been anglicised to the extent that they appear in the Oxford English Dictionary, for example Mahayana, Theravada and nirvana. We have also not used a diacritical on 'Ananda.' Place names in Ceylon and Burma are represented through their contemporary English spellings.

STRUCTURE OF THE BOOK

Chapter One covers Allan Bennett's life from his birth in 1872 to his departure from England around 1900. Calling this time his 'Formative Years,' we begin by examining what his early years were like, when he lived with the support of his grandfather, who was employed in the arts as a theatrical manager. His life changed dramatically with the death of his grandparents and mother. From that point forward, Bennett depended on the support of his sister, while also taking every educational and employment opportunity presented to him. These opportunities, however, were limited by his poverty and poor health. It is during this period that he encountered both Buddhism and occultism. The first group he engaged with was the Theosophical Society, and through it he was introduced to the Golden Dawn. In 1899, he met Aleister Crowley through the Golden Dawn and both lives were changed. Bennett began teaching Crowley the art and science of ceremonial magic, and Crowley gave Bennett a place to live. This relationship continued until the Golden Dawn in London began to deteriorate, and Bennett boarded a steamer for Ceylon. Despite leaving occultism behind in practice, Bennett never fully abandoned thinking like an occultist. As will be shown in the subsequent chapters, ideas and a worldview originating in both the Theosophical Society and the Golden Dawn continued to influence Bennett for the rest of his life.

Chapter Two examines Bennett's brief but important time in Ceylon. He arrived at the beginning of 1900 and almost immediately travelled from Colombo to the south of the island to study Pali and Buddhism at a *vihāra* (Buddhist monastery/temple) in Kamburugamuwa. After about six months, he returned to Colombo. Here, he studied yogic practices under a Hindu politician and Śaivite teacher who was becoming internationally known, Ponnambalam Ramanathan (1851–1930). What he learnt under Ramanathan would also stay with him for the rest of his life. However, it was Buddhism rather than Śaivism that he chose for the lecture he gave at a Theosophical Society lodge in Colombo in July 1901. Shortly afterwards, he travelled to other parts of the island with Aleister Crowley, and then to Burma for ordination as a Buddhist monk. This chapter demonstrates that Bennett's path towards ordination passed through Hindu yoga, meditation and ritual.

Chapter Three charts Allan Bennett's ordination as Venerable Ananda Metteyya in Burma until his mission to Britain in 1908. He gained his novice and higher ordination in Akyab (now Sittwe in Rakkhine State) and, whilst there, wrote two articles that he sent to friends in Ceylon for publication. These laid the foundation for much of his later writing. Soon after his higher ordination, he moved to Mandalay, where he was re-ordained within a relatively new, reformist monastic fraternity. From there, he travelled to Rangoon (now Yangon), from where he developed, with wealthy patronage, his plan to bring Buddhism to the West, through the *Buddhasāsana Samāgama* (International Buddhist Society) and the publication of the journal, *Buddhism*. During this period, Ananda Metteyya, although still hindered by asthma, was productive and energetic. Although unable to speak Burmese, he taught in other parts of the country with the help of translators, and was influential among English-speaking Buddhists in Rangoon, becoming a symbol of Buddhism's resilience under British colonialism and the Christian missionary threat.

Chapter Four focuses on Ananda Metteyya's six-month mission to Britain in 1908 and his last years in Burma. The mission occupied a liminal space between success and failure. Ananda Metteyya's hope that thousands would embrace Buddhism, if it was preached effectively, was always doomed to failure, and he was hard on himself that so few converted. Yet, there were also successes, not least the formation of a functioning, if cash-strapped, Buddhist Society of Great Britain and Ireland, with a nucleus of committed Western Buddhists. After returning to Burma, his last six years in the country were marred by illness, the struggle to keep the Buddhist Society in London financially afloat, disappointed hopes and a legal case that went to court in 1910, which implicated him as a former friend of Aleister Crowley, who, by that time, had acquired a notorious reputation in the eyes of the public. Yet, he continued to write and maintain international contacts, for instance with the Theosophical Society. This chapter uncovers the forces that gathered around Ananda Metteyya in these years, tarnishing his reputation and abilities.

Chapter Five examines the last nine years of Ananda Metteyya's life in Britain. He was forced to return to Britain because of the state of his health, and therefore disrobed (becoming a lay person again), because the journey would involve handling money. His intention was to join his sister on her return to the United States of America. When his passage to America was refused because of his illnesses, Buddhists in the Liverpool area looked after him, with the Buddhist Society raising money for his support. Towards the end of World War I, his health rallied and he returned to London, taking on responsibilities within the Buddhist Society, his passion for Buddhism undiminished. During these years, he struggled with poverty and chronic illness but continued to influence many through lectures, writing and conversation. He died of an intestinal obstruction on 9 March, 1923.

The last chapter explores a selection of the diverse ways in which Ananda Metteyya was appropriated and remembered after his death by both Buddhists and esotericists. In Asia, he was remembered as a pioneer of Buddhist missions to the West, a symbol of the international appeal of Buddhism in the face of Western Christian hegemony. In Western esoteric and occultist circles, he was lauded as a magician who never left occultism behind, becoming an almost mythical role model. Within Western Buddhist groups, his pioneering 1908 mission was not forgotten, but new initiatives, which distanced themselves from his memory, developed. In the 1990s, however, the Sri Saddhatissa International Buddhist Centre in London brought him to the fore again. We argue that few posthumous representations of Ananda Metteyya, including academic ones, brought the whole of his life together, taking into account his significance not only within the transmission of Buddhism to the West but also within Western esotericism.

VOLUME ONE AND VOLUME TWO

Volumes One and Two are closely related. In Volume One, the content of Ananda Metteyya's articles and other writings are summarised in the context of the different stages of his life, in order to demonstrate the intention behind each piece, the progression of his thought, and the way he adapted to different audiences in Asia and the West. Volume Two gives the full text of a selection of his writings to convey the subtleties, complexities and beauty within his writing. We cross-reference to Volume Two at the first mention of each publication in Volume One. The number of technical terms connected with esotericism and occultism in the first four items in Volume Two, which date from the period before Allan Bennett became a Buddhist monk, have necessitated detailed annotations. His articles on Buddhism, on the other hand, are not annotated. The technical terms present in these articles are explained in the Glossary in Volume One. Ananda M's own footnotes remain as footnotes in Volume Two. Annotations from the editors appear as endnotes.

1

The Formative Years

Describing and documenting the early years of Allan Bennett's life is challenging because there is so little information about them, and the material that does exist, including the statements from Bennett himself, are unreliable and contradictory. The reasons for this unreliability vary. Bennett moved frequently when growing up. He struggled with poverty when his maternal grandparents died, and he and his sister may have been illegitimate children. Add to this that, upon taking ordination in the Buddhist monastic Sangha, Bennett gave up all his worldly possessions, and the result is a fragmented history, assembled from a wide variety of sources.

Charles Henry Bennett was born on 8 December, 1872, in the Notting Hill district of London.[1] The name he would go by, Allan, was not part of his name at birth, but was adopted in his adolescence. His mother, according to census records, was named Mary Ann Bennett. However, all evidence indicates that her original name was Charlotte P. Corbyn, and that she was born in 1850 in New York City. It seems that Charlotte Corbyn changed her name to Mary Ann Bennett around the time of her first child's birth, a daughter she named Charlotte Louisa Bennett, on 9 October, 1870, in Brompton, London.[2] Louisa Corbyn (1807–1884) was the name of Mary Ann's mother. 'Charlotte Louisa' was thus a combination of Mary Ann's previous name, and her mother's first name. Bennett claimed his father was named Charles and that he was an engineer. He said that this was where his interests in chemical and electrical engineering stemmed from. However, Charles is not listed as living with Mary Ann in the 1871 census. He is indirectly referenced by her when she states her occupation as 'Civil Engineer's Wife,' but his name is never given. In the 1881 census, Mary Ann is listed as a widow. The only other documentation that mentions Charles is Charlotte Louisa's marriage certificate, which lists her father as Charles Bennett, deceased, and with the profession of electrical engineer. Beyond these fragments, there is no indication Charles Bennett existed. More about Bennett's father is below.

In his earliest years, Bennett grew up in a middle-class environment, supported by his maternal grandfather, Wardle Corbyn (1811-1880). Corbyn was a theatre manager, producer, writer, translator and publisher. He had offices in New York City, London and Paris. Most of the English libretti of musicals and operas he translated and published were from French. In addition to his translation and publishing work, Wardle managed travelling acts. For instance, in February 1845, he travelled to New Orleans to find musicians who played violin, flute or piano. If they were willing to travel, he promised them he would find them consistent performance engagements. At other times, he produced plays in New York and London, some being very successful, and others being complete failures, resulting in the productions going bankrupt. Nevertheless, in New York, he managed talent such as dancers, performing ballet, and actors in opera, performing in Broadway theatres such as Niblo's Garden. In London, he assisted in productions in prestigious venues such as Theatre Royal Drury Lane and The Royal Park Theatre, in Camden Town, as well as less affluent venues, such as in Cremorne Gardens near Battersea Bridge, and the Surrey Gardens Music Hall near Kennington. Due to Wardle Corbyn's occupation, Bennett would have been exposed to drama, in the form of plays, opera, ballet and pantomime. Corbyn's translation of libretti would also have given him access to cultural writings in both English and French, as well as poetry, and other literary forms. Long before he joined any esoteric organisation, Bennett was reading Buddhist and Hindu scriptures. He would have had to obtain them from somewhere, and a good candidate for his access would have been his grandfather. Although Bennett stressed his analytical mind and his love of science, he was also a good writer, despite having limited schooling. All these factors strongly suggest that Bennett had access to a diverse array of performance and literary material connected to culture and the arts. The famous actress Clara Fisher Maeder (1811-1898) notes meeting Wardle in the Drury Lane Theatre in her autobiography. Wardle was the assistant stage manager at the time. She also states that Wardle's father was her 'dancing-master in former days' (Maeder 1897: 39). Involvement with the arts was a family tradition.

Wardle and Louisa Corbyn had seven children. They were Rosa (b. 1832/1833), Sheridan 'Sherry' (1834-1904), Roland (b. 1838), Josephine Madeleine (b. 1840), Harry Wardle (b. 1844), Katherine Blandford 'Kate' (1849-1871) and Charlotte (b. 1850). Bennett's oldest aunt, Rosa, appears to have had some type of cognitive disability that resulted in her living with her parents her whole life. Upon her parent's death, she was institutionalised. The 1891 census lists her as living in the Eastbourne Union workhouse and hospital in Eastbourne, Sussex. Her condition is noted as 'imbecile.' There are no further records relating to her. She most probably died in the 1890s. Rosa would have exposed Bennett to cognitive disability early in his life, and this could have influenced, even if unconsciously, his later interest in the mind.

Bennett's uncle Sherry was born in England but emigrated with his parents to America in 1835. When his parents and siblings returned to the UK around 1860, Sherry remained in America. He followed in his father's footsteps, becoming a theatrical producer in New York City, as well as buying and selling real estate. He often worked with his father, where they both managed the same actors or performers. Wardle managed the European venues and Sherry, the American.[3]

American census records for the 1850s indicate that Bennett had an older uncle named Roland. Born circa 1838, Roland is listed as living with his parents in both 1850 and 1855. However, he fails to show up in any records afterwards. By the time his parents relocated back to England, he was old enough to stay in America. If he had stayed, records would probably exist, as for Sheridan. In contrast, if had travelled with his parents to England, there should be records in England. Yet there are none. Perhaps he died sometime between 1855 and 1860 without his death being recorded. It is simply not clear what happened to Roland.

Allan's second oldest aunt, Josephine Madeleine, was born in New York but moved to England to attend Cambridge University, where she earned a BA in 1849 and an MA in 1852. She remained in London after her graduation and became a lawyer in 1859. In 1863 she married Robert Walter Daysh Stewart (1826-1866), also a barrister, in Chelsea, London. They had two children, Katharine Alexandra (1865-1942), and Walter James Lionel (1866-1854).[4]

Little is known about Allan's uncle, Harry Wardle Corbyn. He was born in New York in about 1844. When Wardle and Louisa moved back to London from New York, Harry joined them. Yet, by 1866, Harry had made his way to San Francisco. Shortly afterwards, he met and married Minnie Loder (b. 1845). The marriage was held in Manhattan in 1868. After the marriage, the couple returned to San Francisco. As he moved to America before Allan was born, it is unlikely they ever met. However, as detailed later, Allan's sister moved to America and married in San Francisco. Perhaps she knew of Harry, and they met when she moved there.

Like Harry, little is known about Allan's aunt, Kate. Born in 1848 in New York, Kate accompanied her parents when they relocated to London.

She lived with Allan's mother after his sister, Charlotte, was first born. Yet, Allan never knew his aunt Kate. She died and was buried in April 1871 in Brompton Cemetery. It is likely that she died of a communicable disease, as the burial register notes that her body was buried at an extra depth of 14 feet, when bodies were typically buried about eight feet deep.

Wardle and Louise Corbyn's last child was Charlotte, Allan's mother. Born in New York, Charlotte joined her parents in relocating to London, living in the Chelsea area, one of the more affluent areas of London.[5] Wardle continued in theatre management and travelled via steamer between London and New York. Despite the ups and downs of theatrical production, the Corbyn family lived a comfortable, middle-class life, which included having live-in servants. This changed for Charlotte in 1870 when she became pregnant. On 9 October, 1870, her first child, Charlotte Louisa, was born, in Brompton, London. After her daughter's birth, Charlotte began residing in her own home, living under the name Mary Ann Bennett. The name change to Mary Ann and Bennett, both very common names, and the fact that she did not return to the Corbyn household, suggests that Charlotte Louisa was born outside of wedlock.

In 2016, author Phil Baker gave a lecture about Allan Bennett to The Buddhist Society in London, in which he claimed Bennett and his sister were illegitimate. Later reprinted in the Society's journal, *The Middle Way* (Baker 2017: 24), Baker claims that Bennett's father, instead of being Charles Bennett, an electrical engineer, was 'an eminent Victorian scientist, or more accurately a technologist,' that he was 'knighted for scientific achievement,' and that he 'maintained more than one family.' Unfortunately, Baker does not name the individual nor his sources, making his statements unverifiable. Nevertheless, there may be some truth to the statements and, if so, they help explain the reason for the paucity of information regarding Allan's and Charlotte Louisa's father. Additionally, it is not clear if Charlotte Louisa and Allan had the same father, as we have no indication of who he was.[6]

The 1871 census lists Mary A. Bennett as the head of a household living at 9 Fulham Road, Brompton, Kensington, London, an upper-middle-class area.[7] Living with her was her five-month-old daughter, Charlotte L., her 22-year-old sister, Kate Corbyn, and their 20-year-old housekeeper, Esther Wharton. As previously mentioned, the census record lists Mary's occupation as 'Civil Engineer's Wife.' The fact that Mary is listed as head of the household and not her husband is uncommon for married couples. It is also no coincidence that Mary Bennett's residence was close to her father's office, which was located half a mile away at 340 Fulham Road.

Wardle continued to provide for his daughter, including paying for a servant. Mary Ann also continued to receive familial support, with her sister, Kate, living with her, at least for a short period of time. As stated above, Mary's second child, Charles Henry 'Allan' Bennett, was born in 1872 in Notting Hill.[8] Wardle died in late October 1880 and was buried on November 11. After his death, Mary and her children moved in with her mother, Louisa, at 46 Warwick Gardens, Kensington, a 'middle-class, well-to-do' area according to Booth's maps (Booth 1889). The Bennetts continued to live a comfortable lifestyle. However, this changed in July 1884 when Louisa Corbyn died. She was buried in Brompton Cemetery, West Brompton, London on 26 July, 1884.

With the death of both her parents, Mary, her children, and Mary's oldest sister, Rosa, were left to fend for themselves. To support her children, Mary Ann began cleaning houses, but this did not last long. Unfortunately for Charlotte and Allan, she died a few months later of ulcerated tuberculosis of the throat (Baker 2022: 49). There is a record of a Mary Ann Bennett, born in 1850, dying in December 1886 in South London, but there is no way to confirm that this was Allan Bennett's mother. Moreover, there are no documents indicating how Charlotte Louisa and Allan were supported in the following years. The next document in which they appear is the 1891 English census, where Charlotte Louisa is listed as living as a boarder at 195 South Lambeth Rd, London, and working as a dressmaker. Their straightened circumstances probably meant they lay within the 30–39% of people in this part of London who lived in comparative poverty (Clout 2000: 102–103).[9]

Throughout his life, Bennett claimed to have been schooled in Bath. This may be true, but we have not been able to verify this. If it were true, it would probably have been in the late 1880s, after the death of his grandmother. One possibility would have been Prior Park College, a Roman Catholic Grammar School. However, 40 years before our research, a fire destroyed much of the school's paper archives. No record was found of Bennett in what survived,[10] and the copies of the *Prior Park Magazine* for the 1880s, held by the Bath Records Office, do not mention Bennett. However, an intriguing detail on Bennett's sister's marriage certificate of 1895 places her in the village of Warkleigh, North Devon, at the time, not so far from Bath. She also lived in Bath with her daughter when her husband was serving in the British army during World War I. Members of the Buddhist Society of Great Britain and Ireland state that she was staying 'with friends' (X. Y. Z. 1916: 218).[11] We have no other evidence of a link between Bennett's family and the south-west of Britain. The link with Warkleigh may have been part of Charlotte Louisa's attempt to hide her background, or it could point to a side of the family that we have not yet uncovered. That she had friends in Bath, though, is highly plausible, and these could have facilitated Bennett going to school in Bath when the situation in London was tough for the family.

However, what is clear is that Bennett went to college in the south-east of Britain in the early 1890s. The 1891 census lists him as living in Ipswich, Suffolk. He was attending the Colonial College in Hollesley Bay, Suffolk. He entered as a 'freshman' in the winter session of 1890 together with 18 others, including L. H. Beamish, who could have been related to H. H. Beamish, who eventually went to Ceylon as a planter (Colonia 1890b: 266). The college was founded in February 1887 by Robert Johnson with just three students. Its aim was to train 'youth for colonial life' as agriculturalists, ranchers, and planters so that they would not become a burden to themselves and others, and it was patronised by the government (Colonia 1890a: 163).[12] By July 1890, student numbers had grown to 69 (Resident Director 1891: 4–7).[13] The college began with just over 1300 acres of land, but within a few years this had grown to over 1800 acres. It offered classes on agriculture, bookkeeping, botany, forestry, geology, horticulture, veterinary surgery, building construction and engineering, and more. Bennett's interest was in courses relating to the sciences, particularly chemistry, and mechanical and electrical engineering, but it is unlikely that the College offered the latter. He would have taken classes in agriculture and similar topics, all of which had an outdoor component together with classroom work. He did not stay long at the College, perhaps less than a year. By the summer session of 1892, he was already an 'old Colonial,' and this most intriguing paragraph appeared in the College magazine:

> Mr Charles Allan Bennett, an old "Colonial," variously celebrated to an older generation for his Buddhist tendencies, his historic falling-out with a bold Dutch student and for his reputed dealings with spirits belonging to a region not mentioned in polite society—who, after a brief stay in the midst of our Arcadian pleasures, forsook them for the odorous realms of chemical analysis—has lately been honourably mentioned in the celebrated Dr Bernard Dyer's thesis "On 'mineral' plant food in Soils" for rendering him valuable assistance in verifying experiments, etc. "Our Spook" is destined to make a name in his new profession. (Colonia 1892: 134)

This indicates, importantly, that Bennett's interest in Buddhism was established by 1890, as were his dealings with the occult. It also suggests that 'chemical analysis' was not offered by the College. This could have been the reason he left. It also confirms that, upon returning to London, he found employment with Dr. Bernard Dyer, an analytical and consulting chemist. Dyer was primarily employed in soil analysis and, with his training at the Colonial College, Bennett would have been of great assistance. The thesis mentioned in the quote is titled *On the Analytical Determination of Probably Available "Mineral" Plant Foods in Soils*. The paper investigates the amount of minerals in soils, pointing out that despite soils often having high mineral content, 'only a very small proportion of this total may be available for plant use.' The paper then gives extensive examples, as well as methods to make greater quantities of minerals available for plant use. It concludes with acknowledgements that mention 'the valuable help rendered to him [Dyer] in the laboratory work by . . . his present assistants, Mr. James Nimmo, F.I.C., Mr. E. H. Roberts, and Mr. C. H. Allan Bennett' (Dyer 1894: 167).[14]

During this time, Bennett also hoped to find additional classes in the sciences. He wrote to his friend and fellow Theosophist, Frederick Leigh Gardner (1857–1930), also an employee of Bernard Dyer's, and inquired if he knew of any schools for chemistry or electrical engineering, because he was 'anxious to get some science teaching in London day-schools.' Despite his eagerness, there is no indication that he ever achieved this.

One of the biggest difficulties we have regarding Bennett is the relationship between his level of education and his living circumstances. All evidence indicates that, after his grandmother and mother died, Bennett and his sister lived in very meagre circumstances. Yet, his writing and knowledge of science indicate he was very educated. Moreover, the Colonial College and the other schools he potentially attended were not charitable institutions. Attending them would have had costly tuition fees, as well as the costs of boarding. Where did the funds for this education come from? They could have been from relatives, although it is clear it was not his uncle Sherry. An 1895 handwritten letter by Sherry to friends claimed he was on his deathbed and requested money for his wife, Angela, and child, Elmire Marie, so they could travel from New York to New Orleans, where Angela had family members who could support them both. A strong possibility could have been his aunt Josephine and her husband, who were both barristers at the time Bennett attended school. There could also have been other relatives and benefactors we do not know of, such as Bennett's father. We simply have no data to answer these questions, and Bennett was silent about the subject. We surmise later in this chapter, however, that Bennett's scientific knowledge was gained on the job, through his employment.

We know much more about Charlotte Louisa and Allan from the beginning of the 1890s. On 19 February, 1895, Charlotte Louisa married Godfrey Barrington Johnson (1872–1940) in Christ Church, Chelsea, London. Mick Brown notes that Godfrey was the son of Robert Johnson, the founder of the Hollesley Bay Colonial College Bennett attended a few years prior to the marriage (Brown 2023: 78). Based on a letter written by Charlotte on the Hollesley Bay Colonial College letterhead regarding Bennett's health, it appears there were times when she stayed with him, perhaps when his illness flared. Charlotte might have met Godfrey at the college while staying with Bennett.

At the time of their marriage, Johnson worked in surveying and lived in Battersea. Initially, they resided in Cedars Terrace, located at the intersection of what is now Cedars Road and Queenstown Road, an upper-middle-class, wealthy area, and then in 24a Albert Mansions, off Albert Bridge Road in Battersea, a road classified as 'middle class. Well-to-do' by Booth (Booth 1889). Within a few years, Johnson had moved the family north of the River Thames, at least briefly living at 17 Rossetti Gardens, Flood Street, Chelsea. They also lived in Sevenoaks, at 1 Holmesdale Villas, Bradbourne Vale Road. Johnson was, therefore, able to house his wife comfortably, in upper- and middle-class areas.

Unfortunately, as time progressed, the relationship between Charlotte Louisa and Godfrey deteriorated. By January 1904, the conflict in the relationship came to a head, with Charlotte filing for divorce and the dissolution of her marriage. According to her petition to the High Court of Justice, Godfrey treated Charlotte 'with great unkindness and cruelty, neglected her, struck and otherwise assaulted her.' She specifically notes that, on 3 January, 1904, Godfrey struck 'a violent blow on her head, with his hand.' Charlotte also claims that Godfrey had committed adultery multiple times, especially with a woman she names as 'Miss Martha.' She notes that, on 18 January, 1904, Godfrey met with Miss Martha in Barrett's Hotel, Craven Street, Strand. What is significant about these details is that Bennett occasionally lived with his sister when she was with Godfrey, and would have witnessed this abusive behaviour. It is not surprising that Bennett chose to stay with others when possible, as indicated by the various letters he wrote during this period, despite the fact that his sister's homes were much more comfortable.

Another indication that Godfrey was earning a decent living is that on the 2 February, 1904, Charlotte refiled her petition for divorce, adding a request for alimony of £2 a week, which is the equivalent of about £250 in 2020, or about $305 USD.[15] By the end of February, the case was set before the court. The nisi, or provisional divorce decree, was granted on 16 May, 1904, and the final decree was given on 28 November, 1904. Just after the divorce decree was finalised, on 3 December, Charlotte boarded the S.S. *New York* in Southampton, and set sail for New York City. She was leaving England to start a new life in America.

Despite being recently divorced, Charlotte travelled under the name Johnson and claimed to be married on the passenger manifest to ensure her safety when travelling unescorted. She arrived in New York City on 12 December, but this was not her destination. It was just the first stop on her way to San Francisco. It is not clear if Charlotte had met William Leonard Bertram Hill (1871–1944) before or after she had filed for divorce. What is clear, however, is that they had planned to relocate to California and marry after Charlotte was officially divorced. W. L. B. Hill, as he preferred to be called, had preceded Charlotte in travelling to San Francisco. Prior to Charlotte sailing to America, she must have sent word ahead that the divorce was complete, because on 10 December, 1904, *The San Francisco Call* newspaper published notice that, on the day before, a marriage licence had been issued to William L. B. Hill, 33 years of age, living in Highland Spring, California, and Charlotte L. Johnson, 33 years of age, of London, England. Upon arriving in San Francisco, Charlotte and William were married on 19 December by Rev. Leavitt of The First Unitarian Church. Afterwards, they began their new life near Kelseyville, Lake County, California.[16] Not long after their marriage, Charlotte became pregnant and on 28 October, 1905, their own child, Alexandria Leslie Hill (1905–1984), was born, although she preferred to be called Leslie.[17] Except for the time W. L. B. Hill was away due to both World Wars, Bennett's sister and brother-in-law lived in Lake County, California for the rest of their lives. Leslie would leave the area, get married twice, but eventually return to Lake County where she remained until her death. She did not have any children.

The violence arising from poverty, and from her spouse, led Charlotte Louisa to flee to America. It would also have had a significant effect on Bennett. For instance, as we have stressed in our Introduction, Allan suffered from acute asthma that debilitated him for weeks at a time, a problem he suffered for his entire life. This would have been exacerbated both by the tensions within his extended family and by London's pollution. The medical field at that time did not understand the causes of asthma. The advised treatment at the end of the nineteenth century often made the condition worse, instead of helping.[18] Most forget that at the end of the nineteenth century, London's air quality was horrific. Burning coal and the construction of buildings were two significant causes of this.[19] With air pollution hitting its peak in 1891, it is not surprising that Bennett suffered from asthma attacks so frequently.[20] The air he was breathing contained massive amounts of soot. The air quality began to improve after the Public Health Act for London in 1891, which encouraged businesses to adopt cleaner and more efficient energy practices, although significant change would not come until the 1950s.[21]

When telling stories about Bennett's childhood, Crowley states that Bennett was already working at a laboratory at age 16, that is around 1888 (Crowley 1989: 180). Bennett continued to work intermittently in similar kinds of employment well into his twenties, both before and after attending the Colonial College. As such, it is reasonable to assume that Bennett's knowledge of chemistry, electricity, and similar subjects was gained on the job and supplemented by any reading material he was able to acquire and classes he was able to attend. Clearly, he became competent in these areas. Letters to Gardner, for instance, show that he was asked to give cost estimates for the analysis of soil samples for an expedition planned for Africa.[22] In these letters, he also discusses a variety of scientific and technical subjects, including creating a 'Poggendorf,'[23] advising Gardner on the proper way of assembling a battery, and creating a variety of inventions with mechanical devices such as lathes and single-phase engines.

Crowley relates that Bennett was devoutly Catholic in his youth, but that his analytical mind caused him to abandon his faith. This series of events was reiterated by Bennett in the speech he gave at his ordination as a Buddhist monk, in which he stated, '[secular knowledge] destroyed my faith in the religious lessons of my childhood' (Ananda Maitriya 1902e: 7). He made a similar statement in an interview with a reporter in London in September 1908 (Daily Telegraph 1908: 12). Crowley's story, however, also notes that it was learning about human procreation that damaged Bennett's faith in God, as well as making him swear to abstain from the opposite sex. Crowley writes:

> When he was about sixteen, the conversation in the laboratory where he was working turned upon childbirth. What he heard disgusted him. He became furiously angry and said that children were brought to earth by angels. The other students laughed at him and tried in vain to convince him. He maintained their theory to be a bestial blasphemy. The next day one of the boys turned up with an illustrated manual of obstetrics. He could no longer doubt the facts. But his reaction was this: "Did the Omnipotent God whom he had been taught to worship devise so revolting and degrading a method of perpetuating the species? Then this God must be a devil, delighting in loathsomeness." To him the existence of God was disproved from that moment. (Crowley 1989: 180)

As Crowley is the only source for this story, it cannot be verified. However, it is true that there is no indication that Bennett ever had a sexual relationship or love interest.

Two important spiritual events are claimed to have happened to Bennett in 1890. The first is related by Crowley:

> When he was about eighteen, Allan had accidentally stumbled into the trance called Shivadarshana, in which the universe, having been perceived in its totality as a single phenomenon, independent of space and time, is then annihilated. This experience had determined the whole course of his life. His one object was to get back into that state. (Crowley 1989: 237; Harris 1998: 5)

While we have no record of this event from Bennett's writing, we do know that Bennett was very interested in Hinduism and Buddhism early within his spiritual practice. This topic is explored in more detail in the chapter covering Bennett's time in Ceylon.

The other important event retold in the many historical sketches of Bennett's life is his reading of Sir Edwin Arnold's *The Light of Asia* (1879) at the age of 18 and his then becoming a Buddhist at heart.[24] While this may be true in some sense, especially in the light of the 1892 report in *Colonia*, throughout his twenties he explored a variety of Eastern religious, and Western mystic and occult systems. Crowley notes that, when Bennett became his teacher in 1899, he had great familiarity with Hindu and Buddhist scriptures.[25] Between 1890 and his relocation to Ceylon at the end of 1899 or beginning of 1900, Buddhism was one part of a spiritual path that included many strands.[26] These interests led him to join two very influential nineteenth-century organisations: the Theosophical Society and the Hermetic Order of the Golden Dawn.

JOINING THE THEOSOPHICAL SOCIETY AND THE HERMETIC ORDER OF THE GOLDEN DAWN

In the summer of 1894, Allan Bennett stood before a room of Theosophists. He was presenting a paper he had written, called 'The Lore of Khem,' in which he was giving his theory about the true meaning of the mystical statements in the Egyptian Papyrus of Ani, commonly known as the Egyptian Book of the Dead. The Book of the Dead is an Egyptian funerary text acquired by the British Library in 1888 that narrates the path the *Ka*, or soul, takes on its way to being judged in the underworld. In both vibrant, colourful illustrations and corresponding hieroglyphics, it presents the scene of judgement by Thoth, the god of wisdom, in the presence of Osiris, the god of the underworld. According to the text, the heart of the deceased is measured on a scale against the weight of a feather, given by Ma'at, the goddess of truth. The scale would show the heart weighing the same as the feather for those who had led a virtuous life; these would proceed to an afterlife in which they were given food, beer and land in the Field of Offerings, a place where Horus could be praised eternally. In contrast, those whose hearts were weighed down by sin, such as by withholding offerings from temples, being deceitful or destroying things that had already been erected for the gods and goddesses, would be given to Ammit, a crocodile-headed demoness, also known as the Devourer of the Dead, and Eater of Hearts.[27]

Bennett was making this presentation at Brixton Lodge, located in Battersea, South London, the lodge through which he joined the Theosophical Society in March 1893. Despite being his home lodge, he had previously presented this paper at Adelphi Lodge just over a week prior. Bennett would go on to present the same paper at additional Theosophical lodges in London, including Chiswick in the west, Bow in the east, and North London Lodge in Islington. Bennett had begun presenting papers at Theosophical lodges in October 1893, when he presented on alchemy, at Bow Lodge, and later on astrology, at Adelphi Lodge. After presenting on Egyptian mythology, Bennett gave a series of presentations about mediaeval magic, which spanned 1894 to 1895.[28]

While these topics may seem unrelated, they were a few of the many religious, philosophical, scientific and mythological subjects examined by the Theosophical Society.[29] In the early nineteenth century, the boundaries between religion, science and myth were porous. The Society aimed to create a 'brotherhood' of seekers, regardless of race, religion or class, which examined a variety of subjects, looking for the universal or perennial truth, an 'Ageless Wisdom' underlying them all, much of which Blavatsky captured under the term 'occultism.'[30]

When the Theosophical Society was founded, members were required to undergo a type of initiation similar to Freemasonry, including the swearing of oaths. However, by the time Bennett joined, the process was generally administrative, with the initiatory system being transferred to a subsection of the Society. Bennett applied for membership on 24 March, 1893, and his application was approved on the 28th. Upon approval, he was a member, no oath needed. The application required two existing members to be sponsors. Bennett's sponsors were William Lindsay and Herbert Coryn (1863–1927).[31] It is not surprising that Bennett joined Brixton Lodge, as it was just two miles from where he lived (Mead 1893: 7).

During the 1880s, Blavatsky had returned to England and begun writing her magnum opus, *The Secret Doctrine*, which was published in 1888 (Blavatsky 1993a;1993b). She had relocated to London after the eruption of an international scandal, in which her psychic powers were labelled fraudulent and her claim that she was in touch with the mystical leaders of the Theosophical Society, the Masters or Mahatmas, imaginary. This scandal created a rift between Blavatsky and Olcott. Being so far from the Society's headquarters in Adyar, India, modern day Chennai, resulted in Blavatsky having much less input into the actions of the Society to which she had dedicated her life. Wanting to return to a leadership role and capitalising on her past reputation as the font of esoteric knowledge in the Society, Blavatsky in 1888 created a new section within the Society—the Esoteric Section (ES),[32] to which she transferred the initiatory process. Within the ES, Blavatsky claimed to give instruction on practising the occultism that had been the core component of the Society's teachings. As a result, many Theosophists requested to be admitted. One of the more famous members of the ES was the poet William Butler Yeats (1865–1939). Another may have been Bennett. In a letter to Gardner, Bennett states that he would not be joining Gardner on a trip to Africa because 'it would have kept me back from admission to the ES till I come back and other occult work.'[33] Gardner had joined the ES in July 1894 and had become a member of its Ananda Lodge (Gilbert 1986a: 14). Ananda Lodge had been established in October/November 1893 by William Wynn Westcott, who was President of the lodge, with Percy Bullock as honorary secretary. While Blavatsky generally considered most people to be ignorant about occultism, she respected Westcott and recognised him as a peer. When Blavatsky created an additional level of esoteric instruction within the ES, called the Inner Group (IG), containing 12 handpicked disciples, six male, six female, she also appointed Westcott as one of the three honorary or 'out-side' members (Cadwell and Spierenburg 1995: xiv–xv).

The ES, as it turned out, gave little practical instruction in occultism. Ever since the beginning of the Society, members had been requesting instruction in practical occultism, always hoping to create observable phenomena to prove occult claims were true. Blavatsky had resisted this, claiming that only advanced adepts should practise occultism and that to do so before one was ready was to invite disaster (Crow 2012). Instead, the members of the Theosophical Society were taught esoteric theories, and encouraged to study comparative religion and philosophy, become vegetarians, practise meditation and adopt altruism as their guiding morality. Within the ES, members hoped to move beyond such teachings and focus on practice. To their dismay, they received three instructions or essays written by Blavatsky, which simply passed on more detailed and complex esoteric knowledge and theory. Even those who were members of the IG were only given additional detailed instruction on esoteric philosophy rather than practice. They were permitted to ask Blavatsky questions and she answered them, relaying her esoteric knowledge in ways that often elicited more questions. The ES, therefore, failed to meet the needs of many who searched for practical and demonstrable occult knowledge. As a result, other organisations arose to meet those needs. The Hermetic Order of the Golden Dawn, or Golden Dawn, was one of them.

The Golden Dawn was an occult initiatory organisation founded in 1888 that promised instruction in practical occultism, in the form of ceremonial magic. It was founded by Samuel Liddell MacGregor Mathers (1854–1918), William Wynn Westcott (1848–1925) and Dr. William Robert Woodman (1828–1891). All three were Freemasons and members of the Societas Rosicruciana in Anglia (SRIA), and studied ceremonial magic. Mathers was not a Theosophist but often attended Theosophical lodge meetings, giving presentations, and had papers published in Theosophical periodicals. Woodman was primarily focused on esoteric Freemasonry and ceremonial magic, but was not interested in Theosophy. The three founders established themselves as the three 'Chiefs' of the Golden Dawn. Similar to Blavatsky's claims that the Theosophical Society was guided by mystical 'Masters,' the Golden Dawn Chiefs claimed they were in contact with and guided by 'the Secret Chiefs of the Order,' also called 'The Great White Brotherhood.' Mathers had found, or created, a cypher manuscript that detailed the first five levels or grades of initiation within the Golden Dawn and whom to contact for more instruction. Upon attempting to gain more information from the cypher manuscript contact, Mathers claimed that a different correspondent replied, saying that the cypher manuscript contact was no longer available and that the Golden Dawn leadership itself had to contact the Secret Chiefs on the astral plane.[34] In 1892, Mathers claimed to have established a link to the hidden Secret Chiefs, and through communication with them, the Second or Inner Order within the Golden Dawn was created, much like the ES was the second level of the Theosophical Society. However, unlike the Theosophical Society, each Golden Dawn initiate was required to demonstrate mastery of occult knowledge and practices to progress to higher grades. These requirements resulted in the practice of occultism that so many sought. To progress in the Golden Dawn, the initiate had to learn the material taught and practise ceremonial magic.

The initiations of the first level, or Outer Order, of the Golden Dawn, were based largely on Egyptian mythology, although a variety of other esoteric topics and material, such as Kabbalah, Freemasonry, astrology, alchemy, magic and tarot were incorporated into them. As the Theosophical Society was a well-established organisation investigating occultism, the crossover membership between the Theosophical Society and the

Golden Dawn was significant. As so many of the people Bennett would have met at Theosophical lodge meetings were also Golden Dawn members, it is highly likely that it was through these Theosophists and meetings that Bennett was invited to take initiation into the Golden Dawn, an invitation Bennett accepted.

In June 1894, Bennett took his first, or Neophyte, initiation into the Golden Dawn, becoming the 187th initiate of the Order. It was a custom for initiates to adopt a motto, usually in Latin, Greek or Hebrew, to use when referring to each other, to ensure the secrecy of the Order's membership. For instance, when Herbert Coryn, one of Bennett's sponsors for admittance to the Theosophical Society, took the Neophyte initiation in August 1893, he adopted the motto *Crescendo*.[35] Bennett adopted the motto *Voco*, meaning, 'I invoke.' Bennett was a fast learner and devoured the Golden Dawn teachings, advancing through the first five grades of the Order in just over a year. Many Golden Dawn members referred to Bennett as one of the best ceremonial magicians in the Order, second only to Mathers. Being proficient in ceremonial magic was one of the primary criteria for advancement into the Inner Order. Following Freemasonic practices, an Outer Order member of the Golden Dawn was evaluated regarding their knowledge before being invited to enter the Inner Order. This invitation process was a way of maintaining control over those who would advance to the higher levels of the Order, where they would have access to powerful esoteric knowledge and potential leadership roles. Initiation was permanent, as in Freemasonry or episcopal consecration. Once given, it could not be taken away. As a result, the members of the Inner Order were cautious as to whom they invited into the Inner Order. Bennett, however, was successful, taking his Adeptus Minor initiation on 22 March, 1895, becoming the 56th Inner Order initiate. Upon entering, Bennett adopted the motto *Iehi Aour* (יהי אור), Hebrew for 'let there be light.' Lastly, the Order adopted the practice of referring to each other as brother or sister, *frater* or *soror* in Latin. As a result, when mentioned in writing, Bennett was usually referred to as Frater I.A.

While Bennett was working his way through the grades of the Golden Dawn, the Theosophical Society was facing a significant internal conflict which ultimately split the Society. The roots of the conflict, however, preceded Bennett's membership. They developed when Blavatsky appointed Annie Besant, in Europe, the Inner Head of the ES, while William Quan Judge (1851–1895), in America, was the Outer Head, or public representative. Judge had been one of the earliest Society members, present at its founding meeting. Some considered him a third founder. Early in the Society's history, Blavatsky and Olcott appointed Judge Vice-President of

Figure 1.1 *42 Dorothy Road, Clapham Junction. Courtesy of Harriet Tait.*

the Society, a position he continued to hold until 1895. In contrast, Besant was a late addition to the Society's leadership. Besant joined in 1888, after reading *The Secret Doctrine*. Because she was an intelligent and capable woman, Blavatsky saw her as a potential successor. To prepare her for a leadership position, Besant advanced quickly through the Society, not only becoming a member of the Inner Group of the ES, but its 'Chief Secretary' and 'Recorder of the Teachings' (Pelletier 2004: 36). As both Judge and Besant had leadership positions in the ES, Blavatsky expected them to cooperate. However, they did not. Instead, they quarrelled. Since Blavatsky was their superior in the ES, she kept the conflict in check. However, with Blavatsky's death on 8 May, 1891, that constraint disappeared.

Immediately after Blavatsky's death, Besant and Judge were recognised as co-leaders of the ES and appeared to work together. Also at this time, the ES changed its name from the Esoteric Section to the Esoteric School. Olcott had always been wary of the ES, and, with Blavatsky's death, he made the ES a separate organisation. Within the ES, Judge was referred to as the head of the 'Western Division' and Besant oversaw the 'Eastern Division.' In 1891, as part of the separation process, Besant found a letter appearing to have been written by one of the Masters overseeing both the Theosophical Society and the ES. The letter claimed that the plan Judge had proposed as to how the ES should proceed 'is right.' At first, Besant accepted this as a letter from the Masters. Later, Besant claimed the letter had been forged by Judge. As this conflict escalated, other leaders, such as Olcott, worked to resolve it. Over time, however, the conflict festered within the ES and the Theosophical Society. Besant, in Europe but with frequent travels to India, was well placed to rally Theosophical leaders to her side, including Olcott. In contrast, Judge, in America, isolated from the majority of the international leadership, was unable to counter the actions of Besant. In 1895, 'The Case Against W. Q. Judge' emerged, wherein Besant called for Judge to resign from the Society due to his dishonest conduct. This charge against Judge was debated by the Theosophical Society membership, and members and lodges began to declare their loyalty, a process in which Bennett participated.

Olcott established an executive committee to investigate the charges against Judge. The committee's membership included Bennett's sponsor, Herbert Coryn, a powerful member of the Society. He was part of Blavatsky's Inner Group and his family had been Theosophical Society members for decades. Coryn supported Judge and opposed all charges against him. Because the committee could not come to a consensus, they sent out a circular letter to all the lodges and leaders of the Society throughout Europe, presenting the case and requesting that the members and lodges vote on how they should proceed.

The conflict between the supporters of Besant and Judge was waged in multiple arenas, the most prominent being periodicals and circular letters. In November 1894, the members of Dublin Lodge sent a circular letter to all the lodges of the European section, arguing that the charges against Judge should be dropped. It also encouraged those who supported Judge to report back to the Dublin Lodge so they could compile a supporters' list. This letter became known as the 'Dublin Lodge Circular.' The English-speaking members of the European Section used a periodical called *The Vâhan*, edited by George Robert Stow Mead (1866–1933). Within *The Vâhan*, the members of the lodges submitted reports, resolutions and other statements regarding their view on the Judge case, as well as responses to the executive committee circular letter and the Dublin Lodge Circular. Mead, a supporter of Besant, refused to publish the Dublin Lodge Circular, but published responses from the lodges and letters from the members.

Herbert Coryn, President of Brixton Lodge, submitted the Lodge's initial reply, dated 30 November, 1894. It was published in the January 1895 edition of *The Vâhan*. Coryn writes, on behalf of the Lodge:

> That the members of this Lodge now present are of opinion that a *prima facie* case has not been made out against Mr. W. Q. Judge.

> That they decline to ask Mr. W. Q. Judge to make any reply to the charges against him.
>
> H.A.W. Coryn, President (Coryn 1895a: 9)

The issues of *The Vâhan* also began reporting the number of people who supported the Dublin Lodge Circular, initially with just a numerical count, but, as the count rose, names started to be included. The February 1895 issue of *The Vâhan*, under the heading 'Additional Signatures to the Dublin Lodge Circular,' contains a long list of names, organised by lodge. Under Brixton Lodge, 20 names are listed, including Allan Bennett, both of Bennett's Theosophical Society application sponsors, as well as past and future Golden Dawn members, Jessie Louisa Horne, Harold John Levett and George Samuel Minson (Green 1895: 12).[36] In the March 1895 edition of *The Vâhan*, Coryn submitted a follow-up resolution from Brixton Lodge:

> At a specially summoned meeting of the Brixton Lodge, held at 196, Clapham Park Road, on February 1st, 1895, the following resolutions were carried unanimously, save for one dissent:—
>
> 1. That this Lodge requests William Q. Judge not to resign from the office of Vice-President of the T.S., it being imperative for the best interests of the Society that he shall remain in the said office for the successful promulgation of Theosophy in America, and generally.
> 2. That in the opinion of this Lodge there is no necessity for the further investigation of the charges made against William Q. Judge.
> 3. That the Lodge expresses its fullest confidence in William Q. Judge personally, and as an official of the T.S., and also in his methods of work, and declares its determination to support him in his efforts therein.
>
> Herbert Coryn, Pres. (Coryn 1895b: 8)

Meanwhile, most American lodges were losing their patience with their Theosophical brethren in other nations. When the American Section of the Theosophical Society held its annual convention in Boston on 28–29 April, 1895, the primary focus was the conflict between Judge and Besant. The central question was whether the American Section should continue to be a part of the Theosophical Society, or whether it should secede, forming its own independent Theosophical organisation. At the end of the convention, most of the American lodges voted to secede from the Theosophical

Society and form the Theosophical Society in America, with W. Q. Judge as its new President.

Word of the secession reached Europe in May, with the June issue of *The Vâhan* publishing both the resolutions issued at the American convention, and Judge's speech, in which he bid goodbye to his role as Vice-President of the Theosophical Society. The next issue contains the Theosophical Society response, which was to annul the charters for the American lodges and members who were part of the secession. In the August 1895 issue, the Society turns its attention to the European members and lodges that supported Judge. Mead writes: 'The following lodges, therefore, unless they repudiate the action of their representatives, are no longer lodges of the Theosophical Society' (Mead 1895: 1-2). The list of lodges includes Brixton Lodge. Because of his support for Judge, Bennett was, therefore, expelled from the Theosophical Society in August 1895. When we consulted the membership roll books, held by the Theosophical Society in London, this expulsion was confirmed. Bennett's membership listing has a long diagonal line drawn through it with 'W. Q. Judge' written on top. From this point, Bennett focused his attention on his Golden Dawn work, but his future interactions suggest that he did not hold a grudge against the Theosophical Society and maintained contact with many Theosophists.

MASTERING GOLDEN DAWN MAGICAL RITUAL

As Bennett had an inquisitive and scientific mind, he explored the occult material learned in the Golden Dawn in a variety of ways, such as by formulating hypotheses based on the ontological claims in the esoteric material and performing ceremonial magic experiments. One of the main principles of occultism is that there are aspects and properties of reality that are generally beyond the reach of material science, but which can be accessed and manipulated through esoteric practices, such as ritual, magic, alchemy and astrology. When Bennett left London at the end of 1899 or beginning of 1900, he gave most of his magical notebooks to his student, Aleister Crowley. It is through these notebooks that we see the various hypotheses, ceremonies and experiments that Bennett was exploring.

The first type of exploration Bennett engaged in related to the esoteric principle of 'correspondences.' Antoine Faivre, scholar of Western esotericism, characterises something as esoteric if it possesses at least four of six characteristics, one of them being systems of correspondences.[37] For millennia, humanity has claimed, in some form, connections, analogies and relationships between the heavens and earth. The belief was accepted by, and was fundamental to, all natural philosophers. Even the Church Fathers accepted the reality of correspondences. In *Summa Contra Gentiles*, Aquinas acknowledges that it is lawful for people to wear amulets which connected to 'the power of celestial bodies' (Aquinas 1956: 93).[38] Aquinas's acceptance of such connections became church doctrine. As a result, we find the notion of correspondences contained in the famous manual instructing clergy in the detection and interrogation of witches, Heinrich Kramer's *The Malleus Maleficarum*, or 'Hammer of Witches' (Kramer and Sprenger 1928: 182). Correspondences underlie many systems of magic, healing and divination. Within Theosophy and the Golden Dawn, the Kabbalistic 'Tree of Life' was the framework upon which all correspondences were mapped. Containing 10 spheres, or *sephiroth*, and 22 paths connecting them, each associated with a Hebrew letter, the Kabbalistic Tree of Life presented 32 different categories through which the cosmos could be organised.

Similar to his occultist contemporaries, Bennett accepted the notion of correspondences, began memorising them, and worked to understand how the various characteristics found in myriad systems could be connected. Entering Theosophy and the Golden Dawn, Bennett was presented with an established system of connections, for example which planets were associated with which colour, plant, Greek deity, zodiac sign and element, such as fire, earth, water or air. However, while general systems of correspondences such as these existed, they were not comprehensive, nor were they all interconnected. Bennett, therefore, began making connections between seemingly unrelated phenomena. In a notebook entry called 'Flashing Sounds,'[39] Bennett presents a set of correspondences between musical notes and various other characteristics, such as astrological signs, colours and letters of the Hebrew alphabet. In the first section, he equates Aries to C major and the colour red. Libra is associated with F# and green. All 12 signs have their musical and chromatic equivalents. In the second section, Bennett lists three important Hebrew letters, called the mother letters, and lists the notes and colours that 'flash' against each other. The colours listed, red and green, yellow and violet, and blue and orange, are complementary colours. The third section gives the complementary correspondences of the planets, their note and colour, as well as the corresponding 'flashing' planet, note and colour. While this may seem confusing to an outsider, what Bennett was attempting was to organise separate sets of correspondences into one coherent system.

Although the system of correspondences may seem academic, this was not how Bennett understood it. For him, and his contemporary occultists, these systems denoted the hidden structures of reality. This becomes

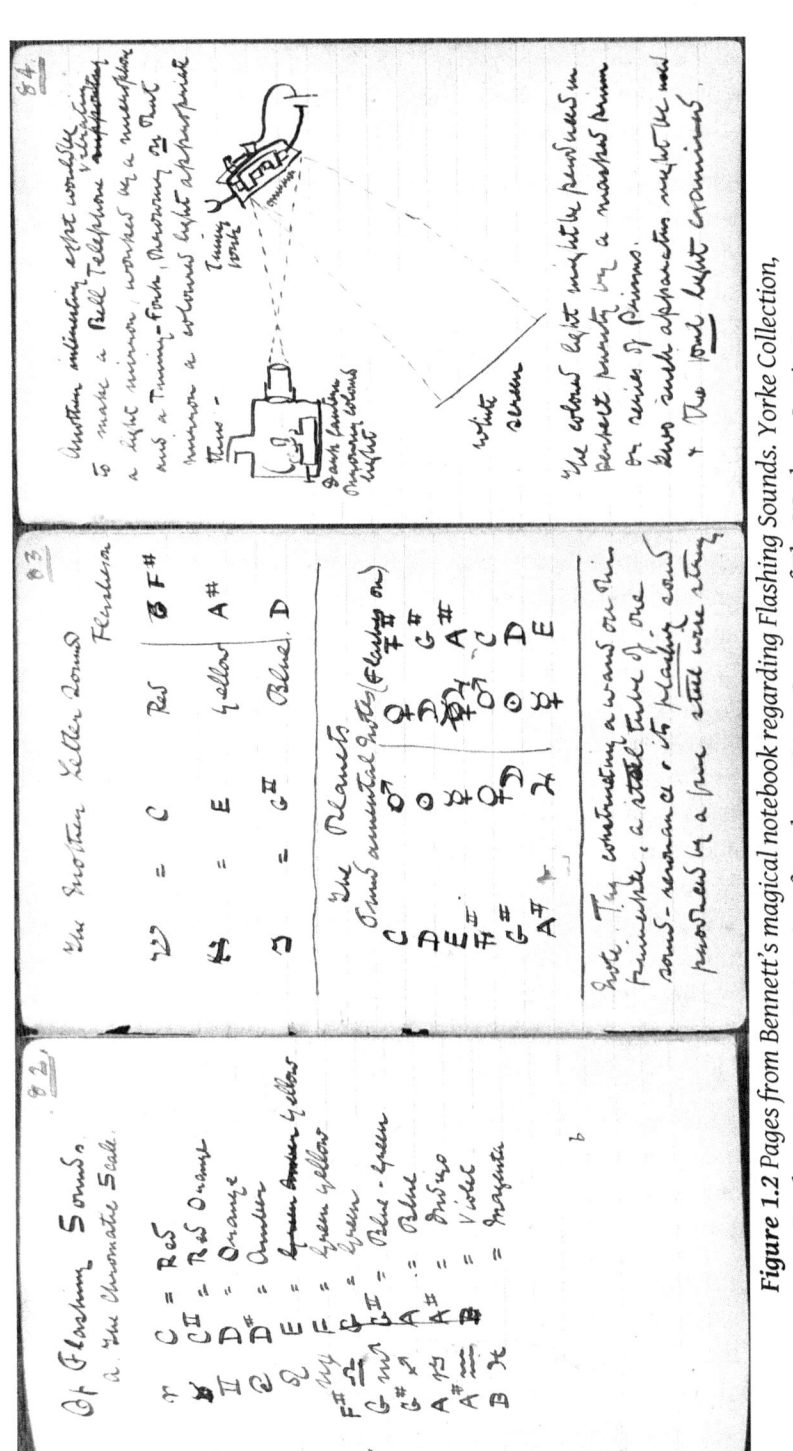

Figure 1.2 Pages from Bennett's magical notebook regarding Flashing Sounds. Yorke Collection, Warburg Institute, University of London, NS 104. Courtesy of The Warburg Institute.

clear when he then posits scientific tests for these correspondences, particularly the colour and sound associations. Bennett writes:

> Another interesting experiment would be to make a Bell telephone vibrating a light mirror worked by a microphone and tuning fork, throwing onto that mirror a colour light appropriate. The coloured light might be produced in perfect purity by a masked prism or a series of prisms. Two such apparatus might be used and the joint light examined. (Bennett 1977: 10)

This description is joined with a diagram he had drawn, with a 'dark lantern throwing coloured light' onto a mirror connected to a tuning fork at the top, and a Bell telephone and microphone on the back. The light is then reflected off the mirror and projected onto a white screen. Bennett's experimental instructions continue, noting that experimental substances may be sensitive to light and that their care needs to be considered.

The same notebook also contains notes for experiments in which electro-magnetism could be integrated into the initiate's wand. Ceremonial magic in the Golden Dawn tradition denoted four primary tools, or elemental weapons, for the magician: the Wand of Fire, the Dagger of Air, the Cup or Chalice for Water, and the Pentacle or Disk for Earth. As the wand was associated with fire, adding elements of electro-magnetism would make sense from an occultist correspondence point of view, as electricity would likely correspond with fire. Bennett writes, 'These [wands] are built upon the principle that the occult powers of a magnet mainly depend on the source of the magnetism, and they are both magnetised by the effect of the will.' He then suggests that the two ways to induce electro-magnetism into the magician's wand are through voltaic and thermo-electric methods. For the first, voltaic, Bennett writes:

> This consists of a doubled wire of copper and zinc, insulated from the other and coiled round a double grooved ebonite rod. The two ends of the upper end of the wires are severally connected to a coil wound round a chilled steel rod to magnetise it. (Bennett 1977: 11)

The second method, thermo-electric, was much more complicated. Bennett notes this after describing the two methods, writing that 'The advantages of the Voltaic form are—that in this the electricity actually passes through the hand, and indeed really takes its rise therein and its much greater simplicity' (Bennett 1977: 11).[40]

Perhaps the best example of how Bennett worked to organise the world through occult correspondences comes from a notebook which was later expanded and published by Crowley with the title *Sepher Sephiroth*

(Bennett and Crowley 1912), meaning 'The Book of Enumerations' in Hebrew. Unlike English, in which numbers and letters are separate and distinct, in Hebrew, the letters are also numbers. As a result, each Hebrew word or phrase also has a corresponding numerical value. The process of calculating and analysing these values is called 'Gematria.' Kabbalists and occultists believe that when two words have the same Gemetria value, they are connected, even if on the surface they seem different. In his notebook, Bennett began to catalogue and organise numerous Hebrew words and phrases by their Gematria value, including their English translation. Pulling from biblical and Kabbalistic sources, Bennett's list became a useful reference guide for the terminology and phrases which could be employed in ceremonial magic. Bennett's list also contains words which were derived from a Kabbalistic process known as 'Notarikon.' Kabbalists would render a phrase into a word by making an acronym. This word would then be considered both important enough to have its own Gematria value, as well as being a representation of the phrase. For example, AGLA (אגלא) is an important Notarikon in Jewish ritual, mediaeval Christian texts and Golden Dawn ceremonies. While what it stands for has been debated, most Kabbalists associate the word with the phrase, *Attah gibbor le'olam 'Adonai'* (אתה גבור לעולם אדני), meaning 'Thou art strong for eternity, Lord' (Regardie 2003: I:55; Hindley 2019: 298).

The other type of esoteric exploration Bennett excelled in was ceremonial magic. Early on, Bennett practised magical ceremonies provided by the Golden Dawn. A notebook written circa 1895 lists numerous rituals which were given by the Golden Dawn or derived from similar rituals. These ceremonies include: Ritual of Consecration of the Lotus Wand; Ritual of the Consecration of the Rose Cross; Ritual for Consecration of the Sword of Art; and The Magical Invocation of the Higher Genius. These would be the kinds of rituals taught to Golden Dawn initiates in the various grades of the Inner and Outer Orders. In fact, it would be expected for initiates to create appropriate rituals for themselves, based on the teachings of the various grades. Initiates would also be expected to create their own elemental weapons. Thus, it is not surprising that Bennett's magical notebooks contain rituals to consecrate magical implements.

The goal of these consecrations was to imbue objects with elemental forces and the will or intentions of the magician. For instance, *The Ritual Magic Manual* (Griffin 1999), a modern how-to book on Golden Dawn ceremonial magic, describes the consecration process for a talisman:

> To consecrate a Talisman by the Ceremonial Formula, first invoke the respective Forces, then charge the talisman with them. Place

the Talisman on the Altar at the point of the Ritual following the Magical Intention. Trace and visualize a circle of white Light around it to confine the Force. Repeatedly project Magical Current into it... Next perform [an] additional Invocation directly over the Talisman... Finally, purify it with water and consecrate it with fire, then wrap the talisman in silk or linen of the corresponding color and put it away before banishing. (Griffin 1999: 527)[41]

In Bennett's time, rituals for consecrating elemental weapons, such as a Lotus Wand, would have been very similar to each other in structure. The Ritual for Talisman of Vision, a ceremony in which Bennett consecrated a talisman to Jupiter, is a good example of the process noted by *The Ritual Magic Manual*, although incomplete in his notebook.[42] Within the Golden Dawn system of correspondences, Jupiter was associated with abundance, growth and expansion, as well as visions, dreams and long journeys. Because of the association with visions and dreams, the Spirit of Jupiter was the appropriate force for Bennett to invoke into the talisman.[43]

Bennett began the Ritual for the Talisman of Vision with his statement of magical intention: 'I Yehi Aour, a Frater of the Order of the GD in the Outer and a Member RR et AC am this day about to consecrate a talisman of Jupiter, which is prepared for assured vision, and to this end have I formulated thereon the appropriate symbols and words.'[44] He then proceeded to prepare the ritual space and talisman by banishing and exorcising all 'impure, evil, and unclean spirits.' Having 'cleaned' his ritual space, he then proceeded to invoke the appropriate forces. The first invocation was of 'The Higher,' or higher powers, that being the name of the spirit or spirits being evoked, as well as the magician's higher or spiritual self. Once these spiritual forces were invoked, Bennett then gave his declaration, specifically stating the reason for the ceremony: 'I, I.A., Do at this time propose to consecrate magically this exorcised vellum as a creature of talismans of great magical virtue and efficacy to cause assured and true visions to whomsoever shall bind it in his hand, and then sleep the magical sleep of Siloam.'[45] Afterwards, to empower the operation, beginning the process of projecting the magical forces into the talisman, Bennett invoked the names of divine power, which derived from Judaism, and at times other religious systems, as well as a series of angelic beings associated with Jupiter. These included the name of the Lord, El (אל), the Archangel, Tzadkiel (צדקיאל), the Angelic Choir, Chashmalim (חשמלים), the Great Angel of Jupiter, Sachiel (another name for Tzadkiel), the Planetary Intelligence or Prince of Jupiter, Iohphiel (יופיאל), and the Great Spirit of Jupiter, Hismael (הסמאל). Having created and empowered the talisman,

Bennett begins an even more 'potent invocation,' or, as *The Ritual Magic Manual* states, an 'additional Invocation directly over the Talisman.' However, after the first paragraph, the manuscript stops. Nevertheless, the formula Bennett started generally matches the format found in other Golden Dawn consecration ceremonies.

Bennett's later notebooks contain rituals that sought outcomes beyond the typical ceremonies created by Golden Dawn initiates. Because Bennett was such a proficient and powerful magician within the Golden Dawn, members in London frequently requested he perform rituals for them. In one example, a Golden Dawn member, Dr. Robert Willliam Felkin, Frater Finem Respie, sought Bennett's assistance in creating a Ceremony to Consecrate a Talisman Against Obsession, a protection talisman. Bennett followed the same general format noted above in consecrating a talisman. However, when it came to the Invocation of The Higher, Bennett included the following:

> Lo, even as I do now physically bind this creature of talismans: so let there be restriction placed upon the larvae of evil. Even as I bind this talisman on Earth, so let the larvae that betimes obsesses Frater F.R. be bound and restrained. . . . And even as I do now veil and envelope with blackness this creature of talismans, so let the larvae that betimes obsesses frater F.R. be blinded in darkness and in fear. And may the holy names, the standards, and ensigns of the mighty God hereon engraven and depicted, create and institute herein an elemental force, which may become powerful with the help of YHShVH to guard and protect Frater F.R. from the larvae that betimes obsesses him.[46]

After the invocation of the Higher, Bennett purified and consecrated the talisman, and then, at length, clearly stated the purpose of the ceremony:

> Hear me, ye divine lords and forces of the Hall of the Twofold Manifestation of Thmaist: Hear me, divine spirit of my God! Osiris glorified and triumphant: hear Thou me, Oh divine genius of my Frater Finem Respice: Ye all spiritual and holy powers, hear my prayer and aid!
>
> I, Yehi Aur, a brother of the Order of the Golden in the Outer and an Initiate of the 5=6 Grade thereof: A lord of the paths in the portal of the Vault of the Adepts; A Zelator Adeptus Minor Ordinis R.R. et A.C.: Do at this time propose to constitute and prepare a holy magical talisman of great virtue and efficiency against obsessions; . . . And I do this thing that I might bring aid unto the soul of my Frater F.R. who betimes is attacked by a terrible

obsession which he is unable to resist. For at time there entereth into his Daath an evil and opposing force of nature of the Qlippoth: causing him to lose control of his thoughts and actions, and establishing itself as lord and master of his reason for a time.[47]

The ritual continued, containing additional stages. First came the Invocation and the circling of the temple, whereby the talisman was taken to each of the cardinal directions and further empowered. It was then placed on the central altar and empowered further with 'a most potent conjuration and invocation,' after which it was 'brought into the light' and invested with more power through additional conjurations until finally the talisman was declared 'duly and properly charged.' When charged, the goal or purpose of the ceremony was once more stated and bound to the talisman. The last step was the closing, in which all the invoked spirits and entities were dismissed in the name of God.[48]

Crowley also describes some of the magical work of Bennett, including his invocations of Goetic entities, in the book *The Key of Solomon*, and his calling spirits into manifestation using the 'Enochian Calls' derived from Dr. John Dee, Queen Elizabeth I's court astrologer and adviser, and his assistant, Edward Kelley. Yet, even though Bennett was considered one of the best magicians in the Golden Dawn, Crowley notes that he did occasionally make mistakes. For instance, on one occasion, he invoked Hismael (הסמאל), a spirit of Jupiter, and accidentally stepped out of the magical circle. Taking one step outside the protection of the circle resulted in Bennett being knocked unconscious for hours. At another time, he created a lunar talisman to invoke rain. To activate rain, the talisman needed to be submerged in water. Bennett had initially done this in a basin and found the talisman to be successful. However, sometime later, he carelessly lost the talisman, and it found its way into the sewer. Crowley states that, as a result, 'London had the wettest summer in the memory of man!' (Crowley 1998: 24).

The most significant Talisman ritual written by Bennett is The Ritual for the Evocation unto Visible Appearance of the Great Spirit Taphthartharath.[49] Taphthartharath was the name of a spirit associated with the planet Mercury. Mercury corresponded with numerous gods related to knowledge and communication, including the Egyptian god, Thoth, the Greek god, Hermes, also called Mercury by the Romans, and the Scandinavian or Norse god, Odin (Crowley 1996). The ritual also mentions the spiritual intelligence, Tiriel, and uses the Hebrew name for Mercury, Kokab. By invoking Taphthartharath into a talisman, the participants were hoping to gain occult knowledge. The ritual states:

Behold! Thou great Powerful Prince & Spirit Taphthartharath. We have conjured Thee hither in this day and Hour to demand of Thee certain matters relating to the secret magical knowledge which may be conveyed to us from Thy great master [Thoth] through Thee.[50]

The talisman was composed of orange lettering and lines, and purple lines for the symbol of Taphthartharath. Orange was associated with the Kabbalistic sphere, Hod, attributed to the planet Mercury, and purple was the complementary, or flashing colour on the colour wheel. The ritual itself was much more elaborate than the talisman used against obsessions. It not only required the typical ritual magic equipment, such as an altar, swords, incense and candles, but also included material related to the spirits they were invoking. For instance, Bennett, acting as the Assistant Magus of Art, wore a white robe and girdle made of a snakeskin. Snakes are associated with Hermes and Mercury, which was why the symbol for Hermes is the Caduceus, which depicts two intertwined snakes. While it is not mentioned in the ritual text itself, the Warburg archive holds letters between Bennett and Gardner in which they discuss the logistics for the ritual. In an undated letter from 1896, Bennett requests to borrow a snake pickled in alcohol from Gardner and also mentions that he needs to create a special candle for the ceremony, a candle that must include spermaceti and 'the fat of a snake.'[51]

The ritual also required a cauldron, in which ingredients were mixed to create a 'hell broth' used as part of the invocation. The ritual text itself only mentions that milk is part of the mixture, but the same letter to Gardner lists other ingredients, including a pint of olive oil, two ounces of coriander seeds and two ounces of ammoniacum gum.[52]

The ritual was meant to take place on Wednesday, 22 April, 1896. However, it was delayed until 13 May, 1896 between 8:32 and 9:10 p.m. In an undated letter to Gardner, Bennett writes that the delay was because 'S.S.D.D. [Farr], Rosher & myself being all suddenly afflicted with grim and horrible diseases.'[53] A delay such as this meant the time and day of the ritual had to be recalculated because they needed to be associated with the planet Mercury. In addition, the ritual had to be performed at a time associated with a particular spirit and the hours of the spirits changed daily, based on the rising and setting sun. This particular ritual was calculated to be the 'hour' of Tafrac, or the eighth Hour of the Night, associated with the Angel of the Hour, the Archangel Michael.[54]

The Ritual for the Evocation unto Visible Appearance of the Great Spirit Taphthartharath is one of the most widely reprinted ceremonies

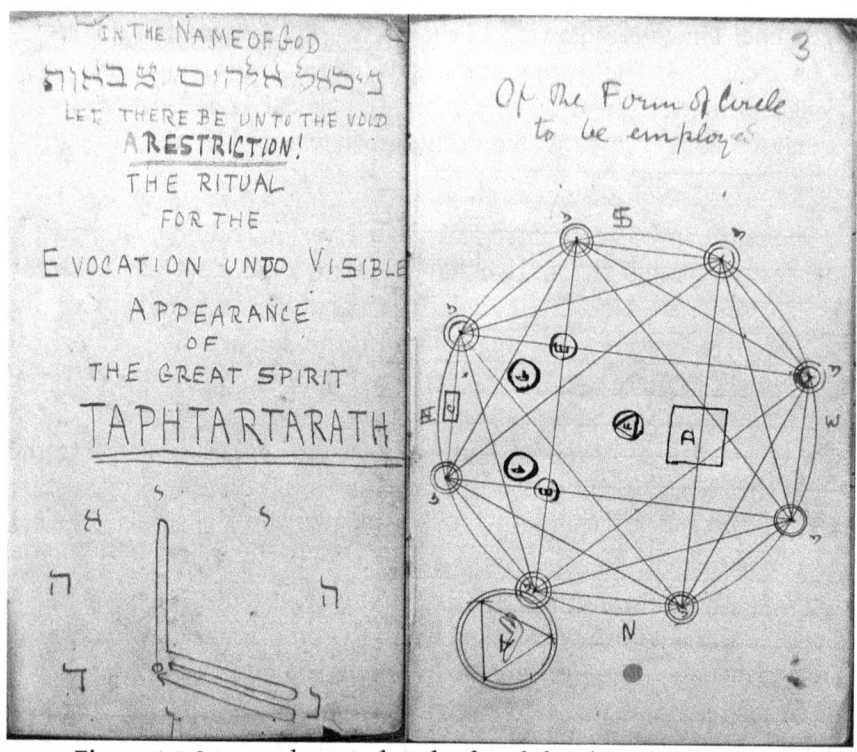

Figure 1.3 Cover and magical circle of Taphthartharath Ritual from Bennett's magical notebooks. Yorke Collection, Warburg Institute, University of London, NS 71. Courtesy of The Warburg Institute.

demonstrating the ceremonial magic of the Golden Dawn. Having Bennett's notebooks, Crowley was the first to publish it. Crowley began publishing a semi-annual journal called *The Equinox*, in 1909. The spring 1910 issue (Vol. 1 No. 3) contains a version of the Taphthartharath ritual. However, Crowley and/or his journal editor made slight changes. Crowley's published version includes a note at the bottom of the first page: 'Soror S.S.D.D. altered Frater I.A.'s ritual, making the operation to form a link between Thoth and the Magus. This is absurd; the correct way is here given, in which the link is formed between the Spirit and the Magus' (Crowley 1910: 170).[55] Most of the reprints of the ritual over the last century have been based on Crowley's version. But four copies of the ritual were made, one by each of the participants, Bennett having the original, and two of the four copies can be found at the Warburg Institute. These are Bennett's and Gardner's versions. As research into the Golden Dawn began in the latter part of the twentieth century, differences between Bennett's, Crowley's, and Gardner's versions began to emerge.

For instance, Pat Zalewsky used both Crowley's and Gardner's versions to create a hybrid one in his *Talismans and Evocations of the Golden Dawn* (Zalewsky 2002). Mary Greer, biographer of the women of the Golden Dawn, notes that Florence Farr made the changes to the ritual intentionally. As Greer writes, '[Farr] hoped that by modifying the ritual to work directly through the gods rather than blind, malleable but often unevolved spirits, she could avoid the use of maledictions,' that is the use of threats to compel the spirit to obey (Greer 1995: 171). Perhaps one of the reasons why the ritual is often reprinted is that the participants claimed the ritual was successful.[56] Another might be because multiple, full copies of the ritual are available. Regardless of why, The Ritual for the Evocation unto Visible Appearance of the Great Spirit Taphthartharath is one of the most well-known Golden Dawn magical ceremonies.

Aleister Crowley met Bennett after Crowley entered the Hermetic Order of the Golden Dawn in 1899. According to Crowley's account, it was at one of Crowley's Golden Dawn initiations that the meeting took place. The first words Bennett said to Crowley were, 'Little Brother, you have been meddling with the Goetia.' Crowley lied, replying that he had not. Bennett replied, 'In that case, the Goetia have been meddling with you' (Crowley 1989: 178).[57] Shortly after, Crowley searched for Bennett and found him living in squalor with another Golden Dawn member, Charles Rosher. Crowley offered Bennett a deal. If he would become his magical teacher, Bennett could become his roommate at Crowley's expense. At the time, Crowley had money, as he had come into his father's inheritance, derived from owning and operating a brewery. Bennett accepted and moved into Crowley's flats, located at 67 and 69 Chancery Lane. There, Bennett began to teach Crowley magic. Crowley wrote that under his tuition he made rapid progress (Crowley 1989: 181). Their activities included analysing magical texts, evoking spirits, creating talismans and various other types of ceremonial magic.

A story Crowley repeated frequently, although the details are slightly different with each telling, is one in which Bennett used a magical wand, a 'lustre,' to demonstrate the power of magic by knocking a person unconscious. The version from Crowley's autobiography, *The Confessions of Aleister Crowley*, is the one most refer to:

> [Bennett] used to carry a "lustre"—a long glass prism with a neck and a pointed knob such as adorned old-fashioned chandeliers. He used this as a wand. One day, a party of theosophists were chatting skeptically about the power of the "blasting rod." Allan promptly produced his and blasted one of them. It took fourteen hours to

> restore the incredulous individual to the use of his mind and his muscles. (Crowley 1989: 180)

In a shortened version of the story, Crowley writes:

> He had a "blasting rod" constructed simply of the lustre of an old-fashioned chandelier, and he was always cheerfully ready to demonstrate its power by pointing it at any convenient skeptic, and paralyzing him for a few hours or days. (Crowley 1998: 23–24)

Finally, in a newspaper article, 'In Search of the Absolute,' in a London newspaper, *The Sunday Referee*, on March 10, 1935, Crowley also describes Bennett's use of the lustre:

> For he was known all over London as the one magician who could really do big-time stuff. There was, for instance, a party at Sidney Colvin's.[58] He was a collector of unusual people. The conversation turned upon the "blasting-rod" and somebody pooh poohed it loudly. Allan produced his pocket wand, a lustre from a chandelier, and pointed it at the incredulous one. Fifteen hours later the doctors got the doubter back to consciousness. (Crowley 1935: 9)

In all these versions, what is consistent is that, when someone doubted the power of magic, Bennett used his magical wand, a lustre from a chandelier, and proved its effectiveness by 'blasting' them unconscious. Whether this story is true or not, it nevertheless demonstrates the consistency with which Crowley promoted Bennett as a powerful magician.

Crowley states that Bennett had an additional wand. This wand was designated for 'serious magical work.' Crowley describes it as 'a rod of almond tipped with a golden star of five points, each engraved with a letter of the Ineffable Name Jeheshua (יהשוה).' In the centre of the wand was a diamond. Crowley claims that Bennett would trace figures in the air with it, which would be visible to the ordinary eye, appearing as a bluish-white light (Crowley 1998: 23–24). Separately, Crowley claims that Bennett's magical work was always visible to the eye because he lacked the ability to visualise, a skill essential to many types of magical work. Crowley writes:

> I ought to premise that [Bennett] suffered from one really terrific handicap—he was simply unable to visualize at all. If he were looking at a picture, a building or even the simplest geometrical pattern, and closed his eyes, no impression remained in his memory. So when he did see a thing, it was at least objective, even though his impression of what he saw might be false. (Crowley 1935: 9)

Because both Crowley and Bennett were close to the head of the Golden Dawn, Samuel Liddell MacGregor Mathers, they began adding MacGregor to their names while rooming together. Some of those who have written about Bennett have claimed that MacGregor Mathers adopted Bennett.[59] This is unlikely. Nevertheless, it is probable that Bennett met Mathers in 1894, when Bennett joined the Theosophical Society. This would place Bennett in his very early twenties, a time when he was already supporting himself, to the best of his ability, and was too old to be adopted. That said, these statements about adoption could indicate that Mathers acted as a father figure for Bennett, especially since Bennett grew up fatherless. Moreover, there is strong evidence that Bennett was close to Mathers personally. Bennett stayed with him in Paris for a period at least twice in 1895 and 1897 (Howe 1972: 155, 187). When Mathers's leadership of the Hermetic Order of the Golden Dawn was challenged, Bennett sided with Mathers in opposition to almost all his peers.[60] Claims would also emerge that Bennett was Scottish, based on the use of the name MacGregor (e.g., Daily Telegraph 1908: 12).

While Bennett was Crowley's roommate, he pursued his experiments in electricity and other areas of science. One area he investigated was self-hypnosis as a means of treating insomnia, a condition he might have suffered from. With Crowley's financial help, Bennett patented the device he imagined. The patent documentation describes 'An Improved Means for Use in or connected with the Cure of Insomnia' as the following:

> By means of this oscilating [sic] or revolving shutter for instance, which is actuated by clockwork mechanism ... the word "sleep," or other adopted device is as aforesaid intermittently illuminated and this intermittent illumination produces that fatigue of the optic nerves which is the readiest cause of hypnosis.
>
> It will be understood that in operation the patient lying on his or her right side and the illumination of the device proceeding from left to right, there will be induced a continual tendency to gaze upward, an act which in itself is highly conducive to hypnosis and the utilization of a word such as "sleep," being continually conveyed to the mind of the patient further acts as a powerful hypnotic suggestion to that end.
>
> Having now particularly described and ascertained the nature of my said invention, and in what manner the same is to be performed, I declare that what I claim is:—
>
> 1. The means for the effectual cure of insomnia consisting of an apparatus for use in combination with a lamp or other source

of light not contained by the apparatus, whereby the light from the said lamp or other source of light is reflected from a design or device caused to revolve in a horizontal plane in a direction contrary to that of the hands of a clock, directly into the eyes of a patient, the patient being situated in such a position as to induce a continual tendency to gaze upward, substantially as and for the purposes specified.
2. The modified apparatus for use in the cure of insomnia, whereby a transparent device in an opaque background is caused to be intermittently illuminated by a source of light contained in the apparatus, the illumination proceeding from left to right, substantially as and for the purposes hereinbefore specified.
3. In apparatus for the cure of insomnia of the class described, the utilization of a particular class of device such as the word "sleep," for the purpose of conveying the desired suggestion to the mind of the patient, substantially as and for the purpose specified.[61]

The name on the patent description is Allan Bennett MacGregor, and the lawyers filing for the patent were Hughes and Young, located at 55 and 56 Chancery Lane, London. This was the law office Crowley used and was located just down the street from where Crowley and Bennett lived.

THE ABANDONMENT OF OCCULTISM

Towards the end of 1899, it was clear that Bennett's health was waning, and that he needed to leave London for a better climate. Additionally, Crowley notes that Bennett was losing interest in occultism and was becoming more interested in Eastern traditions. As we have shown, he had already become familiar with Hinduism and Buddhism through the Theosophical Society and from directly reading scriptures, in translation, from both. George Cecil Jones, Jr. (1873–1960), a chemist and one time member of the Golden Dawn, along with Crowley, performed a Goetic evocation of Buer to obtain funds for Bennett's trip. While a Goetic entity appeared, it did not match their expectation and thus they dismissed it (Crowley 1989: 181).[62] Shortly after, Crowley claims to have obtained the funds, £100, from a former mistress. He gave this to Bennett, who began his preparations to leave for Ceylon.

Before he left London, Bennett gave most of his magical notebooks to Crowley, perhaps keeping an incomplete one back. From them, Crowley

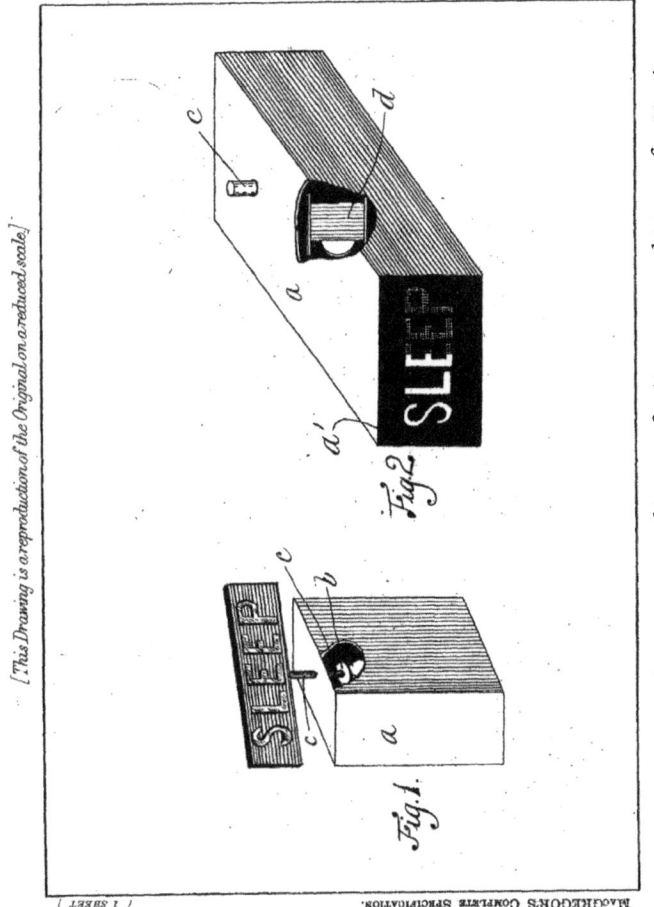

Figure 1.4 Bennett's 1899 patent diagram for 'An Improved Means for Use in or Connected with the Cure of Insomnia.' Courtesy of European Patent Organisation, https://worldwide.espacenet.com/

extracted numerous rituals and other texts. *A Note on Genesis*, in which Bennett presents a study of the Hebrew Kabbalah, was one of these.⁶³ Crowley reprinted the essay in his journal *The Equinox* in 1909. In the essay, Bennett describes his interpretation of the first verse of the first chapter of Genesis, 'In the beginning, created, God, the Essence of the Heavens, and the Essence of the Earth,' in Hebrew (בראשית ברא אלהים את השמים ואת הארץ; Frater I.A. 1909: 167). In summary, the essay examines how seven Hebrew words describe the way God created being from nothing. Bennett begins with a prefatory note:

> But before I may proceed unto the Qabalistical enumeration and analysis of the Text, a certain preamble in the fruitful fields of that Science will become necessary. The Evolution of the Numbers is the Evolution of the Worlds, for as it is written in the *Clavicula Salomonis*, "The Numbers are Ideas; and the Ideas are the Powers, and the Powers are the Holy Elohim of Life." That which is behind and beyond all Number and all thought (even as the Ain Soph with its Mighty Veils depending back from Kether is behind and beyond all Manifestation) is the Number 0. Its symbol is the very Emblem of Infinite Space and Infinite Time. (Frater I.A. 1909: 168)⁶⁴

Crowley also used other notebook entries of Bennett's to create a Kabbalistic dictionary, the previously mentioned *Sepher Sephiroth*, which Crowley published in *The Equinox* in 1912 (Bennett and Crowley 1912). Crowley claims that Bennett had created the basis of the dictionary and that he and others had contributed to it.

Bennett's notebooks have been a source of inspiration to magicians and occultists for the last century. By containing The Ritual for the Evocation unto Visible Appearance of the Great Spirit Taphthartharath, and other talismanic ceremonies, as well as other ritual fragments, essays and notes, the notebooks have been reproduced, in whole or part, by individuals and magical groups around the world. The material Bennett authored also contributed greatly to the magical revival that began in the 1950s in America, which resulted in the reestablishment of the Golden Dawn by modern magicians. As Crowley integrated much of the material into his own rituals and practices, the thousands of occultists that have continued to be members of the groups he started have also carried on Bennett's magical work. Despite giving up occultism in pursuit of Buddhism, by giving his magical notebooks to Crowley, Bennett established a magical legacy that continues today. We examine this in Chapter Six.

With the money obtained by Crowley, Bennett was able to book his passage out of England for Ceylon, a trip he embarked upon either at the end of 1899 or the first part of 1900.⁶⁵ Bennett never looked back to his days practising occultism. Crowley would come to visit him several times after he left England, first in Ceylon and then in Burma. When they first met up in Ceylon, Bennett was already focused on meditation and Buddhism. When they met again, Bennett had fully focused on Buddhism. Following his teacher, Crowley began to seriously consider the merits of Buddhism, but ultimately rejected it. Their last meeting seems to have been in 1905 in Burma, although there is some indication that they may have met in 1908 during Ananda M's mission in London.⁶⁶ Bennett also wrote letters to Crowley, at least up to 1905.⁶⁷ While Bennett pursued the dharma and its spread to the West, Crowley embarked on the life of a magician, focused on occultism. Although they would likely never meet again after 1905, the time they spent together had a great impact on both of them. Unfortunately, as will be shown, their past involvement with each other, and Crowley's flamboyant and controversial life, created problems for Bennett in the future.

2

Allan Bennett in Ceylon

In July 1901, Allan Bennett, who at the time was calling himself Allan MacGregor, still evoking his relationship with MacGregor Mathers, read a paper on the 'Four Noble Truths' at the Hope Lodge of the Theosophical Society in Colombo (MacGregor 1902).[1] It was the first time he had spoken in Colombo and it is obvious that he took the responsibility seriously. It was not, of course, the first time he had spoken publicly in a Theosophical Society lodge or taken a leading role in ritual. He had done so numerous times in the 1890s. But this was the first time he had spoken to Buddhists about Buddhism. The audience would have largely been middle-class and English-speaking Buddhists, with perhaps a handful of Western Theosophists who had come to aid the Buddhist revival in the country.[2] It is highly unlikely that any Sri Lankan converts to Christianity or Christian missionaries were present, since both could have been reprimanded for entering Buddhist 'spaces' and thereby setting a negative example to other converts, who were encouraged to reject their former religion completely (Harris 2006: 53–61; 2018: 25–42).

Up until this point, he had largely passed under the radar of the English-speaking Buddhist elite in Colombo, who would have come to hear him out of curiosity and perhaps with some scepticism.[3] By his own admission, he spoke with 'diffidence' (MacGregor 1902: 9) and presented himself as 'an alien,' whose knowledge of Buddhism was inferior to those who were 'Buddhist-born' (MacGregor 1902: 10), although there can be no doubt that he now saw himself as Buddhist. He warned his listeners that they 'must look for nothing new' in what he said and craved indulgence for what he may have 'understood wrongly' (MacGregor 1902: 10). What he presented, however, on the evidence of the printed text, was fluent and poetic, a foreshadowing of his later writing in Burma, although his presentation might have been rather timid. Throughout his life, he found it difficult to speak loudly, without shyness, in public.

The paper he gave demonstrated an awareness of Pali literature and justified, with clarity, his decision to focus on the Four Noble Truths. For those sensitive enough to hear, the time he spent on the first 'truth,' the realisation that there is 'pity and woe' in 'all sentient existence' (MacGregor 1902: 13), betrayed his own intimate encounters with suffering.[4] His mention that all other religions except Islam taught 'the utter misery and futility of all earthly existence' (MacGregor 1902: 11) pointed to his spiritual explorations before he came to Ceylon, typical of Theosophists, who were encouraged to study all the world's religions comparatively. If there were any Theosophists in the audience, they would have warmed to this. He also referred to the 'Oneness' of all life, a common theme in Theosophical literature but not so common within Theravada Buddhism (Blavatsky 1993a: 20). For Bennett, this 'Oneness' made the suffering of others almost unbearable:

> And knowing that great truth of the Oneness of all—not merely of all humanity, but of all holiest and meanest lives—have you learned this, and can you say, this day I have no sorrow? No sorrow, when the eyes of your brothers are filled with tears? When the whole face of fair-seeing nature is but the mask of an intolerable and a continuous cruelty when the air vibrates with the cry of living helpless things in pain? ... What woe greater than to feel apart from other life, to feel that one is against these other lives, and for himself alone, to be without pity for the weak, and sorrow for the sorrow of all. (MacGregor 1902: 13)[5]

Significantly, he urged his listeners to give up the 'belief in a soul' and presented the concept of a 'great God, away somewhere there in heaven' as a fiction born of desire that hindered a person who sought the 'Law of Love and Truth' (MacGregor 1902: 15). With this, he dramatically moved away from Theosophy and indeed some rituals of the Order of the Golden Dawn that he once judged to be 'true and sacred' (Howe 1972: 141–142), affirming his identification with Buddhism. In The Ritual for the Evocation unto Visible Appearance of the Great Spirit Taphthartharath, for instance, the idea of non-self was implicitly present but within a framework through which selfhood was gained through submission to a higher power.[6] Now, in 1901, he stressed the Buddhist concept of *anattā* (non-self),[7] stripped of any higher power framework, and this difference regarding the soul would be a frequent topic of disagreement between Bennett and Theosophists for years to come. He then, nevertheless, made a spirited defence of devotion, 'of adoration,' not to a deity but to the Buddha, as an expression of sheer love for what the Buddha had given to the world and a tribute to 'the incomparable life and pity and love of our Great Teacher' (MacGregor 1902: 15–16).

Bennett's words were spoken with passion. Commitment shone through, especially when he set himself the task of summarising Buddhism in one word and chose—'Pity, because it implies Love, as well as the Sorrow which stands at the foundation of our Faith' (MacGregor 1902: 18). He ended with *nibbāna* (enlightenment/liberation), 'the Silence, and the Great Peace' (MacGregor 1902: 20).

ARRIVAL IN CEYLON

Bennett arrived in Colombo in early 1900, at a time when Ceylon had been under British rule for just over 100 years. Two cameos from his journey to Ceylon survive. Years later, he would tell Edgar Bradford, a Wesleyan Methodist missionary in Burma, that 'when he first came out East it was a great surprise to him to meet on the steamer intelligent folk who still adhered to Christianity' (Purser and Saunders 1914: 86), suggesting that he met Christian missionaries on the ship and engaged in conversation with them. The second comes from Aleister Crowley, who states that Bennett's asthma disappeared on the voyage, so much so that he threw 'overboard his entire apparatus of drugs' (Crowley 1989: 238).

As previously noted, Bennett gave most of his magical notebooks to Crowley before leaving London, suggesting that Bennett wanted a new start. Yet, he could not jettison his past completely. The rituals of the Golden Dawn had become part of him, as had the mindset of an occultist. These combined with his long-standing interest in Buddhism and Hinduism. There was also one experience from his past that he could have wanted to rediscover in Asia, namely the previously mentioned experience of 'Shivadarshana' that, according to Crowley, occurred in 1890.[8] Crowley's judgement, that this experience 'determined the whole course of his life' (Crowley 1989: 238), only partially hits the truth, but the search for methods of meditation that led to higher states of consciousness and insight marked Bennett's time in Asia.

Ceylon was Bennett's first direct experience of Britain's imperial power. His freethought background and innate sensitivity to suffering meant that he would have quickly realised that he had entered a context of struggle and discontent among the Ceylonese. In future years, this, together with his experience in Burma, would make him a vocal critic of British imperial arrogance. His experience at Hollesley College might have prepared him for some of this, but certainly not all. The College, after all, would have stressed the opportunities within the 'colonies,' not the discontent of the native inhabitants.

The British administration, for instance, was boasting considerable achievements in building the island's economic infrastructure. The Governor, Joseph West Ridgeway, reviewing the public works undertaken between 1896 and 1903, during Bennett's time there, states that 300 bridges 'had been built in places where previously no bridges at all existed,' and that 'over 400 timber bridges had been converted into more permanent structures' (West Ridgeway 1903: 37). Fourteen hospitals had been established in the same period and a sizeable number of new police stations. His review also boasts a marked reduction in the number of cholera and smallpox cases (West Ridgeway 1903: 94) and the introduction, in 1901, of electric street lights in Kandy, the main town in the central hill country, which Bennett visited towards the end of his stay in the country. West Ridgeway's review regrets, however, that the import of opium had increased, and describes ways in which the government was seeking to restrict its abuse (West Ridgeway 1903: 115).[9]

This official narrative, however, masked the religious re-awakening, and consequent inter-religious tension, that was occurring in Ceylon, both in the predominantly Buddhist south and the majority Hindu north. For instance, West Ridgeway states of education:

> The harmony with which the present system works is remarkable. There is no conscience clause, but all schools are bound to devote certain hours to secular education, attendance at other hours being optional. There is no friction in the towns and larger villages—only healthy rivalry and competition. Protestant and Roman Catholic in particular avoid conflict and trespassing on each other's field of labour. The tolerance with which Buddhists and even Mohammedans send their children to mission schools is remarkable, and has no parallel in any country with which I am acquainted. (West Ridgeway 1903: 61)

West Ridgeway was right to point to the fact that many Buddhists and Muslims were willing to send their children to schools run by Roman Catholics and Protestant missionaries, and that there was no compulsion for Buddhist and Muslim students to attend classes on Christianity. However, a Buddhist revival, predicated on anti-missionary sentiment and aided by Western Theosophists, was transforming education in the country, through the founding of Buddhist schools, which were at first located so that they would be in direct competition to those run by the missionaries and convert Ceylonese Christians (Harris 2018: 57–62). Some of these eventually flourished, for example Mahinda College in the southern port of Galle. Founded in 1892, it struggled under a number of foreign and local principals until 1903, when it came under the inspired leadership of a British Theosophist, Frank Lee Woodward (1871–1952), who remained in post for 16 years (Gunewardene 1973). Others collapsed, because local Buddhists could not sustain the cost. The atmosphere between Buddhists and Christians in the field of education, therefore, was not one of 'healthy rivalry and competition,' but acrimonious competition.[10]

There were other causes of discontent under West Ridgeway, for instance the Waste Land Ordinances that judged communally owned village land to be waste land and, therefore, state property (Lewis 1926: 365; Harris 2018: 110). Additionally, when Bennett was in Ceylon, there were significant increases in the cases brought to court involving murder and homicide, robbery, burglary, arson and riot, and the number of these cases referred to the Supreme Court increased.[11]

As a former Theosophist, it is significant that Bennett did not offer himself to the educational projects of Buddhist revivalists in Ceylon, as many European Theosophists had done. Crowley asserts that Bennett's 'first idea had been to take the Yellow Robe' (Crowley 1989: 237). Two decades later, Ananda M would share at a Buddhist meeting in London that, on his first day in Ceylon, he went to a Buddhist temple in Maradana, a part of Colombo, and met an English-speaking Thai monk there, experiencing for the first time the 'all-but palpable power' of Buddhism's presence (The Buddhist Review 1920a: 214–215).[12] This would seem to support Crowley's words. Yet, Crowley also states that Bennett, during his time in Ceylon, was offered the management of a coconut plantation but refused because he would have needed to kill vermin (Crowley 1989: 238). This is not far-fetched. In the 1890s, there were several old boys of the Colonial College in Ceylon, working as planters, to the extent that one of them, H. H. Beamish, hoped to arrange a 'College Dinner' at the beginning of 1900.[13] Beamish could have been related to Ananda M's batchmate, L. H. Beamish, and it is not impossible that he offered Bennett this post. Crowley additionally states that Bennett had also been offered 'the post of treasurer to a famous monastery outside Colombo,' because they could not trust a Ceylonese to do the job (Crowley 1989: 237).

Most of the information about Bennett's early months in Ceylon, however, comes from Cassius Pereira, a Ceylonese Buddhist who became one of his closest friends. One of the first choices Bennett made, in line with his thoughts about ordination as a Buddhist monk, was to spend several months at Divigalahēna Dēvāgiri Purāna Vihāraya in Kamburugamuwa on the south coast of Ceylon, one of a number of small vegetable-exporting villages between the towns of Matara and Weligama (Cave 1908: 170), which were, by the end of the nineteenth century, accessible by train (Wright 1907: 195–196). The Vihāraya traced its history to about 700 CE according to an informant in Kamburugamuwa, Hewadiddenige Mahindaratne.[14] In 1900, it had a respected scholar monk at its head, Veragampita Rēvata Thera, and belonged to the reformist body of monks, the Amarapura Nikāya.[15]

Cassius Pereira states that Bennett gained an introduction to the Vihāraya from J. E. Richard Pereira, namely Cassius's own father (Pereira 1923a: 6). Bennett met the Pereira family early into his time in Ceylon, perhaps because he was presenting himself as Scottish through the name MacGregor. Richard Pereira had married a woman of Scottish descent, Jeannie Mary Wilson, Cassius's mother.[16] There are three other possibilities. In 1899, Richard Pereira had founded the Buddhist Aid Association, with a group of like-minded people. He was also involved with the Vajirarāma Vihāraya at Bambalapitiya, south of the centre of Colombo, near his home in Havelock Road,[17] which a reformist monk of the Amarapura Nikāya, Pelene Vajirañāna, was in the process of founding. Both of these things could have drawn Bennett to the Pereira family.[18] Given Pereira's involvement with Pelene Vajirañāna's project, it is also not surprising that Pereira recommended Rēvata Thera, although he was not widely known to Western orientalists.[19] Pelene Vajirañāna was closely connected

Figure 2.1 Venerable Veragampita Rēvata Thera, courtesy of the Sri Saddhatissa International Buddhist Centre, London.

to the temple in Kamburugamuwa. Indeed, Rēvata Thera was probably his Pali teacher.[20] Research done by Handupelpola Mahinda Nayake Thera for the commemoration of the centenary of Ananda M's mission to Britain by the Sri Saddhatissa International Buddhist Centre in London offers the third possibility, namely that a prominent Sri Lankan Buddhist living in London in the 1890s, Wilmot Arthur de Silva (1869–1942), gave Ananda M accommodation in Ceylon and introduced him to Richard Pereira, who, in turn, took him to Kamburugamuwa (Madawela 2008; Mahinda 2008: 47).[21] We consider this to be a strong possibility, especially since de Silva, together with Richard Pereira, became the Ceylonese representatives of Ananda M's *Buddhasāsana Samāgama* (International Buddhist Society), which he inaugurated in Burma.[22]

Gaining information about this period of Bennett's life is difficult. When Elizabeth visited the Kamburugamuwa Vihāraya in 2018, the Head Monk, Malandeniye Vipassi Thera, claimed that Rēvata had written diaries that mentioned Bennett and that these had been in the possession of the Vihāraya. He added with bitterness that they had been removed by another scholar, who had not returned them. She was shown, however, a book giving the lineage of the Vihāraya, which contained the name of Allan Bennett (not MacGregor this time) but without a date. She was also shown a pamphlet with a versification of the *Mahā Supina Jātaka*,[23] produced jointly by Rēvata and Bennett.[24] According to Vipassi Thera, Rēvata had been known for his knowledge of Pali, his holiness, and even miracles. Apparently, there was a tradition that a snake came to listen to his preaching, waiting in the *bana maḍuva* (preaching hall) for him to speak.

Drawing on what his father had gleaned from the oral memory of the Kamburugamuwa villagers, Mahindaratne stated that some people had reacted badly when Bennett had tried to preach as a foreigner and when posters were displayed about a foreign person preaching *dhamma* (the truth, the teaching of the Buddha). He had also been known for the thinness of his body. However, he must have won over the villagers, because, eventually, he became famous for his preaching and his attempts to use Pali. Cassius Pereira states that Bennett could converse fluently in Pali after learning the language for six months (Pereira 1923a: 6). That he could use Pali fluently in written and spoken forms after such a short period is highly unlikely. That he learnt some Pali in Kamburugamuwa and could use it in a colloquial context, however, is almost certain, and he took this forward into his later monastic training. At the end of the nineteenth century, Pali was still used colloquially within some monastic settings across the Theravada world.

We can imagine Bennett spending a lot of his time attempting to learn Pali and delving into the Pali texts, some no doubt in translation, knowledge of which he demonstrated at the Hope Lodge lecture. The Harry Ransom Centre in Austin, Texas, holds an intriguing notebook that belonged to Bennett. It is not dated but internal evidence suggests that it was one of the few notebooks he took to Ceylon, because it was only half full. It begins with ceremonial magic, including a ritual entitled The Ascent unto Daath. After a few blank pages, there are then translations from the *Dhammapada* with the Pali, written in pen, on the right-hand side and the translation, written in pencil, on the left. Many scholars of Pali begin with accessible texts such as the *Dhammapada*, and Bennett may also have done so, careful to use only pencil on the left-hand side so that mistakes could be erased. After these translations, there are scientific diagrams and calculations but no further ceremonial magic.[25]

Bennett's time in Kamburugamuwa, however, might not have been easy. It was a small village, although only three miles from one of the main towns in the South, Matara,[26] where evangelical Christian missionaries were active and Buddhist revivalism was strong. He would have been in an almost entirely Sinhala-speaking environment, although Rēvata himself might have conversed quite well in English. Although his aim was to learn Pali rather than Sinhala, this meant he would have learnt some colloquial Sinhala to communicate with the villagers in his day-to-day activity. For he would certainly have walked into the surrounding villages and agricultural land, given the appreciation of the natural environment that permeated his later writing.

After about six months in the south of the country, Bennett returned to Colombo (Pereira 1923a: 6), without opting for novice ordination. Crowley states that 'Allan' became 'fearfully disappointed by the degeneracy of the Singalese bhikkhus' (Crowley 1989: 237). He does not mention when this happened. If it was in Kamburugamuwa, and this is probable, this might explain Bennett's decision. Residing alongside the monastic Sangha (community) in Ceylon could have disillusioned him, bringing him face-to-face with laxity in monastic discipline or a lack of interest in meditation and spiritual practice.[27] Both would have sorely disappointed him. It was the reformist Rāmañña Nikāya, not the Amarapura Nikāya, which pursued meditation practice at the time (Crosby 2020: 83). As Crowley remarks, 'Allan was almost puritanically strict' and he would have applied this to the practice of Buddhism (Crowley 1989: 238). In 1903, when Bennett returned to Ceylon as Ananda Metteyya to open Maitriya Hall, he would say publicly:

> When, aforetime, I lived amongst you, I saw many things in this land concerning your religion and your lives—and some I fear, that filled me with surprise and shame to see in holy Lanka—the last things I had expected to see in a Buddhist land. I saw men who were held in honour amongst you—the leaders of your people, men of power and wealth—grown heedless of the faith which was aforetime the glory and the pride of Lanka—or, worse still ashamed to bear the name of Buddhist (Ananda Maitriya 1903n: 182).

Although he was mainly referring to the breaking of the five precepts through the drinking of alcohol, his words could have embraced other sources of disappointment. He also stated that only two things told a story that was different from the negative picture he had painted—the establishing of Buddhist schools and the forerunner of Maitriya Hall, namely 'a thatched shed as a school where Bhikkhus might learn what Western knowledge can teach them' (Ananda Maitriya 1903n: 182–183).[28]

According to a letter Bennett wrote to a British friend, he left Kamburugamuwa in about August 1900, when he had already decided what his next step would be—to go to a Śaivite guru and politician, Ponnambalam Ramanathan (1851–1930), who was Solicitor General of the country.[29] That Bennett chose Ramanathan indicated a wish to continue his earlier interest in meditation and yoga. Bennett could have known about Ramanathan, cousin of Ananda Coomaraswamy (1877–1947), before coming to Ceylon, through Ramanathan's links with Theosophy and the Golden Dawn.[30] Ramanathan was not only a politician and a lawyer, but also an expert in Tamil and Sanskrit, and a Hindu Śaivite spiritual teacher/guru, who was becoming known internationally for his ability to draw Hindu and Christian teaching together (e.g., Parānanda 1898; 1902; Ramanathan 1905).[31]

In Ceylon, Ramanathan was appreciated both by Buddhists and Theosophists, because of his support for Buddhist education, evidenced in his speeches to the Legislative Council. For instance, on 11 February, 1884, he spoke 'On the Religious Intolerance of Certain Christian missionary managers of Grant-in-Aid-Schools in the Northern Province of Ceylon,' namely in the predominantly Hindu north (Anon 1929a: 85–88), but his words also had a message for education in the Buddhist south. In 1888, he spoke stridently in favour of better management of lands held by Buddhist temples, 'as a question of remedying a great social evil which is daily gnawing into the vitals of the Sinhalese' (Anon 1929a: 169–170). As for the Theosophists, Ramanathan's biographer claims that 'Olcott's faith in Ramanathan was so unbounded that he made him joint treasurer with himself of the immense funds he raised for the furtherance of Buddhist education' (Vythilingam 1971: 476–477).[32]

Ramanathan visited Europe twice, once in 1886 for five months (Vythilingam 1971: 298) and again in 1897 to represent Ceylon at Queen Victoria's Diamond Jubilee celebrations. It is possible that he made informal contact with Theosophists on both visits, and possibly with members of the Golden Dawn on the second.[33] In 1886, Bennett, still a teenager, was not yet involved with Theosophy. In 1897, however, he might well have heard about him or even met him. Ramanathan, therefore, was someone to whom Bennett would naturally have been drawn when he returned to Colombo, disillusioned perhaps with the lack of meditation practice within Ceylonese Buddhist monasticism.

Ramanathan's biographer does not mention Bennett but does write, 'Many a Westerner, thirsting for religious knowledge or seeking enlightenment, was drawn to his [Ramanathan's] home in Colombo and had the satisfaction of certainties dispelled' (Vythilingam 1971: 495). One of them, in 1903, was the lawyer, Myron Phelps, Director of the Monsalvat School for the Comparative Study of Religion (Ramanathan 1907: iii–iv), who studied with Ramanathan for about a year (Vythilingam 1971: 514). He was then instrumental in bringing Ramanathan to America in 1906. Bennett was another. Whether he was employed, however, to tutor Ramanathan's younger son/s, as Crowley states (Crowley 1989: 237), is questionable. Ramanathan's first marriage took place in 1874 when he was 23 (Vythilingam 1971:105) The three sons and three daughters from this marriage would have passed beyond the age for tutoring by the time of Bennett's arrival, although we have not been able to find their exact dates of birth. That there were children within Ramanathan's extended family, however, is highly likely.

Whether Bennett actually tutored Ramanathan's sons or not, he certainly went to Ramanathan for instruction in yoga and yogic meditation. Ramanathan may also have shared his personal religious philosophy with Bennett, namely that underlying all true religion was an esoteric, inner message and path about the release of the 'soul' from mind and body into boundless love (Ramanathan 1907: 247–248). Bennett would have been familiar with this view of the soul from Theosophy, but had rejected it by the time of his Hope Lodge lecture.

That Bennett was combining Buddhist and Hindu methods of meditation at this time is confirmed by Cassius Pereira. Bennett visited the Pereira household (Pereira 1947: 67) and taught meditation to the teenage Cassius. Cassius had initially thought everything he learnt was Buddhist. Only later did he realise that it combined a number of traditions. His conclusion was that Bennett was then 'vague, wonder-seeking, and really only played about the fringe of a truly marvellous avenue for study and practice' (Pereira 1947: 67). He would much later tell Alec Robertson, a lay Buddhist who became key to an organisation that Cassius Pereira founded, the Servants of the Buddha, that Allan experimented with an Indian form of *prāṇāyāma*, which involved taking in deep breaths and holding. This is most significant. It looks back to Bennett's practice in Britain and points to what he sought and practised under Ramanathan.

Aleister Crowley visited Bennett in August 1901, arriving on the 6th, during Bennett's work with Ramanathan—'the pupil of a Shaivite guru,' in Crowley's terminology (Crowley 1989: 234)—but when his mind was turning once more to ordination as a *bhikkhu* (Pali: Buddhist monk). On 17 August, the two of them, Bennett having left his work with Ramanathan, lived in a rented, furnished bungalow called Marlborough that was situated above the man-made lake in Kandy, an administrative centre in the hill country of the island. We only have Crowley's account of this period and a notebook, to which both contributed. Kandy would have been an obvious choice for the yoga retreat that Crowley suggested, and paid for, with Bennett as teacher (Crowley 1989: 238). It was easily accessible by train, cooler than Colombo—Crowley was again worried by 'Allan's' health—beautifully located, accustomed to visitors from all over the world, and landscaped with paths for walking. Communication in English would also not have been difficult. One eloquent but excessive tourist guide of the town, written by Henry Cave, founder of an important publishing firm within Ceylon, points to the 'botanical wonders' on walks from the town (Cave 1894: 61) and the unforgettable experience of seeing 'the overhanging hillsides, sparkling with the fairy lights of fireflies' on an evening stroll around the lake (Cave 1894: 53). Of the bungalows of Kandy, he writes:

> An attractive feature of this scenery will be found in the neat little bungalows, with their deep pillared verandahs and their luxuriant gardens, bright with the endless variety of gorgeous crotons, which grow to perfection of colour in the sunny clime of this mountain region. (Cave 1894: 53)

Marlborough was just such a bungalow.[34] High above the lake, the present owner stripped the doors and walls of numerous coats of paint when he occupied it in the 1980s, returning them to what they might originally have been—dark oak doors and windows, and walls painted in a mellow sandstone colour. It is a sizeable, one-storeyed dwelling with a 'deep pillared verandah' on the two sides that overlook the lake, although thick foliage now obscures the lake itself. In 2018, when Elizabeth visited it, the bungalow was surrounded on the other two sides by new building developments, mostly apartments of the type that now scale the Kandyan hills, coveted because they are above the rather polluted town centre. In 1901, the bungalow would have been completely surrounded by green, possibly with a more open view down to the lake and Kandy itself. There would have been some smaller dwellings along the paths that led to Marlborough and perhaps a few other bungalows. Bennett and Crowley, however, would have found themselves in a haven of peace, except for the 'headman' they hired and the 'servants' the headman sub-hired (Crowley 1989: 236).

The present owner remembers a newspaper article in the 1980s that claimed two princes from the UK had come to Marlborough and practised voodoo. We have not been able to find this. In 1996, a serialised article on Crowley's links to Ceylon appeared in the Sri Lankan press, drawn mainly from his *Confessions*, with no mention of voodoo (Boyle 1996) and, in 1999, a further article on Crowley was published that completely omits his link with Ceylon (Patterson 1999). The possibility that there was such an article in the 1980s, however, points to the presence of oral memory about the months that Bennett and Crowley stayed there, watched no doubt by their headman and servants, who would not have been silent about their experiences.

Crowley's formal account of the time that he and Bennett spent in Kandy mentions the practice of *prāṇāyāma* (breathing practice), *āsana* (correct sitting), *pratyāhāra* ('introspection' according to Crowley but, traditionally, withdrawal of consciousness from the senses and external world), *dhāraṇā* (concentration), *dhyāna* (meditative absorption) and *samādhi* (one-pointed concentration), which Crowley describes as the final 'trance' and 'Union with the Lord' (Crowley 1989: 238–243; 246–248). His notebook from this time additionally mentions the *cakra*, or chakras, (centres of energy in the body), different forms of breathing, *mokṣa* (release from rebirth in Hinduism), *atman*, described by Crowley as 'the Self or Knower,' and the five *kośa* (coverings or sheaths of the *atman*). All these terms are Sanskrit, not Pali, although *samādhi* is shared by both languages. This, together with Crowley's description, suggests that the two of them practised the largely Hindu methods Bennett had been taught under Ramanathan, although these could have been combined with the Buddhist practice of *dhyāna* (*jhāna* in Pali), since, at one point, Crowley describes *dhyāna* as beginning with bliss and ending in 'indifference,' the correct Buddhist progression (Crowley 1989: 244).[35]

That their practice mainly drew from Hinduism is further confirmed by material inserted into Crowley's notebook by Bennett. Although this contains the Tibetan Buddhist mantra, *Oṃ maṇi padme hum*, its focus is worship of the divine feminine principle in Hinduism. Bennett writes, for instance, 'Aum! Let us meditate on the Adorable Light of That divine

Savitri. May She enlighten our minds.'[36] In line with this, the notebook also includes, in Bennett's hand, a Sanskrit hymn of praise to Gauri (Pārvatī), representing the Divine Mother, from the *Lalitā Sahasranāma* of the *Brāhmaṇḍa Purāṇa*.

The practice that Crowley and Bennett undertook was intense. Crowley shares one moment in Kandy when he found Bennett tipped up, away from his meditation mat: 'I found him, not seated on his meditation mat . . . but in a distant corner ten or twelve feet off, still in his knotted position, resting on his head and right shoulder, exactly like an image [of the Buddha] overturned' (Crowley 1989: 246). If this had been seen by their Ceylonese helpers, it might indeed have been seen as some form of spirit possession, and if the two were combining yoga with occultism, this would have confirmed their fears.

With reference to their period in Kandy, however, Crowley also writes this:

> Allan had become more and more convinced that he ought to take the Yellow Robe. The phenomenon of Dhyana and Samadhi had ceased to exercise their first fascination. It seemed to him that they were insidious obstacles to true spiritual progress; that their occurrence, in reality, broke the control of the mind which he was trying to establish and prevented him from reaching the ultimate truth which he sought. He had the strength of mind to resist the appeal of even these intense spiritual joys. (Crowley 1989: 249)

Crowley's implication is that Bennett had begun to seek more than the methods he had practised under Ramanathan. Yet, Crowley's words could be misunderstood. The *jhānas* (Pali; Sanskrit: *dhyāna*) and *samādhi* (concentration or one-pointedness of mind) are central to Buddhist meditative practice and feature in many Pali texts. The Pali texts list four meditative absorptions or *jhānas*, together with four further *arūpa* or formless/immaterial states.[37] Furthermore, the *jhānas* are the gateway to *iddhi* or supernormal knowledges and powers, which can include producing 'a mind-made body' by 'drawing the body out of this body,' developing the power to pass through walls and mountains, and knowing other people's minds.[38] Bennett might have glimpsed these extraordinary powers through his practice of meditation in Kandy. The occultist in him might have identified these types of practices as astral travel, a core teaching in the Golden Dawn. Through his growing closeness to Buddhism, however, he might have realised that they were a hindrance to perceiving truth. Buddhist traditions do not deny the importance of *iddhi*, but normatively stress that they can draw practitioners away from the main path to enlightenment because of their tendency to reinforce the ego. Bennett's later writings as a Buddhist monastic play down the existence of *iddhi*.[39]

The evidence of Crowley's account and the notebook, therefore, suggests that the two friends mainly practised Hindu yoga, informed by Buddhist *jhāna* practice, during which Bennett realised that these methods had limitations. Although he probably never gave up the practices he perfected under Ramanathan, they were not articulated in his later writings, most probably because of his fear that they could reinforce the ego rather than lead to realisation of the Buddhist non-self doctrine that he held dear.

The two had a number of diversions from meditation. According to Crowley, they went to the *Daḷadā Māligāva* (The Temple of the Tooth) in Kandy, where they were granted a viewing of the tooth 'at the annual inspection by the trustees,' and also witnessed the annual Äsala Perahära, when the tooth is taken from the temple and placed within an elaborate procession, with numerous elephants, torches, drums and performers. Crowley was energised and made almost delirious by its 'gigantic jollification' and the 'savage noise and blaze of the ceremony' but, of his companion, he says, 'Poor, serious, single-minded Allan, with his whole soul set on alleviating the sufferings of humanity and helping them to reach a higher plane of existence, was saddened and disillusioned' (Crowley

Figure 2.2 Magic Lantern slide from the collection that Ananda M brought to England, showing the Temple of the Tooth in Kandy, courtesy of The Buddhist Society, London.

1989: 250–251). The experience of the Perahära, a ceremony originally connected to the gods, which had only been buddhicised in the mid-eighteenth century by the addition of the tooth relic (Duncan 1990: 128), could have been another reason for his decision to be ordained in Burma. The perception of Burma among some Ceylonese was that Buddhism there was purer than in Ceylon, less adulterated by Hindu elements and in possession of a purer monastic community.[40]

From Kandy, the two visited, by horse-drawn coach, some of the ancient Buddhist sites further to the north: the caves at Dambulla filled with Buddha images; Sigiriya rock topped by the ruins of a palace, although they were unable to climb it; Mihintale, where tradition says Buddhism first arrived on the island; and Anuradhapura, the first Buddhist capital of the island, home to a bodhi tree grown, Buddhists believe, from a sapling of the very tree under which the Buddha gained enlightenment in India (Crowley 1989: 254–255). Bennett was certainly impressed by Anuradhapura. His magic lantern slides of the city that he took to Burma and then brought to England demonstrate this.[41] His later writings about the city, however, avoid his own religious experience, concentrating in preference on the political, including British encroachments into the holy areas and Buddhist resistance to these.[42]

Soon after the period in Kandy, Crowley travelled to India. Bennett remained in Ceylon, making preparations to take a steamer to Akyab in Burma, where Crowley would visit him, after his sojourn in India.

Figure 2.3 Magic Lantern slide from the collection that Ananda M brought to England, showing the monastic Sangha in what appears to be Ceylon, courtesy of The Buddhist Society, London.

Before moving to Bennett's journey to Burma, it is important to say more about his friendship with the Pereira family, particularly Cassius Pereira, who was just 15 when Bennett gave his Hope Lodge lecture.[43] He and Bennett became very close, particularly after Bennett left Ceylon. Pereira told Alec Robertson that they had an almost telepathic communication with each other, knowing what the other was writing and thinking, and even when one of them was writing a letter to the other.[44] That Bennett and Pereira corresponded on more than religious matters is clear from the letters that have survived. Science was one of their passions, possibly started by Bennett's enthusiasm for scientific experimentation. For instance, on 10 February, 1905, Bennett writes to 'Cash' from Burma:

> I would much like to know in what paper appeared the prophecy relative to discoveries in psychology you mention, if you can get at this:—where did you see about it? I can do nothing with the crude appliances at my disposal here,—it is a matter of very delicate measurements, and have written to my friend Crowley to see if he will get the apparatus required and come out and try the experiments with me. Meanwhile I am pottering about in other directions of a minor order, mainly in the matter of trying to produce a substance which shall fluoresce to my hypothetical radiations. Not much of this, even, at present as I am very extra asthmatic.[45]

According to Robertson, Cassius Pereira, as a lay person and as a monk, saw himself as a custodian of Theravada Buddhist orthodoxy. He lamented the laxity of the modern Buddhist monastic Sangha (e.g., Pereira 1918) and was against linking the supernatural with Buddhism, severely criticising a young Robertson on this issue.[46] Most significantly, he championed *samatha* (tranquillity) meditation over *vipassanā* (insight meditation) and taught concentration on the in and out breath (*ānāpāna-sati*) and on the 'bright' objects such as loving kindness (*mettā*).[47] He was part of a controversy over the import of a Burmese method of meditation that involved watching the breath as it entered the belly, arguing that it was inaccurate and that it stimulated sexual feelings (Dirilakuru 1978: 223–224; Bond 1988: 162–171).

Although Pereira was critical of Bennett's practice of *prāṇāyāma*, the writings of the two friends show remarkable similarities, witnessing to a common sense of purpose. For instance, both defend Buddhist devotion against the accusation of some Western orientalists that it was futile and non-Buddhist, if the Buddha had passed into *parinibbāna* (further *nibbāna*), beyond engagement with humans. Bennett touched on this in his Hope Lodge lecture and would defend it again in Burma when speaking to the

Rangoon College Buddhist Association.[48] Pereira, in a lecture on 'The Simpler Side of Buddhist Doctrine,' given in 1945, did something similar by focussing on *saddhā* (faith) and *sīla* (virtue). His message was that faith was not blind. 'Saddhā is rather the mature Love and Confidence, the true heart's adoration that comes in the train of understanding, when we have gained a little of self-mastery and begin to understand the value of self-sacrifice,' he declared. It was when we 'begin to gain some glimpse of the meaning of that infinite Love that *for us* resulted in some slight knowledge of the Law, our treasure' (Pereira 1945: 4).

He adds, later, 'We all need it [*saddhā*], for the mental power it alone can yield,—for none of us has escaped the fangs of self, and Saddhā is the antidote to its poison' (Pereira 1945: 6). This could have been written by Bennett, after he became Ananda Metteyya. Bennett also stressed the self-sacrifice of the Buddha as warranting not 'blind faith' but absolute devotion and love, particularly in the lectures he gave in London in 1919–1920, a copy of which we know Pereira possessed (e.g., Bennett 1923: 7, 111).[49] The two were also eventually united in their attitude to Buddhist meditation, and in their interpretation of non-self (*anattā*).[50]

Bennett sailed for colonial Burma fairly soon after Crowley left for India. His choice of Burma for ordination was probably due to his experience of village Buddhist monasticism in Kamburugamuwa, the request that he should become the treasurer of a monastery, his experience of alcohol abuse in Ceylon, and his conviction both that Sri Lankan Buddhism had become tarnished by non-Buddhist elements and that Burmese Buddhism was purer (e.g., Ananda M 1911c: 133). As Balangoda Ananda Maitreya shared with Elizabeth in 1994, Ceylon at the time was a centre for Pali studies and not Abhidhamma or meditation. Burma, on the other hand, was known for both of the latter.[51] From the writings of a Wesleyan Methodist missionary, however, a further interesting possibility emerges. Robert Spence Hardy wrote in 1850, 'In Arrakan [the part of colonial Burma to which Bennett travelled] candidates for the priesthood are received without any regard to their country, caste, or previous religion' (Spence Hardy 1850: 368). Christmas Humphreys, pioneer of Buddhism in England, claims, years later, that Bennett chose Burma in the light of his envisioned mission to the West, because of 'the limitations imposed on the Sangha in Ceylon, where ordination into one of the principal sects would automatically exclude him from free intercourse with those of other sects' (Humphreys 1937: 14).

Caste factors certainly surrounded monastic ordination in Sri Lanka. As for Akyab, it was a cosmopolitan and reformist city at this time, somewhat separate from the rest of Burma, and could well have had greater openness in this matter.⁵² It is possible that Bennett heard that the situation was different in Arakan. His final decision may have been taken, however, because he met in Ceylon the person who would be his main ordination sponsor, Dr. Tha Nu, of Akyab, an intellectual who supported the Maha-Bodhi Society, founded by the Ceylonese revivalist, the Anagārika Dharmapāla. According to Turner, Cox and Bocking, it was Dr. Tha Nu who facilitated Bennett's journey to Burma (Turner, Cox and Bocking 2020: 139). Richard Pereira also helped.⁵³ Bennett sailed to the port of Akyab (now Sittwe) in Arakan (now Rakkhine State), in September or October, 1901.

ANANDA METTEYYA'S RETURN TO COLONIAL CEYLON

Allan Bennett was better known among the Ceylonese Buddhists who drove the country's Buddhist revival after he sailed to Burma than when he lived in the country. This is hardly surprising. The publication of his Hope Lodge lecture by Cassius Pereira's father would have convinced many in Colombo that Bennett was a foreigner with a large heart, who knew something about and loved the devotion of the people, unlike some Theosophists who decried it.⁵⁴ Additionally, the news that Bennett was going to Burma to be ordained would have increased his appeal. Not one of the Theosophists who had aided the Sri Lankan Buddhist revival had gone this far in affirming the institutional structure of Buddhism in Asia. Bennett's decision to become a wearer of the 'robe,' and, therefore, part of the third 'refuge,' the Sangha, was the ultimate sign of respect for the Theravada Buddhist tradition. Its symbolic significance went beyond that of Colonel Olcott and the Theosophists.

One means through which Bennett was kept in the minds of revivalist Ceylonese Buddhists was through the Buddhist media, particularly *Sarasavi Sandaresa*, the Sinhala journal of the Buddhist Theosophical Society, and *The Buddhist*, the English supplement to this. In 1902, the latter was taken over by the Young Men's Buddhist Association (YMBA). In the first volume after this change, almost every issue includes something written by Bennett, now 'Ananda Maitriya.' The first issue reprints his Hope Lodge talk (MacGregor 1902). The second carries an article by him entitled 'Animism and Law' (Ananda Maitriya 1902a) and the third, one entitled, 'On the Culture of Mind' (Ananda Maitriya 1902b), both written from Akyab.⁵⁵ The latter was then published as a booklet. The fourth number, July–August 1902, carries Bennett's ordination address (Ananda Maitriya 1902d) and a description of the ordination (Anon 1902a;

see also Anon 1902b) and the fifth, September–October 1902, a short piece by him, 'From Beyond the Graves' (Ananda Maitriya 1902f). In this volume, Ananda M is the principal focus. This was not only because Ananda M was, by this time, a persuasive writer on Buddhism but also because his orange robe was a powerful and confidence-building symbol of resistance against British imperialism and the hegemony of Christianity in the island, at a point when Buddhist-Christian competition was high.

Ananda M returned to Ceylon on 6 April, 1903 (Sarasavi Sandaresa 1903a: 1), to open the previously mentioned Maitriya Hall, a new preaching hall in Bambalapitiya, on the outskirts of Colombo,[56] which was named after him. The hall was built by Richard Pereira, on his own land, and the foundation stone was laid by his wife, Jeannie.[57] Pereira sponsored Ananda M's return.[58] According to Ananda M, the hall cost 6000 rupees. The whole project had begun unpretentiously, with the thatched building that Bennett had seen in Bambalapitiya before he left for Burma (Ananda Maitriya 1903n: 183). The aim of the new hall was to create a Westernised venue that could instruct members of the monastic Sangha in 'English and in Western learning,' and offer lectures on Buddhism in English to lay Buddhists educated in that medium and accustomed to more Western 'modes' (Ananda Maitriya 1903n: 182), for instance, sitting on chairs rather than the floor. Both its exterior and interior, therefore, were modelled on a church, in order, as Alec Robertson explains much later, to wean Buddhists away from Christian churches (Ratnayake 1992: I).[59]

Even before the opening of the hall, the *Sarasavi Sandaresa* mentioned Ananda M. An anonymous *upāsaka* (male lay follower) praises his booklet, 'On the Culture of Mind,' writing that all English-speaking monks and lay Buddhists should read it, but asking, at the same time, for more information about some of its key terms and for confirmation of the correctness of parts of its argument (Sarasavi Sandaresa 1903b: 3).

Ananda M's address at the opening, given on 25 April, 1903 (Sarasavi Sandaresa 1903c: 5), took the theme of 'Western Education for Buddhist Bhikshus' (Ananda Maitriya 1903n). The Hall was packed with Sinhala, Tamil, Burgher and English people. At the head table sat three of the most famous revivalist Buddhist monks in the country: Mahāgoda Ñānissara, Hikkaḍuvē Sumaṅgala and Doḍandūvē Piyaratana (Sarasavi Sandaresa 1903d: 7; see also Sarasavi Sandaresa 1903a: 1). After the *bhikkhus* had chanted and a preliminary speech had been presented, Ananda M, 'with a tall body and pleasant facial appearance' entered the decorated 'pulpit' (Sarasavi Sandaresa 1903d: 7).

Notable again was his diffidence, which was not surprising given the stature of a monk such as Hikkaḍuvē Sumaṅgala (see Blackburn 2010). In his own eyes, he was a newly ordained monk, 'little learned in the law he [the Buddha] taught,' speaking in a context within which each member of the monastic Sangha present was his 'superior alike in knowledge of the law, and in seniority in the Sangha' (Ananda Maitriya 1903n: 181). He presented the English ethos of the hall as 'an outer court where men may learn the nature of the Palace of the Truth that lies within,' and himself as 'of that outer court, a watcher at the gate,' although of 'the yellow robe,' 'able to speak with men in the gate, to tell them, in a tongue they understand, a little of our Palace of the Truth' (Ananda Maitriya 1903n: 182). This speaks volumes of Ananda M's perception of himself as occupying a liminal space between East and West. Yet, in the eyes of the monastic and lay Buddhists present, he was a potent symbol of their own revitalised confidence in a colonial setting. And we suspect his talk did not disappoint in terms of its content, although he read from a written script, probably with his eyes down (Sarasavi Sandaresa 1903d: 7).

The heart of his presentation was a spirited defence of the need to teach *bhikkhus* English and Western learning, if Buddhism was 'to hold its own today' (Ananda Maitriya 1903n: 184). *Bhikkhus* able to illustrate Buddhism using 'modern similes' and to be effective 'in a controversy' were needed. Today, he continued, *bhikkhus* should not wait for lay people to come to them. Because of the threat of Christianised education aimed at alienating Buddhist children from their religion, they should reject the path of solitary meditation and go out to teach, with knowledge of Western arguments and learning (Ananda Maitriya 1903n: 185–187). Since the audience was not entirely Buddhist, he spoke more generally about Buddhism at the end. He also carefully stated that he did not seek to 'reproach' Christian teachers; he acknowledged their devotion and the sincerity of their belief, although he added that Buddhists believed these beliefs were 'mistaken' (Ananda Maitriya 1903n: 185). His final exhortation was this:

> Make of this, then, O men of Lanka, make of this a national work, the germ and centre of a new life for Ceylon, give to it of your wealth and leisure that have these to give, infuse into it that old fire of your race that aforetime wrought those mighty works in Lanka that to-day are testified to only by stupendous ruins. Are your hearts also in ruins, ye of the Lion Race, whose pride and hope was in this Buddhist Faith, is the old spirit dead amongst you that are the descendants of those great of old? Nay, surely, for their blood runs in your veins, their energy and their devotion are the spirit of your national life. (Ananda Maitriya 1903n:199)

He added, 'make of this work the germ of a great national religious movement . . . till there shall not remain one heir to that great and immemorial civilisation that shall not glory in the name of Buddhist' (Ananda Maitriya 1903n: 199). Into this speech, Ananda M poured both the sadness he felt when he saw the influence of Western materialism in Ceylon, and his hope for effective Buddhist revivalism under colonialism.

Ananda M remained in the country until 8 June, giving sermons every Sunday at Maitriya Hall at 5.00 p.m., with an entry fee of 10 cents, which no doubt went towards paying the outstanding debts on the building (Sarasavi Sandaresa 1903f: 1). On 26 April, for instance, the day after the opening, he gave a sermon on *nibbāna* (Sarasavi Sandaresa 1903d: 7).

During his time in Ceylon, he also travelled out of Colombo. In late May, he was in Kandy. On the 27th, he gave a significant sermon on drinking alcohol at the Buddhist boys' school, Dharmaraja College, and, on the 29th, spoke again on 'Nirvana' at the Town Hall (Sarasavi Sandaresa 1903h: 2). The *Sarasavi Sandaresa* claims that the former impressed the audience so much that they committed themselves to forming a Temperance Society,

Figure 2.4 *Ananda M in Sri Lanka in 1903 (taken by the colonial The Colombo Apothecaries Co. Ltd., Kandy and reprinted in* The Buddhist Annual of Ceylon 1923, *p. 35)*

following 'a suggestion by the newly appointed lawyer, Mr. Edward Lionel Vijegunawardhana' (Sarasavi Sandaresa 1903h: 2).

Rogers argues that the upsurge of temperance activity among Buddhists in Ceylon at this time started in 1904, in the south-west of the island, driven by a P. A. de Silva, and spread from his village, among the elites, along the south-western coastal strip and from there to other parts of the country, including Colombo and Kandy, in connection with which he mentions 'Wijegoonewardene, a twenty-four-year-old lawyer' (Rogers 1989: 330). Ananda M's influence in 1903 is not mentioned but could nevertheless have been important. It is also significant that Christian missionaries, particularly the Wesleyan Methodists, had been encouraging abstention from alcohol for a long time, setting up Temperance Societies and, in their schools, Bands of Hope.[60]

If an advanced notice is to be trusted, on 31 May, Ananda M was in Nittambuwa, a town between Kandy and Colombo, distributing prizes and giving a 'special Dhamma sermon' at Vidyānanda Pirivena, a monastic school sponsored by the Mahā Dhammadāna Society (lit. Great Society for the Giving of the Dhamma; Sarasavi Sandaresa 1903e: 5). Back in Colombo, he gave his last Maitriya Hall sermon on Sunday, 7 June, on 'Right Living' (Sarasavi Sandaresa 1903f: 1; 1903g: 1). A synopsis of this in *Sarasavi Sandaresa* indicates that he spoke about both morality and meditation, within the latter mentioning 'four *kasina bhāvanās*'—which four is not stated—out of which his listeners were encouraged to choose the one most suitable for them. When he shared that he was leaving, the report continues, 'many wept. They came to the room where the monk was and bid farewell to him and left with heavy hearts' (Sarasavi Sandaresa 1903g: 1).

Ananda M's mention of the *kasinas* in his last lecture is significant, since they would have evoked in his mind the Golden Dawn tattwas. *Kasinas* are devices that are used as meditation objects, the best description of which appears in the *Visuddhimagga* (The Path of Purification).[61] There are traditionally 10 *kasinas*: earth, water, fire, wind, blue, yellow, red, white, space and consciousness. *Kasina* practice can include concentrating on a coloured disk until a mental image of it arises, which in turn produces a counter-image. Such concentration is believed to lead into the meditative absorptions or *jhānas*, which became important in Ananda M's spiritual practice. Within the Golden Dawn, the five tattwas were coloured symbols representing the five elements that were used to practise concentration and develop clairvoyant abilities. The symbols were a yellow square for earth, a blue disc for air, a red triangle for fire, a silver crescent for water and a black, egg-shaped oval for spirit. Golden Dawn members were encouraged to create these symbols out of coloured paper and affix them to a white background. They then focussed their vision on the symbol for approximately 20 seconds, before shifting their attention to a white surface, on which the shape would appear in its complementary colour. This was then held in the mind and used as a portal to enter the astral realm behind the shape. In explaining how to use tattwas, Mathers writes:

> Transfer the vital effort from the optic nerve to the mental perception, or thought-seeing as distinct from the seeing with the eye. Let one form of apprehension glide on into the other. Produce the reality of the dream vision by positive will in the waking state ... Then maintaining your abstraction from your surroundings, still concentrated upon the symbol and its correlated ideas, you are to seek a perception of a scene or panorama or view of the plane. This may also be brought on by a sense of tearing open, as a curtain is drawn aside, and seeing the 'within' of the symbol before you. (Regardie 1995: 459)

The astral realm accessed through the tattwa in the mind of the 'seer' or practitioner would tend to correspond to the associations of the colour, element, astrological sign and planets, as well as many other attributes found within the Golden Dawn's system of correspondences. Moreover, the seer was encouraged to internally name the entities that corresponded with the realm and to seek a spirit guide to assist with the journey in the astral plane. Finally, when the time came to leave the astral realm, the seer was instructed to exit the plane through the symbol and return to the physical world in a calm and deliberate manner. Upon returning, the seer had to reestablish their connection with their physical surroundings. Later, upon reflection, the seer should review their journey, analysing what was seen and encountered. This last step was necessary because, as the instructions warn, 'under no circumstances accept them [the visions] on their face value or neglect his tests [of the imagery's correspondences], for the whole astral plane, apparently, seeks to delude the seer and if he open himself, by neglecting the tests, he is lost' (Regardie 1995: 462). By these means and symbols were Golden Dawn members taught to meditate and develop their clairvoyant abilities. This Golden Dawn practice was different from that described by Bhadantācariya Buddhaghosa in the *Visuddhimagga*, but the parallels would not have been lost on Ananda M.

Ananda M's return visit to Ceylon lasted almost two months and ended with an emotional farewell. It overshadowed his earlier visit and his first lecture on the Four Noble Truths, to the extent that one notice of his death published in Ceylon only mentions the 1903 visit:

It was in 1903 that the Bhikku visited the Island and made a long stay lecturing and studying and doing the spade work for laying the foundation of the *Buddhasasana Samagama* (Buddhist International Society) of Rangoon and preparing the material for his Illustrated quarterly, *"Buddhism,"* which for many years played a very important part in making known the Dhamma in English-speaking countries. (The Buddhist Annual of Ceylon 1923: 69)

On Ananda M's return to Burma, his link with Ceylon continued, particularly through Cassius Pereira and the Ceylonese Buddhist revivalist, the Anagārika Dharmapāla (1864–1933). Maitriya Hall continued to host meetings but an entry in the diaries of Dharmapāla suggests that, in 1904, there was a period when it was uncared for.[62] The journal Ananda M started in Burma, *Buddhism*, contained news of Buddhist anti-imperialist activities in Ceylon and, when back in Britain, he continued to reach out to his friends there. While it seems that he never returned to the island, he certainly never forgot what it did for him.

Figure 2.5 Magic Lantern slide from the collection that Ananda M brought to England, showing a Buddha image at Anuradhapura, courtesy of The Buddhist Society, London.

3

Ananda Metteyya in Burma

AKYAB

When Allan Bennett arrived at the port of Akyab (Sittwe), the fourth largest town in Burma, in the region then called Arakan, he met as cosmopolitan, multi-ethnic and hybrid a port as he had left. Mythologically, Akyab's links with Buddhism were strong. 'Akyab' is a corruption of the name of a 'pagoda which is supposed to house the shrine of the jawbone of the Buddha,' states the British civil servant who wrote the Gazetteer for the District in 1917 (Smart 1957: 216). 'Hazy traditions' existed, he continues, that four small temples to the north-west of Akyab had links with the 'Selâgîri tradition of Gotama' (lit. rocky mountain tradition; Smart 1957: 36–37, 49), referring to Selagiri Hill, which local tradition links with a visit of the Buddha with 500 followers.[1]

Akyab, however, might have had a different feel from Colombo, mainly because of the number of migrants from Bengal and China. Arakan was annexed by Burma in the 1780s (Harvey 1946: 18–19; Furnivall 1948: 23; Smart 1957: 27). This pushed refugees into British territory and eventually instigated the British conquest of Arakan in the first Burmese War of 1824–1825. The British chose the fishing community of Akyab as their main Arakanese base and consequently many Muslims and Hindus entered from British India, increasing a trend of cultural exchange and migration that had been present for centuries, and which had nurtured architectural and religious hybridity.[2] Taking the Akyab District as a whole, between 1872 and the census in 1901, the Muslim population increased from 58,255 to 154,887 (Smart 1957: 83). In Akyab town itself, there were fewer Buddhists than Hindus and Muslims when Bennett arrived (Smart 1957: 215–217). Indians were taking over commerce and fishing, and, outside the town, were displacing the Arakanese in rice production (Smart 1957: 137). The Arakanese, many of whom were Buddhists, were, therefore, under demographic pressure, in danger of being commercially marginalised by new models of global trade within the British Empire (Smart 1957: 85).[3]

Nevertheless, Akyab had energy, with goods arriving by steamship daily from Calcutta and Madras, and other parts of the British Empire. It had also caught the 'fashion for organizing' and, by 1899, had 'the Arakan Jubilee Club, the Hypocris Club, a literary society, and a half dozen others' plus a Young Arakanese Student's Club of Rangoon (Turner 2014: 76).[4]

Bennett's main sponsor in Akyab was the previously mentioned 'modernist intellectual' and humanitarian, Dr. Tha Nu, the resident medical officer, together with his wife, Ma Mra Nyo (Ananda Maitriya 1902e: 6; Harcourt Butler 1927: 166; Turner, Cox and Bocking 2020: 139). According to one newspaper report, Tha Nu was related to the person who would become Bennett's main sponsor in Rangoon (Yangon), Mrs. May Hla Oung, also known as Daw Mya May (Straits Times 1908: 5). On 12 December, 1901, his birthday, Bennett received novice ordination, with the name Ananda Metteya Sāsanajotika.[5] At this point, as previously mentioned, his address to the monks and lay supporters who were present explained how his secular knowledge of science had destroyed the Christian faith of his childhood, particularly its exclusivist attitude to religious others (Ananda Maitriya 1902e: 7-8).

After this ordination, according to the account of his higher ordination, he lived in Akyab:

> [I]mproving his knowledge of the Páli language, learning the duties of a Bhikkhu, and writing a few papers on Buddhism, which have been printed in Ceylon. He lately moved to Kyarook Kyoung [Kyayouq Kyaung], and it was Kyarook Sayadaw, who, together with Shwe Zedi Saradaw, assembled together the many eminent Theras who took part in the conferring of the full ordination [*upasampadā*].[6] (Anon 1902b: 2)

He might also have begun recitation from books in Pali on Abhidhamma, the scholastic set of texts within the Pali Canon that focuses particularly on meditation and the nature of mind. It was a central part of monastic training in Burma and was undergoing a revival as part of a defensive strategy to strengthen Buddhism under colonialism (Turner 2014: 34-40, 106). Ananda M would later write that the Abhidhamma's 'profound metaphysics often form the subject of the keenest discussion even by the laity, and at the *Uposatha*-day reunions [when monks recite their monastic rules] in every monastic rest-house' (Ananda M 1911c: 133; Braun 2013: 64). Abhidhamma's attraction for Ananda M would later find expression in his scientific experiments.

Aleister Crowley, after visiting India, arrived in Akyab on the evening of 14 February, 1902. He stayed the first night at Ananda M's monastery but was then given accommodation by Tha Nu. Through Crowley, we see another aspect of Ananda M's novitiate, namely that 'people of all sorts trooped in incessantly to pay their respects to the European *bhikkhu*,' prostrating themselves 'at his feet' with reverence and affection, bringing him gifts of food and literature (Crowley 1989: 271–272). In monastic robes, Crowley declares, 'Allan' seemed to be of 'gigantic height as compared to the diminutive Burmese,' adding, 'The old gentleness was still there' (Crowley 1989: 270). He also notes that 'Allan's' asthma had returned, putting it down to the coolness of his pre-dawn alms-rounds. His response was to wish that 'sanctity was not so incompatible with sanity' (Crowley 1989: 271).

The period between Ananda M's novice and higher ordination, therefore, combined study, writing, training in Buddhist ritual culture, and interactions with both his monastic community and the laity. As mentioned in the previous chapter, he sent at least two articles to Ceylon for publication through the Pereira family: 'Animism and Law' and 'On the Culture of Mind.'[7] He probably also gave copies to Crowley. They appeared first in *The Buddhist* (Ananda Maitriya 1902a; 1902b), and then at least one was reprinted for free circulation by J. D. Fernando (e.g., Ananda Maitriya 1902c). According to Ananda M's own record, he stayed in the Kyayouq Kyaung for four months, with robes, foods and books donated by lay Buddhists, and was taught all he 'knew of the duties of a Priest' by U Tejarama Thera (Ananda Maitriya 1902e: 6). Tha Nu and his wife, however, continued to be his main donors, feeding and nursing him when he was ill (Ananda Metteyya 1902e: 6). In addition, Pali scholar Tha Do Aung gave him a Pali Grammar and helped him with his studies (Ananda Maitriya 1902e: 6). In Akyab, he was no less than a celebrity, a potent symbol of Buddhism's resilience under colonialism.

The two articles that we know Ananda M sent to Ceylon are highly significant. Both were written for a Buddhist rather than a Western readership. 'Animism and Law' entered the debates in Ceylon between Buddhists and Christian missionaries, with Ananda M arguing that monotheism was the 'highest manifestation' of animism, which he defines as the belief that events are caused by gods and demons. He admits that Jesus 'was a very loving and merciful man' (Ananda Maitriya 1902a: 33) but argues that the 'animistic trait' in Christianity awoke a 'latent savagery,' which killed heretics, scientific investigators and those believed to be witches (Ananda Maitriya 1902a: 34–35). This strong indictment of the Christianity that had accompanied British imperialism would develop into an evolutionary theory, which placed Christianity within humanity's childhood because of its appeal to 'blind faith.'[8] Significantly, his argument also challenged the reverence given to philosophical Brahmanism by Theosophy and the theistic underpinnings of the Golden Dawn. Ananda M then enthusiastically contrasted such animism with the 'Rule of Law,' present not only in the scientific discoveries of Newton and Lavoisier, but also, supremely, in the principle of karma (action) within Buddhism. Ananda M claims, for instance, that the ethical dimension of karma paves the way for anger to give way to compassion (Ananda Maitriya 1902a: 37), through practices such as *samādhi*, which he has no problem translating as 'meditation.'[9]

In this article, Ananda M sought to mediate between Western science and Buddhism, by placing both in the context of 'Law.'[10] He ends with the concept of *sankhāra*, a complex Pali term usually translated as 'mental formations.' Ananda M, however, defines the term as ever-changing 'tendencies' and, more controversially, suggests that they linked together our rebirths.

'On the Culture of Mind' begins where 'Animism and Law' ends, with the 'reproductive energy' of the 'tendencies' (Ananda Maitriya 1902b: 54) and meditation as a way of transforming, re-directing and controlling them. Taking *Dhammapada* verse 183, which would become key to modernist definitions of Buddhism (Trainor 2012), he concentrates on its last clause, translating it as 'the purification of all our thoughts.'[11] Twentieth-century Western appropriations of Buddhism prioritised insight meditation (*vipassanā*) over *samatha* (tranquillity, serenity) practice.[12] In this article, however, Ananda M does not mention the term *vipassanā*, although the growth of insight is mentioned at the end as a fruit of meditative practice (Ananda Maitriya 1902b: 67).[13] He largely concentrates on *samatha*, which traditionally involves concentrating on an object. For him, Buddhist meditation was not divided into *vipassanā* and *samatha* but rather into the components found in the Eightfold Path—*sammāsati*, which he describes as 'accurate reflection upon things in order to ascertain their nature,'[14] and *sammāsamādhi*, explained as 'bringing to bear upon the mind the powers of concentration' to bring good states of mind into being (Ananda Maitriya 1902b: 58). He gives practical advice on how these should be carried out, for instance choosing a particular time of day when the stomach is empty, and sitting or adopting a 'cross-legged posture in a quiet place other than one's bedroom.' When it comes to objects of meditation, Ananda M demonstrates knowledge of the *Visuddhimagga*, and its description of *kammaṭṭhāna* (lit: working ground, namely of meditation), with its 40 types of meditation objects.[15] The objects he recommends for his readership are the four *brahmavihāras*, namely *mettā*, *karunā*, *muditā* and *upekkhā*, which he translates as love, pity, sympathy and indifference.[16] This, argues Ananda M, is transformative of the mind. At the end, he outlines a rigorous mental practice for remembering past births, also from the *Visuddhimagga*, although the *Visuddhimagga* may have drawn on the *Vimuttimagga*.[17] It involves the cultivation of memory, with Ananda M claiming that there is nothing 'miraculous' about it (Ananda Maitriya 1902b: 63). The cause of our brain-structure, he stresses, comes from our past lives, from our *sankhāra*, and this means that 'all our karmic ancestry,' including memory of our past lives, lie in our brains. The method involves thinking backwards, beginning with entering the room one was meditating in and then going through all the activities of that day. He recommends beginning with only one day but then gradually going further backwards into childhood until one reaches the moment of birth. In line with the *Visuddhimagga*, Ananda M stresses that proceeding further than this is difficult and could take many attempts, but that there would come a time when 'you will suddenly find yourself remembering your death *in your last life*' and would be able to go further. He continues that with practice:

> You will see yourself living a thousand lives, you will feel yourself dying a thousand deaths, you will suffer with the suffering of a myriad existences, you will see how fleeting were their little joys, what price you had again and again to pay for a little happiness. (Ananda Maitriya 1902b: 66)

Ananda M, therefore, places this practice firmly within a Buddhist framework, namely realisation of the pain and suffering of existence with its repeated rebirths (*dukkha*), and commitment to the Buddhist path of liberation. He translates the practice from the monastic setting that is evoked in the *Visuddhimagga* into a form that his Ceylonese lay readers might have been able to understand. It is probable that the practice would nevertheless have been new and strange to them, touching the esoteric. Ananda M, however, even at this early stage, was able to communicate the heart of this practice, namely that it was not an egotistic curiosity trip but a way of realising the truth of *dukkha*.

If 'Animism and Law' entered Buddhist-Christian debate, 'On the Culture of Mind' sought to fill a lacuna Ananda M perceived in Ceylonese lay Buddhist practice, through drawing on the *Sutta Piṭaka* and the *Visuddhimagga*. Through his concentration on *samatha* rather than *vipassanā*, he reflected traditional Buddhist practice in Ceylon and Burma at this time rooted in historical precedent (e.g., Harris 2019; Cousins 2022), the methods that Cassius Pereira would also champion as he grew older. At this point, he does not stress that the practice of *sammāsati* and *sammāsamādhi* could lead to 'the inner, higher, mental realms' (the *jhānas*), as he does in later years (e.g., Bennett 1923: 77). However, what he advocates is not a complete break from his esoteric past. The meditation to remember past lives, although rooted in the *Visuddhimagga*, certainly evokes it, and there are remarkable similarities between his suggested meditation on loving kindness and the magical rituals of the Order of the Golden Dawn. In effect, he places the heart of the canonical *Karaniya Mettā Sutta* (Discourse on Loving Kindness; *Sutta Nipāta* v. 143-152) within a spatial structure from his past ritual culture. Key to the *Sutta* are the following verses:

> Just as a mother would protect her only child at the risk of her own life, even so, cultivate a boundless heart towards all beings.
> Let thoughts of boundless love pervade the whole world: above, below and across without any obstruction, without any hatred, without any enmity (verses 149-150, adapted from Saddhatissa 1985:16)

Ananda M, in response to the directional emphasis of the second verse, recommends that the meditator should first flood the 'Eastern Quarter of the World' with 'love,' likened to 'a great spreading ray of light,' so that 'there is not one being in all the Eastern Quarter of the world whom he has passed over.' The same was to be repeated for the Southern, the Western and the Northern Quarters. The use of 'light' and the term 'quarters,' and the sequence in which the 'quarters' were to be addressed, echoes a preliminary ritual that was used by the Order of the Golden Dawn to purify space, The Opening of the Watchtowers, and also parts of the Ritual of the Pentagram (Regardie 1995: 258-259, 280-284).[18] The content of the meditation is in complete harmony with the message of the *Karaniya Mettā Sutta*, namely that the meditator should flood the world with loving kindness, but the structure of the meditation is taken from Ananda M's ritual past, demonstrating its continued hold on Ananda M's psyche.

'On the Culture of Mind' also became a seminal text within Crowley's magical system. As the essay was originally published in a Ceylonese journal in 1902, Crowley probably obtained a copy from Ananda M when he visited him in Burma. Crowley changed the name to 'Training the Mind' and published it in his journal, *The Equinox* (Ananda Metteya 1911). In doing so, he made changes throughout. In most cases they are small edits, such as changing punctuation, or rephrasing portions of sentences. However, in two instances, Crowley makes a change that dramatically alters the text and puts words into the mouth of Ananda M that he would have never said. In a section in which Ananda M is illustrating how one person with power can have a great effect on others, he writes,

> ... but who can estimate the power of one human mind, whether for good or for evil? One such mind, the mind of a man like Napoleon,

may bring about the tortured death of three million men, may wreck states and religions and dynasties, and cause untold misery and suffering... It is by use of this energy that the child learns how to speak; it is by its power that Napoleon could bring sorrow into thousands of lives... (Ananda Maitriya 1902b: 55–56)

In the version Crowley published, he changes Napoleon to Jesus Christ, a change that presents Ananda M as disparaging Christianity, something he would never have done. Crowley's change reads:

... but who can estimate the power of one human mind, whether for good or for evil? One such mind, the mind of a man like Jesus Christ, may bring about the tortured death of many million men, may wreck states and religions and dynasties, and cause untold misery and suffering... It is by use of this energy that the child learns how to speak; it is by its power that Christ could bring sorrow into thousands of lives... (Ananda Metteya 1911: 33–34)

In later years, Crowley focused specifically on the section about remembering previous lives. He references the text frequently within his magical instructions and lists the essay on reading lists given to his magical students. For example, in his magical instructions, titled *Liber Thisharb*, Crowley discusses the importance of developing one's memory:[19]

Memory is essential to the individual consciousness; otherwise the mind were but a blank sheet on which shadows are cast. But we see that not only does the mind retain impressions, but that it is so constituted that its tendency is to retain some more excellently than others.... The first method to be described has been detailed in Bhikkhu Ananda Metteya's 'Training of the Mind.' We have little to alter or to add. (Crowley 1912: 108)

After giving more context, Crowley describes the first method of enhancing one's memory, summarising the practice Ananda M described in the essay, while also adding his own suggestions. Summarising this method with the phrase, 'Let the Exempt Adept first train himself to think backwards' (Crowley 1912: 109), he suggests everything from walking backwards, writing backwards, to thinking backwards in time, starting by remembering the last five minutes, then prior days, years, events, and then finally, past lives.

Liber Thisharb was published in *The Equinox* in 1912, along with a large collection of texts intended to be instructional material for Crowley's magical order known by the initials A∴A∴. Throughout his life, he made repeated reference to *Liber Thisharb*, and thus indirectly to 'Training of the Mind.' In his letters to magical students in the 1940s, Crowley makes statements such as this, written in 1943:

> In conformity with the practice which you may perhaps choose to adopt later, given in "Liber Thisharb," sub figura CMXIII . . . you must find an answer to the question: "How did I come to be in this place at this time, engaged in this particular work?" As you will see from the book, this will start you on the discovery of who you really are, and eventually lead you to your recovering the memory of previous incarnations. (Crowley 1954: xii)

Similarly, Crowley makes reference to *Liber Thisharb* in a letter focusing on magical memory, where he asks, 'for how else could one have reasonable "certainty," as contrary to "faith," . . . otherwise than by the acquisition of the "Magical Memory"—the memory of former lives' (Crowley 1954: 243). In another letter on the topic of reincarnation, he makes multiple references to *Liber Thisharb* (Crowley 1954: 297–301). Lastly, he references it in a letter that discusses the record keeping of one's magical work (Crowley 1954: 491–492).

Not only was Bennett the greatest influence on Crowley in terms of his training within ceremonial magic and meditation, but 'On the Culture of Mind' was also a seminal text within Crowley's personal magical system, which is still practised today. For example, one of Crowley's magical students, Charles Standsfeld Jones, practised 'thinking backwards' as part of his magical work and recorded his experience in his magical diary,[20] a portion of which Crowley published within *The Equinox*, as an example to other students:

> June 12, 1911. On Saturday night, in bed I attempted "thinking backwards" and successfully managed two days, with no breaks in the first day, and practically none for the day before, except a few little incidents during office hours in the morning. When I came to thoughts on waking of Saturday morning and got to the "blank" I experienced some mental visions and 'telephone-cross voices,' but cannot say if they were connected with any dream; then suddenly I found myself lying in bed with the last thoughts of the previous night in mind. Yesterday, I read the article on the subject (Training of the Mind) carefully, also learnt the formula of the four great meditations on Love, Pity, Happiness and Indifference. At night, I again attempted "thinking backwards," but experienced rather more difficulty as conditions were bad. However, once started, I

got back through Sunday and very nearly, if not quite as fully, over the two previous days; then, having got into the swing, I roughly attempted a short and incomplete review of my whole life, which although brief, was much fuller than I expected. I remembered things connected with early childhood quite accurately, but of course not with full connections. Then something occurred that I really did not expect, and only later trials will prove if it was an illusion or not. Having tried hard to pierce the blank, back of all, I had a sudden clear sensation of lying on a bed with people around, and in particular an elderly man in black velvet and knee breeches, whom I at once felt was my Tutor, leaning over me. The ideas that came with this were that I was quite young, and had some disease like consumption, that the family was wealthy, and the house a Country Residence. These impressions were very real and quite unexpected, but as I used to have a dread of consumption, and still young, and meditation took place lying down, it would seem that very little imagination would make up the rest. However, I mention it, as the experience was different from anything I can previously remember. (Frater V.I.O. 1919: 149–150)

While Ananda M did not intend 'On the Culture of Mind' to be used in the context of ceremonial magic, it has nevertheless, through Crowley, become an important text in modern occultism.[21]

ANANDA M'S HIGHER ORDINATION

Ananda M's higher ordination took place on the full moon day of Vesak, 12 May, 1902, conferred by Ven. Shwe Bya Sayadaw Khemālaṅkāra Mahāthera (Ananda Maitriya 1902e). In the detailed report that comes down to us of the event, we are told that numerous members of the monastic Sangha congregated in Akyab, staying in the Buddhist monasteries there, lavishly provided for by lay devotees, organised by Htoon-Chan and others. 'When there were twenty priests' the report states, 'the townspeople brought enough food for thirty,—when, on the last few days, some seventy Priests were present, there was food enough for a hundred and fifty' (Anon 1902b: 2). We are also told that Htoon-Chan initiated the monastic visitors into the 'mysteries of the Phonograph and the Telescope,' entertaining them 'with magic-lantern pictures of some of the great Buddhist Shrines in Ceylon' (Anon 1902b: 2). Behind this, no doubt, was Ananda M's fascination with such scientific developments, and his photography of Anuradhapura and other Buddhist sites when he was in Ceylon.

In 1902 Akyab, therefore, the spectacle of a white person receiving *upasampadā*, attracting numerous *bhikkhus*, many from outside the town, complemented the usual Vesak celebrations. An added novelty was that the actual ordination took place on water, on a steamer of the Arakan Flotilla Company, to avoid dissension over the *sīmā*, the monastic boundary within which monastic acts such as an *upasampadā* can be performed (Anon 1902b: 3).[22] The 'Cutting of a Sima' was done on the boat with 'Shwe Zedi Saradaw' scattering water around the boat to mark 'its separation from the world without and its consecration as a water-sima' (Anon 1902b: 3).

The ordination address Ananda M gave is worth examination, because of the light it throws on what was driving him at this point. It laid out what we will call his 'Akyab Plan.'[23] He began with adoration of the Triple Gem (Buddha, *Dhamma* and Sangha), and then expressed intense gratitude, naming the *bhikkhus* and lay people who had helped him: 'From a far distant land I came, an alien and unknown; and I have been received amongst you as a brother, and as one well-loved, for the sole sake of this our common Faith' (Ananda Maitriya 1902e: 5). He then immediately passed to his role:

> If, as is my chiefest hope, and the ambition of my life, the all-ruling Power of Karma shall place in my hands the blessing that I crave, the giving of our Master's Law of Pity and of Love unto the Lands of the West; you, who have all helped me thus lovingly to obtain the position and the knowledge necessary to that gift, have also a share in the giving:—for without your aid, what could I alone have accomplished? (Ananda Maitriya 1902e: 7)

Revisiting the theme of his novice ordination speech, he then stressed the 'bitterness' that came into his life when he lost his Christian faith, and his conviction that the West was imprisoned in this bitterness.[24] It possessed scientific knowledge but no wisdom of the 'World Beyond, the World of Pure Consciousness' (Ananda Maitriya 1902e: 13), and so filled the gap with destructive forms of materialism and commercialism. Only Buddhism had the answer to this spiritual impasse (Ananda Maitriya 1902e: 13–14). His aim, therefore, was to establish, 10 years from that date—at the beginning of the twenty-sixth century, in Buddhist terms, since the Buddha preached his first sermon in Sarnath—'the Sangha of His Priests [*bhikkhus*] in England, America, France and Germany; and perchance in other countries' (Ananda Maitriya 1902e: 14). By then, he would be able to confer novice and higher ordinations in these countries (Ananda Maitriya 1902e: 14) and act as teacher (*ācariya* or *upajjhāya*).[25] He was convinced the West was ready for Buddhism, probably believing already what Jayasundara reported him to have said: that some persons had taken birth in 'Western lands' with 'prenatal Buddhist proclivities' (Jayasundara 1920: 10).

The first step in this plan was to gain 'postulants for the Priesthood' from the West, through the founding of 'an international Buddhist Society, to be known as the *Buddhasāsana Samāgama*,—at first in these countries of the East and later extending to the West.' He would then issue a monthly subsidised journal to be sent free to 'great Libraries, and to all eminent Buddhists.' He gave himself six months to start this and stressed the benefit for 'the East' of having European Buddhists 'going about here and there, working for Buddhism and preaching the Good Law' (Ananda Maitriya 1902e: 14-15). His aim, therefore, was to create a European monastic community, a 'New Sangha of the West,' made up of educated men—the uneducated would bring Buddhism into 'ridicule'— who would be trained in Asia in order to move to Europe and America. He added of this Sangha:

> [W]e would in like manner answer any attacks which might be made against our Faith; but would never permit that any of our members should revile or abuse any form of religious belief held by others; believing always that the Truth is all-conquering, and will triumph in the end; whilst abuse and ridicule of the Faiths of others can breed but hatred and heart-burning; and is a method, moreover, opposed alike to the letter and the spirit of our Master's Teaching. (Ananda Maitriya 1902e: 15-16)

He finished with a rousing call for financial support, directed to the richer members of the laity, since, without wealthy sponsors, he knew that his project would fail. The images and metaphors he used, however, could have been taken from the rituals of the Golden Dawn: 'bringing from the East even unto the West the splendour of a Dawn beyond our deeming;— bringing joy from sorrow, and out of Darkness, LIGHT!' (Ananda Maitriya 1902e: 18).[26]

This speech had been in the making since the point in Ceylon when he had determined to travel to Burma for *upasampadā*, and it inspired his whole period in the country. His focus would be the 'saving' of the West through Buddhism. As a missionary teacher at Rangoon College, Professor G. R. T. Ross, writes, 'He had no special interest in the Burmese though charmed with his first reception, but sought to direct a propaganda from Burma which was to regenerate western society' (Purser and Saunders 1914: 86). It was no doubt for this reason that he continued to study Pali but not Burmese, that most of the writing he completed in Burma was not directed towards the Burmese market but to the West,[27] although there were exceptions to this, and that his principal sponsors were elite, English-educated Burmese who were equally at home in western and eastern contexts.

SECOND ORDINATION IN MANDALAY

Ananda M did not stay long in Akyab. Soon after his *upasampadā*, he travelled to Mandalay in time for the rains retreat (*vassa*), which traditionally lasts three months during the period between June and October. There were several reasons for this. First, Mandalay lay at the heart of Burmese Buddhism, whereas Arakan, as a previously independent regional kingdom, lay at the periphery. As at Akyab, Mandalay's population certainly contained Indian and Chinese traders and money-lenders but, as Talbot Kelly, a British 'tourist' who painted and described Burma, remarks, 'It is a Burmese city built for Burmans, and, excepting for a few of the commercial streets, almost solely occupied by them' (Kelly 1905: 157). In Mandalay, Ananda M knew he would be living in a Buddhist milieu, rich in temples and monasteries.

Second, Mandalay was the centre of a respected, scholarly Buddhist tradition of intellectual inquiry and reform (Braun 2013: 16–28). He possibly believed he had learnt as much as he could from his teachers in Akyab and needed further training in the *Vinaya* (monastic discipline) or Abhidhamma in the home of Burmese Buddhism. Third, he sought a further ordination in a reformist monastic fraternity, the Shwegyin Nikāya, supported by lay Buddhists in Mandalay. Although his ordination in Akyab would have been sufficient for his life as a *bhikkhu*, it was not out of the ordinary for a monk in Burma to have two ordinations. Ananda M could have seen an ordination in Mandalay as more prestigious and authentic than the water ordination in Akyab. As Janaka points out, Burmese Buddhism at the time placed great importance on 'monastic purity,' which was dependent on 'the validity of monastic ordination and *sīma*' (Janaka 2016: 33–34). On the other hand, Ananda M could have wanted to strengthen social bonds with his patrons, who would have gained merit from the auspicious act of sponsoring an ordination in their favoured lineage. There are several Burmese words to refer to such a re-ordination, including *theik-hka-htat* (reaffirming monastic discipline or training), *thein-htat* (reaffirming the act of ordination within a *sīmā*) and *kan-htat* (reaffirming the action of ordination).[28]

Ananda M's first ordination, according to Ananda M's records (see Ananda Metteyya 1908h), had been within the majority Thudhamma fraternity. The Shwegyin Nikāya had split away from the Thudhamma in the mid-nineteenth century, during the reign of the reformist King Mindon (reigned 1853–1878), ostensibly to preserve the Buddha's teaching through strict observance of the *Vinaya* in the context of the British threat to Buddhism (Mendelson 1975: 85; Schober 2011: 32; Turner 2014: 26, 94; Dhammasami 2018: 55), although power politics were also present within this and other instances of sectarianism (Mendelson 1975: 101–102). To seek training with the Shwegyin Fraternity, therefore, was consistent with Ananda M's continual search for authentic Buddhism, his personal strictness and his wish to be seen as an exemplary follower of monastic discipline.[29] Ananda M would later claim, when defending himself against an accusation that he was not regarded in Burma as a 'properly ordained Bhikkhu,' that he had 'twice received the Upasampada Ordination, so as to secure the advantage of belonging to both of the two schools of Monks prevalent in Burma.'[30] He further stated that he had been ordained in Mandalay by 'the Engan Sayadaw,' the head of 'the stricter or Reformed School' (Ananda Metteyya 1908e), whom Mendelson named the 'Ingan Mahawithudayon Sayadaw' (Mendelson 1975: 365, Appendix E).

Most of the information that we have of Ananda M in Mandalay comes from Sankin Sayadaw and accounts that derive from Sankin. Born in 1870, Sankin was only two to three years older than Ananda M. Later in his life, he would become head of the Shwegyin Nikāya. A biography that includes interviews with him was written before his death by two monks, Mānitasirī and Nandamālābhivaṁsa. Sankin told them that Ananda M could have been re-ordained in Mandalay, under the preceptorship of the Visuddharama East Monastery (Mānitasirī and Nandamālābhivaṁsa 1972: 177).[31] We consider this to be a strong possibility, as we will show later.

According to Sankin, Ananda M's sponsors in Mandalay included Shwe Lat War U Kyaw Yan, U Kar and U Yin Ka Lay (Mānitasirī and Nandamālābhivaṁsa 1972: 177). Min Yu Wai repeats this information (Min Yu Wai 2011: 18–19). U Kyaw Yan (1867–1946) was a key figure in Mandalay and indeed Burma. Zay Yar's biographical note mentions only his skill in Burmese traditional medicine and astrology, for which he gained titles: *Sīribhāsakkarakavidhaja* (outstanding and wise astrologer) for his astrological knowledge and *Bhisakkasiddhijeyya Kyaw Htin* (famous, excellent and accomplished physician) for his medical skill (Zay Yar 2010: 17). However, he was a man of 'multiple identities': a teacher; an educational administrator in the colonial system, gaining an honourable mention in the 1899–1900 Public Instruction Report (Report on Public Instruction in Burma 1900: 14); and the founder of a number of Buddhist Anglo-vernacular schools and also the Mandalay Society for Promoting Buddhism (*Buddhabatha Thathana*

Pyu Athin), which had branches in other towns (Turner 2011: 272-279; 2014: 67-69).[32] Again, therefore, Ananda M was sponsored by one of the most prominent Buddhist laypersons in the region.

There were three Buddhist institutions in Mandalay with which Ananda M developed links—the Shwekyimyin Pagoda, the Visuddharama East Monastery and the Visuddharama West Monastery, the last two being affiliated with the Shwegyin Nikāya. Sankin Sayadaw claimed that Ananda M spent his rains retreat in the Shwekyimyin Pagoda (Mānitasirī and Nandamālābhivaṁsa 1972: 177). This is again repeated by Min Yu Wai (Min Yu Wai 2011: 17-23). Sankin added that he learnt Pali from Sayadaw U Vicāra, who would become the second abbot of the Visuddharama West Monastery. Min Yu Wai additionally adds that, after the rains retreat, he went to the Visuddharama East Monastery for *pavāraṇā*, the formal ceremony that ends the rains retreat (Min Yu Wai 2011: 18). At what point in this process Ananda M's further ordination took place is not clear, but, as we have already surmised, it is probable that it took place in the Visuddharama East Monastery under Ingan Mahāwithudayon Sayadaw, Ananda M's 'Engan Sayadaw' (Mendelson 1975: Appendix E).[33] That Ananda M's main link was with the Visuddharama East Monastery was confirmed when Elizabeth visited Mandalay in 2018.[34] Therefore, whilst recognising that Ananda M probably stayed for the rains retreat at the Shwekyimyin Pagoda, with Sayadaw U Vicāra of the Visuddharama West Monastery coming there to teach him monastic discipline and Pali[35]—and his monastic rules would have mandated him to remain in one place during this period—it is almost beyond doubt that he moved to the Visuddharama East Monastery after the rains retreat, again experiencing life as part of a monastic community.

From Sankin Sayadaw's biographers, who quote Sankin's words, comes a vivid and disturbing picture of Ananda M at the *pavāraṇā* ceremony. His lack of seniority in the monastic order meant that he was last in the line of monks. In this position, he apparently found the ritual culture so difficult that he fainted (Mānitasirī and Nandamālābhivaṁsa 1972: 177). This could have been due to the length of time a seated posture had to be maintained, the posture itself, or lack of food or water. This suggests, however, that Ananda M, although only just over 30, was so weakened by his asthma that the ritual culture of the monastic Sangha was difficult for him. Yet, he would again have made a deep symbolic impression on those present. As Min Yu Wai stresses, the sight of a tall, handsome, white English man, with head shaved and in a saffron robe, humbly practising the Buddha's teachings, made everyone happy and 'they praised him' (Min Yu Wai 2011: 20-21).

On 19 July, 1902, during the rains retreat, Ananda M took the initial step in his Akyab Plan, through the founding, with the help of sponsors such as U Kyaw Yan, of the *Buddhasāsana Samāgama* (International Buddhist Society). It was only when he relocated to Rangoon, however, that the Society truly started the work he had envisaged in Akyab.

RELOCATING TO RANGOON

Ananda M was living in Rangoon by 1903. He could have completed the whole journey by river using the Irawaddy Flotilla Company, or have combined river-travel with a train from Prome (Caine 1898: 615–616; Wright 1910: 140–145). There were at least three reasons for this move. First, Rangoon was an international port networked both with other parts of Asia (Keck 2015: 125) and with the target of his missionary hopes, the West. It took three to four days, for instance, to travel between Calcutta and Rangoon on the daily services of the British India Steam Navigation Company, and Bibby's steamers brought travellers from Liverpool, first class, for £50 (Caine 1898: 613).[36] Rangoon, in fact, epitomised the aspirations of the British in Burma, through its economic expansion and modernisation (Keck 2015: 37), and was 'the third busiest city in all India—Calcutta and Bombay alone surpassing it.'[37] During Ananda M's time there, Rangoon would see its first motor cars (1905), its first electric tram car (1906), electric street lighting (1907 onwards) and the motor bus, through the Rangoon Electric Tramway and Supply Company (1913; Pearn 1939: 278–279). Second, Ananda M no doubt believed that the *Buddhasāsana Samāgama* would have a better chance of success in this cosmopolitan port, because, thirdly, he already knew that his wealthiest sponsors were there.

On the evidence of Ananda M's writings and the nature of monastic training in Burma, Ananda M entered Rangoon trained in the Vinaya, the rudiments of Pali, Abhidhamma and Buddhist forms of meditation, particularly *kammaṭṭhāna* (the *samatha* practice outlined in the *Visuddhimagga*),[38] although his personal meditation practice would also have included yogic and possibly esoteric methods to access 'the World of Pure Consciousness' mentioned in his ordination address. The teaching of *vipassanā* meditation in its modernist form was in its infancy in Burma at this point (Houtman 1990). This and his Abhidhamma studies would stimulate a wish to use Western science to verify the potential of the mind. In addition, he had become a keen advocate of Buddhist education in Burma, influenced perhaps by U Kyaw Yan, and had probably already written all or part of a paper called 'On Religious Education in Burma' (Ananda Maitriya 1903m). He was also convinced that the West was spiritually and morally less civilised than the Buddhist Burmese, however advanced its scientific discoveries (Ananda Metteyya 1908a).

Ananda M had nevertheless bought into one racist, orientalist discourse that he had no doubt met in Ceylon, if not before, through his link with Theosophy: that Indians, and indeed Ceylonese Buddhists, were Aryan, one branch of a 'superior' Aryan 'race' that had spread to the East and the West from a point in Central Europe. His interpretation of this was that the Aryans of the West, including Britain, were inferior to the Aryans of the East, because they had chosen material gain in preference to the spiritual development that characterised the East (Ananda M 1910: 103–104; Ananda Metteyya 1910a: 7).[39] This interpretation inverted race in the hierarchy of Theosophy, which placed Europeans above Asian Aryans. His view was combined with orientalist ideas about 'race' that drew from the concept of evolution, namely that 'races' progressed through a process of mental and moral evolution from childhood to adulthood or maturity, and could rise and fall according to their level of evolution. The roots of this are present in 'Animism and Law' (Ananda Maitriya 1902a; see also Ananda Metteyya 1908a). He saw the Burmese, for instance, as 'young in racial development' (Ananda M 1910: 103), whilst nevertheless remaining in awe of their devotion and their charity. This view was similar to that of Theosophists and other Westerners in Burma at the time.[40]

In addition to this combination of orientalism and critique of Empire, Ananda M also brought to Rangoon a very practical burden, his illness. Although in Ceylon he had been largely free of asthma, evidence of recurrence peppers the accounts of his time in Burma, with other health problems added. A letter received by the Anagārika Dharmapāla from May Hla Oung shows that it was particularly bad in 1904.[41] In 1905, Ananda M wrote to 'Cash,' 'I am very extra asthmatic.'[42] When Dharmapāla visits him in April 1907, he writes 'He seems very weak,' but does not refer to asthma.[43] Another clutch of evidence comes in 1910 and 1911. Caroline Rhys Davids received a letter from the scholar U Shwe Zan Aung in 1911 stating that 'Ananda Mittehha was seriously ill lately,' hindering his review of work that Rhys Davids and Zan Aung were doing, most probably a follow-up to their collaboration on a translation from the *Abhidhamma Piṭaka*, which was published as *A Compendium of Philosophy* (Shwe Zan Aung 1910).[44] Additionally, Ananda M, in his correspondence, makes repeated references to his illness. In December 1908, to friends in England, he describes himself as a 'chronic invalid living a life very difficult, from merely physical considerations, for an Occidental to live' (Ananda Metteyya 1930: 270) and, in December 1910, he refers to 'this wearisome ill-health' (Ananda Metteyya 1929: 175). To counter the severity of his asthma attacks, it is probable that he continued to use opium, heroin and morphine, together with asthma and tobacco cigarettes, although the dangers of addiction were realised.[45]

Rangoon was as ethnically diverse as Akyab. Talbot Kelly, for instance, remarks on Rangoon's prosperity and kaleidoscopic attractiveness (Kelly 1905: 5) but judges it to be 'hardly Burmese' (Kelly: 1905: 8). His first impression at the wharf was its *'Indian* character.' The police were predominantly Sikhs, the 'Government messengers' were predominantly Indian (Kelly 1905: 6), and the Chinese dominated commerce and river trade. Kelly had to travel further out of the port to find what he calls 'the Burman in his purity' (Kelly: 1905: 11). Reading between the lines of Kelly and others who directed their orientalist gaze towards the city (e.g., Caine 1898: 620; Harvey 1946: 69–72; Powell-Brown 1911: 110–111), Rangoon under the British was communally fractured. By the census of 1901, its population had increased from the 1881 number of 134,176 to 248,060, out of which only 77,825 were ethnically Burmese (Keck 2015: 123; see also Pearn 1939: 286). The asymmetry between Indians and Burmese in Rangoon increased in the years that followed. In 1911, Indians and other immigrants would make up 56% of Rangoon's population and Burmese, only 31% (Pearn 1939: 286).[46] The downtown part of the city was the most cosmopolitan but, even here, different communities were spatially separated. Muslim and Hindu South Asians lived in the central downtown area and Chinese, to the west of this area, with the more prosperous Chinese separated from those who were economically poorer (Keck 2015: 124). A communal riot between Muslims and Hindus occurred in June 1893, after Muslims had 'killed a cow outside the Hindu temple in 29th Street' on the occasion of 'Bakr'id' (the Muslim festival of the sacrifice, otherwise known as Eid al-Adha). When the military fired into the protestors, some lives were lost (Pearn 1939: 259). More riots occurred in the early twentieth century, sometimes between rival gangs of criminals and, in 1930, between Burmese and Indians over employment (Pearn 1939: 271, 290–291). Some of these downtown commercial areas were known for prostitution and the trafficking of women, crowded conditions and disease. Pearn, referring to a period later than that of Ananda M, could still call 'the housing conditions of the poor' as nothing less than 'slums' (Pearn 1939: 286)[47] and points to a 'severe epidemic of plague' in 1905–1906, during Ananda M's time there (Pearn 1939: 288).[48]

The relationship between Burmese Buddhists and immigrants from South India and China was mainly commercial. Many Burmese found themselves in debt to the Indian Chettiyars, a group of Indian bankers (Keck 2015: 146), who became the butt of Burmese cartoonists (Harvey

1946: 55). The voluntary organisations that arose in the city were also largely ethnically defined. For instance, the Theosophical Society in Myanmar, unlike in Sri Lanka, was maintained mainly by the Indian community rather than Buddhists, and was not part of Buddhist revivalism. The boundaries between religions and communities were less porous in Rangoon than in Akyab.

One side of Rangoon life that was rarely brought under the scrutiny of British writers was their own imposed presence and the comforts they built around themselves. According to the 1901 census, there were 3,805 Europeans in Rangoon (Pearn 1939: 287). With the exception of working-class seamen and labourers, few lived in the commercial areas. They gravitated to the leafy and spacious 'Cantonment,' where gardens and other opportunities for leisure were developed. There was the 'Cantonment Garden,' situated below the Shwedagon Pagoda, and the nearby Dalhousie Park, laid out around the 'Royal Lake' in the 1890s (Bird 1897: 145; Wright 1910: 280-282; Pearn 1939: 285), together with a golf club and the Gymkhana Club. Daily rhythms were developed. As the afternoon moved towards evening, for instance, expatriate life included tennis or a walk around the shaded paths of Dalhousie Park, where a volunteer band played, followed by time at the Gymkhana Club, with its reading rooms, billiard tables and ballroom (Kelly 2005: 25-26). Polo was also indulged in (Headlam 1903: 273). The British had servants but, according to Johnston, one of the more empathetic Westerners in Burma, the Buddhist Burmese would only work for British people who knew the language and could sympathise with Burmese 'customs and ideals' (Johnston 1908: 333), leaving Indians to suffer the contempt that other expatriates were likely to show 'the natives' (Johnston 1908: 334-339).[49]

Ananda M would rarely have engaged with this expatriate British culture, and indeed critiqued it, although his visits to the Shwedagon Pagoda would have meant moving into the Cantonment, and his first monastery, close to the Pagoda, might even have been within it. Yet, due to his monastic robes, he did not pass beneath the radar of the British, as he had done in Ceylon. Crowley, on a visit to Rangoon, noted that the British saw political dangers in any European who 'thought Burmese beliefs better than their European equivalents' (Crowley 1989: 462; Harris 1998: 9). There were exceptions to this, for example the pro-Buddhist Harold Fielding Hall (1859-1917), who wrote several books that sought to contest negative stereotypes of Buddhism and the Burmese people (e.g., Fielding Hall 1898; 1913).[50] Fielding Hall donated at least two of these to the *Buddhasāsana Samāgama*, suggesting he was in contact with Ananda M (Buddhism 1903: 338; 1904: 696). He was forced to leave Burma in 1906 due to ill-health, meaning that personal contact between them could have been restricted to about four years.⁵¹ Additionally, Ananda M certainly came under the scrutiny of the British and American missionaries in the city, for whom he was an ambivalent figure, a challenge to their mission, but also a source of fascination. It is worth examining this aspect of Rangoon.

By the time Ananda M arrived in Rangoon, Burmese Buddhists were no longer seeking a non-confrontational coexistence with Christian missionaries, as they had done in the mid-nineteenth century in order to benefit from Christian schooling (e.g., Marks 1917: 73–74). Passive forms of 'resistance' (Leigh 2011: 78) had given way to vocal opposition, as Buddhists reconfigured their sense of identity in the face of the threat from Christian missionaries, particularly their undermining of Buddhism (Houtman 1990: 55–75). For instance, Cochrane, an American Baptist missionary in Burma, in his memoir of his 15 years of service, repeats the nihilistic missionary stereotypes that had been present in colonial Asia for decades, whilst nevertheless boasting that he is describing 'Buddhism As It Is.'⁵² Lived Buddhism, he states, was *'rotten to the core,'* with the people evading their moral precepts and the monks growing fat by preying upon 'the superstitions of their people' (Cochrane 1904: 139, 143). When Buddhism was practised with diligence, as at funerals, he judges it powerless 'to meet the needs of the human heart' (Cochrane 1904: 140). He ends his description with the normative missionary representation of *nibbāna* as complete annihilation: 'The Gift of Gautama is eternal death' (Cochrane 1904: 145).⁵³

The British missionaries in Rangoon, however, were mainly from the Anglican Society for the Propagation of the Gospel (SPG). By the beginning of the twentieth century, their theology was less strident than Cochrane's. 'We do not regard the non-Christian religions as wholly evil, and the creation of the Devil but consider them to be a preparation for Christianity,' SPG missionary William Purser declared in 1912, when reviewing a new book on Buddhism by his friend, Kenneth Saunders (Purser 1912: 322). This 'fulfilment' approach, however, did not prevent SPG missionaries from pointing out what they saw as the weaknesses of Buddhism, and they carefully watched Ananda M's moves in Rangoon.⁵⁴

News of Ananda M also reached church bodies internationally. For instance, the *Baptist Missionary Magazine* in the United States of America gained information about him from *The Rangoon Gazette* and used editorials in the Gazette to undermine Ananda M's conviction that Buddhism in Burma was pure and had the capacity to gain a foothold in the West (e.g., Baptist Missionary Magazine 1904: 779–780).

Ananda M was well aware of these Christian missionary representations of Buddhism. and also that they went hand-in-hand with strategies to convert every Buddhist (e.g., Smith 1914: 54).[55] Yet, he was able to say that missionary attacks on Buddhism had, in fact, been a benefit, since people had 'hastened to learn what their Scriptures could say in reply' (Ananda Maitriya 1903e: 142). In this context, he did not see missionary schools as a grave threat, given that 'no Buddhist who rightly comprehends his own Religion would ever abandon it for another' (Ananda Maitriya 1903m: 5). Maybe he knew that the missionaries continually spoke of the difficulty of converting Buddhists[56] and realised that, although Buddhists would listen to missionaries out of courtesy and curiosity, they rarely followed this up (e.g., Bestall 1905: 44).[57] When interacting with the missionaries in Rangoon, therefore, missionary records suggest that Ananda M was courteous and polite, and gained their respect. We will return to this later. Suffice to say here that, as Ananda M entered Rangoon, the relationship between Buddhists and Christian missionaries was becoming more antagonistic, and that this was an important conditioning factor for his work and his writings.

In the context of Buddhist-Christian tension, the presence in Burma of U Dhammaloka, (?1856–?1913), an Irish labourer and seaman, who was ordained in Burma on 8 July, 1900, almost two years before Ananda M, is most significant. The two diverged in character and background. They rarely met, although they tussled in the press. A short article in the *Madras Weekly Mail*, in July 1903 (Madras Weekly Mail 1903: 20), repeated in the *Bangkok Times and Weekly Mail*, declares that Ananda M was 'a decided improvement' over U Dhammaloka and this led to one of the spats between them (Turner, Cox and Bocking 2020: 140). The SPG missionary, Purser, drew a similar distinction (Purser 1911: 217). It was their attitude to Christian missionaries in Burma that most divided the two. U Dhammaloka defined himself through flamboyant denunciations of 'missionary Christianity' (Turner 2013: 69) and Western values (Turner, Cox and Bocking 2020), with Purser claiming that Dhammaloka regarded it 'as his mission in life not to preach Buddhism but to vilify Christianity' (Purser 1911: 217). He left Buddhist doctrine to others, prioritising the translation of Western anti-Christian literature into Burmese over the study of Buddhist texts (Purser 1911: 217). Ananda M, in contrast, mounted a devastating doctrinal critique of monotheistic religions in his writing but was courteous to Christians in his day-to-day relationships.

The 1910 Mandalay Circuit Report of the Wesleyan Methodist Missionary Society (WMMS) refers to 'European Buddhists' distributing tracts with antagonistic 'caricatures of Christianity and European social life' (Leigh 2011: 80), almost certainly a reference to U Dhammaloka, as was this diatribe by Cochrane:

The presence of a European clad in yellow robes, parading through the chief towns of Burma, making great pretensions, and reviling the Christian missionaries, created a sensation for a time. But his claim to be the head of Buddhism was not quite to the taste of the many native priests who, locally, or for the province, aspired to that position. Hardly more to their taste was his departure, taking with him a generous sum of money collected during his tours. (Cochrane 1904: 270)

U Dhammaloka is presented by his biographers as a pioneering, energetic and effective anti-colonial campaigner, not only in Burma but throughout Asia (Turner, Cox and Bocking 2020). He grew to detest the more urbane manner of Ananda M, and could well have seen him as a hypocrite, who 'neither understood nor approved of the real Buddhism lived by the Burmese people' (Turner, Cox and Bocking 2020: 143). When Dhammaloka visited Ceylon in 1909, one of the Anagārika Dharmapāla's diary entries about him reads, 'Passed the night at Akuressa. Dhammaloka for hours & hours will continue talking agst. Ananda Maitreeya & shows an abnormal spirit of vengeance.'[58] We have not found any direct references to U Dhammaloka in Ananda M's writings on Buddhism, but subtle references to Dhammaloka's mode of operation are present, as early as his ordination address in Akyab, when he stressed that uneducated Western *bhikkhu*s would bring Buddhism into ridicule and that any Buddhist monastic community in the West would not 'revile or abuse any form of religious belief held by others.' U Dhammaloka became, in effect, the foil for Ananda M's stance towards the presence of Christianity in Burma.

In addition to the spat after the *Madras Weekly Mail* article, Ananda M and Dhammaloka traded blows in the press at other times, both in Burma and elsewhere. Turner, Cox and Bocking note multiple instances where the two made claims about the other. For instance, in 1903, Ananda M sent complaints about Dhammaloka to English-language newspapers in Bangkok, causing them to be sceptical of Dhammaloka's press releases (Turner, Cox and Bocking 2020: 113). Another exchange took place in the *Burma Echo* in 1907, in which Dhammaloka dismisses Ananda M's interpretations of Buddhism (Turner, Cox and Bocking 2020: 142). However, the most important, and the one that had unanticipated consequences, took place in 1908, when Ananda Metteyya was on his mission in London and Dhammaloka wrote to the British newspaper, *The Truth*, making claims that Ananda M's ordination was illegitimate. This exchange would seriously hurt Ananda M's reputation when it was resurrected in the yellow press, and connected to his former magical student, Aleister Crowley, who, by then, had already earned a less-than-favourable reputation with the public. We examine this in the next chapter.

The two main sponsors of Ananda M in Rangoon, according to Burmese sources, were the previously mentioned U Shwe Zan Aung and Mrs. May Hla Oung (Min Yu Wei 2011: 21). An additional sponsor was Dr. Ernest or Ernst Reinhold Rost (1872–1930), the son of the orientalist, Reinhold Rost (1822–1896).[59] Zan Aung, a scholar and philosopher, who was one year older than Ananda M, had just entered the Rangoon civil service when Ananda M arrived in the city.[60] He would become the first Burmese Executive Commissioner. Rost was appointed Resident Medical Officer at Rangoon Central Hospital in November 1901.[61]

Mrs. May Hla Oung (Daw Mya May),[62] is the only Burmese person mentioned under the 'Social: Burmese' category in the who's who section of the chapter on Rangoon in the prestigious *Twentieth Century Impressions of Burma*, published by Lloyds (Wright 1910: 304–307). Daughter of a military general who had transferred his allegiance to the British in the second Burmese war, she came from one of the wealthiest families in Burma and married U Hla Oung, who became the Controller of the Indian Treasuries, the first Burmese person to hold the post. According to Ñāṇatiloka, who will be mentioned later in this section, U Hla Oung spent most of his time in Calcutta (Hecker and Ñāṇatusita 2008: 24) and died in 1906. They had one son, Ba Hla Oung, who studied in Eton and Oxford and became a noted barrister.[63] He also died young, in July 1910. In addition, the Hla Oungs

Figure 3.1 Mrs. May Hla Oung (Daw Mya May), Buddhism Vol. 1, No. 4: p. 673.

also raised Daw Ma May's nephew, May Oung (1880–1926), after his parents died. May Oung became one of only two Burmese judges appointed to the High Court when it was established by the British in 1922, and was an expert in Buddhist law (e.g., May Oung 1916; Harcourt Butler 1927: 192).[64] Both young men knew and worked with Ananda M, Ba Hla Oung as a member of the Executive Council of the *Buddhasāsana Samāgama*.

As Turner argues, Daw Mya May 'was anything but defined by the men in her life' (Turner 2014: 66). She was presented to the British royal family twice outside Burma, once in 1877 in Madras and again in 1889 in England and, on the visit of the Prince and Princess of Wales to Burma in January 1906, she led a group of Burmese ladies in erecting a 'pandol' and met their Royal Highnesses.[65] She established the Society for the Prevention of Infant Mortality in Burma (Wright 2010: 307) and, together with her son, founded the Empress Victoria Buddhist Boys' School in 1897 in York Street (Ananda Maitriya 1903e: 174), which taught boys until they were about 13. She then opened, in the same year, the Empress Victoria Buddhist Girls' School in Canal Street, taking over a Municipal School that was due to be dismantled. This taught girls up to the age of about 11 years (Ananda Maitriya 1903h: 174; Turner 2014: 67).[66] The names of these schools, in themselves, indicate her 'positive identification' with both British rule and Buddhism (Turner 2014: 67). She was a generous patron, not only of Ananda M and other Western *bhikkhus* but also of others, for example, a notable Burmese artist, Ba Myan (1897–1945). A painting by him of a matronly Daw Mya May hangs in the Myanmar Museum. She epitomised the colonial representation of Burmese women, namely that they were exceptionally independent and liberated (Ikeya 2011: 46–55).

Ananda M needed to be supported by wealthy Burmese citizens such as Daw Mya May if his Akyab Plan was to be realised. In the second issue of *Buddhism*, he includes a photograph of 'the little monastery close by Shwé Dagon where BUDDHISM [his journal] first saw light.' He describes the noisy atmosphere with novices loudly chanting from the Vinaya, the *suttas* and Abhidhamma, and thanks Burmese donors for finding a new Editorial Office, still in sight of the Pagoda (Ananda Maitriya 1903j). The latter was at 1 Pagoda Road, adjacent to Daw Mya May's home.[67] We have been unable to find either the monastery or the buildings in Pagoda Road, and surmise that both have been replaced by modern constructions.

On the evidence of a letter sent to Charles Lanman in 1907, it is probable that the monastery was also his home at first, and that the conditions were basic, although he may have had some sort of a laboratory there.[68] In 1906 or 1907, Daw Mya May solved Ananda M's accommodation difficulties by building a 'dwelling place' in 'a quiet secluded area,' on her own land in Rangoon,[69] for Western *bhikkhus*, which, at that time, included Ananda M, Ñāṇatiloka and Sīlācāra, to whom we will return (Hecker and Ñāṇatusita 2008: 29).[70] On the evidence of a prominent Burmese Buddhist, P Monin, who was a Buddhist monk at the time, it was named the U Byar Tawya [Forest] Monastery (P Monin 2009: 51–52). The Anagārika Dharmapāla simply called it 'the new Temple built by Mrs Oung,' when he visited Ananda M there on 10 October 1907.[71]

Letters sent to Capt. J. Powell-Brown and another to his wife Ethel Powell-Brown in 1913 give the following address for this new dwelling place: European Kyoung, Bodhigun, Boundary Road, P.O. Rangoon.[72] Boundary Road circled the Shwe Dagon Pagoda, Dalhousie Park and the Royal Lake and was sparsely developed. According to Pearn, in 1890, only 'one or two houses' lay along it (Pearn 1939: 276).

The best description of Ananda M's new accommodation comes from Ethel Powell-Brown, who visited Ananda M with her husband, when they were in Rangoon.[73] Writing for a London journal, she describes it as 'beneath the shadow of the Sh[w]e Dagone Pagoda, in a jungle clearing, as remote and peaceful as if it were a hundred miles from Rangoon.' It was reached by steps and consisted of 'scattered wooden buildings,' each housing one European monk.[74] Terming it a hermitage rather than a monastery, Powell-Brown states that each building consisted of a 'room below and a room above connected by a steep outer staircase.' Surrounded by 'bodhi and mango trees' and 'blossoming shrubs,' it combined in her eyes 'into one spacious and inclusive habitation.' Ananda M used the lower room as a laboratory, the room above being his living quarters. When Powell-Brown visited, probably after 1908, it was lined with overflowing bookcases, with 'cascading piles of magazines' on the floor and chairs.[75]

An interesting cameo of Ananda M at this new monastery comes from a letter of W. B. Yeats, written in 1907 to Florence Farr: 'Bennett goes out every morning with his begging bowl as a monk, but always gives the contents of his bowl to some less well-provided for brother. His own meals are sent in every day to the workshop.'[76] This suggests that Ananda M perhaps preferred or needed a diet different from traditional Burmese cooking (Bax 1946: 58–59; reprinted in Kelly and Schuchard 2005: 747–749).[77]

In the purpose-built monastery, Ananda M was able to combine his knowledge of Buddhist mental culture with psychology and science, carrying out his scientific experiments in a more congenial laboratory. P Monin, whom we have quoted above, writes:

> While I was wondering in this way, I reached U Byar Tawya Monastery. I found out that the abbot was an English monk called

Ananda Metteyya. He could not speak Burmese so that there was no one who could have a conversation with him. When he came to know that I could fluently speak English, he let me stay at his monastery. As he was a chemist, he made a laboratory in the monastery and he was endeavouring to take a photo of how the *vīthi* process [process of consciousness] works as mentioned in the Abhidhamma. (P Monin 2009: 51–52)[78]

P Monin had obviously not encountered Ananda M before this. His words shed an interesting light on Ananda M's continuing scientific experimentation, confirming that at least one of his projects involved examining the process of consciousness as detailed in Abhidhamma. P Monin adds a footnote to say that Ananda M's experimentation was aimed at demonstrating to Westerners, through photography, the accuracy of Abhidhamma. He adds that this project did not succeed—he was asthmatic, returned to Britain and passed away, suggesting that the visit was after 1908 (P Monin 2009: 51–52).

Ananda M conducted many different types of experiments, both before and after his move to the new monastery. His letter of February 1905 to Cassius Pereira indicates his early interest in scientifically measuring mental processes.[79] One thing he sought to show was that consciousness not only consisted of particles, *dhammas*, as described in the Abhidhamma, but also measurable waves. Greenly records that, before his 1908 mission to Britain, he had devised an 'electrical apparatus' that could cause 'a light spot' to move on a screen through concentrated thought, when it was connected to a galvanometer (Greenly 1945: 85; see also Humphreys 1937: 33). Yeats also states to Farr in 1907 that Ananda M was working on 'N Rays' (Bax 1946: 58; reprinted in Kelly and Schuchard 2005: 747–749).[80] Whether this was linked to his work on the mind is not known. What he frequently lacked were the tools to accomplish these experiments, and he would occasionally ask correspondents for assistance. His aim was to patent and then sell the results of his experiments and so gain funds for his Akyab Plan.[81]

Ananda M also continued extensive meditation practice, evidenced by the emergence of stories similar to the one that Crowley recorded in Kandy. The first is again linked with Crowley. Ted Bryant, recalling a conversation with Crowley, writes that Crowley had visited Rangoon at a time when Ananda M had decided to have a retreat 'in a little bungalow about half-a-mile from the main buildings.' If, as we believe, the last visit of Crowley to Burma was in 1905, then it is probable that this occurred before Ananda M moved into his new monastery. Food and water were put outside the bungalow so that Ananda M need not be disturbed. Crowley was approached when food had not been taken in for three days. When Crowley opened the door, in the words of Bryant, he 'saw him [Ananda M] suspended in the air at eye level. He had no longer any weight and in the draught from the open door, he was 'blown about like a dry leaf' (I remember Aleister's phrase).' Bryant adds that he was convinced Crowley was being 'sincere in his belief that it actually happened.'[82] Ethel Powell-Brown records another instance, writing that, on one visit to Ananda M's monastery, she and her husband found his Burmese servants in 'a state of excitement,' because 'the Bhikkhu had levitated while in meditation, and they had all seen him.'[83] Additionally, she reports an undated conversation with Ananda M, when he, unusually, shared a meditation experience:

> It seemed to be an illumination, he said, an exaltation, and a liberation. Every step was a step both up and out. He likened it to travelling upwards in an elevator. And at each stage in the journey, the four walls fell outwards and he found himself in an immensely larger, lighter space, which itself began to move upwards until the walls of that fell out, and the roof rolled back, and he was again in immensities, but moving higher ...[84]

With meditation practice at the heart of Ananda M's personal religious life, his eyes were nevertheless turned towards the West on his arrival in Rangoon. An account of his activities in Rangoon must, therefore, begin with the international links he maintained and created. We will then examine his impact on Burma before moving, in the next chapter, to his mission to Britain in 1908 and his last years in Burma.

ANANDA METTEYYA'S INTERNATIONAL IMPACT WHILST IN RANGOON

On 15 March, 1903, just three weeks before he returned to Ceylon, Ananda M, together with an executive of four others and a council of eight, reorganised the *Buddhasāsana Samāgama* with a new constitution and set of rules. The Constitution states that the Society's objects were:

> to promote a wider knowledge of the tenets of Buddhism, and the study of Pāli and Sanskrit Buddhist Literature. These Objects the Samāgama will prosecute (*a*) by printing and circulating works on Buddhism, Pāli Text[s], and translations of Buddhist Scriptures, etc., (*b*) by promoting Buddhist Education, and (*c*) by arranging for the delivery of Lectures, etc., on Buddhist subjects, and in such

other manners as may hereafter commend itself to the Council. (Buddhasāsana Samāgama 1903b: 6)

Within the same 'Revised Prospectus,' in a section entitled 'Information for Enquirers,' the Society further adds that its 'chief work' was publication, in the belief that 'an extension of the system of ethic and philosophy known as Buddhism will prove a remedy for many of the evils of the present age' (Buddhasāsana Samāgama 1903b: 1). It was already in the process of publishing six pamphlets through the Hanthawaddy Press. These include the already-cited account of Ananda M's ordination (No. 1; Anon 1902b), the previously mentioned paper by Ananda M entitled 'Religious Education in Burma' (No. 2), to which we will return, a reprint of Ananda M's 1901 lecture on the Four Noble Truths (Pamphlet No. 3), a reprint of 'Animism and Law,' as it had appeared in Ceylon (No. 4), and two papers by European scholars: 'Buddhism and Science' by Dr. R. Ernest (No. 5–probably Dr. Ernst Rost) and 'The Will in Buddhism' by Caroline Rhys Davids (No. 6).[85]

Significant also was that membership of the Society was not restricted to Buddhists. It was to be 'eclectic.' The only condition was that members had to be 'interested in some branch of the Society's work' (Buddhasāsana Samāgama 1903b: 1). No mention is made in the Prospectus of a mission to the West, but the term 'eclectic' was certainly directed towards the West, where many who did not label themselves Buddhist were interested in its philosophy. Additionally, in line with Ananda M's Akyab Plan, the fact that the 'Official Organ of the Society' was a journal in English—*Buddhism: An Illustrated Quarterly Review*—implied its anticipated international reach, just as much as the name of the Society. The following clause in the Constitution of the *Buddhasāsana Samāgama* was also in line with Ananda M's Akyab Plan, and probably includes an indirect reference to U Dhammaloka:

> Endeavouring to follow the example of the Great Founder of the Buddhist Religion, it shall be the policy of this Samāgama in its official publications, and in lectures, etc., given under its auspices, to avoid any abuse or ridicule of any form of Religious Belief; which, as it would bring about hatred or heart-burning, is opposed both to the letter and the Spirit of the Buddhist Law. (Buddhasāsana Samāgama 1903b: 7)[86]

A photograph included in the third issue of *Buddhism* (March 1904) of the *Samāgama* shows a serious, pale, robed but untonsured Ananda M, surrounded by the principal members and sponsors of the Society, including Daw Mya May and Rost.

Figure 3.2 Council of the Buddhasāsana Samāgama with Ananda M seated in the centre, Buddhism Vol. 1, No. 3: opposite p. 473.

A considerable amount of international correspondence preceded this reformulation, continuing until the first issue of *Buddhism*, which contains a list of the Society's representatives and honorary members. Outside Asia, the Society had representatives in Austria (Karl Neumann), Germany (Arthur Pfungst) and Italy (Giuseppe de Lorenzo), and honorary members in London (Edwin Arnold, Caroline Rhys Davids, T. W. Rhys Davids and D. M. Strong), the United States (Paul Carus, K. Hori and H. C. Vetterling) and Denmark (V. Fausböll). Within Asia, there were representatives in Sri Lanka (W. Arthur de Silva and Richard Pereira)[87] and China (Kong Yu Wei). Hikkaḍuvē Sumaṃgala, who had been present at the opening of Maitriya Hall, was an honorary member (Buddhasāsana Samāgama 1903a: iii). Further names were added in subsequent issues.

THE FIRST ISSUE OF *BUDDHISM*: AN ILLUSTRATED REVIEW

The first edition of *Buddhism* appeared in September 1903, just six months after the reformulation of the Society. The primary aim was to set 'before the world the true principles of our Religion believing, as we do, that these need only to be better known to meet with a widespread acceptance

Figure 3.3 Ananda M outside the first headquarters of the Buddhasāsana Samāgama, Buddhism Vol. 1, No. 1: p. 163.

among the peoples of the West' (Ananda Maitriya 1903g: 163–164). Two further objectives are also outlined: the promotion of 'humanitarian activities' and the creation of an international network to unite 'as by a common bond of mutual interest and brotherhood, the many Associations with Buddhist aims which now exist' (Ananda Maitriya 1903g: 164). In line with the Akyab Plan, the journal also invites Westerners to Burma for ordination as *bhikkhus*, Ananda M aspiring to receive five each from the United States, England, France and Germany. His hope was that they would eventually return to the West in teams to propagate Buddhism.

The main articles in the first issue, three by Ananda M, one by Caroline Rhys Davids, one by Daw Mya May and one by Moung Po Me, are not a random collection but were carefully selected to contest the misrepresentations of Buddhism that Ananda M perceived in contemporary discourses (Harris 2008).[88] For him, this had to be the first step in communicating Buddhism to the West. They are, therefore, worth examining.

The first article, 'The Faith of the Future,'[89] by Ananda M, combines his passionate advocacy of Buddhism, the West's moral bankruptcy and its misrepresentation of Buddhism, and his engagement with social issues. It begins in much the same way as 'Animism and Law,' with the conviction that scientific discovery would sweep away the irrationalities of theistic

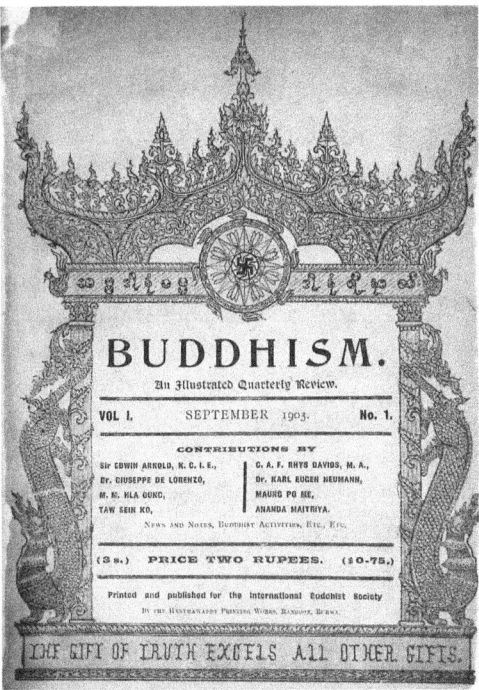

Figure 3.4 Cover of Buddhism, *courtesy of John L. Crow.*

faith. He adds, however, that this was also killing the praiseworthy ethics of 'the old-time beliefs,' which had led to more 'real poverty, more starvation, more utter misery in England and America to-day than yet exists in any Buddhist land' (Ananda Maitriya 1903a: 11). A denunciation of Western society for its lack of humane values, its promotion of 'the curse of competition' and its pedalling of 'the arts of death and devastation' follows (Ananda Maitriya 1903a: 12). Unsurprisingly, Ananda M then presents Buddhism as the sole answer, appealing, as before, to its 'Reign of Law' and its potential to create a society where people could live 'in harmony, in self-restraint, in mutual forbearance' (Ananda Maitriya 1903a: 14). Stressing that Buddhism is a religion of 'the here and now' rather than of philosophical speculation, he then outlines the Four Noble Truths as 'a profound and an accurate analysis of existence as we know it' (Ananda Maitriya 1903a: 20), pointing towards 'salvation founded upon *works*, and not on faith; a deliverance born of self-conquest, the living of a life of good' (Ananda Maitriya 1903a: 22). He then appeals in lyrical tones to the necessity of diminishing the 'I,' the ego, in the realisation that 'All life is one,' echoing his Hope Lodge lecture (Ananda Maitriya 1903a: 22).

Only then does he move to misconceptions, naming three: that Buddhism is 'heathen' and idolatrous—the view of Christian missionaries; that it is mysterious, 'miracle-mongering' and esoteric—the view of many Theosophists; and that it is apathetic, pessimistic and annihilationist and is, therefore, unsuitable for the energetic West—the view of some British colonialists. He then demolishes each. Buddha images are not idols but beautiful reminders of the teaching of the Buddha. Controversially, he attributes the view that Buddhism is mysterious and esoteric to the Western discovery of Mahayana Buddhist literature.[90] He then critiques Theosophy for appropriating this, focussing on their distortion of the Buddhist teaching of *anattā*, non-self, through their conviction that the Buddha taught the reincarnation of a soul (Ananda Maitriya 1903a: 28). He then adopts a supersessionist approach: Theosophy prepared the way for Buddhism in the West. Westerners would not have listened to the East had the truth of *anattā* been preached first! (Ananda Maitriya 1903a: 29). As for the accusation of nihilism, he declares Buddhism to be 'the proudest Optimism' (Ananda Maitriya 1903a: 30). It encourages neither apathy nor indifference but rather strenuous effort to 'induce new good to arise' (Ananda Maitriya 1903a: 31). The last part of the article offers the now discredited view that Buddhism had spread without being stained 'with human blood,' unlike other religions, which had been 'scourges' rather 'than blessings in the world' (Ananda Maitriya 1903a: 32). Buddhism had ennobled the peoples it had touched and could fill another lacuna in the west, namely the 'exercise and development of the higher faculties of mind,' such as love and compassion as an antidote to anger, which could lead, for instance, to the more humane treatment of criminals (Ananda Maitriya 1903a: 34–37).

Next comes Caroline Rhys David's 'The Threshold of Buddhist Ethics' (C. A. F. Rhys Davids 1903), which argues that the psychological introspection of Buddhism has an ethical dimension that encourages a reduction of egoism. After this comes Daw Mya May's article on 'The Women of Burma,' commissioned by Ananda M to illustrate the reasons behind the 'freedom' and 'happiness' of Burmese women.[91] Daw Mya May claims the 'secret' lies in Buddhism, within which women were not 'the slave of man' but 'his loved co-worker, his dear companion in the work and play of life' (Hla Oung 1903: 62). She admits that village girls do not have the educational opportunities of boys, but claims that few are unable to read and write (Hla Oung 1903: 63).

The next article, by Moung Po Me, 'Animism and Agnosticism,' contests the Christian missionary view that Buddhism has no 'consolation' because it had no God, and so had to create objects of worship, such as the Nats (nature spirits; Po Me 1903). The Prologue and Part One of a serialised article, 'In the Shadow of Shwe Dagon,' by Ananda M, come next (Ananda Maitriya 1903b).[92] It voices another of Ananda M's messages to the West—that Buddhism is not only a rational philosophy but also a total way of life, a lived religion, which involves ritual, devotion, community and aesthetics. The 'Prologue' centres on a single evening visit to the Shwe Dagon Pagoda, with an unnamed friend, at a Buddhist full-moon festival, probably Vesak, when they passed 'up the terraced path that leads from our Temple to the Great Pagoda' (Ananda Maitriya 1903b: 107).

Ananda M begins this by contrasting the commercial activism of lower Rangoon with 'the City of the Great Pagoda, true capital of Burma for six million hearts' (Ananda Maitriya 1903b: 101). He dismisses the missionary view that the Shwe Dagon is a hive of idolatry, representing it as a space where the Burmese touched the 'promise of the Dawn of Love' (Ananda Maitriya 1903b: 102). He then describes what happened around the pagoda—phonographs, music, flags, paper dragons, horoscope readers and story-tellers, together with surging, colourful, laughing crowds that would flatten themselves to let a *bhikkhu* pass—and contrasts this positively with the Western idea of reverence, 'the sad respectful countenance and slow gait' (Ananda Maitriya 1903b: 108). In the pagoda itself, Ananda M knelt with his companion and turned his thoughts inwards to observe his feelings and perceptions, perhaps using the meditation techniques described in 'On the Culture of Mind.' He found that the image of London's Battersea Park on an Easter Monday played on the fringes of his consciousness, particularly the drunkenness and lewdness of the people, and his own sense of shame when he had witnessed it. The last paragraphs then gently criticises those in the West who believe that the Burmese have to be civilised or Christianised.

A postcolonial lens might dismiss this representation as an orientalist, romanticised othering of colonial Burma. We would differ from this view. Ananda M's turn of phrase was certainly lyrical and romantic but what he perceived was both 'other' and part of his adopted identity. He was both insider and outsider, inhabiting a liminal space, and it is obvious that he describes an authentic 'religious experience,' which led him to see even more clearly the folly of British white supremacism. And he used this to challenge those who would split Buddhist philosophy from its lived devotional base.

The last significant article in this issue, again by Ananda M, who was still calling himself 'Maitriya,' is on 'Nibbāna.' Most probably adapting the lectures he had given in Ceylon, his aim is again to correct what he sees as 'misapprehensions' (Ananda Maitriya 1903c: 113). The continuously stated conviction of Christian missionaries in Asia was that *nibbāna* was the annihilation of life. With these and other orientalist scholars in mind, he advises against using the Sanskrit, *nirvāṇa*, because it could encourage people to conflate the Buddhist concept with the Hindu goal of absorption into Brahma. He then challenges the view that there were two or three types of *nibbāna*, particularly Robert Childers's distinction between 'Arahatship' (Pali: *arahant/arahat*; Skt: *arhat*—the gaining of enlightenment through the teaching of a Buddha) in this life and the 'annihilation' of the 'arahat' at death.[93] Prefiguring the mid-twentieth century tussle between theology and the emerging discipline of religious studies, he then proposes that readers should place themselves 'in the mental attitude of the Buddhist' (Ananda Maitriya 1903c: 117). If this was done, then discussion of *nibbāna* would begin from the right premise, namely the doctrine of *anattā* (not-self; Ananda Maitriya 1903c: 119). Rebirth was to be understood not through the concept of a soul or ego but through the principle of *kamma* (action) and, repeating earlier writing, the transference of energy or 'tendencies' (*sankhāra*) (Ananda Maitriya 1903c: 119–120). He then presents *nibbāna* as liberation from the round of birth and rebirth, driven by the principle of *kamma* and cites positive textual descriptions of it, particularly from the *Milindapañha*, a canonical text within the Burmese tradition. Only then does he turn to *nibbāna* after death, arguing that humans cannot, with their finite minds, grasp 'that Light beyond,' that 'Unconditioned, Unchanging and Unknown' state, which certainly exists but only in a form beyond human conceptions of the 'existent' (Ananda Maitriya 1903c: 128). His conclusion demonstrates that this article was not only an academic intervention but a statement of Ananda M's aspiration, hope, joy and truth:

> And so to conclude. If I am asked, 'Is the Nibbāna Annihilation? Is it Cessation? Is it the End of All?' I reply, thus even have we learned. It is Annihilation—the annihilation of the threefold fatal fire of Passion, Wrath and Ignorance. It is Annihilation—the annihilation of conditioned being, of all that has bound and fettered us; the Cessation of the dire delusion of life that has veiled from us the splendour of the Light Beyond. It is the End of All—the end of the long tortuous pilgrimage through worlds of interminable illusion; the End of Sorrow, of Impermanence, of Self-deceit. From the torment of the sad Dream of Life an everlasting Awakening,—from the torture of selfhood an eternal Liberation;—a Being, an Existence, that to name Life were sacrilege, and to name Death a lie:—unnameable, unthinkable, yet even in this life to be realised and entered into:—thus is the glory of Nibbāṇa by our Lord declared, and such the Goal of this our Buddhist Faith. (Ananda Maitriya 1903c: 133)

The selection of articles for the first edition of *Buddhism* was, therefore, driven by pragmatic decision-making about what to convey to the West and how to convey it. Into this, Ananda M poured his own experience, informed both by his fascination with scientific discovery and his passion that Buddhism should challenge the moral failings of his day. Most of his later writing was prefigured in it and, after his death, articles such as 'The Faith of the Future' were republished in a variety of publications, both Buddhist and theosophical.

The first issue of *Buddhism* and those that followed also offer considerable evidence of Ananda M's ongoing international contacts and interests, for example, his concern for the state of Buddhism throughout the world, his wish to keep abreast with scientific advances, his receipt of international journals, and his ability to gain an international cohort of contributors, including Thomas and Caroline Rhys Davids (United Kingdom) and Paul Carus (United States).[94] His ongoing contact with Buddhist revivalists in Ceylon, including the Anagārika Dharmapāla, is seen in his critique of British actions in Anuradhapura and the inclusion of articles by Ceylonese friends.[95] His willingness to defy the proclamations of the British monarch, who had commanded his subjects to 'observe a strict Neutrality' in the 1904 war between Russia and Japan[96] is seen in his passionate support for Japan, as the 'first of the Oriental states to fight on equal terms with any western race within the last two centuries.' He casts Japan as 'the champion of weakness against tyranny. . . . fighting the battles of Civilization against the most despotic, the most reactionary, and the most ruthless of the Christian Powers' (Ananda Metteyya 1904f: 649).[97] As for science, he engages with Marie Curie's discovery of radium (Ananda Maitriya 1903f: 158),[98] gives a scholarly commentary on the work of Herbert Spencer at his death (Ananda Metteyya 1904c: 503–509) and covers the work of the Cavendish Laboratory in Cambridge (Ananda Metteyya 1905a: 119). In 1908, in collaboration with T. W. Rhys Davids, he appeals to the Burmese to donate to the 'Pitaka Translation Scheme,' namely the Pali Text Society, in preference to pagoda or shrine building (Ananda Metteyya 1908d: 340).

Ananda M's relationships with international Buddhist scholars, however, was not always harmonious. Karl Neumann withdrew after the first issue of *Buddhism* because Ananda M had edited his translation of the *Mahārāhulavāda Sutta* (Neumann 1903); Neumann had wanted it to be printed exactly as he had sent it and took 'serious offence.' Ananda M justifies the editing on the grounds that Neumann had not been using his 'mother-tongue' and had included 'many curious idioms' that English readers would not have understood (Ananda Maitriya 1903j: 315). His name appears as both a representative and a patron in the first edition of the journal but is absent thereafter.

ONGOING LINKS WITH INTERNATIONAL THEOSOPHISTS

The pamphlets published by the *Buddhasāsana Samāgama* and the issues of *Buddhism* were sent to both the international headquarters of the Theosophical Society in Adyar and to the European headquarters in London. Olcott, the International President, reviewed in *The Theosophist* the publications sent to Adyar. The first was the pamphlet that describes Ananda M's ordination and gives his ordination address. Olcott begins by noting who 'Allan MacGregor' is, and how he came to Buddhism. He then reprints large quotations from the pamphlet, with a few annotations. For instance, after quoting the section of the ordination where Ananda M received his new name, Olcott writes:

> One can't help but remarking that the priestly name—Ananda Metteya (Maitriya)—conferred upon the young Englishman, was rather pretentious, for Maitriya is the name of the Buddha who is to come at the end of the Yuga and lead mankind into the full knowledge

of the Arya Dharma, and into the peace which will result. (Olcott 1902: 686)

Olcott then quotes and comments on the 'very ambitious programme' contained in the pamphlet, ending the review with:

> Well, let the young man dream his dreams in peace and let us all hope that when his day of disillusionment comes, as it has to all of us his predecessors, he may have the pluck and perseverance to stand alone and fight his fight and, if it need be, die at his post, courageous and undaunted. (Olcott 1902: 688)

These comments clearly show that Olcott was frustrated by Ananda M's eagerness to bring Buddhism to the West, no doubt because his speech and plan failed to acknowledge those who had made similar attempts, including Olcott himself. Yet, despite the sarcastic remarks, the fact that he reprinted large portions of the pamphlet in the journal was useful to Ananda M's cause.

Olcott also reviewed the first issue of *Buddhism* in the October 1903 edition of *The Theosophist*. His review is generally positive. He writes that the journal is 'beautifully illustrated,' 'ably edited,' and 'calculated to fill a long-felt want among the adherents of this faith throughout the world' (Olcott 1903: 56). In his discussion of 'Faith of the Future,' he adds a parenthetical note, 'we may notice further, hereafter,' indicating he would return to the issue of *anattā* brought up in the essay. Subsequent issues show that this did not happen. Notably, the sarcasm present in Olcott's review of Ananda M's ordination pamphlet is absent.

In contrast to Olcott, the Theosophists in London engaged with Ananda M's comments about Theosophy directly, with snide comments of their own. In the November 1903 issue of *The Theosophical Review*, the journal editor, G. R. S. Mead, dedicates eight pages to the virtues of the first edition of *Buddhism*, while also refuting Ananda M's claims regarding *anattā*. The review begins:

> We offer our cordial congratulations and a hearty welcome to our new contemporary *Buddhism*. *Buddhism* is an illustrated quarterly review of some 200 quarto pages, excellently printed and illustrated, published at 1, Pagoda Road, Rangoon, under the auspices of the International Buddhist Society (Buddhasâsana Samâgama), and edited by Bhikkhu Ânanda Maitriya. (Mead 1903: 193)

The editors then declare that Theosophists would enjoy the issue, not because they favoured Buddhism over any other faith, but because 'we desire to learn from all men who have a living faith in the tradition of any great teacher or teachers what they have to say for themselves about the fundamentals of that tradition' (Mead 1903: 193-194). They then note how wonderful it is that a Westerner, with an occidental mind, can learn what the living members of the great Eastern faiths had to say about solutions to the world's problems (Mead 1903: 194). A generally positive review of each article follows. When the review comes to 'The Faith of the Future,' however, they first summarise its content, including Ananda M's view that Buddhism was compatible with science. They then dissect his second assertion, namely that Buddhism had no mysteries and was not esoteric. First, they refute his claim that in Buddhism, 'There is no Noumenon behind Phenomena' (Mead 1903: 195-196). Next, they return to the claim that Buddhism was compatible with science and question it, stating, 'Ânanda M. is out of touch with the signs of the times in things scientific in the West' (Mead 1903: 197). This finally leads them to address Ananda M's criticism of Theosophy, namely that Theosophists misunderstood the Buddha when they claimed that he taught that there was a soul:

> Even when we meet with such sayings as that which directs us even with regard to the utmost limits of consciousness to declare: "This is not Mine; this am I not; this is not my Self"—it is not to be supposed that this was taught by the Buddha to prove that there was *no* "I," no "Self"; but rather to encourage His Bhikkhus to ever greater and greater efforts to realise the true "I," the true "Self"—the Noumenon of noumena—as it really is, and to transcend not only the most transcendent phenomena of "I"-ness or "Self-hood," but even the noumena of these phenomena. This Noumenon is not "an immeasurable clergyman in a white tie," or a material soul hidden in a body as a needle in a bundle of hay.... Why, in the very magazine before us we have what is practically an apologia by Ânanda M. for the Burman's belief in Nats! (Mead 1903: 198)

The editors next direct their criticism to Ananda M's refutation that Buddhism contains the esoteric. One of the earliest popular books to promote the Theosophical teachings given by the 'Masters' was A. P. Sinnett's, *Esoteric Buddhism* (Sinnett 1883). About this, the editors write:

> And why a Buddhist who is studying the problem of the nature of ignorance should object so furiously to the term, we cannot for the life of us imagine, except that a certain famous book was (in our opinion unfortunately) called *Esoteric Buddhism*.... We believe from our own studies in comparative Theosophy, and from our

own teaching, that we see in the obscurity of the traditions traces of what we consider to be the great truths of general religion, philosophy and science, and this point of view we call "esoteric." ... Finally, if there is no tradition of esotericism in Buddhism, we should like to know how Ânanda Bhikkhu accounts for the three treatises which H. P. Blavatsky printed under the general title *The Voice of the Silence*? The late Professor Max Müller was unable to answer this question when challenged to do so; what has Ânanda Maitriya to say on the subject? Perhaps he had better settle the dispute of Hînayâna with Mahâyâna before he asserts that he alone is in possession of "Right Views." (Mead 1903: 200, 276)

Despite their voluminous criticism, they end the review with a conciliatory tone, writing:

In so far as *Buddhism* may serve to make this divine universalism familiar to the world, it has our sympathy and thanks, our goodwill and our love; for this, we believe, was the Dharma of the Tathâgata [a name used in the texts to denote the Buddha], this the Good Law that those who thus walk have ever taught. (Mead 1903: 277)

In the second issue of *Buddhism*, Ananda M refers to this critique, claiming that he would reply to it in detail, although he never did (Ananda Maitriya 1903k: 320–321).

Olcott gives a full page review of the second issue of *Buddhism* within *The Theosophist*, in which he resumes his tongue-in-cheek comments. The review begins:

Our friend Ananda Maitriya, whilom Mr. Macgregor, of Scotland, is going ahead in his new role of a Burmese Buddhist Priest, with a rush that is calculated to make the conservative Burmans, and especially the old fashioned Hpongyis [Buddhist monks], his colleagues, catch their breath. The ancient policy of quietism, that sort of pleasant, Oriental, dream-life, he changes at one crack of the editorial whip, into a policy of international propaganda. Its first fruit is the issuing of this new quarterly, which makes a really grand appearance and offers to its readers an intellectual banquet. If the Editor keeps his health, and goes on at this rate, he must soon become a power in the Buddhist world. (Olcott 1904a: 374)

Olcott then lists the contributions to both the first and second issue, mentioning at the end the previous editorial exchange with the editor of the *Theosophical Review*, G. R. S. Mead. Finally, he comments on Ananda M's health and denigrates the Burmese, while praising his own revivalist work in Ceylon:

> Unhappily the Editor's health is precarious, and this gives the element of uncertainty to all his new life-work. There is also an enormous contrast between the propaganda which his militant enthusiasm impels him to enter upon, and the heart-breaking passivity of the Sangha in general of the "Southern Church" so-called. Twenty-three years of work in the same field has taught us what that means. Ananda Maitriya's best, if not only, chance is to get around him a considerable body of the same class of earnest laies who have won the marvellous success which has crowned the attempt at Buddhist revival in Ceylon. (Olcott 1904a: 374–375)

The multiple references to Ananda M's health suggest that Olcott was not only kept informed about Ananda M's activities but also his health struggles. Indeed, the review of the third issue of *Buddhism* begins with Ananda M's health, with Olcott writing of his astonishment:

> that in so short a time, a young Scotchman, turned monk of Buddha, could have gathered around him a devoted band of Burmese men and women, ready to make every sacrifice for the production of this quarterly in the English language, which, of necessity, would appeal to a very limited reading-public in their own country, but must be regarded as an agency of propaganda to carry the teachings of Buddhism to the chief countries of the world. (Olcott 1904b: 571)

The review continues by questioning the wisdom of creating 'copies of his expensive magazine' to be sent to the tables of reading-rooms and libraries in the West. He mocks Ananda M's statement that he had frequently received letters from people who had found the magazine in one of these venues. The end of the review returns to Ananda M's health:

> There cannot be two opinions as to the intellectual brightness and literary ability of Ananda Maitriya; while one must admire the dauntless courage with which he undertook the very serious responsibility of starting an International Buddhist Society, and he deserves compliments and congratulations on the success which has, so far, rewarded him. The darkest cloud at present on his horizon is his enfeebled health, which we are sorry to learn from him, is getting worse instead of better. His life is indispensable to the welfare of his Society, and we most heartily pray that he may be long spared to push on his useful work. (Olcott 1904b: 572)

Ananda M's obituary for Olcott, published in the second volume of *Buddhism*, is the most telling of Ananda M's responses to Theosophy during his time in Burma.[99] He is glowing in his praise for Olcott's contribution to the Buddhist revival in Ceylon. He then states that his readers would be aware that 'there are profound differences between Theosophical teachings and those of the Master' [the Buddha]. He then repeats a point he had made in 'The Faith of the Future,'[100] namely that Theosophy had laid the groundwork for Buddhism in the West, by encouraging people to look beyond 'Graeco-Judaic civilisation' towards the East, whilst retaining belief in a soul. Without this, Buddhism, with its teaching of 'Selflessness,' would have had a much harder time (Ananda Metteyya 1908c: 337). In effect, he presents Buddhism as the fulfilment of Theosophy, the ultimate truth that could build on but went beyond Theosophy.

Interestingly, the editors of *The Theosophical Review* decided to republish this obituary. The only additions are an introductory note explaining the source of the obituary, appreciation for Ananda M's 'kindly words' about Olcott, and a sentence on the contrast made between Theosophy and Buddhism regarding *anattā* (no soul): 'These are two of the "profound differences" between Bhikkhu Ananda Metteya's view of the Dhamma of the Buddha and Theosophy' (Ananda Metteyya 1908g: 366).

Under the editorial direction of the second International President, Annie Besant, the representation of Ananda M in *The Theosophist* became more positive. For instance, in June 1909, a large portion of Ananda M's 1908 address to the *Buddhasāsana Samāgama*, which we cover in the next chapter, entitled 'Extension of the Empire of Righteousness to Western Lands' (Ananda Metteyya 1909b),[101] was published in *The Theosophist*. The editorial footnote reads:

> Reprinted from the pamphlet of this name by the Bhikkhu Ananda Metteya. The unusual interest of this statement must be our excuse for reproducing it here. The author was lately engaged in a Buddhist Mission to England. Ed. (Ananda Metteya 1909: 302)

The portion reprinted includes Ananda M's plan for Burma in terms of support for the spread of Buddhism in the West but omits many other sections. Later in this chapter we cover the 1911 reprint of Ananda M's essay 'The Religion of Burma' in *The Theosophist*.

Ananda M also met with Charles Webster Leadbeater for the first time in 1906. Leadbeater was conducting a tour of India and South Asia. He was accompanied by two young Theosophists, Fritz Kunz and Basil Hodgson Smith. In a letter to his sister, sent from Calcutta, dated 17 January, 1906, Fritz writes that their itinerary has them in Burma from January 24th to

February 10th. It is on the last day of their time in Burma that Leadbeater met Ananda M.

Smith's journal entry for the day includes notes about their meeting:

> At 1.30 [Leadbeater] called to take us to see the white monk Ananda Mitriya. He is an interesting man and has a good laboratory & in fact he seems much more of a scientist than a monk. He wanted L. to test his experiments. He is looked upon with some doubt because of all this, but he is trying to work for Buddhism along his own line.' [Personal diary, Basil Hodgson Smith, 10 February 1906.]

The statement about Leadbeater testing Ananda M's experiments indicates that Ananda M asked Leadbeater to use his clairvoyance to examine the laboratory and experiments. The entry does not state Leadbeater's responses, but it does indicate that Ananda M still considered occult abilities as real and was willing to use them to his advantage if it helped further his goals of earning money to support his Akyab plan. This would not be the last time Ananda M would meet with C. W. Leadbeater. He was also with Annie Besant when she met Ananda M in 1911, discussed later in this chapter.[102]

WESTERNERS COME TO BURMA

By 1904, *Buddhism* was being sent free to between 500 and 600 libraries in Europe, on the condition that each copy was left on the reading room table until the next was received (Ananda Metteyya 1904b: 473). The first Westerner to respond, attracted by Ananda M's article on *nibbāna*, was John McKechnie (1871-1951), a Theosophist, who offered his services in business management for free. In 1904, he took over this aspect of the Society's work. Ordination as a Buddhist monk was not immediately in his mind. Yet, his knowledge of Buddhism was such that he spoke at the Second Annual Convention of the Society in July 1904 on the potential for Buddhism to be a 'propagandising Religion in the West' (Ananda Metteyya 1904g: 675), and contributed articles to the fourth and fifth issues of *Buddhism* (McKechnie 1904; 1905). By the March 1908 issue of *Buddhism*, he was Ven. Sīlācāra, and would play a significant role in the propagation of Buddhism both in Rangoon and the West.

At least two other Westerners linked to Ananda M were in robes by 1907: Anton Gueth (1878-1957), who became Ven. Ñāṇatiloka, and Walter Markgraf (d.1914), who became Ven. Dhammānusāri.[103] On the evidence of his autobiography, Gueth actually arrived in Asia before McKechnie

Figure 3.5 From left to right, the Western bhikkhus Sīlācāra, Ñāṇatiloka and Dhammānusāri, Creative Commons (CC BY-SA 3.0), submitted to Wikimedia Commons by Ven. Nyanatusita of the Buddhist Publication Society in Kandy, Sri Lanka.

and had been attracted to Buddhism after hearing a lecture by the Theosophist Edwin Böhme, in Hamburg, at the end of the 1890s (Hecker and Ñāṇatusita 2008: 19). In 1902, he travelled overland to Asia to become a Buddhist monk. In Ceylon, he found a monk, Sīlānanda, who was willing to ordain him, but he desisted, saying 'that he wanted to discuss this first with a Scotsman he had heard about,' namely Ananda M. Richard Pereira gave him the necessary addresses (Hecker and Ñāṇatusita 2008: 24; see also Nyanaponika Mahathera 1978: 2–3). On arrival in Burma, he stayed in Daw Mya May's 'villa,' from where he met Ananda M and prepared for novice ordination, which took place in September 1903, under U Āsabha Thera 'at a monastery close to the Ngada Khi Pagoda' (Nyanaponika Mahathera 1978: 3). After this, he 'lived for one month in a single room with Ānanda Metteyya' (Hecker and Ñāṇatusita 2008: 25), before moving to 'Kyundaw Kyaung monastery, not far from the Shwe Dagon Pagoda' (Nyanaponika Mahathera 1978: 3), where, in January or February 1904, he received *upasampadā*, under U Kumāra Mahāthera, most probably within the Thudhamma fraternity.

In the following years, Ñāṇatiloka travelled in Burma and more widely in Asia. A year after his *upasampadā*, Ananda M shared with Cassius Pereira that Ñāṇatiloka wished to come to Ceylon to study Pali under an English-speaking *bhikkhu*, asking 'Cash' to help him gain 'his support and dwelling place whilst in Ceylon.'[104] Ananda M spoke here as the senior monk, commending someone less experienced. However, according to Ñāṇatiloka's records, it was Ñāṇatiloka who gave novice ordination to Sīlācāra (Hecker and Ñāṇatusita 2008: 29), disregarding the traditional 10-year principle.[105] After spending time in Ceylon in 1906, Ñāṇatiloka returned to Burma, eventually to the monastery built by Daw Mya May, where Ananda M and Sīlācāra already lived. From there, he accepted Walter Markgraf for ordination (Hecker and Ñāṇatusita 2008: 29). A photograph of the three of them, Sīlācāra, Ñāṇatiloka and Dhammānusārī (Markgraf), was reproduced in Ñāṇatiloka's autobiography (Hecker and Ñāṇatusita 2008: after p. 54). By 1908, Bhikkhu Sāsana-Dhaja was also in Rangoon, attending the Sixth Annual Convention of the *Samāgama* (Ananda Metteyya 1909b: 1). Sāsana-Dhaja was E. H. Stevenson, from Peterborough in the UK, who was ordained on 13 September, 1908, in Burma, having converted to Buddhism after working in Asia as 'an earnest Christian Churchworker' (The Buddhist Review 1909a: 144).

Ananda M's vision of Westerners coming to Burma for ordination was thus being realised by 1907, but it is significant that it was Ñāṇatiloka rather than Ananda M who claimed agency for their ordinations, because he was willing to ignore traditional monastic conventions. Ananda M had no doubt envisaged Westerners being ordained by senior Burmese monks, as in the case of Ñāṇatiloka. Tensions could have existed between Ananda M and Ñāṇatiloka because of this. Ñāṇatiloka eventually made Ceylon his home, where, from an island hermitage, he ordained some of the most notable Western *bhikkhus* of the early twentieth century, such as Ñāṇamoli (Osbert Moore 1905–1960) and Ñāṇaponika (Siegmund Feniger 1901–1994).

Ananda M also influenced Western lay people in Rangoon, such as the previously mentioned Ethel Powell-Brown, who stayed in a boarding house in Rangoon when her husband was at sea. A free-thinking suffragette sympathiser, she published a memoir in 1911 of her travels up the Irrawaddy river (Powell-Brown 1911). She does not mention Ananda M in this, but her representation of Buddhism betrays conversations with him. She stresses, for instance, that 'Buddhists do not worship idols' or pray to Buddha images, explains the Buddhist doctrine of *anicca* (impermanence), quotes verse 183 from the *Dhammapada*, and condemns the Christian missionary representation of Buddhism as 'our blundering misconception of the noble religion of a noble race' (Powell-Brown 1911: 99–102). Rather than try to convert Buddhists, Christians should be fighting 'against the dirt, disease, crime, intemperance and ignorance of the slums of our large cities,' she adds (Powell-Brown 1911: 102–103) In a later section, her criticism of Christian 'intolerance and self-righteousness' is more strident.

With a reference to Aśoka's edicts, she argues that Buddhists 'never ridicule the religion of another' and, citing Paul Carus, accuses Christians of misunderstanding their own religion. In her eyes, Buddhists, in their tolerance, were 'superior to average Christians.' Comparing the two religions, she writes:

> Where absolute knowledge is, there also is infinite compassion, and that is what the Buddhist is striving to reach when he tries to attain Supreme Enlightenment, and that too is the ideal of Christianity,— infinite compassion, universal love ...
>
> When any one has advanced sufficiently to be able to see the inward similarity between Buddhism and Christianity, he will perceive better the real significance of both, and so become alive to a little more of eternal truth. (Powell-Brown 1911: 193–194)

All these themes are present in the writings of Ananda M, except her argument that 'to be "one with God" is to attain Nirvana' (Powell-Brown 1911: 194).

The portrait painter and society artist, Gerald Festus Kelly (1879–1972), President of the Royal Academy from 1949–1954, also visited Ananda M in Burma, as a young man. A friend of Aleister Crowley, he came to Burma in 1908–1909,[106] after Ananda M's mission to Britain. The only record we have of the impact of this encounter is Kelly's sensitive portrait of Ananda M, which we have used on the cover of this biography and reproduced below. No doubt he knew about Ananda M through Crowley. Significantly, his sister, Rose Edith Kelly (1874–1932), was married to Crowley at the time of his visit, although they divorced in 1909.[107] They had two daughters, one of whom died young. The other, Lola Zaza Crowley (1907–1990) was eventually looked after by Gerald.

METTEYYA'S LINKS WITH CEYLON AND THE ANAGĀRIKA DHARMAPĀLA

Throughout his life, Ananda M maintained contact with Ceylon, particularly through the Pereira family, such that reports of the *Samāgama*'s activities reached the Sinhala and English Buddhist press of the country,[108] as did news of the Buddhist Society of Great Britain and Ireland, formed to greet Ananda M's mission to Britain.[109] A German visitor to Ceylon in 1903, for instance, stated that the *Buddhasāsana Samāgama*, although based in Burma, had 'a certain importance' in Ceylon, mostly among 'cultured people' striving 'after a purer, more inward Buddhism, one more in accordance ... with European taste' (Hackmann 1910: 119–120). In

Figure 3.6 Painting of Ananda M by Gerald Festus Kelly, courtesy of John Randall.

addition, Cassius Pereira occasionally sent reports from Ceylon for inclusion in *Buddhism* (e.g., Pereira 1905).

Ananda M's relationship with the Anagārika Dharmapāla, and his family, the Hewavitarnes, was also significant. If, as we believe, Ananda M met Dr. Tha Nu in Ceylon through his involvement with the Maha-Bodhi Society, it is not impossible that Ananda M met Dharmapāla in Ceylon before 1901. Dharmapāla was well-aware of Ananda M's ordination (*upasampadā*) and his work in Rangoon, perhaps through Tha Nu. A reprint of the account of his *upasampadā* appears in the 1902 editions of Dharmapāla's journal, *The Maha-Bodhi and the United Buddhist World* (The Maha-Bodhi and the United Buddhist World 1902)[110] and Ananda M's article on *nibbāna* appeared in the following year (Ananda Maitriya 1903d).[111] In May 1904, Dharmapāla praised the third issue of *Buddhism*, particularly 'The Law of Righteousness' (Ananda Metteyya 1904a). It prompted him to send a cheque to Ananda M for 50 rupees 'for his personal expenses.'[112] In the August of that year, he lamented that Ananda M's asthma and want of funds was threatening the publication of *Buddhism*, continuing:

This is sad. In 1902 from Los Angeles I wrote to him not to begin a new work, that I was willing to place M.B.J. [Maha Bodhi Journal] and M.B. [Maha Bodhi Society] fund at his disposal. He was then supremely ambitious and he had friends to back him up; and he rejected the proposal. I hope friends will come forward to push on the publication.[113]

Dharmapāla, however, continued to help Ananda M financially in future years, for instance, when he was in distress in London in the early 1920s,[114] and Dharmapāla's diaries record many letters to him, although rarely the content.[115] When Ananda M was preparing his mission to Britain, for instance, Dharmapāla impulsively wrote that he intended to sell his property and go to England to help 'A Metteyyo'[116] and a few days later sent a letter.[117] Although this never materialised, Dharmapāla records, on 2 June, 1908, that he 'Wrote a long letter to Revd. Ananda M. expressing my sincere delight at the great work he is doing in London,' suggesting, in addition, that the 'King of Siam' should be approached for financial help. Then, on 12 July, 1909, comes, 'Revd: A. M. writes me a long letter that I should work with him when he opens his mission in England.'[118] Dharmapāla did not record his response, and they never collaborated in England.

The two were also brought together through Dharmapāla's campaign to wrest Buddhist sites in India from Hindu and British control, particularly the temple at Bodh Gaya, the traditional site of the Buddha's enlightenment. In the 1890s, Dharmapāla lost a legal case against the Hindu 'Mahant,' proprietor of the Bodh Gaya temple, after Dharmapāla controversially placed in the temple a Buddha image gifted by Japan. Burma was directly involved in this, because the image was then placed in its 'Rest House' at Bodh Gaya (Amunugama 2016: 32–40), built in the 1870s by King Mindon. During Ananda M's time in Burma, there were further legal tussles over where the Japanese image should be placed, and the very existence of the Burmese Rest House (Amunugama 2016: 42). In 1907, for instance, the Mahant successfully ejected the resident Burmese monks through a court order (The Maha-Bodhi and the United Buddhist World 1924: 218).

Ananda M and the group of educated Burmese around him, including M. M. Ohn Ghine, a magistrate and member of the Rangoon Municipality (Wright 1910: 288; Pearn 1939: Plate 40), were involved with these legal cases and their funding, Dharmapāla contacting them from Bodh Gaya.[119] At one point, Dharmapāla suspected Ananda M of 'playing a game,' by not retaining 'a copy of the Burmese Record extract.'[120] Later, he feared Ananda M was overlooking or subordinating the work of the Maha-Bodhi Society in the West.[121] However, when he arrived in Rangoon on 12 April,

1907,[122] he met Ananda M two days afterwards[123] and again on 17 April, when Dharmapāla records a much longer conversation, in which Ananda M apparently assures him that his praise of the work of the Maha-Bodhi Society was 'not flattery.' Dharmapāla adds, 'He advised me to preach Buddhism to the Western people; and to spend my money on my maintenance, that he will do his best to supply me with literature.'[124] Dharmapāla left for 'Calcutta' on the 22 April only to return in October of the same year, still working on the Bodh Gaya case. As the next chapters demonstrate, he not only took a keen interest in Ananda M's visit to Britain but also in the subsequent efforts of Buddhists in Britain to raise money for the propagation of Buddhism.

ANANDA METTEYYA'S IMPACT ON BURMA

Ananda M's dependence on a network of Burmese donors for his Akyab Plan mandated engagement with the Burmese. Ananda M was also sincerely committed to strengthening Buddhism in Burma as a defence against British imperialism. Although *Buddhism* was aimed at a Western audience, it was also sent to libraries in Burma, for instance, those of English-speaking schools and colleges. In addition, the *Buddhasāsana Samāgama* at first had a regional representative in Mandalay and sub-representatives in Kyaukpyu, Moulmein, Meiktila, Pegu (Bago), Tharrawaddy, Thaton and Katha (Buddhasāsana Samāgama 1903a;). The brief of these representatives had national and international dimensions. To the Third Annual Convention of the Society held in October 1905, for instance, Ananda M made an impassioned plea for financial aid and more members, evoking a missionary image of Buddhism with *viriya* (energy) at its heart and an ability to reach the whole world (Ananda Metteyya 1905b: 7–11). He urged the 'representatives' to draw members and 'associates' together in weekly or monthly local meetings to discuss the aims of the Society and the Society's publications as well as to gain donations (Ananda Metteyya 1905b: 11–13). Recognising no doubt that the lack of Burmese material within the *Samāgama*'s publication list was a hindrance, he mentioned 'the Burmese pamphlets which we will soon be able to issue' if funds became available (Ananda Metteyya 1905b: 12–13). We have found no evidence in Burma or Britain that these pamphlets were published.

Ananda M's social interactions in Burma were nevertheless limited by his inability to speak Burmese. This was a severe handicap. For instance, as Janaka points out, Burmese Buddhist monks resisted learning English under British rule (Janaka 2016: 107–107). Yet, in the early years of the *Samāgama*, Ananda M certainly travelled outside Rangoon to teach and promote the Society. In 1903, he visited Pegu [Bago] and Mandalay, funded by lay donors, so he could witness the 'installation of the Thathanabaing' (lit: keeper of the *Sāsana*—Buddhist dispensation; Ananda Maitriya 1903j: 317).[125] Later in the year, he expressed an optimistic wish to visit every town in Burma, having just returned from another unnamed part of the country (Ananda Metteyya 1904b: 477–478). In April 1905, he visited 'Dawei Township' in Lower Burma, accessible at that time only by sea. It was a place rich in Buddhist history and sacred geography, preserved in chronicles that began with a visit of the Buddha (see Howard Moore 2013). When he disembarked on 6 April, he was greeted warmly by a reception party of 100 and rested in a local monastery. During the visit, he gave talks and sermons, translated by a devotee called Maung Ba Cho, and stayed at least until the 9th, since he was scheduled to give another sermon then (Hanthawaddy Bi-Weekly Review 1905: 945–946).[126] After 1905, however, reports of visits outside Rangoon are few. He must have visited the ancient Buddhist site of Pagan [Bagan], however, since the collection of magic lantern slides that he brought to Britain includes pictures of Pagan. Tike Soe, a Burmese author and university librarian who evidently knew Ananda M, includes an intriguing reference to Ananda M in Volume II of his *Collection of a Bookworm*:

> Sometimes, Venerable Ananda Metteyya travelled to other towns for dhamma talks. We faced funny things sometimes. An elephant broker from one of the towns where the Yangon-Mandalay railway line passed invited Venerable Ananda Metteyya. At that time Venerable P Monin, Venerable Vaayama and Dr Ross accompanied him. Venerable Ananda Metteyya firstly preached the Dhamma. (Tike Soe 2018: 383)

This observation has no date, but we can place it after P. Monin visited Ananda M in the monastery built by Daw Mya May, suggesting that he travelled outside Rangoon after 1905. Ananda M's wish to travel throughout the whole of Burma, however, was another hope that was not realised, most probably due to a lack of funds and his poor health.

His impact on Burmese society emerged in other ways. These included the conventions of the *Samāgama* in Rangoon and his role in English-speaking organisations such as the Rangoon College Buddhist Society and the Burma Research Society. His promotion of Buddhist education and his relationships with key Buddhist monks and lay people were also important.

Figure 3.7 Ananda M with his alms-bowl in Burma, reproduced from 'The Clubman,' The Sketch, 14 October 1908: p. 8.

RANGOON COLLEGE BUDDHIST ASSOCIATION AND THE BURMA RESEARCH SOCIETY

In 1905, Ananda M assisted in founding the Rangoon College Buddhist Association. Rangoon College, if we have correctly located 1 Pagoda Road at the road's downtown end, was very close to the administrative office of the *Samāgama* (Bird 1897: 145).[127] When Ananda M arrived in Rangoon, it was the city's elite educational institution, offering education up to Bachelor of Arts level, through Calcutta University, with about 160 pupils.[128] The founding of the Association was a potent symbol that Buddhism would not be pushed out of education in colonial Rangoon. Ananda M spoke there regularly in English,[129] at least until 1911; the meetings were advertised in local newspapers, with many attending (Vijja Mg Nyan Shin 1962: 46). He used the platform to alert educated Burmese to what he perceived as failings or misunderstandings within Burmese Buddhism. For instance, in December 1906, he spoke on *anattā* (non-self), arguing that the soul theory present in all other religions was a dangerous and evil illusion. He therefore urged his listeners to help eradicate 'the local form of the Soul-theory' in the villages, which he saw as threatening the Buddhist nature of the country, in spite of the compassionate action of the people (Ananda Metteyya 1906: 32). His words were hard-hitting and had a reformist zeal that was very different from the work of his rival, U Dhammaloka, who refused to criticise popular Buddhist practice. The target of his 1909 lecture on devotion in Buddhism, however, was different—not popular Buddhist practice but the orientalist idea that Buddhism was a philosophy and nothing else.[130] Building both on his Hope Lodge lecture (MacGregor 1902) and 'In the Shadow of Shwe Dagon' (Ananda Maitriya 1903b), he contested those who argued that Buddhism's repudiation of 'blind faith' made devotion obsolete. There were higher and lower forms of devotion, he argued. The lower could lead no further than a birth in the heavens, whereas the higher form could energise the whole Buddhist path, by reminding devotees of the selflessness of the Buddha (Ananda Metteyya 1910a: 15–16).

In 1909, Ananda M was elected a 'Patron' of the Association, together with eight others including Ledi Sayadaw, U Vayama, U May Oung and U Shwe Zan Aung (Ngwe Gaing 1910: 2). The Association was significant enough for reports of its activities to travel beyond Burma, for instance through Dharmapāla's journal, *The Maha-Bodhi and the United Buddhist World*, and *The Open Court*, which reviewed the lecture Ananda M gave to the Association in 1911 on 'The Three Signata' (Anon 1912: 382).[131]

This 1911 lecture was possibly Ananda M's last. The 1913 Association report makes no mention of Ananda M, only of Sīlacāra, a lecture by whom had been published in 1910 (Sīlacārā 1910; The Maha-Bodhi and the United Buddhist World 1913: 211–212). A Rangoon College magazine began in April 1914 but, by that time, Ananda M was too ill to be involved, such that the report of the Annual General Meeting of 1 March, 1914, states, 'The Association, however, regretted that neither Bhikkhu Ananda Metteyya nor Bhikkhu Sīlacāra was able to give lectures, the former owing to ill-health, and the latter owing to the fact that he was leaving the country' (Rangoon College Magazine 1914: 71).

The Burma Research Society was inaugurated in March 1910 by prominent British and Burmese scholars. Civil servant and educationalist, J. S. Furnivall, initiated the idea, working with Burmese scholars such as Maung Tun Nyein (the first Treasurer) and Daw Mya May's nephew, May Oung, who gave the inaugural address (May Oung 1911) and later became editor of the Society's journal (Journal of the Burma Research Society 1911; Than Aung 1978). The Society began late in Ananda M's time in Burma, but he was a member from the outset and contributed a review of Shwe

Zan Aung's *Compendium of Philosophy* to the first issue of the Society's journal (Ananda M 1911c).[132] It is possible, however, that his glowing praise for the work of one of his sponsors in Rangoon—an annotated translation within Buddhist Abhidhamma—was what led the editors to commission another, less flattering, review in the next issue (Ross 1911),[133] no doubt souring the relationship between Ananda M and the Christian-dominated council of the Society.[134]

THE THEOSOPHISTS OF RANGOON

Ananda M was rarely in contact with the Theosophical Society in Rangoon. Burmese Theosophists showed little interest in him. A Burma Section of the Theosophical Society was inaugurated only in 1912, but the history of Theosophy in Burma started with a visit by Colonel Olcott in 1885 (Po Lat 2012: 69). A Burmese Theosophical journal began in 1904: *The Message of Theosophy*. It is striking that Ananda M is not mentioned in this journal until 1911, after the visit of Annie Besant in January and February of that year. His 1908 mission to Britain, for instance, goes unrecorded, although an article by Sīlācāra appears in almost every issue that year (e.g., Sīlācāra 1908a; 1908b; 1908c; 1908d). In 1911, however, the same year that Sīlācāra became the Chairman of the Section, the journal reprinted, in serialised form, beginning in April (Ananda M 1911a), Ananda M's chapter in *Twentieth Century Impressions of Burma*, 'The Religion of Burma' (Ananda M 1910),[135] the content of which we address in the next chapter. This was probably not due to Sīlācāra's influence as Chair. He gave his inaugural address only in October 1911, suggesting that he took up the post in September. It was probably due to Besant, in that she reprinted 'The Religion of Burma' in *The Theosophist* in April and May 1911. This allowed the Burma Section simply to state that the article came from *The Theosophist*, without any acknowledgement that Ananda M was a *bhikkhu* in Rangoon.

Besant arrived in Rangoon from India on 28 January, 1911,[136] with a group that included Charles W. Leadbeater, Krishnamurti and the Secretary of the Central Hindu Girls' School in what was then Benares (Lat 1911: 225). Besant and Ananda M certainly met during her visit, with Besant agreeing to print 'The Religion of Burma' in *The Theosophist* and to help the *Samāgama* with a local edition (Ananda M 1911b: 6–7). The glowing report of Besant's visit by Maung Lat in the January–March 1911 issue of *The Message of Theosophy*, however, does not mention this communication or any relationship between Besant and Ananda M (Lat 1911). According to Maung Lat, Besant spoke in Moulmein, Maymyo (now Pyin-Oo-Lwin) and Mandalay, as well as Rangoon, in 22 public meetings, 12 Lodge meetings, seven private meetings, in addition 'to private conversations' (Lat 1911: 240).[137] One of those private meetings was with Ananda M. Besant also gives an interesting account in the *Theosophist* of a visit to Daw Mya May's girls' school on the 30 January:

> On the 30th we had a Lodge meeting in the morning, and an address on Temperance—alas! that such an address should be needed in Buddhist Burma—in the evening, and between these we visited a school for Buddhist girls maintained for the last 16 years by Ma Hla Oung, a wealthy Buddhist lady. She is not, unfortunately, supported in this good work by her fellow-religionists, and deserves the more credit in that she stands alone; she maintains also a school for Buddhist boys. (Besant 1911: 870)

We would suggest that the distance between Ananda M and Burmese Theosophists was not due simply to his critique of Theosophy in 'The Faith of the Future,' although this played a part. As previously mentioned, Theosophy in Burma was mainly embraced by the Indian community, with Hindu backgrounds, as shown in the lists of office holders recorded in its journal. Additionally, Theosophy in Burma, unlike Ceylon, was not a significant arm of Buddhist revivalism in the country, although Burmese Theosophists established a girls' school and a boys' school, to which some Buddhist children would have been sent (Lat 1911: 232–234; Turner 2014: 69).[138] The names of Ananda M's sponsors and other Buddhists in Rangoon, therefore, are absent from Burmese Theosophical records. The involvement of Sīlācāra is an exception, and it was not uncontroversial. For instance, an article by Sīlācāra on *anattā*, published in *The Message of Theosophy* in 1908 (Sīlācāra 1908c), was placed by the editor alongside a serialised article entitled 'The Persistence of the Individual according to the Pali Pitakas—Did the Buddha Deny It?' by J. C. Chattopadhyaya, who argues, in opposition to Sīlācāra, that the Buddha 'taught the identity of the reincarnating Ego' (Chattopadhyaya 1908: 187). The lack of communication between Ananda M and Theosophists in Burma can be contrasted with the ongoing relationship with Theosophists outside Burma, as we have shown in a previous section.

BUDDHIST EDUCATION IN BURMA

All secondary schools registered in Burma in 1891 were under Christian missionary management (Ikeya 2011: 31). In this context, one of the first booklets published by the *Buddhasāsana Samāgama* was Ananda M's previously mentioned pamphlet, 'On Religious Education in Burma.' His argument is that it is irreligion rather than Christianity that is threatening Buddhism in Burma, through education in the English medium. His remedy is fourfold, listed 'in order of immediate practicability, and in inverse order of cost': weekly classes in Buddhist temples for younger children; Buddhist education in the Anglo-Vernacular schools; the founding and endowment of Buddhist Secular Schools with an English education coupled with daily religious instruction; and the founding of a Buddhist College [University] for higher education to degree level (Ananda Maitriya 1903m: 7–8; Turner 2014: 69). Each is described in detail. For instance, to push forward the first, he encourages lay people in each district to form a committee 'to promote Buddhist education,' by arranging for a monk able to 'talk in very simple language' to give an hour's instruction per week' to the children (Ananda Maitriya 1903m: 9). His approach is child-centred and progressive. When describing 'a Buddhist College or University,' he envisages school teachers being trained there, and uses the same argument as he later uses to encourage donations to the Pali Text Society, namely that funding the project would be equally, if not more, meritorious than 'gilding a great Cetiya' [*stūpa*] (Ananda Maitriya 1903m: 14):

> It is the better gift, that Best Gift of the Master's Law—the greatest Merit, and the most enduring Shrine! A hundred years, and your brickwork will be an heap of ruins—your gilding washed off by a century's rains; but if you will so work as to enshrine the Image of the Lord, not in buildings of brick and stone, but in houses not made with hands,—in these your children's hearts, surely He will not lack for Shrines so long as the people of Burma exists. (Ananda Maitriya 1903m: 14)

Progress in Buddhist education had occurred before 1903, as Ananda M recognised, by citing the Anglo-Vernacular Schools in Pegu, where the Municipal Committee had already allowed religious instruction (Ananda Maitriya 1903f: 11; Turner 2014: 69). Additionally, specifically Buddhist schools had been in existence for several years, for example, those founded by the Hla Oung family and the Buddha Thathana Noggaha School in Mandalay (Turner 2014: 68), all of which Ananda M experienced. Yet, the decline of Buddhist education in Burma was nevertheless serious, the traditional system of monastic education having been seriously undermined under the British (Ikeya 2011: 30), in spite of the view of Knight, an SPG missionary, in 1903, that 'The teaching of Buddhism in the monastic schools is tremendously effective.'[139] To complement his 1903 pamphlet, therefore, Ananda M published in *Buddhism* a hard-hitting article by an unnamed Christian, British 'official' (Anon 1904: 404), perhaps Fielding Hall, which outlines the decline in morality within Burmese society, due to the system of vernacular lay schools and Anglo-Vernacular schools introduced by the British, and the 'retrogression' of education in the monasteries.[140] Condemning both forms of schools, the author imagines what they could be if they taught Burmese culture and ethics rather than British history and geography: 'Unless we as rulers of this country give some moral teaching in the schools we have established, the people will either learn to despise morals or despise us' (Anon 1904: 404). Such moral training, he adds, had to use Burmese 'materials and modes of thought.'

As editor, Ananda M added comments of his own to this anonymous contribution, confirming that he was indeed an early pioneer of child-centred education. Arguing that the author's main point was that education should be 'an organic and not a mechanical process,' he stresses that teaching has to use examples from the child's experience to establish a relationship between 'the child's mind and the world by which it is surrounded' (Postscript by Ananda M in Anon 1904: 407–410).

Ananda M's interventions on education were pertinent, but whether they had a direct influence on the British administration is doubtful. We examine this further in the next chapter. There is no doubt, however, that he contributed to a growing Burmese movement both for Buddhism to be taught in government schools and for the establishment of Buddhist schools. His address on 'Western Education for Buddhist Bhikshus' (Ananda Maitriya 1903a), given in 1903 in Ceylon, should also not be forgotten, although we have not found evidence that he gave similar addresses in Burma.

METTEYYA'S RELATIONSHIPS WITH KEY BURMESE BUDDHIST THINKERS AND BHIKKHUS IN BURMA

Information about Ananda M's relationships with key Burmese monastic and lay figures in early twentieth century Burma is scant, with the exception of his donors and partners in the *Buddhasāsana Samāgama*. What is available, however, suggests that Ananda M enjoyed conversation with those who could speak English. His encounter with P. Monin has already been discussed. Given Ananda M's interest in Abhidhamma and meditation, it must be asked whether he met Ledi Sayadaw (1846–1923). Initially, Ledi was attached to a monastery in Mandalay, but Ananda M would probably not have met him there: in 1901–1902, Ledi was teaching and writing in a cave complex near the Chindwin River, not far from his home area of

Monywa, in Upper Burma.[141] Ananda M, however, would have been aware of Ledi's influence when he was in Mandalay. If Ananda M met Ledi, it probably happened on one of Ledi's visits to Rangoon, for instance in 1905 (Braun 2013: 53), when he was travelling around Burma, teaching meditation and popularising Buddhist learning (Braun 2013: 88),[142] or between 1908 and 1910, when Ledi is reported to have spoken to the Rangoon College Buddhist Association, at a point when both him and Ananda M were made patrons (Ngwe Gaing 1910: 2). Ananda M demonstrates knowledge of his work in his previously mentioned contribution to *Twentieth Century Impressions of Burma* (Ananda M 1910), where he favourably comments on monks going 'forth among the people' stirring them 'to better their ways' (Ananda M 1910: 116). They also had at least one attitude in common. Ledi Sayadaw was convinced that if Burmese Buddhists could be strengthened in their own religion, Buddhism could respond to and contest British imperialism. Ledi's eventual popularisation of *vipassanā* was linked to this defensive strategy (Houtman 1990: 35-36). Contemporary reports claim that he did this without antagonising the British authorities.[143] Ananda M followed this example.

In Mandalay, Ananda M had identified himself with the reformist Shwegyin monastic fraternity. In Rangoon, it is probable that he did the same. Ven. Dr. Khammai Dhammasami[144] alerted us to Ven. Ādiccavaṃsa (1881-1950; Adeiksawuntha in Burmese), and his pupil U Thitthila (1896-1997). Both were English-speaking reformist monks, who positively engaged with the West. The former, according to Dhammasami, had known Ananda M and had helped him prepare for his 1908 mission to Britain. We have not been able to confirm this independently. The biography of Ādiccavamsa, released on the centennial anniversary of the monastery he founded in Rangoon in 1916 (Ādiccavamsa Monastery) does not mention Ananda M (Myint Swe 2017). When Elizabeth visited the monastery in 2018, the monks there did not know if Ādiccavamsa had known Ananda M.[145] Records of Buddhism in Britain in the 1920s, however, mention a visit of a 'Venerable Ardissa Wuntha,' no doubt Ādiccavamsa, and the support he gave to Buddhism in England (e.g., Buddhism in England 1926a: 2; Humphreys 1937: 60). As for U Thitthila, he was a child when Ananda M arrived in Burma, but gained novice ordination at the age of 15, within Ananda M's time in Rangoon. Thitthila, after he gained higher ordination, *upasampadā*, became a missionary scholar monk in the West (Buddhist Studies Review 1997). It is not impossible that he was inspired by Ananda M. During the bombing of London in World War II, for instance, he was in Britain and volunteered to work as a stretcher-bearer (Buddhist Studies Review 1997).[146]

The last issue of *Buddhism* contains a significant article about a Burmese Pali scholar, Sayā U Pyé (1850–1930), then editor of Pyi Gye Mandai Press (Ananda Metteyya 1908b). He had been a teacher of Pali at Rangoon College and Ananda M may have first met him there. Ananda M claims he had an accuracy in Pali surpassing that of the Pali Text Society and was 'responsible for the great bulk of the printed Pāli Texts in Burma' (Ananda Metteyya 1908b: 229), including a version of the *Visuddhimagga* that was almost error-free. Ananda M wishes to place him 'in the front ranks of the Pāli scholars of the world' (Ananda Metteyya 1908b: 332).[147] U Pyé gained international mentions, although his scholarship was largely restricted to Burma.[148]

RELATIONSHIPS WITH THE CHRISTIAN MISSIONARIES IN BURMA

William Purser, in 1911, contrasts U Dhammaloka and Ananda M, claiming Ananda M is a 'man of quite different character. He is a scholarly Agnostic who has sought for a historic religious system which is compatible with Agnosticism and has found it in Buddhism' (Purser 1911: 218). Several years later, he published with Kenneth Saunders an account of Burmese Buddhism, drawing on answers to 63 questions from about 30 Burmese and Western missionaries, and civil servants. Ananda M appears mainly towards the end of this compilation, when the questions turn towards Western Buddhists. A person named E. Colston, who was almost certainly a civil servant sympathetic to Buddhism rather than a missionary, writes that he had known 'Ananda Meittreya' since he had arrived in 'Burma' and found him 'a man of uncommon powers of observation and insight' (Purser and Saunders 1914: 39).[149] He refers particularly to Ananda M's growing realisation that 'Deva worship' (worship of gods and spirits—the nats) had a place in Buddhism, a perspective similar to that of Fielding Hall (Fielding Hall 1898: 250–271).

Question 59 of the compilation asks, 'With what motives do certain Europeans take the yellow robe?' When the editors introduce the question, they mention several distinct types of European Buddhist monks: 'some are scholars, one is a mystic, one at least an infidel,' because his mission is 'not to preach Buddhism but to vilify Christianity' (Purser and Saunders 1914: 86). The latter was no doubt U Dhammaloka and 'the mystic' or perhaps the 'scholar' could have been Ananda M.

Ananda M is named in the answers to this question as one 'whom all respect.' The previously mentioned Professor Ross, who would have known Ananda M through Rangoon College, claims that he 'took the robe out of a sincere interest in religion, believing that Buddhism was the only religion which could be reconciled with modern science and philosophy' (Purser and Saunders 1914: 86). The previously mentioned Edgar Bradford, who worked in Burma from 1899–1914 (Leigh 2011: 205), and to whom Ananda M had expressed surprise that there could still be intelligent Christians,[150] places him in the context of his earlier spiritual search, claiming that he had had long talks with Ananda M:

> Among other things he said that he would be a Christian if there existed any motive power in Christianity ... He professed to be quite satisfied with Buddhist cosmogony which he said was quite in harmony with scientific positions to-day. He drifted into Buddhism via Agnosticism and Theosophy, and was greatly influenced by 'The Light of Asia.' (Purser and Saunders 1914: 86)

The next question concerns how the Burmese see European monks. The missionary respondents, unsurprisingly, minimise their influence, citing their ignorance of Burmese—in contrast to the missionaries who invariably learnt the language. So SPG missionary, G. Whitehead, claims that 'the European monk' 'is to them [the Burmese] rather like a white elephant, of which they are proud, but from which they get no real service' (Purser and Saunders 1914: 87). Ross claims, 'There are not a dozen of the laity in Burma capable of understanding the teachings of neo-Buddhists, and even fewer who if they understood would be in sympathy with a world-wide propaganda' (Purser and Saunders 1914: 87). The editors comment after this, with obvious reference to Ananda M, 'So the good Bhikkhu with all his obvious sincerity has been declared "unorthodox" and "unintelligible" by those who have been most closely connected with him' (Purser and Saunders 1914: 87). A few lines later, they quote an unnamed leading Burmese Buddhist, who said to them, 'We feel that Buddhism is pessimistic but Silacara and Ananda Metteyya will not have us say so.'

It is obvious from these reflections that Ananda M was willing to have respectful conversation with the missionaries and, through them, we rightly glimpse the restricted nature of Ananda M's influence in Burma, because of his inability to speak Burmese. It was not true, however, that he was no more than a 'white elephant,' a symbol rather than an agent. Ananda M, in Burma, related to a not insignificant number of the English-speaking Burmese middle class through the *Buddhasāsana Samāgama*, his early visits to other parts of Burma, the Rangoon College Buddhist Association, and other initiatives. What is less certain is the extent to which his teaching created change.

MISSION TO BRITAIN

An important chapter of Ananda M's time in Burma was his relatively short mission to Britain in 1908. In July 1907, he wrote a candid letter to Charles Lanman, in which he laments the lack of missionary zeal among the Burmese, which meant that gaining money for his Akyab Plan had proved more difficult than he had hoped when he took on the robes of a *bhikkhu*. He even wonders whether it had been a mistake to become ordained.[151] Yet, by 1908, he had enough sponsorship from Daw Mya May to travel to England. His hopes concerning the mission are encapsulated in a preparatory article published in *Buddhism*—'Propaganda' (Ananda Metteyya 1908a).[152] This sketches a history of decline in Buddhism after its first energetic expansion but anticipates a 'new era of intense activity,' as Buddhism is accepted in the West (Ananda Metteyya 1908a: 177). With a passion that betrays autobiography, he describes the horror experienced by those who lost faith in God or the goodness of the world—the context of many in the West he believed—and the solution that Buddhism could bring. Buddhism is needed most particularly, he argues, to challenge the West's selfishness, its poverty and the 'ever-rising tide of human agony' that is threatening 'Western civilisation with ruin' (Ananda Metteyya 1908a: 192). What actually happened forced him to review this optimism, as the next chapter examines.

4

Ananda M's Mission to Britain and Return to Burma

Britain had changed in the decade since Ananda M had left London. With the death of Queen Victoria in January 1901 and the accession of Edward VII, one era had ended and another had begun. In terms of infrastructure, London, now the world's biggest city, bore a different face. When Ananda M had left, most licensed buses were horse-drawn with only the occasional motorised vehicle. By 1907, 1205 of the 3742 licensed buses on London's streets were motorised. In 1901, the first electric tramway appeared. In 1904, there was the first double decker bus and in 1907, the first taxicabs (Clout 2000: 12). Horse-drawn vehicles were still on the streets, however, and could cause severe traffic jams (Barker 1995: 76). Furthermore, the development of new thoroughfares in the centre of the city, for example, Kingsway and the Aldwych, had meant the destruction not only of slums but also of 'vestiges of overhanging Tudor houses' (Barker 1995: 77). The underground railway system had also expanded in this decade, with the Bakerloo, Piccadilly and Northern lines opening in 1906–1907, criss-crossing London from north to south and east to west. For the capital's elite, new theatres in London's 'West End' had opened and the London Symphony Orchestra had been founded in 1904 (Clout 2000: 12). In less affluent areas, there were more music halls (Barker 1895: 117). At this level, the Edwardian decade (1901–1910) was one of 'astonishing growth and change, of strong protest and daring creativeness in many fields' (Cooke 1995: 10).

For the majority of Londoners, however, little had changed since the end of the nineteenth century. Although the formation of the Metropolitan Water Board eased the threat of water-borne diseases such as typhoid, and an education act was giving the whole country a national secondary school system (Barker 1995: 12), London's air remained polluted. There would be little improvement until the Clean Air Acts of 1956 and 1968 (Clout 2000: 134), although London's numerous parks and open spaces mitigated pollution to some extent. Cycling in Battersea Park, for instance, was a popular pastime (Weinrebb and Hibbert 1983: 45). The gap between rich and poor also remained large, with many of the slums concentrated in the East End of the city. It was because of poverty that protest emerged. A protest march in Trafalgar Square in 1908 bore placards carrying the message 'Starved to Death in a Land of Plenty' (Barker 1995: 180–181). It is possible that Ananda M witnessed this (Ananda Metteyya 1909b: 11–15). A third edition of Charles James Booth's magisterial work, *Labour and Life of the People of London* was published in 1902–1903 (see Booth 1889). It mapped the levels of affluence and poverty in the city, and indicated both that the level of poverty was unacceptable and that enlightened social administration could ameliorate the situation.[1] We have used these poverty maps to assess the poverty level in the areas of London in which Ananda M lived.

When Ananda M arrived in this changed city in 1908, his mission had been anticipated for several months. One of the most informative accounts of the preparation for it was written by Rost, although by the time he compiled it for publication in 1930, he was misremembering some of the facts. He claims, for instance, that Ananda M had arrived in May 1908 (Rost 1930: 273). It was, in fact, April 1908. Not in doubt, however, is that preparation for the visit began in 1907, when Rost was on leave in London and inaugurated a London Branch of the *Buddhasāsana Samāgama*, after opening a Buddhist book shop at 14 Bury Street, near the British Museum. He worked with a group of people who were already interested in Buddhism, including R. J. Jackson, Francis Payne and Professor Edmund Mills, a fellow of the Royal Society and a Professor of Chemistry (Humphreys 1968: 4–5). A few months later, on 26 November, 1907, this became the Buddhist Society for Great Britain and Ireland, with Thomas W. Rhys Davids, founder of the Pali Text Society (1881), as President, and Captain John E. Ellam as Honorary Secretary.[2] The 'Constitution and Rules' were modelled on the *Buddhasāsana Samāgama* (Ellam 1909: 1) and stressed that the Society did not expect 'members to become Buddhists' (Ananda Metteyya 1908d: 338). According to Rost, about 60 people were interested in the Society by this time (Rost 1930: 273). In a pattern that would be repeated when Ananda M arrived, the Press was informed. The *Pall Mall Gazette*, for instance, reports that 'all those who were known to be Buddhists in London' met in Harley Street on 3 November to inaugurate the Society, and that Ananda M's visit would create 'a Buddhist church.' Also conveyed to the press was that there were 'over five hundred known Buddhists, excluding natives of Eastern countries, now in Great Britain' (Occasional Correspondent: 1907: 10). The Anagārika Dharmapāla, however, would later report that only 'some twenty-five persons' were actually present at the first meeting. More were present at the 'Foundation Meeting' on 26 November, which was held in the Cavendish Rooms in Mortimer Street West, with Rhys Davids the speaker (Dharmapala 1909a: 10).[3] On 17 February, 1908, the Bury Street premises and bookshop were taken over by the Society (Ellam 1909: 2).

Rost claims that it was he who arranged the mission from Burma, headed by Ananda M, engaging 'two small houses in Barnes,' one of them being 101 Elm Grove Road. This was to the south-west of central London, south of the Thames, close to the open space of Barnes Common, with far less pollution than inner-city areas. It is more likely, however, that he suggested the timing of the visit and coordinated arrangements at the London end, rather than initiated the idea. Ananda M had wanted to bring a mission to the West since his time in Akyab and had worked hard in a difficult situation to gain the necessary Burmese sponsorship. Rost also made contacts with internationally known scholar monks in Asia, for instance with requests for 'presentation Buddhist books and articles for publication' to aid the mission.[4]

Even before Ananda M arrived, the press carried anticipatory pieces, primed no doubt by Rost and the Buddhist Society. The *Western Chronicle*

Figure 4.1 The storefront of the Buddhist Society, Bury Street, London,
The Sphere, 2 May 1908, p. 16.

Figure 4.2 101 Elm Grove Road, courtesy of the Sri Saddhatissa International Buddhist Centre, London.

(Somerset) could have been the first, with a short notice on 7 February, 1908 (Western Chronicle 1908: 5). This was followed by the *Morning Post* (Morning Post 1908a: 6), the *Birmingham Daily Gazette* (Birmingham Daily Gazette 1908: 3), the *Dublin Daily Express* (Dublin Daily Express 1908: 2), the *South Wales Daily Post* (South Wales Daily Post 1908: 6), the *London Daily News* (London Daily News 1908: 7) and, finally, a fuller report in the *Daily Mail* (Daily Mail 1908a: 3). Some of these repeat the claim in the *Pall Mall Gazette* (15 November, 1907) that the aim was to establish a 'Buddhist Church.' Others state that only with the formation of the Buddhist Society of Great Britain and Ireland was the mission possible, some adding that the *Buddhasāsana Samāgama* would be transferred to London. The *Daily Mail* focussed on an interview given by Rost on 21 April, which covered the Eightfold Path and gender equality in Buddhism. Rost also appears to have stated that Ananda M was a Scotsman.

Ananda M arrived on the evening of 22 April, 1908 by the steamship *Ava*, together with 23 Burmese disciples, including Mrs. Hla Oung, her son, Bah Hla Oung, and her daughter-in-law. The passenger list simply states that his port of arrival is London and that he is English. Although at least two accounts claim that he arrived at Tilbury Dock, further down the Thames in Essex (Daily Mirror 1908: 13; Homeward Mail from India, China and the East 1908: 528), the most reliable sources state that he arrived at the Royal Albert Dock, closer to the centre of London. One of these is the *Daily Mail*, which sent a representative to write about his arrival

(Daily Mail 1908b: 5). According to this account, a group of English and Burmese Buddhists welcomed the ship with a Buddhist flag and Burmese greetings. Ananda M did not come out with the other passengers and so Rost, together with the journalist from the *Mail* and perhaps some others, went on board and a preliminary interview was conducted in his cabin. The *Mail*'s journalist describes Ananda M as looking 'deathly pale, as he nervously fitted a cigarette into his amber holder, dropped it, took up his beads and again nervously fingered them.' He wore only his yellow robe and his feet were bare. The journalist also records him as saying:

> As regards my object in visiting this country, it is to spread the tenets of Buddhism and to let them be known in the West. Buddhism is not opposed to Christianity or to any religion. It goes further than any religion or creed. (Daily Mail 1908b: 5)

The report adds that, when he came out, he 'averted his eyes' from the women at the dockside and was taken by 'motor-car' to Barnes: 'Thus landed, Mr Allan Bennett MacGregor, graduate of Cambridge and late assistant to Dr. Dyer—the first Buddhist monk to visit these shores' (Daily Mail 1908b: 5). Another account states that the women amongst Ananda M's group were presented with 'bouquets and flowers' from the welcome delegation (Lloyds Weekly Newspaper 1908: 5). By the evening of 23 April, reports had reached local papers such as the *The Evening Telegraph and Post*, Dundee, which adds that an old friend had addressed Ananda M as 'Allan' on his arrival, at which point he had lowered his eyes, bowed and turned away (The Evening Telegraph and Post, Dundee 1908: 4).

Reading between the lines of these reports, Ananda M arrived exhausted and perhaps apprehensive. He was also determined not to make concessions either to the coolness of the London evening or to his past life as a lay person. As a Buddhist monastic, his lay name, Allan, belonged to the past.

On the following day, again according to the *Daily Mail*, a Buddhist temple was established at 101 Elm Grove Road, in the front bedroom, sheltered from the view of the street by green chintz (Daily Mail 1908c: 6). The *Daily Express*, at this point, sent its own journalist to Barnes. The result was quite a lengthy piece in which Ananda M is asked about his monastic discipline and meditation. The reporter states, 'Everything he says and does is intended to lead to concentration of thought till he attains the highest of the "five trances" and can hammer out abstruse mental problems without the intrusion of "self" or the limitation of mere personality.' He is represented as eating mostly 'oranges, tomatoes, apples and rice,' and as wishing to return in two and a half years, when he would be able to ordain others, to establish a monastery together with monks from Burma. The journalist also states, anticipating that there would be antagonism to his visit, that 'He is preparing for the conflict that is to come—the conflict that aims at the breakdown of Occidental custom and tradition and the substitution of the slow-won wisdom of the Orient' (Daily Express 1908c: 5).

A plethora of other reports appeared throughout Britain and Ireland, drawing on these accounts and other news stories, sometimes including line drawings and photographs of Ananda M. As well as describing Ananda M, some newspapers comment on the 'sensation' he caused, as one local paper in the southwest of England puts it (Warminster and Westbury Journal 1908: 2). *The Bystander* claims that the papers were 'making fun of him—as is the fashion with regard to religious innovators' (The Bystander 1908a: 213). *The Falkirk Herald* states that the 'English Buddhist' came to London 'exactly at the right time,' when newspapers were looking for 'some thing new,' the holidays [Easter] being over and Parliamentary business not yet begun (The Falkirk Herald 1908: 5). The *Oxfordshire Weekly News* claims, tongue in cheek, that Ananda M may provide 'the "serious" boom of the present season,' given that other attractions had ceased (Oxfordshire Weekly News 1908: 2).

The Rangoon Times, catering to a largely expatriate British readership, took a month to report Ananda M's arrival in England, giving an outline of the 'Bhikkhu's first day,' from his rising at 4.30 a.m. to his retirement at 10.00 p.m. Significantly, the piece does not indicate that Ananda M had travelled from Rangoon or had any link whatsoever with Burma (The Rangoon Times 1908a: 12). The Anagārika Dharmapāla's journal, *The Maha-Bodhi and the United Buddhist World*, contains a report in its June 1908 issue. It stresses what was important from a Buddhist perspective, namely that the first Buddhist temple had been established in Great Britain: 'Anything more unlike the atmosphere or surroundings of the places of worship at Rangoon or Kandy could not be imagined than the first Buddhist temple to be established in Great Britain' (The Maha-Bodhi and the United Buddhist World 1908: 88–90).

Verbal cameos of his appearance are also given in some reports. At least two mention his dark, large, brilliant or 'soulful eyes under heavily-marked brows' (Lloyds Weekly Newspaper 1908: 5). The *Dundee Evening Telegraph* adds to this:

> Though he is only thirty-five years old his hair is white and is closely shaven. His eyes are large, brilliant and soulful. He speaks in low unimpassioned tones, but with a musical softness that charms the listener. His face is full of expression. One instinctively gains the

impression that he is a man who has suffered long and intensely. (The Evening Telegraph and Post, Dundee 1908: 4)

That his hair was white is not likely. He was reported to have black hair, after his return to Britain in 1914.

News of his mission also reached the USA, with *The Montgomery Advertiser* stating, 'he has a face that is oval and of highly intellectual type with a complexion as delicate as a woman's and an expression that is a fine blend of welcome and aloofness' (The Montgomery Advertiser 1908: 24). *The Kansas City Star*, on the other hand, in a lengthy piece entitled 'This Buddhist Priest Would Convert "Heathen" America,' calls Ananda M 'a strange new missionary,' who has 'a smooth, hollow-cheeked face tanned to a hue intermediate between the average white man's and that which one sees in the Chinaman and his neighbors in Asia' (The Kansas City Star 1908: 8C). Additionally, several reports mention his smoking and the discoloration of his fingers (e.g., The Kansas City Star 1908: 8C).

Almost all the newspapers that featured Ananda M were also fascinated by the rules he had to follow, for instance, that they precluded riding behind a horse, making motor car travel the best option (e.g., Westminster Gazette 1908a: 3).[5] The fact that he returned money put in his bowl by well-wishers convinced some of 'the genuineness and severity of his self-denial' (Oxfordshire Weekly News 1908: 2).

Two or three different accounts of his life emerge in these reports. The *Daily Express* records him as saying to its reporter, 'I am no one.... I have no name, no self, no ego. I cannot, I must not discuss Ananda Metteyya' (Daily Express 1908: 5). Most newspapers, therefore, had to rely on alternative sources, for example Rost and other members of the Buddhist Society. Some adamantly claim Ananda M is Scottish.[6] Others stress that he was born in London and that he is definitely not Scottish.[7] Some state that he was brought up a Christian, became an agnostic, travelled in Asia and there read *The Light of Asia*, which prompted his conversion to Buddhism.[8] Newspapers that feature this narrative sometimes add, 'His object in coming to England, he has said, "is to show that ignorance reigns wherever a man looks upon himself as something apart from the universe"' (The Courier 1908: 11).[9] Another narrative concentrates on Burma, stating that he had three Europeans studying under him in Rangoon.[10] One newspaper claims that he visited China before Burma to cure his asthma and that it was there that he converted to Buddhism (The Evening Telegraph and Post, Dundee 1908: 4). Yet another claims that Ananda M's parents had died in infancy and that he had been raised by Cyrus Field (Lloyds Weekly Newspaper 1908: 5).[11]

Some reports additionally state, based this time on Ananda M's words to the *Daily Express*, that the mission was to last six months and that he hoped to return in two and half years to establish a Buddhist monastery (Daily Express 1908: 5; Lloyds Weekly Newspaper 1908: 5). As for his first lecture, all agree that it would be at the rooms of the Royal Asiatic Society (RAS) but the date varies, some saying that it would be on 6 May and others, 8 May. Those that opted for the former were right. The *Hull Daily Mail* reported on 8 May that Ananda M had spoken at the RAS on Wednesday, 6 May, and that his message had included that 'Buddhism would conquer as a religion rather than as a system of philosophy, for its philosophy appealed only to a rare type of human mind' (Hull Daily Mail 1908: 3). The lecture was published by the Buddhist Society of Great Britain and Ireland in 1908. According to this text, Ananda M additionally stated that Buddhism was a 'Religion' that can 'alter men's hearts and ways for what is nobler and higher' (Ananda Metteyya 1908f: 6) and, evoking his ordination address, presented the Buddha as the only teacher who 'ever won to the Beyond of Consciousness' (Ananda Metteyya 1908f: 10), which he described as an 'Infinitude' that was beyond any notion of Self (Ananda Metteyya 1908f: 21). In an implicit attack on Theosophy, he also claimed that other indic traditions had not gone far enough. Although they had reached 'tremendous realms of consciousness,' they had mistakenly thought 'Brahma' and 'Consciousness enselfed' was the ultimate truth, when it was not 'the final liberation from Ignorance and change' (Ananda Metteyya 1908f: 19–21). His listeners also heard him say this:

> That attitude [the Buddhist attitude to other religions] is, as will I hope be clear to you, that the Same One Light—That Light which shines beyond the shadow-play of Life—which is Life's Hope and Life's excuse and goal—has been seen, known, lived by all the Great, by the Founders of all the World-Religions. Where, then, these seek to turn men to the Light; where they give hope, so needed in this darkling world; where, in the outer world, they teach love, charity, compassion, all that makes for Oneness—there is our Buddhist Religion in absolute concordance with them . . . But where, beyond this teaching of the Light, whether in the heart within or as made manifest in deeds of love in the world without—where you shall find one word that seeks to define, to limit, to bring down to man's comprehension as something like himself, if vaster or more powerful, That Light Beyond, there, thinks the Buddhist, you have only the tinting of the mind of the Great One who founded that Faith. When, then, one should say to the Buddhist, "Only Red Light is

Light"—there the Buddhist would consider him wrong; wrong, in that he deemed it possible to define the Undefinable; to limit the Illimitable; to express in terms of thought That which is far beyond all consciousness you know. (Ananda Metteyya 1908f: 10–11)

ANANDA M'S ACTIVITIES WHILE IN ENGLAND

Ananda M's activities during his five to six months in England were diverse. He conversed with individuals and groups, and gave interviews from his house in Barnes. One interview, for instance, was with Dudley Wright and an unnamed other for the journal, *Light: A Journal of Psychical, Occult, and Mystical Research*, during which he was asked whether Buddhism was in conflict with spiritualism and whether it held that the 'highest state of all' was 'extinction of individuality.' To the first of these, Ananda M replied that there was no conflict between Buddhism and spiritualism, since Buddhism asserted 'the existence of a ghost-world.' He nevertheless added, 'Spiritualists are in error in the deductions they make from this fact; they do not go far enough.' As for the second, he agreed that Buddhism did indeed work towards the extinction of individuality but stressed that this was not annihilation—Buddhas were reborn in 'a higher world' (Wright 1908: 225). Informal group settings included an 'at home' that he gave to 'a large assemblage' at 53 Grosvenor Street West, a prestigious part of London, 'by kind permission of Lady Cavendish Bentinck' (Westminster Gazette 1908b: 5).[12]

He also contributed academically, giving a paper in mid-September on 'Religious Experience in Buddhism'[13] at the 'Third International Conference for the History of Religions' in Oxford (Nature 1908: 552–553),[14] attended by nearly 600 people and with 140 papers. The *Morning Post*'s report of the conference mentions Ananda M as attending, describing him as 'A Scotsman turned Buddhist' (Morning Post 1908c: 7). Significantly, this enabled Ananda M to meet with a large number of academics, orientalists, and practitioners teaching Buddhism and other religions in the West. These included Ananda Coomaraswamy, James Hope Moulton (a Methodist scholar interested in comparative religion, particularly Zoroastrianism), Louis de La Vallee Poussin (a Belgian scholar of Buddhism), D. T. Suzuki, T. W. Rhys Davids, Caroline Rhys Davids and Charles Lanman from Harvard, who had been a friend and confidante for several years, as shown at the end of the last chapter (LeRoy Perreira 2012: 545–549). These encounters would have brought him into the heart of contemporary discourse concerning the encounter between the West and religions such as Buddhism and Hinduism. Before he left Burma, he had expressed the wish to form in England a committee of Buddhist and Pali scholars to work on a unified approach to the translation of Pali terms, which could be shared globally among all translators of Buddhist texts (Ananda Metteyya 1908d: 341). We have not found evidence that he succeeded in this laudable project, although such a meeting would have been the ideal context within which to explore it.

Ananda M's main point of contact with the general public, however, was through lectures, some more intimate than others. To give a handful of examples, soon after his lecture at the RAS, he spoke at Kensington Town Hall during the week of 17 May (The Bystander 1908b: 422) and also on 3 June (The Spectator 1908: 876). On 10 June, he lectured on 'Buddhism' at the Helena P. Blavatsky Lodge of the Theosophical Society, demonstrating his ongoing willingness to engage with Theosophists. On 9 July, he gave a presentation to the Spes Bono Club at the Holborn Restaurant, London, on 'Buddhist Self-Culture' (Ananda Metteyya 1914). On 13 September, he was scheduled to give a talk on 'Buddhism' at Hampshire House, Hammersmith (The Clarion 1908: 7) and, on 20 September, he spoke at Highgate Unitarian Church.[15] In addition to these, he lectured almost weekly at the Sunday evening meetings of the Buddhist Society of Great Britain and Ireland, organised by Alexander Fisher and held at The Studio, 17 Warwick Gardens, Kensington.[16] Taken together, the locations of these lectures stretched right across London, from Highgate in the northern suburbs to Holborn in the centre, Hammersmith to the west of the centre, and Battersea to the south.

Rost gives an appealing cameo of one of Ananda M's talks, in Clapham, South London, suggesting that, although Ananda M was a missionary monk and sought converts, more important for him was that the message of the Buddha was communicated, with or without the label 'Buddhism':

> One of these [lectures] I remember well, as it was a very wonderful meeting, at which an address was given by him in a Congregational Church in Clapham, which was filled with working men. He taught them the Master's words, but no one could tell till the end that he was not preaching Christianity. That was indeed an example of the divine love of the Bhikkhu, who never says anything against any other form of religious belief, but preaches the Dhamma in its pure reasoning, its compassion, and its middle path. (Rost 1930: 273)[17]

A diary entry from Basil Hodgeson Smith, a Theosophist, throws light on his lecture to the Theosophical Society in Albemarle Street: '[H]e gave an interesting lecture though one did not entirely agree with it, as he was so very materialistic.' He adds that 'We were there quite in force,'

Figure 4.3 1908 Crayon drawing of Ananda M whilst in England, by Alexander Fisher, courtesy of The Buddhist Society, London.

suggesting that Ananda M had a sizeable audience.'[18] We know from Ananda M's letters to Dr. George Watson MacGregor Reid (c. 1850–1946), who presided 'at the first meetings he held in London' (W. A. P. 1946: 3), that his lecture topics included Buddhist ethics, karma and re-birth, and mind-culture.[19] These letters also confirm that he was not free of asthma during his visit and was painfully aware that the strength of his voice was affected.[20] As he was giving the lectures, he sent the texts to MacGregor Reid for possible publication and wider circulation, reviewing them when necessary, in the light of his experience of lecturing.[21]

These examples alone suggest that Ananda M and his elite Burmese team gained aristocratic support in England, *The Bystander* speaking of his 'distinguished patronage' (The Bystander 1908b: 422). They also suggest the breadth of his contacts, ranging from those connected with spiritualism to Christians willing to give him space in a church.

Ananda M did not escape opposition during the mission, but the conflictual model anticipated by *The Daily Express* did not materialise. After all, Ananda M was consistently adamant during his visit that Buddhism did not oppose any other religion. The first challenge, in fact, did not come from England but from Burma. As mentioned in the last chapter, in June 1908, U Dhammaloka, upon learning of Ananda M's mission from newspaper coverage, wrote from Bassein to the journal *Truth*, claiming he had been asked to comment on the mission, in his role as President of the Buddhist Tract Society in Rangoon. His letter states that Buddhists in Burma had been astonished by reports of the mission, because Ananda M was not regarded in Burma as 'a properly ordained mendicant' and had been turned out of 'three monasteries in this province—one in Akyab and two in Rangoon,' partly because of his asthma, which should have precluded him from ordination (Dhammaloka 1908: 65). Dhammaloka's insinuation is that Ananda M had lied at his ordination about his asthma. He further challenges Ananda M's apparent claim that he was the first Western Buddhist monk, listing several ordained Western Buddhists who had preceded him (Dhammaloka 1908).

The editors of *Truth* stated that they could not confirm the allegations made in the letter. They therefore invited Ananda M to respond and published what he submitted the following week (Ananda Metteyya 1908e: 130; Turner, Cox and Bocking 2020: 283). Ananda M's approach is firm, as we have already intimated. He had received higher ordination twice 'so as to secure the advantage of belonging to both of the two schools of Monks in Burma,' one of them within 'the stricter or Reformed School.' He had been quite open, he states, about his asthma but had 'imagined' himself 'cured of it' when he was ordained. He also claims that it is 'untrue' that he had been turned out of 'various monasteries' or that he had met his sister on arrival. The only point he concedes is that other Buddhist monks had visited England, but he adds that he had never claimed to be the first: 'It is probably a newspaper misquotation, of which, of course, many have appeared.' He could have cited *The Daily Mail* (Daily Mail 1908b: 5). He does consider himself, however, to be the first Buddhist monk to have 'appeared *in public* in the country' (Ananda Metteyya 1908h: 130). At the end, Ananda M notes that other newspapers have reprinted U Dhammaloka's accusations and requests that these same papers publish his reply. Whether they did this or not, U Dhammaloka's accusations would become the basis for Ananda M being repeatedly called a 'rascally sham Buddhist monk' in the press during a 1911 defamation case brought against the publishers of the periodical, *The Looking Glass*, by Ananda M's friend, George Cecil Jones. The court case is discussed later in this chapter.

In June 1908, a Theosophical magazine weighs in, with the judgement that Ananda M 'does not understand what he has come to teach,' because of his denial of 'an indwelling divine self'—a not unfamiliar accusation. Quoting an interview with the Ceylonese scholar monk, Hikkaḍuvē Sumaṅgala, published by Blavatsky, the anonymous writer argues that even Sumaṅgala did not deny 'an overshadowing Soul or "*True Self*"' (Century Path 1908: 3).

Then, on 15 August 1908, an intriguing notice appears in *The Rangoon Times* that a new Buddhist association was to be formed in Rangoon 'for the promotion of Buddhist affairs,' with a meeting to be held at the 'Upasaka Zayat' (an assembly place for lay Buddhists), perhaps indicating that the *Buddhasāsana Samāgama* was seen as ineffectual. One interpretation of this would be that it was an indirect criticism of Ananda M's mission (The Rangoon Times 1908b: 10).

As for the Christian response to the mission, the notice for Ananda M's last London lecture actually quoted a popular 'Clergyman in South London,' who had said that Ananda M was 'one of the most Intellectual Men who has yet visited England.' This unnamed cleric could have been the same person who had given him permission to lecture in the previously mentioned church in Clapham. *The Open Court*, the magazine founded by Paul Carus, mentioned another positive Christian response in a periodical called the *Christian Commonwealth*. We have not been able to find this, but *The Open Court* describes it 'as free from all bitterness as was customary with missionaries in former days when speaking of other religions' (The Open Court 1908: 573). During and after his visit, however, *The Church Times* included a number of items on Buddhism that sought to alert readers to the dangers of being 'misled' by Buddhism. Ananda M's visit no doubt lay behind these, although he was not named. On March 27, those 'misled' by Edwin Arnold's poem, *The Light of Asia*, are pointed towards Bishop Reginald Copleston's negative examination of Buddhism (The Church Times 1908a: 401; see Copleston 1892).[22] H. Fielding Hall's book, *The Inward Light*, is advertised on 1 May (The Church Times 1908b: 569). On 9 October, the second edition of Copleston's book is advertised (The Church Times 1908c: 476). On 20 November, John Campbell Oman's, *Cults, Customs and Superstitions of India* (Oman 1908) is positively reviewed, with readers directed particularly towards the chapter on Buddhism, at a time 'when Buddhist missionaries are seeking to establish themselves in England' (The Church Times 1908d: 691). Additionally, in April 1909, *The Buddhist Review* reports an attack on the Buddhist Society of Great Britain and Ireland by Rev. W. St. Clair Tisdall in *The Churchman*, which claimed that Buddhism was 'a freak religion' (The Buddhist Review 1909a: 149). Further afield, an American Methodist periodical that published news from England carried a piece that regretted that people were finding time 'to be lured by Christian Scientists and even by Buddhists, for a Buddhist propaganda has been seriously opened in London by Bikuya Ananda Metteyya—a renegade Scotsman' (Zion's Herald 1908: 1131). A more neutral report in *The Missionary Review of the World* was nevertheless entitled 'England Invaded by Buddhists' (The Missionary Review of the World 1909: 66–67).

In Burma, the SPG missionaries were also watching closely. *The Rangoon Diocesan Magazine* of April 1908 carries an article by the editor, Francis Trotman, which reviews Ananda M's article, 'Propaganda,' in the light of the mission. He contests Ananda M's view that Buddhism is not a rival to any other 'form of religious belief,' by arguing that Buddhism's denial of God means 'that Christianity and Buddhism do, and must always, remain opposed' (Trotman 1908: 142). He casts doubt on the success of the mission—the West is not egocentric but theocentric, he argues—and challenges Ananda M's views on the superiority of the East, accusing him of false comparisons and the wish to spread to the West a Buddhism very different from that of the ordinary Burmese (Trotman 1908: 145–146). His article is followed in the magazine by summaries of four lectures given by Rollestone Fyffe on 'Christianity and Buddhism,' each of which seeks to defend Christianity in the face of the activities of the *Buddhasāsana Samāgama*. The first lecture, for instance, quotes from the journal *Buddhism*, and judges Buddhism to be a useful ethical philosophy but not a religion that could offer people hope (Fyffe 1908: 235–237). This tone continues throughout. Although the author stresses that he does not want to decry other systems (Fyffe 1908: 275), his undoubted aim was to do just that.[23]

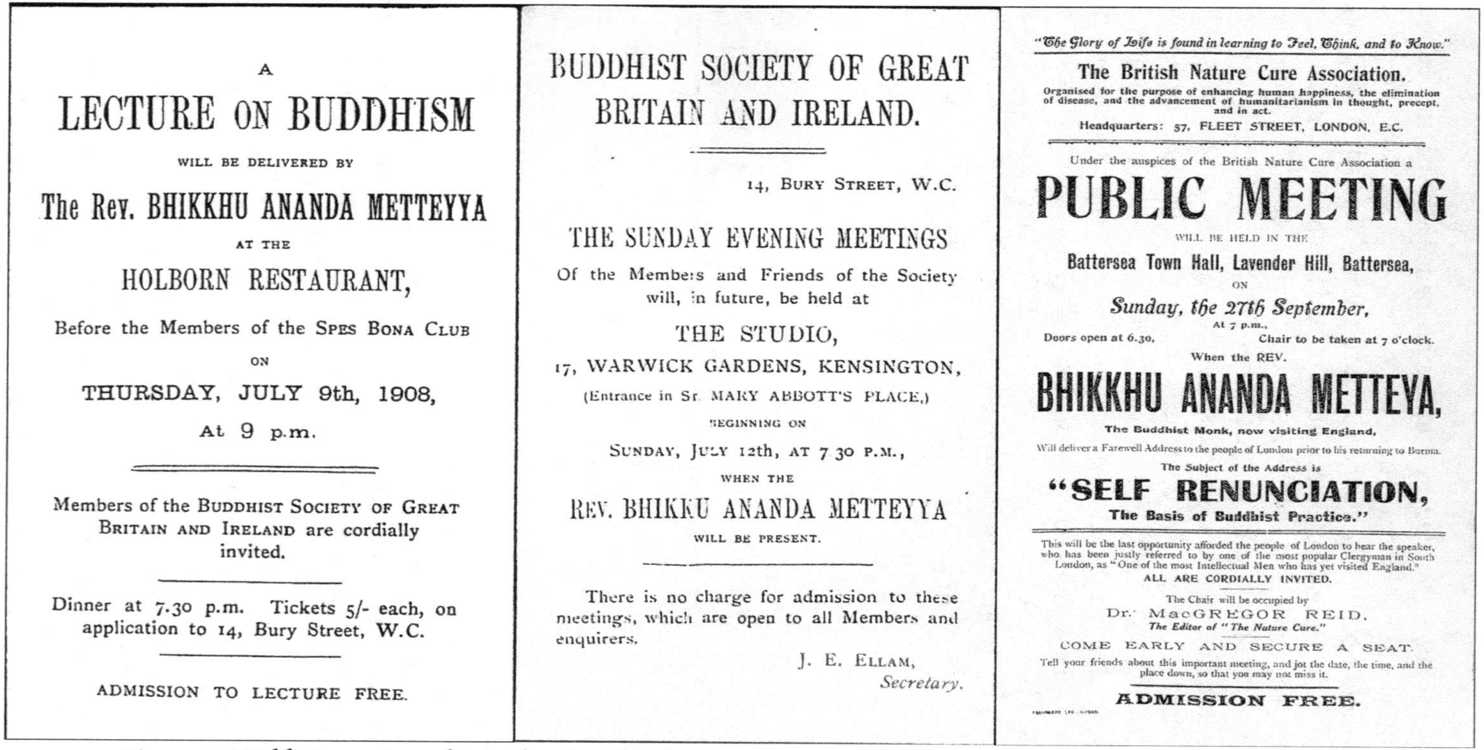

A

LECTURE ON BUDDHISM

WILL BE DELIVERED BY

The Rev. BHIKKHU ANANDA METTEYYA

AT THE

HOLBORN RESTAURANT,

ON

Before the Members of the SPES BONA CLUB

THURSDAY, JULY 9th, 1908,

At 9 p.m.

Members of the BUDDHIST SOCIETY OF GREAT BRITAIN AND IRELAND are cordially invited.

Dinner at 7.30 p.m. Tickets 5/- each, on application to 14, Bury Street, W.C.

ADMISSION TO LECTURE FREE.

BUDDHIST SOCIETY OF GREAT BRITAIN AND IRELAND.

14, BURY STREET, W.C.

THE SUNDAY EVENING MEETINGS

Of the Members and Friends of the Society will, in future, be held at

THE STUDIO,

17, WARWICK GARDENS, KENSINGTON,

(Entrance in ST. MARY ABBOTT'S PLACE,)

BEGINNING ON

SUNDAY, JULY 12th, AT 7.30 P.M.

WHEN THE

REV. BHIKKU ANANDA METTEYYA

WILL BE PRESENT.

There is no charge for admission to these meetings, which are open to all Members and enquirers.

J. E. ELLAM,
Secretary.

"The Glory of Life is found in learning to Feel, Think, and to Know."

The British Nature Cure Association.

Organised for the purpose of enhancing human happiness, the elimination of disease, and the advancement of humanitarianism in thought, precept and in act.

Headquarters: 57, FLEET STREET, LONDON, E.C.

Under the auspices of the British Nature Cure Association a

PUBLIC MEETING

WILL BE HELD IN THE

Battersea Town Hall, Lavender Hill, Battersea,

ON

Sunday, the 27th September,

AT 7 p.m.

Doors open at 6.30. Chair to be taken at 7 o'clock.

When the REV.

BHIKKHU ANANDA METTEYA,

The Buddhist Monk, now visiting England,

Will deliver a Farewell Address to the people of London prior to his returning to Burma. The Subject of the Address is

"SELF RENUNCIATION,

The Basis of Buddhist Practices."

This will be the last opportunity afforded the people of London to hear the speaker, who has been justly referred to by one of the most popular Clergymen in South London, as "One of the most intellectual Men who has yet visited England."

ALL ARE CORDIALLY INVITED.

The Chair will be occupied by

Dr. MacGREGOR REID,
The Editor of "The Nature Cure."

COME EARLY AND SECURE A SEAT.

Tell your friends about this important meeting, and put the date, the time, and the place down, so that you may not miss it.

ADMISSION FREE.

Figure 4.4 *Publicity notices of Ananda M's public lectures during his mission. Yorke Collection, Warburg Institute, University of London, NS 101 15. Courtesy of The Warburg Institute.*

THE MISSION DRAWS TO A CLOSE

As the mission drew towards its end, Ananda M gave more interviews to the Press. As early as 14 August, the *London and China Express* reports that Ananda M would return to 'the East' in October and that he had expressed satisfaction 'with the fruit of his labours' (London and China Express 1908b: 603). The *Cornish and Devon Post* repeats this on 29 August, adding that it was a 'strange anomaly' that there was a Buddhist missionary in England when the British were doing their best to convert 'the heathen' (Cornish and Devon Post 1908: 3). Both repeat that Ananda M would return in two years to establish a Buddhist monastery. Towards the end of September, more reports appear, stimulated by a significant interview that Ananda M offered from his home to *The Daily Telegraph* on 28 September. The report of this interview repeats that Ananda M was 'a Scotchman' and claims that he still had a 'highland brogue.' He is described as tall and handsome in a room that 'had no affectation of Orientalism' about it, although he seemed to 'wear his unbecoming garment uneasily.' He smoked continuously and is again reported as saying that he saw 'no reason to be dissatisfied.' He had made only about 28 or 30 converts but 'everywhere amongst the more thoughtful class has been a desire to inquire into the principles underlying the teaching.' As he talked, the report continues, he stroked a kitten that had jumped onto his robes and became much more animated when he was describing Buddhism, particularly the evil of individualism, striding from 'one end of the tiny room to the other.' When asked how he had become Buddhist, he stated that he had studied science, become an agnostic, chanced upon *The Light of Asia*, and then had studied Buddhism for 10 years before going to the East, a reinvention of himself that edited out his involvement with occultism (The Daily Telegraph 1908: 12).[24]

Ananda M also sought to prepare his British followers for his departure. On 24 September, 1908, he wrote a pastoral 'letter' to those in the Buddhist Society who considered themselves committed Buddhists. He first stresses that Buddhism is surely 'destined to become the Guide of all the West' (Ananda Metteyya 1909a: 8). He then appeals to his readers in poetic language that they should express their Buddhist convictions in action, 'not the vain claim that we are Followers of the Buddha, whilst yet our lives are empty of the pity and the love and helpfulness He taught... remembering that the world can only judge of Buddhism by your actions, by your love, your life' (Ananda Metteyya 1909a: 11). On 26 September there was an informal meeting of the Buddhist Society to bid him farewell.[25]

Ananda M gave his last public London lecture on Sunday, 27 September at Battersea Town Hall in South London. It is possible that the first venue suggested by MacGregor Reid for this was a theatre, which prompted a dismayed response from Ananda M. A Buddhist monk could not lecture at a place linked with a 'class of entertainment' that even 'pious Buddhist laymen' would not go to![26] The title resonated with the message he had consistently given in London about the dangers of individualism: 'Self Renunciation: The Basis of Buddhist Practice.'[27] It was chaired by Macgregor Reid under the umbrella of the British Nature Cure Association, the association which Macgregor Reid founded, and admission was free.

This was not, however, his last presentation in London; on 28 September, he was booked at the City Temple Debating Society.[28] He left London for Liverpool on 29 September[29] and, additionally, gave an evening lecture the following day in the Alexandra Hall, Islington Square, Liverpool (Birkenhead News 1908: 1).[30] Admission was again free but one could reserve a seat for a penny.

Rost claims that the mission ended in November 1908, 'due to lack of funds' at the same time as Rost, himself, returned to Burma at the end of his leave. Again, Rost is wrong. Ananda M sailed back to Burma at the beginning of October 1908, from Liverpool, according to his letters to MacGregor Reid.[31] We have no doubt that his funds had run low by this time, but the early newspaper reports of his mission indicate that Ananda M had always intended to stay about six months (Ananda Metteyya 1929: 171). The shortage of funds is confirmed by a story that the geologist and sympathiser Edward Greenly (1861–1951) recalls, namely that a Burmese well-wisher had given Ananda M a large 'ruby' before his departure from Rangoon, saying that it had been given to his father in repayment of a debt and that Ananda M should realise its value to help fund the mission. When this was tried in London at the end of the mission to meet the costs accrued, it proved to be a fake. To defray the debt, money was raised by the Buddhist Society, with Mrs. Annie Greenly playing an important part (Greenly 1945: 85; Bax 1951: 163).[32]

Whether the mission was a success gained different answers according to the context in which the question was asked. Rost, having known Ananda M since the founding of the *Buddhasāsana Samāgama*, had the deepest respect for him, to the extent that he could see him as filled with a love that was 'divine.'[33] For Rost, therefore, the visit was a success. *The Buddhist Review*, the journal of the Buddhist Society of Great Britain and Ireland, could say in 1909 that Ananda M left behind 'golden opinions and the friendship and respect of all who had the privilege of meeting him' (Ellam 1909: 3). Yet, there was an ambivalence about their stance, because of Ananda M's past occultism. So, the report continues:

> [S]ome attempts have been made to surround him with mystery. There is no more mystery attending Bhikkhu Ananda Metteyya than any other person. It should always be remembered that there is no mystery, as such—there is nothing "esoteric"—in true Buddhism. (Ellam 1909: 3)

In the next issue of the journal, the Society feels it necessary to stress that it gave no encouragement to the practice of 'occultism, mystery, or thaumaturgy' (The Buddhist Review 1909a: 142).

Retrospective accounts of the mission are also restrained. Christmas Humphreys, for instance, points to the difficulties of accommodating Ananda M's strict adherence to Buddhist monastic discipline, the *Vinaya*, such as not eating after noon, and not sleeping in the same house as a woman or on 'high and soft beds.' Outside the houses in Barnes, the difficulties were compounded, because his refusal to handle money meant he had to be accompanied wherever he went. And if he walked in the streets in his 'bright yellow robes,' he faced 'ribald comments from small boys.' Humphreys actually speaks of 'harassed lay supporters' (Humphreys 1937: 22).

Clifford Bax, whose friendship with Ananda M we discuss in Chapter Five, proposes that the paucity of converts could have been due to Ananda M's teaching of *anattā*, stating, 'Nothing is harder for the mind of a Westerner than to regard his apparent individuality as the last illusion' (Bax 1951: 163). As for his preaching style, we know from Greenly that Ananda M did not engage with his audience, reading his lectures with downcast eyes in line with traditional monastic practice in Burma and Ceylon. Greenly attended a meeting in Holborn in September 1908 and writes, retrospectively:

> At this meeting I perceived one of his chief defects as a leader; perhaps it was the only one. To me it mattered little or nothing, but it should be recorded here, because it is one of the principal reasons why the mission did not accomplish all that had been hoped for it. Here was a Buddhist monk, tall, graceful, dignified, and with noble features whereon commanding intellect was written. . . . But Nature, when bestowing on him such a wonderful shower of gifts—man of science, philosopher, poet—had fatally omitted the essential gift of eloquence. So far did this go that he read his addresses. We sat in the front rank, hardly a couple of yards from him, and saw that he never once lifted his eyes from his paper to his audience. (Greenly 1945: 85)

Newspaper reports confirm this. *The Sketch*, for instance, claims he read his lectures 'whilst seated' in accordance with 'Buddhist custom' (The Sketch 1908: 8), whilst *The Daily Telegraph* mentions his 'rapid, melodious, and slightly monotonous voice' (The Daily Telegraph 1908: 12). The effect of his asthma cigarettes, containing opiates, cannot be discounted either, as a contributing factor to his unimpressive lecturing style. The density of the lectures could also have been a problem in some contexts, in spite of Rost's praise of the Clapham lecture. This can be glimpsed in the reprint in *The Buddhist Review* of his address at the Spes Bona Club on 'Buddhist Self Culture' (Ananda Metteyya 1914). In private interviews, he was much more animated, willing to talk at length both about Buddhism and his scientific experiments (Greenly 1945: 85).

As for Ananda M himself, what he said to the media, stressing his future hopes for Buddhism in England, must be distinguished from what he shared in private correspondence. In a letter to MacGregor Reid before he left England, he laments that he would only leave behind 'a poor nucleus,' and adds later:

> The work here has,—with the exception that it has brought me a few earnest and devoted colleagues, like yourself,—been a failure; financially,—just as with your own movement, none of the wealthy members will do anything,—nothing can be got even to keep the movement bar[r]el floated. So the only remedy seems to be, to make the money myself. This I hope to do by developing to commercial point one or other, or both of my inventions.[34]

On 28 November, however, he writes to a friend in Colombo, possibly Cassius Pereira:

> Taking into consideration the smallness of our resources, and the lack of any special ability for the work on the part of all members of this Buddhist Mission, I think we may fairly consider the results as most remarkable. We have left behind us a well-established Buddhist Society, including amongst its members some thirty actual Buddhists; perhaps thirty of whom have received the *Tisarana* [Three Refuges] and *Pancha Sila* [Five Precepts]. (Ananda M 1908: 180–181)

He sees this as 'the first tiny wavelet of the returning Buddhist flood' (Ananda M 1908: 181). A month later, writing of his conviction that the West had to be saved from 'self-destruction' and that his mission had been one poor start, he nevertheless states that 'hampered for want of means, where I had hoped to reach thousands, I was able only to reach tens with my poor rendering of that great message' (Ananda Metteyya 1930: 270). He had also failed to produce a further issue of *Buddhism*, perhaps made up of his lectures. Before he had left Rangoon, he had hoped to produce another issue in Britain (Ananda Metteyya 1908d: 342).

Late twentieth-century accounts, for instance, that by Sandra Bell, read between the lines of Humphreys's words, which were doubtless rooted in oral tradition, and Ananda M's own personal feelings, to conclude that the mission 'ended in failure' because of 'cultural dissonance' (Bell 1994). Yet, it would do an injustice to the mission to emphasise only its negative aspects. Ananda M's hopes for the mass dissemination of Buddhism in the West, founded on the belief that Westerners only had to hear the message of Buddhism to be converted (Ananda Metteyya 1908a), were doomed to failure from the start, and could have hidden from him the mission's positive sides. From the standpoint of the twenty-first century, the mission occupied a more liminal ground between success and failure.

Dharmapāla, for instance, stresses the mission's potential: 'If even a small portion of the British people embrace the Dhamma we shall then see the dawn of a better era, an era of peace and plenty, of human brotherhood' (Dharmapala 1909a: 11). Humphreys refers to Ananda M's 'immense' work output when he was well, his correspondence, and the constant interviews he held, which enabled him to gather a body of supportive scholars around him. He writes this:

> Those who stared at Ānanda at this time had good reason to stare. He was then thirty-six years of age, tall, slim, graceful and dignified. The deep-set eyes and somewhat ascetic features, surmounted by the shaven head, made a great impression on all who met him, and all who remember him speak of his pleasing voice and beautiful enunciation. It seems his conversation was always interesting; in his lighter moments he showed a delightful sense of humour, while his deep comprehension of the Dhamma, his fund of analogy from contemporary science, and power and range of thought, combined to form a most exceptional personality. (Humphreys 1937: 22)

Greenly claims that his conversations with Ananda M put him 'under a spell, the spell of a personality of the most "magnetic" sort,' which left a 'deep' impression that lasted throughout his life 'due, not only to his personality, but to his profoundly mystical interpretation of the Teaching' (Greenly 1945: 85). In 1945, Greenly claims that he had known two 'geniuses,' one of whom was Ananda M (Greenly 1945: 87).

No doubt some lay supporters felt 'harassed' by the requirements of Ananda M's strict adherence to the *Vinaya*, and some certainly experienced 'cultural dissonance.' Yet, the new London-based Buddhist Society would not have been taken off guard completely by Ananda M's requirements, since some of its members were familiar with Buddhism in Asia and were acquainted with the needs of Buddhist monks. Rost, for instance, knew in advance that two houses were necessary for the mission, to accommodate male and female members of the Burmese delegation, and T. W. Rhys Davids had been a civil servant in Sri Lanka, working in Buddhist majority areas. To the mission's credit, when Ananda M left, the number of Western Buddhists to keep the work of the Buddhist Society going had increased. Francis Payne, writing to the Anagārika Dharmapāla in December 1908, claims there are 150 people in England who were 'believers of Buddhism' and that some 600 had inquired about Buddhism as a result of the mission. He also speaks of 'dear Ananda.'[35] To the *Buddhasāsana Samāgama*, in December 1908, Ananda M said, 'we left behind us, perhaps, some hundred and fifty; and out of these, there are perhaps twenty or thirty persons who have gone with us *all* the way we went to shew; and have become actual Buddhists' (Ananda Metteyya 1909b: 7). This was not something of which he should have been ashamed, however downcast he might have been as he sailed back to Burma through the Suez Canal, grieving that the fruit of his mission, the result of 'seven years of unremitting work,' had been one small Buddhist Society, which had few funds (Ananda Metteyya 1930: 270).[36]

RETURN TO BURMA

On his return to Burma, Ananda M's orientation towards the West was stronger than ever. He felt a keen sense of responsibility towards the Buddhist Society of Great Britain and Ireland, and its fledgling group of Buddhist converts, and continually sought new ways of communicating the truths he believed could 'save' the West. MacGregor Reid had offered to publish some of the lectures Ananda M had given during the mission, and Ananda M wrote repeatedly to him about the logistics and potential of this. Writing on the return journey, he mentions five lectures to MacGregor Reid, three of which he had revised as the most important: 'The Message of Buddhism to the West,' 'Buddhist Self-Culture' and 'Religious Experience in Buddhism.'[37] He was to be disappointed. MacGregor Reid's interests were always larger than Buddhism. He eventually became a Universalist minister (W. A. P. 1946: 3), and later helped revive Druidism in Great Britain (Stout 2011). Some of Ananda M's lectures were, nevertheless, published in *The Buddhist Review* (Ananda Metteyya 1910b; 1913a;[38] 1914) and the Anagārika Dharmapāla's journal, *The Maha-Bodhi and the United Buddhist World* (Ananda Metteyya 1910c; 1913b).

A key consideration for Ananda M was that the London-based society was short of money. To MacGregor Reid, he spoke of 'the heavy burden of indebtedness with which the early management had saddled the

Buddhist Society,' which had been made good by the 'better-off Buddhists in England' at his request, leaving few other resources for the eventual establishment of a monastery in the West.[39] The Society, for instance, did not renew its tenancy of the Bury Street premises when it expired on 29 September, 1908, judging 'an establishment of this kind' to be 'rather too ambitious' (Ellam 1909: 2).[40]

Ananda M's address to the *Buddhasāsana Samāgama* in December 1908 was, therefore, a passionate appeal to his Burmese listeners to donate, claiming that 'the spread of Buddhism in the West' was 'not only a possibility but a moral certainty,' partly because he was convinced that many people in the West had been Buddhists in former lives and felt 'at variance' with the western values around them (Ananda Metteyya 1909b: 8-10).[41] To help the West move towards Buddhism was, therefore, a moral duty of the Burmese, as 'custodians of all the earth's fairest and greatest light.' His plea was for nothing less than a continuous reverse mission from Buddhist Asia to the West's 'darkness,' caused by individualistic competition and seen in the 'Hunger March' he had witnessed in London, organised by those without enough to eat in the 'wealthiest city in the world' (Ananda Metteyya 1909b: 11-15).[42] The *Buddhasāsana Samāgama* printed it, as did the Buddhist Society for Great Britain and Ireland, under its own cover.[43] *The Theosophist* notified its readers of the Rangoon publication, as well as reprinting a portion of it, demonstrating their ongoing interest in Ananda M (Besant 1909).

Daw Mya May and her family continued to be Ananda M's main supporters in Burma, but their other commitments meant that their generosity was limited, although Daw Mya May would later make further gestures of goodwill to London. On 25 December, 1908, therefore, Ananda M writes an open letter to the Buddhists in London appealing to their generosity.[44] Drawing on what he would say three days later to the *Buddhasāsana Samāgama*, he again shares something of his own journey into Buddhism, giving the same reduced account that he had given to reporters in London, adding that it was only when he travelled to Asia that he saw Buddhism's 'living power.' He then explains that he had come to the West as a monk because of his conviction that only 'one wearing that Yellow Robe which has been the greatest civilising agency the earth has ever known' would be able to embody the full truth of Buddhism in the West (Ananda Metteyya 1909b: 3-5; 1930: 269). He urges his readers to support the Buddhist Society financially so that the work he had begun would grow from 'a feeble seedling' into 'a stalwart sapling' and then, eventually, into 'a great tree of life' (Ananda Metteyya 1930: 270).

Ananda M knew, however, that not all the support needed could come from London, Burma or Ceylon. Putting his scientific knowledge to use became the only other option for him. As we have shown, he wrote about this to MacGregor-Reid before the end of the mission. The letter mentions two scientific inventions with 'commercial value,' for which he needs 'apparatus,' although he admits, 'even if both [inventions] fail the apparatus will still enable me to go on another step in my consciousness research.'[45] Whilst still in England, he obtained support from 'Prof. Mills and an engineering friend' to gain some of the equipment he needed.[46] Other items were only ordered after his return. The first oil-engine he ordered was 'an utter fraud' but, by April 1909, the 'lathe-tools' he had ordered were in port.[47] Later, he enlisted Greenly to send another oil engine to pursue a method he had devised for extracting oxygen from air, which he believed could be worth 'thousands of pounds' (Greenly 1945: 86, quoting from a letter from Ananda M). Greenly contacted a friend who located a second-hand oil engine, which they sent out to their 'Prince of Cranks,' namely Ananda M (Greenly 1945: 86).

The last example shows that Ananda M was not working only on inventions connected with the mind. Ethel Powell-Brown remembers him saying that he could make ice more cheaply than 'the manufacturers of refrigerators' but was convinced these same manufacturers would kill the project, and also that he could 'sterilise food to preserve it ... by means of rays from a special lamp.' She was writing in 1952 and claims that this was 40 years ago, placing it after Ananda M had returned from the mission.[48]

These inventions proved to be another unfulfilled aspiration. Greenly, for instance, laments that he heard nothing more from Ananda M about oxygen, putting it down to his deteriorating health (Greenly 1945: 86). Again, one can only speculate what the consequences of success would have been. Greenly apparently took information that Ananda M sent to Rhys Davids about his electrical apparatus that could measure aspects of thought when connected to a galvanometer to two physics professors after Rhys Davids's death, only to be told that the experiment was unrepeatable without further information (Greenly 1945: 85).[49] From the vantage point of the twenty-first century, however, Ananda M can be seen as a precursor of the contemporary interest among neuroscientists, and cognitive and clinical scientists, in Buddhist meditation and Buddhist theories of mind.[50]

In England, the Buddhist Society was gradually building up its resources. On 18 June, 1909, their account held £37, seven shillings and eight pence, with £2 in petty cash and a £20 donation expected.[51] That would be the equivalent of almost £8,000 today—a comfortable amount but not enough to fulfil the Society's aims. Tenders to print 1000 copies of *The Buddhist Review* alone were coming in at about £25, over one third of their total assets.[52] Soon after the mission, Payne appeals to Dharmapāla for financial help for *The Buddhist Review*, asking him, rather than Ananda M, to approach friends in Burma.[53] In June 1909, the Society hears that Dharmapāla and the Western *bhikkhu* Sāsana Dhaja[54] had launched 'a special appeal' in Ceylon and Burma 'on behalf of the Society.'[55] In August 1909, Dharmapāla records in his diary that Richard Pereira was raising funds for London Buddhists.[56] Help came from individuals, such as a Mrs. Jeremias Dias of Panadura, on the south coast of Ceylon.[57] That J. D. Fernando reprinted in Colombo in 1909 Ananda M's lecture on the Four Noble Truths, together with two popular devotional discourses, the *Mahā Maṅgala* and the *Vasala Suttas*, would have been no coincidence, raising Ananda M's profile (Ananda Metteyya 1909c). In January 1910, Maung Mya U successfully requests authorisation to collect funds in Burma.[58]

By May 1910, the average balance held by the Society was between £50 and £60, an increased amount on which the Society could survive but not flourish.[59] By 1911, however, the balance was more likely to be over £80.[60] In April 1912, Payne refers both to 'the magnificent help received from Ceylon both financially and in respect of literary matter' and also to that which had come from the Burmese.[61] By this time, Ceylonese Buddhists resident in London were also helping, for instance, the previously mentioned Wilmot Arthur de Silva, who had 'defrayed the expenses of a series of meetings held at Chandos Hall,' the Society having given up the room they had rented at 11 Hart Street in Bloomsbury.[62] In April 1913, a further cheque, this time for £25.18.8d, was received from Mrs. Dias.[63] The brother of the Anagārika Dharmapāla, Charles Hewavitarne, was also giving generously. For these Asian revivalists, supporting Buddhism in Britain was a symbolic reversal of the power relationships of British imperialism, and their actions would no doubt have warmed Ananda M's heart.

The Buddhist Society at first expects Ananda M to return in two to three years, to establish a monastery (The Buddhist Review 1909a: 144). Ananda M's November 1908 letter to Ceylon speaks of the 'not less than five monks' needed, 'to form a chapter or Sangha' (Ananda M 1908: 182). Attached to Ananda M's 1908 appeal to the *Buddhasāsana Samāgama* was a full-page illustrated advert for the monastery and the £4,000 or 60,000 rupees needed for its realisation (Ananda Metteyya 1909b). Dharmapāla reprinted it in *The Maha-Bodhi and the United Buddhist World*, praising Ananda M for his efforts and urging all Sinhala Buddhists to contribute to the 'London Monastery Building Fund' (Dharmapāla 1909b: 103–104.) Sāsana Dhaja was in line to help Ananda M in this work of 'establishing the Sasana in Western lands,' although his removal to Australia prevented this.[64]

Doubts, however, emerged within the Society about the financial feasibility of the monastery project. As early as 1909, it was giving way to the idea of inviting one *bhikkhu* to London. Rost seems to have suggested this, without mentioning Ananda M.[65] The sculptor and artist Alexander Fisher was particularly keen, and gained agreement in 1910 that the Society should create a Renunciation Fund for this purpose, with Fisher taking charge of it.[66] At the start of 1911, Mills was tasked with providing an estimate for the project.[67]

By this time, Ananda M probably realised that his poor health and lack of finance would make a return in 1911 or 1912 to establish a monastery impossible, but his initial reaction to the idea of one *bhikkhu* being invited was negative. In an emotional letter sent to a friend in December 1910, he argues that it would be far better for the Society to spend the small amount of money it held on literature rather than on bringing a single *bhikkhu* to London, although he nevertheless states that he wants to come to England again 'some time' (Ananda Metteyya 1929: 171). Claiming

Figure 4.5 Line drawing of "The Proposed New London Buddhist Monastery," pictured at the back of the 1909 pamphlet, Extension of the Empire of Righteousness to Western Lands: Address of Bhikkhu Ananda Metteyya, Director of the Buddhasasana Samagama at the Sixth Annual Convention of the International Buddhist Society, December 27, 1908.

that he is the only person qualified to fulfil such a request, his argument against it cites both the *Vinaya*-based concept that he should not leave the place of his ordination to reside elsewhere until 10 rain seasons had passed, and his fear that what the Buddhists in Britain really wanted was the equivalent of a resident priest and a 'Buddhist "Church,"' moulded on Christian precedent (Ananda Metteyya 1929: 176). This was anathema to him, given his belief that only a community of monks could truly communicate Buddhism's message to the West through embodying it in their lives (Ananda Metteyya 1909b: 4). He writes:

> The first thing, for example, without doubt would be just those "services,"—that was the cry, even when I was in London before. How much more would it be so if I (or another, if there were another) were being supported by those very persons? And, once one analyses the psychology of that demand, one sees at once how fatal would compliance be, how impossible it would make the already-so-difficult task of diffusing the Buddhist spirit in an alien land. (Ananda Metteyya 1929: 176)

His fear is that Buddhists in Britain would attend the Sunday 'service' and be attracted to the ritual, perhaps imported from Mahayana Buddhism, and ignore the teaching for the rest of the week, as Christians did when they went to a mass (Ananda Metteyya 1929: 177). Buddhism had to be lived every day, he argues, without 'crutches' and, for this, a *bhikkhu* was not needed (Ananda Metteyya 1929: 178).

It is probable that Ananda M's views were communicated to the Society even if his full text was not. On 12 May, 1911, the Minutes of the Society show that there was a heated discussion in London. Fisher urged that every effort should be made to 'obtain a Bhikkhu.' Wilmot Arthur de Silva stressed the difficulties of doing this and a person called Barsky argued that the project was simply not feasible. It was probably not coincidental that Daw Mya May is also reported at this meeting as having offered £40 a year towards the upkeep of a residence for a *bhikkhu* in England.[68] Fisher, nevertheless, gained agreement in December 1911 that his Renunciation Fund should be used for a *bhikkhu* and, in 1912, Charles Hewavitarne and Paul Dahlke added their support.[69] The Society was also openly sharing this aim more widely, with Mills stating to the press that they were looking for a 'bikkhu who is also a good orator, to carry on the work of Ananda Metteyya' (e.g., The Telegraph 1912). On 25 January, 1913, the Society placed a short advertisement on the front page of *The Times*, which was republished and expanded in English speaking newspapers around the world. The advert simply states:

> BUDDHISM—WANTED, a YOUNG MAN (graduate of a British University) to proceed to Ceylon and TRAIN there as a BHIKKHU, for subsequent service in this country. All expenses paid,—x, 64 Twyford avenue, West Acton, London, W. (The Times 1913—capitalisation as printed in *The Times*).

Other newspapers gained further information from Professor Mills and the Society, possibly through press releases. The *Gisborne Times* (New Zealand), for instance, states that the successful applicant, in Ceylon, would live in a cell with no comfort, must beg for his food, and then return to England, adding that 'a wealthy Cingalese' had offered to support the monk (Gisborne Times 1913: 7). *The Londonderry Sentinel*, on the other hand, quoting Professor Mills, claims that one patron is 'the King of Siam' (The Londonderry Sentinel 1913: 8). Several newspapers add that Ananda Metteyya would have been an ideal choice but that his asthma had made it impossible (e.g., Overland China Mail 1913).[70]

Despite actively advertising for a person to train for ordination, there was still division within the Society as late as January 1914, when the Committee discussed houses for the proposed *bhikkhu*. Oswald Reeves referred to 'the great services rendered by Ānanda Metteyya in his mission as a reason for obtaining such help again' but Caroline Rhys Davids, the President, argued that bringing a *bhikkhu* was unnecessary.[71] Although the precedent of Ananda M's mission was mentioned in this discussion, it is significant that it was not suggested that Ananda M should be the desired *bhikkhu*. In December 1913, Mills specifically stated that he considered it 'inadvisable to accept a visit from Ānanda Metteyya or at present Silācāra.'[72]

The heat in this discussion was partly because the wish to welcome a Buddhist monk to England had to compete with the Society's need to gain permanent headquarters, perhaps with enough room for a *bhikkhu*. In 1911, a Housing Fund was established, with Asian Buddhists such as Charles Hewavitarne raising healthy amounts for it. By January 1914, the Fund stood at £611.16.7d.[73] Forty-four donations, for instance, are mentioned in *The Maha-Bodhi and the United Buddhist World* in October 1913 and over 30 in November, amounting to over 8,000 rupees.[74]

Ananda M's letter concerning the *bhikkhu* project voices his agonising about Buddhism and the West, due in part to his realisation that the West would not embrace Buddhism as easily as he had originally imagined. Something about Buddhism was alienating Westerners, or at least failing to attract their interest. *The Open Court* in 1908 reports that Ananda M was intending to compile a pamphlet 'which will explain to the Western world the tenets of Buddhism, freed from Oriental expressions' (The Open Court 1908: 574). In 1910 or thereabouts, Ananda M, intending at this point to write not a pamphlet but a manual of the Dhamma for a Western audience, uses a letter to a friend to reflect on how Buddhism could be communicated to the West without 'frightening people away.'[75] It is worth quoting from this at length, since it clearly reflects the point that Ananda M had reached almost two years after the mission:

> I am in entire accordance as to the advisability of introducing the great ideal of Buddhism (or rather, of the Truth: our own Dhamma is a far more appropriate word than the foreign term 'Buddhism') without mentioning the word Buddhism at all. In England with its great mental inertia especially, not a few of the best minds even, are likely to be frightened off at the start by a word which unfortunately has come to be associated with so much mystery-making and mythology. Where, of course, *my* work is concerned, that line can't be taken. But to no true Buddhist does it at all matter whether that label is born by men or no. The only question is, to get the Truth home to our fellows' hearts; to help—so far as our own small knowledge of the Dhamma goes—to plant seeds in others minds. (Ananda Metteyya 1931: 62)

He had experimented with this approach in England, according to Rost's account of the meeting in Clapham, and hints at it in his ordination address and subsequent articles, referring to Buddhism as the 'Good Law,' the 'Law of Pity and Love,' 'His Eternal Dharma' (Ananda Maitriya 1902d; Anon 1902b: 7).

Once again, however, Ananda M's aspiration, this time to write a manual of the 'Dhamma' that eschewed 'mystery-making and mythology' in favour of a message that could transform society, did not materialise. According to Cassius Pereira, his health failed rapidly on his return to Burma in 1908, because of asthma and gallstone trouble, leading to two operations (Pereira 1923a: 6).[76] One of these was in December 1911, with the Buddhist Society describing it as 'severe' (The Buddhist Review 1912: 80). The combination of this with lack of funds meant disappointment was almost inevitable.

As for the *Buddhasāsana Samāgama*, it published no further issues of *Buddhism* after 1908. The final edition came out before the mission, in March 1908, funded with the mission in mind by a Chinese Buddhist living in Burma, Tan Hmaw Yan (Ananda Metteyya 1908d: 340), who died before the issue was complete. The *Buddhasāsana Samāgama*, however, remained active in furthering Buddhist education and Ananda M, at least for a few years, retained his involvement with the Rangoon College Buddhist Association, outlined in the last chapter. In 1909, the Buddhist Society of Great Britain and Ireland congratulated Ananda M and his colleagues for successfully campaigning for Buddhism to be taught in schools.[77] A 1910 circular from the Burmese Office of Public Instruction, however, raises a question mark over this achievement, in that it outlines tight conditions for Religious Education in government schools, in line with India.[78] Nevertheless, Ananda M and the *Buddhasāsana Samāgama* continued to align themselves with Buddhists and others concerned for education in the country, for example, H. Fielding Hall, who writes in 1906 that 'the higher education [in Burma] now is artificial. A real education is an incorporation into the life of a nation, and that is not yet even in sight' (Fielding-Hall 1913: 231). Together, they campaigned for an educational system that exposed children and young people to Burmese culture and religion, in a context where there were very few Buddhist schools, apart from those attached to Buddhist monasteries, which gave an elementary standard of education.[79]

The hope of the *Buddhasāsana Samāgama* that it would have regional representatives promoting Buddhism throughout Burma also evaporated. Ledi Sayadaw filled the gap. In 1913 he founded the World Buddhist Missionary Association in Mandalay, which developed 24 regional groups in larger cities throughout Burma and published a journal in Burmese (Janaka 2016: 96).

Ananda M's presence in Rangoon was, however, still considered significant enough by SPG for a further piece by Trotman to be published in 1909, this time in the Society's main journal. It consists of extracts from a lecture Trotman gave in Whitby, entitled 'The Church's Message to Buddhists' and it focusses on God, the soul and sin. Again, the journal, *Buddhism*, and Ananda M's writings are pivotal to Trotman's argument. He calls Ananda M 'a thoughtful English Buddhist' and 'a learned Buddhist' but uses Ananda M's words on the reality of pain (*dukkha*), non-self (*anattā*) and the 'mental and moral progress' needed for the acceptance of Buddhism to argue for the superiority of Christianity and the inability of Buddhism to address 'the deeper thoughts of humanity' (Trotman 1909: 271–275).

The longest piece of writing Ananda M completed after his return to Burma was 'The Religion of Burma,' written for the previously mentioned *Twentieth Century Impressions of Burma*.[80] It is the first time he identifies himself publicly with the British imperial project. There were several reasons why Ananda M was asked to contribute to this publication and, more significantly, why he accepted. First, his main sponsors, the Hla Oung family, were part of the Rangoon elite, on good terms with the British authorities. May Oung wrote the chapter on 'Manners and Customs' in the book (May Oung 1910) and Daw Mya May features prominently, as previously mentioned. Second, Ananda M's contribution was placed within the 'Ecclesiastical' section, alongside Christian writers—the presence of Hinduism and Islam in Burma was not recognised. Ananda M was respected, but probably not understood, by Christian missionaries in Rangoon, but they would probably have supported the idea that he should write on Buddhism adjacent to their own representations of Christianity. As for Ananda M's acceptance, the Western-facing nature of the series would have attracted him. It was one more opportunity to convey 'the real nature of Buddhist Teaching' and to remove some 'of the immense burden of misunderstanding and misapprehension' with which Buddhism was saddled in the West (Ananda M 1911b: 5). Perhaps he saw it as a preparation for his anticipated manual.

It is worth examining what Ananda M selected at this point in his life for 'The Religion of Burma,' since the omissions are as significant as what he includes. In his introductory note to the accessible edition that was published by the *Buddhasāsana Samāgama* with the help of Annie Besant, he states that it should be regarded as 'altogether rudimentary' (Ananda M 1911b: 5). This, however, makes his selection even more important. He first makes the scandalously imperialistic distinction between the 'civilised' Buddhists of Upper and Lower Burma and the 'savage or semi-civilised tribes' in the remoter parts of the country (Ananda M 1910: 102). He then seeks to make sense of Buddhism's diversity, stressing that the Buddhism found in 'Burma, Ceylon and Siam' is 'the pure and original religion propounded by the Buddha' (Ananda M 1910: 103) and repeating that it should be called Theravada Buddhism (Ananda M 1910: 102), a point he had also made in 'Propaganda' (Ananda Metteyya 1908a: 175).[81] He then reiterates his view that Buddhism is 'the greatest product of Aryan thought' (Ananda M 1910: 103). The Burmese, at this point, therefore, are not praised for themselves but because they preserved Indian Aryan thought (Ananda M 1910: 104).

From this, Ananda M returns to the message of 'Animism and Law' (Ananda Maitriya 1902a), namely that at the heart of Buddhism is 'the principle of causation,' the 'law of karma,' which is totally in harmony with science. He then lists what Buddhism is not, echoing 'The Faith of the Future' (Ananda Maitriya 1903a). It is a religion without 'a god' and without the conception 'of a subtler and immortal spirit.' It is 'empty of prayer, yet giving to its followers the solace prayer so surely brings, void of all dogma, yet offering to the fullest extent the sense of surety which dogma brings to those who can accept it' and 'asking of its followers not faith but understanding' (Ananda M 1910: 104). He adds, in line with the letter we have previously cited, that there is no word equivalent to 'our "Buddhism" at all,' only the Dhamma, Truth, and the Law or Discipline. So he presents 'the religion of Burma' as 'Truth and Discipline,' with nothing to 'correspond to the creeds and sacraments' of the West (Ananda M 1910: 104), save for the three refuges or jewels, the 'Ti-ratana' (Skt. *Triratna*).

After this, he takes the *ti-ratana*—the Buddha, the *Dhamma* and the Sangha—one at a time. Under the first, he predictably links the achievement of Buddhahood with compassion and offers readers, in lyrical prose reminiscent of Edwin Arnold, a fairly standard orientalist Buddha biography up until the enlightenment, drawing on canonical and non-canonical traditions. It is the hold of this section of the Buddha biography over the minds of Burmese Buddhists, he stresses, that nurtures their intense devotion to the Buddha (Ananda M 1910: 109). At the end of this part, he again stresses that 'not one drop of blood' has been shed in Buddhism's name, adding that, 'To the Buddhist, that fact, did it stand alone, were proof beyond traversing of his religion's truth' (Ananda M 1910: 109). He evidently did not place the war between Japan and Russia in this category.

When outlining the *dhamma*, echoing 'On the Culture of Mind' (Ananda Maitriya 1902b), Ananda M begins with *Dhammapada* verse 183.[82] This time, however, he emphasises the first two clauses on ethical teaching rather than the last, with its focus on meditation. 'Avoiding evil' is explained in terms of the five and the eight precepts, and the activities of lay people on days of religious observance. All ethical training, he stresses, involves 'the beginning of self-restraint,' namely the giving up of actions that cause suffering to others (Ananda M 1910: 110). 'Cultivating good' is linked to *dāna*, generosity: 'charity in every sense of the word.' He describes this as 'the essence of love, which, like a magnet, grows but stronger the more it is employed in imparting its magnetism to other bars of steel' (Ananda M 1910: 110–111). He then idealistically praises the Burmese for the heights of their charity, which render poverty unknown in Burma, in contrast to the poverty of a London slum or an Indian village, which he sees as a curse on Western nations, breeding 'crime and cruelty' and starving 'even little children to death' (Ananda M 1910: 111).[83] The hardship present among non-Buddhist communities in downtown Rangoon is not mentioned.

When he reaches the last clause of verse 183, purification of the mind, Ananda M attempts, through scientific analogy, to explain *anattā*, 'non-self,' as holding within it the truth that all life is one. The term 'meditation' is not mentioned. Only then does he describe the Four Noble Truths as given in the Buddha's first sermon, explaining each element of the Noble Eightfold Path, and the goal—'the incomparable security of Nirvana' (Ananda M 1910: 114). When he comes to the elements connected with meditation, he explains *sammāsati* as 'right watchfulness,' namely watchfulness 'of all our mental operations,' and *sammāsamādhi* as 'right ecstasy,' saying only that this refers to methods of mental culture leading to 'various realms of conscious life' and 'Arahantship' (Ananda M 1910: 114). In this explanation, *kammaṭṭhāna* (subjects of meditation covered in commentaries such as the *Visuddhimagga*) and the *jhānas* (meditative absorptions/higher stages of consciousness) are implied but not named or explained. At this point, Ananda M does not see them as essential for his Western audience, in contrast to the Buddhist readership of 'On the Culture of Mind,' to whom he described mental culture in detail (Ananda Maitriya 1902b). Moral living and the lessening of selfishness were more important. In a similar way to the section on the Buddha, this part ends with an invitation to recognise truth:

> Enter, then, on this way of peace; enter it by self-restraint, by self-renunciation. Live, work, strive, no more for self but for pity of all life; so, by reforming yourself, may you help to relieve the pain of all, and bring your little wave of life to break at last upon the further shore. (Ananda M 1910: 114)

In the last part of the paper, he outlines the role of the monastic community, distinguishing it from the priesthood within 'theistic creeds' and taking a lived religion approach. Significantly, only in this context is 'the practice of Bhavana or meditation' specifically mentioned, albeit only with the claim that it was too large a subject to deal with.[84] Here, again, he states that a monk cannot ordain other monks until he has 'ten year's standing in the Order,' becoming a Thera, a point on which we know he diverges from Western monks such as Ñāṇatiloka. At the end, he speaks both of Buddhist revival in Burma, naming Ledi Sayadaw, and of his own mission to Britain, referring readers to the 'Secretary of the Buddhist Society of Great Britain and Ireland' (Ananda M 1910: 116). He also laments the effect of some aspects of 'Western civilisation' on the Burmese, most notably the introduction of alcohol. In a footnote, he draws attention to the 'cheap Manchester goods' that have all but killed the village weaving industry (Ananda M 1910: 116).[85]

In this article, Ananda M attempts to communicate what he feels the West needs to know about Buddhism, stressing rationality, ethics, social activism, compassion, non-violence, self-restraint, the letting go of selfishness, and the ultimate peace of 'Nirvana.' Significantly, he does not stress the practice of meditation, judging that the West does not need to know about it, or that the vocabulary connected with it is foreign and unknown, or that readers would dismiss it as esoteric or 'mysterious.' In his treatment of *anattā* (non-self), however, he implicitly conveys meditation's fruits. Themes that had been present throughout his time as a monk reappear, particularly Buddhism's non-violent character. Most significantly, he takes the opportunity to go beyond describing the Buddhism of Burma to inviting a Western response to it. The whole article expresses Ananda M's conviction that the message the West needs to hear if it is to avoid catastrophic consumerism, materialism and self-centredness is humanitarian and activist, involving the development of love, compassion and self-restraint. The development of higher planes of consciousness is important but not essential to this message, and could in fact deflect attention away from what might change Western society.

Annie Besant's visit, as previously mentioned, enabled an accessible version of 'The Religion of Burma' to be printed internationally and in Burma itself, although, as we explain in the last chapter, Besant made some editorial changes to make Ananda M's words more compatible with Theosophical thought.[86] In 1911–1912, Ananda M sent free copies of it to the Buddhist Society of Great Britain and Ireland, with the Society paying the carriage.[87] However, when he suggested that he should send 1500 copies of his anticipated 'handbook to Buddhism,' the following was minuted, demonstrating that boundaries between Theosophy and Buddhism were already being drawn in the West: 'It was agreed to accept the offer on condition that the book was not identified with Theosophy in any way.' The Society had no doubt noticed Besant's link with the version of 'An Outline of Buddhism or the Religion of Burma' sent to them.[88]

After this local publication of 'The Religion of Burma' in 1911, Ananda M's communication with the West and his links with Burmese associations weakened. In London, his name was mentioned less than that of Sīlācāra, who contributed much more than Ananda M to *The Buddhist Review* at this time. Additionally, in 1913, the Buddhist Society agreed to approach Sīlācāra to be spiritual adviser to its members and not Ananda M.[89] The Society's minutes do not record the outcome of this but rather suggest division of opinion, as previously described.[90] In 1914, however, after the Society had taken the tenancy of a property in 43 Penywern Road, Earls Court, London, they were hoping to welcome Sīlācāra. This is examined further in the next chapter.

ANANDA M'S REPUTATION DAMAGED BY TRIAL IN LONDON

While the difficulty of managing Ananda M's mission and his uncharismatic speaking style might account for some of the Buddhist Society's eventual reluctance to seek Ananda M's return, his associations with Theosophy, the Hermetic Order of the Golden Dawn and Aleister Crowley were also possible influences. These associations came to public attention through a legal case that highlighted Ananda M's prior association with Aleister Crowley, who, by 1910, had already garnered a dubious reputation, although he had not yet been dubbed the 'Wickedest Man in the World' by the yellow press.

The legal case arose when *The Looking Glass*, a British periodical, published, in October 1910, an article called 'An Amazing Sect.' The article discusses the first of a series of magical ceremonies that Crowley and his associates performed publicly at Caxton Hall in October and November, collectively called 'The Rites of Eleusis.' Each of these ceremonies, or rites, was an invocation related to an astrological 'planet,' such as the moon, the sun, Mercury, Venus or Jupiter. At the end of article, the reviewer writes:

> We leave it to our readers, . . . after reading our plain, unvarnished account of the happenings of which we were an actual eye-witness, to say whether this was not a blasphemous sect whose proceedings conceivably lend themselves to immorality of the most revolting character. (The Looking Glass 1910a: 142)

Two weeks later, *The Looking Glass* published a follow-up article, 'An Amazing Sect—No 2,' in which they detail the meaning of the rites and their symbolism. This includes the beginnings of a brief biography of Crowley. In part three, they continue their biography of Crowley, including his involvement with the Hermetic Order of the Golden Dawn, although they call it 'the Rosicrucian Order.' In a section headed 'By their friends Ye Shall Know Them,' the article notes two associates of Crowley—George Cecil Jones and Allan Bennett:

> Two of Crowley's friends and introducers are still associated with him; one, the rascally sham Buddhist monk, Allan Bennett, whose imposture was shown up in "Truth" some years ago; the other a person of the name of George Cecil Jones, who was for some time employed as [in] Basingstoke in metallurgy, but of late has had some sort of small merchant's business in the City. Crowley and Bennett lived together, and there were rumours of unmentionable

immoralities which were carried on under their roof. (The Looking Glass 1910b: 203)

The next section, 'An Exposure in "Truth,"' elaborates on the accusations against Ananda M made in *Truth* two years prior by U Dhammaloka. It also claims that Crowley and Bennett are thieves who stole money from a woman under a false pretext to pay for Bennett's trip to Ceylon, and that Ananda M's 'drug-taking to excess' is among his other 'vices.'

While we have no record of Ananda M discussing *The Looking Glass* articles, we can assume that members of the Buddhist Society alerted him to them, although there was nothing he could do, being both in Burma and restricted by the *Vinaya* from suing for libel. Crowley and Jones, however, could sue for libel; Crowley deferred but Jones pursued legal action.

The *Jones vs. The Looking Glass* suit went to trial in November 1910. The trial was widely covered in the London papers, with frequent republishing of the accusation that Bennett was a 'rascally sham Buddhist monk,' although most omitted the insinuation that Bennett and Crowley had a homosexual relationship. Within the trial itself, the fact that Crowley and Bennett refused to respond to the articles was taken as an admission of the truth of the accusations against them. When Jones was asked about the claims of U Dhammaloka, he repeatedly noted that the lawyer for *The Looking Glass* omitted reference to Ananda M's response.[91] Nevertheless, as proof of U Dhammaloka's bad reputation, Jones only had the statement of Buddhist Society members to go by, and these were quickly dismissed as friends of Bennett, who would be 'prejudiced' against U Dhammaloka. Jones lost the libel suit and the media coverage of it dramatically hurt Ananda M's standing with members of the Buddhist Society. This probably contributed to the Society's desire to find an alternative monk to Ananda M.

Just before the articles in *The Looking Glass* and the Jones libel trial verdict in April 1911, Crowley released the next issue of his magical periodical, *The Equinox*, in March, in which he republished, with only slight editorial changes, Ananda M's article 'On the Culture of Mind' (Ananda Maitrya 1902b), entitling it, as we have previously stated, 'The Training of the Mind' (Ananda Metteya 1911).

Despite the trial besmirching Ananda M's name, the 1911 issues of *The Buddhist Review* contain favourable references to him. For instance, Francis Payne, as editor, positively reviews 'An Outline of Buddhism or The Religion of Burma' (Payne 1911) and Ananda M's review of 'The Compendium of Philosophy' is included (The Buddhist Review 1911).

As for Ananda M's relationship with Crowley, the two had already drifted apart. Crowley was aware of his mentor's mission in London, and they may have met, but there is no indication there was significant interaction.⁹² If there had been, it would have likely been noted in Crowley's magical journals or been included in his autobiography, written a little over a decade after Bennett's mission. Instead, Crowley wrote an essay nostalgically relating events within their past interactions, including Bennett's involvement with the Golden Dawn, the invocation of the Spirit of the astrological planet Mercury named Taphthartharath, and how Bennett gave it all up to adopt 'the Yellow Robe' and 'the Begging-Bowl.' He concludes the essay praising Ananda M by saying that any serious person who is dissatisfied with faith and doubt should know 'that here is a Man who has passed through all the ways of death and life, a man who has torn the heart of Truth bleeding from the dead body of the Universe, who has known, who has attained' (Crowley 1908). This essay, connecting Ananda M to occultism during his mission, may have been an additional reason the Buddhist Society needed to reassure readers in 1909 that there was nothing esoteric or mysterious in what Ananda M taught.

Despite growing apart, Crowley always praised and looked up to Bennett. When he corresponded with an Australian student of occultism named Frank Bennett in 1910, Crowley asked if he was related to Allan.⁹³ In a series of letters Crowley wrote to various occult students in the 1940s, posthumously published with the title, *Magick Without Tears*, Bennett is a frequent topic.⁹⁴ Yet, the version of Bennett that Crowley describes is an Allan Bennett that fails to change or mature. Crowley's Bennett is stuck somewhere between 1897 and 1905, occupying the role of his unchanging magical teacher. While Allan Bennett assumed the role of a *bhikkhu* and struggled to spread the message of Buddhism, Crowley continued to see him through his occultist lens. Crowley's Bennett would forever be his 'white knight' in a yellow robe.⁹⁵

ANANDA M'S HEALTH CONTINUES TO DETERIORATE

Another reason for the Buddhist Society's side-lining of Ananda M was that he was an invalid by 1913. We have already mentioned the operation carried out in December 1911. The second of the operations mentioned by Cassius Pereira (Pereira 1923a: 6) was performed in December 1913 by Rost (Humphreys 1937: 33). Any improvement, however, was short-lived, and the burden on his sponsors would have become increasingly unsustainable,⁹⁶ not to mention the pain that Ananda M suffered. As Clifford Bax writes to Crowley in 1944, 'His liver was in a desperate condition, and of course he had violent asthma.'⁹⁷ Ethel Powell-Brown gives the following description of him at this time:

Our friend (Allan Bennett) was ill and suffering. When he appeared there showed an alarming change for the worse since our last visit. The skin that should have been white was yellow as a Burman's with jaundice. The arm that the monkish robe left bare was incredibly thin and from the bony shoulder the robe itself hung in gaunt and angular lines like the folded wings of an adjutant bird. But the black eyes under the up-tilted eyebrows were as burningly alive as ever and the words just as cordial.[98]

In 1914, therefore, according to Humphreys, the decision was taken that Ananda M should live with his sister in Lake County, California, a drier and less humid climate than Rangoon. Bax writes that 'Allan always said that he left Burma on account of his health.'[99] Correspondence connected with the Powell-Browns confirms and clarifies this picture. Ethel Powell-Brown writes in 1952 that 'It was my husband who initiated the move to get Allan Bennett sent home. He was undoubtedly very ill, and, I think, often under the influence of cocaine.'[100] A later letter by Ethel, this time to Gerald Yorke, states that, before he left Burma, Ananda M sent them a letter that 'was full of suspicion of everyone around him.' She adds, 'I think his mind was clouded by then by his painful illness and the drugs he used to alleviate it.'[101] She destroyed the letter but sent Yorke two others from Ananda M, written in May 1913, after Ananda M knew that Capt. Powell Brown would facilitate his journey to America.

Both of these letters offer insight into what was going on in Ananda M's troubled mind. To Ethel Powell-Brown, he states that his first letter of appeal to the Powell-Browns had been in the midst of 'horrible illness,' and mentions 'discoveries of a most serious kind' concerning a friend of Mrs. Powell-Brown. He urges her not to credit as true anything that the person told her about him and also shares that his health was improving after 'the last gall-stones-pass,' although the pain had been so severe that he had thought he could not pull through it. To Captain Powell-Brown, he expresses his deepest thanks for setting him free 'from the terrible state you found me in.' He speaks of being a prisoner when ill, of friends being kept away from him, of 'malevolent lies' being spread about him, of resources being stolen from his 'Samāgama' and of experiencing 'unspeakable agony of body and mind alike.' He also refers to a fund of money that had been made safe through Edwin Arnold's son, who worked at the *Rangoon Times* and had agreed to become a trustee of it.[102] He claims that Powell-Brown had literally saved his life, adding 'all I have or am is at your disposal.' His words to the couple make it quite clear that he was longing to leave Burma.[103]

It is very likely, therefore, that the drugs he took to curb the pain of both gallstones and asthma during a particularly severe bout of illness affected his perception of reality. Ethel Powell-Brown calls it 'a matter of some delicacy,' probably because one of the people he suspected, of reading his letters for instance, was Mrs. May Hla Oung, who had introduced the Powell-Browns to Ananda M.[104]

Powell-Brown headed a subscription list to raise money for Ananda M's passage, and Arnold 'asked for further help through his paper.'[105] Ananda M sailed to Plymouth, from where he travelled to Liverpool to meet his sister and niece before the passage to North America. According to Sankin Sayadaw and Humphreys, it was the fact that he travelled alone that necessitated him disrobing and leaving the monastic Sangha. If he had remained a *bhikkhu* on the journey, he would have been forced to break his monastic discipline by handling money (Humphreys 1937: 35; Mānitasirī and Nandamālābhivaṁsa 1972: 179), and this would have been an unacceptable violation of his monastic vows. In the end, however, and much by chance, he sailed on the same ship as the Powell-Browns, Captain Powell-Brown having failed to secure an earlier leave for himself.[106] Ethel Powell-Brown was later to write that they never saw him again, and her letters express sadness at this.[107] An intriguing notice in the journal *Light* suggests that the Buddhist Society for Great Britain and Ireland was expecting him. In January 1914, the journal published a list of the Society's lectures for the coming months. 'Ananda Metteyya' was due to give a talk on 'Buddhist Self-Culture' on 29 March, 1914 (Light 1914: ii). Yet, he would not arrive until May. It is possible that Ananda M had planned to come to England earlier, in better health, although it could just have been a typographical mistake.

5

In Britain

1914–1923

[W]hole days go by when I can do nothing, so wretched a physical inheritance did my parents give me. Ah, women, women—if they would think of the consequences when they summon so wantonly, a new creature into this world! (Ananda M to Clifford Bax, 1923; Bax 1933: 321)

Ananda M was 41 years old when he arrived in Plymouth in May 1914 and travelled to Liverpool, probably by train—the UK rail network was at its height in Edwardian Britain. According to Humphreys, he 'was altered beyond belief.' Humphreys quotes an unnamed 'friend,' who remarked that the former *bhikkhu* 'was a bent and shambling figure with an unkempt shock of hair, in a badly cut, badly fitting coat and trousers' (Humphreys 1937: 35).[1] His Western clothes had no doubt been sewn in Burma, rather badly, after he realised that his need to handle money on the voyage necessitated the traumatic decision that he disrobe. Further attacks of asthma may also have occurred on the voyage, aggravated by a worsening stoop. Yet, in contrast to this picture, Ethel Powell-Brown writes retrospectively of the voyage that 'A number of passengers came up to ask questions about the Bhikkhu and to tell me what a remarkable knowledge he had displayed in conversation with them.'[2]

The plan was that Ananda M should wait for his sister in Liverpool and sail with her back to America in September. According to Humphreys, he stayed with 'various members of the local branch' of the Buddhist Society of Great Britain and Ireland (Humphreys 1937: 35).[3] The anonymous writers of a later appeal for Ananda M are more exact, stating that he was hosted by 'two members' of the Branch (X. Y. Z. 1916: 217). There was optimism at this point, since Ananda M's future seemed to be secure, with his sister in California. Things did not go to plan. In July 1914, Edward Greenly appeals to the Buddhist Society 'in the sad case of Ananda Metteyya,' the Society responding with a £5 grant to help his supporters in Liverpool.[4]

The very fact that this appeal refers to 'Ananda Metteyya,' however, rather than 'Allan Bennett,' and that Ethel Powell-Brown still calls him a 'bhikkhu' in her memories of the voyage, suggests that British Buddhists were unwilling to see him as a lay person. To coincide with his arrival, *The Buddhist Review* published Ananda M's article on 'Buddhist Self Culture' (Ananda Metteya 1914) under the name 'Ānanda Metteyya Thera.' In October 1914, an intriguing letter from Greenly was read to the board of the Buddhist Society, denying that Ananda M had 'left the Order,' although a concurrent letter from the President, Edmund Mills, considered that he had.[5] Having disrobed for the voyage, Ananda M could not have worn robes again without a further ordination, and this was not possible in Britain. What was true, however, was that Ananda M did not jettison his inner monastic demeanour. Mentally and emotionally, he remained a monk, which is why he continued to style himself, Ananda M, the name we will continue to use.[6] In practical terms also, he remained a renunciate, since he had no independent source of income and had to be supported financially by others. As this chapter demonstrates, several of those who came to know him well in the final years of his life continued to see him as a *bhikkhu* or a 'yogi' or even a saint (Bax 1933: 273). To Mrs. Green, his landlady when he moved to London, he was simply a 'kind' man who never gave any trouble (Bax 1933: 325), although a later account goes further, claiming that one of his London landladies had said, 'Just like a saint, he is. . . . never seen the like of it' (Bax 1951 164). Others, however, saw him as prematurely old, with disabling chronic illness, living in relative poverty.

Whilst he waited for his sister, World War I broke out. Great Britain entered the conflict on 4 August, 1914 with its declaration of war on Germany.[7] Liverpool, at this point, was a global trading hub, the maritime heart of Britain and 'the second city of the Empire,' dealing with 30% of Britain's imports and exports (Russell 2018: 28), its wealth advertised through monumental architecture and a world-famous waterfront.[8] The first impact of the war on the city was an influx of refugees from Belgium (Russell 2018: 23),[9] although 6 August saw the first deaths of Liverpool seamen on a cruiser that ran into a minefield (Russell 2018: 31). Liverpool's port status meant that recruitment to the navy for the war effort was immediate and considerable. Recruitment to the army began at the end of August at the large St George's Hall in the centre of the city and, within five days, 3,000 had signed up, in one of 'the most successful and earliest recruitment campaigns' in the country (Russell 2018: 42–43). Enlistment for many was an escape from poverty and unemployment. Despite the city's commercial wealth, the docks were run on poorly paid, casual labour. Liverpool's slums were at least as miserable as those in Rangoon, and the poverty within them was the seedbed of racism and brutality, together with sectarianism between Roman Catholics and Protestants (Lees 2011: 120–125). The Association of Religious Agencies in Liverpool, for instance, founded in the late nineteenth century, aimed only to bring together 'the Protestant and Evangelical Religious Agencies in Liverpool and neighbourhood,' which included philanthropic organisations but not Roman Catholic bodies.[10]

The sight of the city mobilising for war with an almost euphoric enthusiasm would have further affected Ananda M's health and state of mind, given his antipathy to violence. He would later say that the war 'was the most cruel and terrible calamity that the individualistic greed of man ever in history has succeeded in inflicting upon himself' (Bennett 1923: x).

On 12 September, 1914, Ananda M went to the Liverpool docks to sail for America. It was then that 'the tragedy' occurred (Humphreys 1937: 35). His passage was refused by the ship's doctor, who feared that the state of his health would mean a denial of entry to the United States by the American Immigration Authorities (X. Y. Z. 1916: 217; Humphreys 1937: 35–36). Sister and brother met for the first time in many years. Also, for the first time, Ananda M met his niece, Alexandra Leslie.[11] The pain caused by Ananda M's inability to travel onwards, not only to the two relatives but also to those who had given hospitality to him, is hard to imagine. The small Liverpool Branch of the Buddhist Society was left with a prematurely old man, albeit with a gentle and compassionate nature, who was penniless, ill and homeless. According to *The Buddhist Review*, at this moment of crisis, Ananda M was taken in by 'a third member of the Liverpool branch, a medical man' (X. Y. Z. 1916: 217). His name was Dr. Leonard Youatt. He was married to Hannah Edith Faraday Youatt (neé Whitaker), great-great niece of Michael Faraday, the well-known scientist of electromagnetism and electrochemistry. With five children, they lived on the outskirts of Liverpool, in Prescot, Youatt working for at least some of this time at Oakdene Hospital in nearby Rainhill. He and his wife cared for Ananda M for at least three years.[12]

We have little information about Ananda M at this time. A twentieth-century, independent scholar and artist who worked on Ananda M, Jean Pemberton (neé Bell), traced a female member of the Youatt family and visited her with her husband, Tom Pemberton. Jean had died by the time we started our work, but her husband wrote, 'Sadly the lady, who was a young girl at the time, had only vague memories of an ill, old man whose arrival had meant the children of the family sharing a bedroom and a growing atmosphere of concern and worry surrounding his presence.'[13]

This was probably Marjorie or Norah Youatt, Dr. Youatt's youngest daughters, who were around 14 at the time Ananda M came to stay with the family. Jean also heard that no one was willing to 'take personal or financial responsibility' for Ananda M, save for the host family,[14] which was also giving him 'incessant medical care' (X. Y. Z. 1916: 218). At some point, 'an attempt was made to get him to America by means of the United States Embassy' but the war 'frustrated' this, since his brother-in-law had re-joined the British army, being awarded the temporary rank of Captain (X. Y. Z. 1916: 218).

If Ananda M had travelled into the centre of Liverpool whilst in Prescot, he would have witnessed the growth of eight munitions factories in the city, staffed by women (Russell 2018: 59), and incessant fund-raising activities for the war and charities connected with it. The rising death toll on the front would not have escaped him either. After conscription was introduced in 1916, he might also have been aware of the discrimination experienced by conscientious objectors, some being imprisoned (Russell 2018: 109). We have found no record of him lecturing on Buddhism at this time, probably because of illness. It came to the point in 1916 when asthma attacks were occurring 'more than once a day,' brought on 'even by crossing the room' (X. Y. Z. 1916: 218). That Liverpool was located within the damper and wetter part of Britain might have worsened his condition.

By 1916, the Youatts had come to the end of what they could tolerate financially and emotionally. The money refunded from the shipping company for the passage to the United States did not last long. Their sons and daughters were 'just going out into life' (X. Y. Z. 1916: 218) and needed resources from their parents. Leonard and Hannah's oldest daughter, Gwen, was 20, and the oldest son, Brian Dinsdale, was 18. World War I was also tearing at the economic heart of Liverpool, with the price of commodities, especially medical supplies, considerably inflated.

In this context, a group of anonymous well-wishers published an appeal for money to maintain Ananda M with the level of medication he needed. They state that Mrs. Hla Oung had offered £10 per year towards his maintenance, but stress that that was not enough and that Ananda M might have to be placed 'in some institution supported by public charity' if funds were not found (X. Y. Z. 1916: 218). The most notorious of these in Liverpool would have been the Brownlow Hill Workhouse, a town within a town, where the destitute were forced to work for no pay and poor food (Lees 2011: 85). They continue:

> In any case, we appeal for a sum of money to reimburse the generous friend who has done so much. He ought not to have to bear

expense when he is already giving housing and the constant care of a patient. Yet he has already spent far more than he can properly afford. Towards this several friends have now contributed about £8, and another member of the Liverpool Branch has given, in three instalments, a sum of £50.

To raise the remainder, about £40, we appeal to the members of the Buddhist Society of Great Britain and Ireland, a society which owes its existence to the movement which was started and long carried on by the ex-thera. We appeal to all, whether in West or East, who take an interest in the movement for making known the Buddhist teachings in the West. And finally, we appeal to all who have themselves profited by the ex-thera's own writings—writings that express in such a high degree his genius, energy and devotion. (X. Y. Z. 1916: 218–219)

Help did come, from Asia and the West, which meant that Ananda M did not have to suffer the indignity of a public institution.[15] Kenneth Mullen suggests that he stayed in Liverpool throughout the war and came to London only in 1920 (Mullen 1989: 92). This is unlikely. Ananda M himself writes that he came to London 'during the earlier and terrible years of the Great War' (Bennett 1923: v). Brown claims it was 1916 without citing his source (Brown 2023: 93). This, however, would accord with the anonymous appeal, which implies that Ananda M was still in Liverpool in 1916 (X. Y. Z. 1916: 217–218). In 1916, we also know that Ananda M's sister, Charlotte, sailed from the United States to Liverpool with her daughter and from there travelled to Bath, where she lived until 1919, whilst her husband served in the British army.[16] They would have met during this time but, according to the 'appeal,' she was unable to offer accommodation to Ananda M because she was staying 'with friends' (X. Y. Z. 1916: 218).

It is not until 1918 that Ananda M can definitely be placed in London, where he rented a 'small, dingy room' in Lavender Hill, Battersea, from a female landlord, a Mrs. Green, and her companion, who lived below him (Bax 1933: 274). The address according to his death certificate was 90 Eccles Road, within easy reach of Clapham Common and Clapham Junction railway station, which had made that part of London a major commuter centre. Interestingly, it was the general area in which Ananda M and his sister had lived after their mother died. Eccles Road lay in Booth's category of the 'fairly comfortable—good, ordinary earnings' (Booth 1889).

The reason for his move from Liverpool to London was probably to help the Buddhist Society of Great Britain and Ireland and to relieve the pressure on the Youatt family. Just as the war was beginning, the Society

Figure 5.1 90 Eccles Road, Clapham Junction, courtesy of the Sri Saddhatissa International Buddhist Centre, London.

optimistically rented a house on a 14-year lease (with a break at the end of five years) at 43 Penywern Road, Earls Court.[17] By October 1914, with the lease of the house complete, the Society agreed that they should welcome Sīlācāra.[18] There is no evidence, however, that he came, although it is probable that he intended to. After all, the *Rangoon College Magazine* reported in 1913 that Sīlācāra had not given any lectures because he was preparing to leave the country (Rangoon College Magazine 1914). In 1914, he was living in Tumlong near the Tibetan border (Hecker and Ñāṇatusita 2008: 41–42).

Without a resident monk, it soon became clear that the house was too far from the centre of London to be regularly used. Suggestions that local societies could also make use of it were turned down (Humphreys 1937: 38). As the war continued, *The Buddhist Review* became intermittent and reduced in size, hit by the inflated cost of printing and reduced revenue (Ananda M 1920a: 181–182).[19] The Society's weekly meetings were maintained, held together by the Secretary and Treasurer, Frank E. Balls, with the help of Francis Payne, but with a reduced number of attendees, sometimes with none at all (Ananda M 1920a: 181). Publicly advertised 'Buddha Day' or Vesak celebrations, however, continued each May,[20] and Payne gave a series of lectures early in 1917 (Humphreys 1937: 39).

Ananda M addressed the Society at Vesak (May) 1918, 10 years after his 1908 mission. Humphreys calls it 'a fighting speech' that gave fresh enthusiasm to his listeners (Humphreys 1968: 14). Yet, it was more pastoral than 'fighting.' It was an intimate talk to 'a handful of followers' (Ananda M 1918: 144), whilst war continued. May 1918 was not long after the devastatingly brutal second battle of the Somme, in which a total of over 400,000 men died. At the beginning of the presentation, therefore, Ananda M spoke both of the crisis through which the Buddhist Society was passing and the war, in which he saw 'the apparent triumph of Force over Reason, of Hate over Truth and Love, of heartless Greed over the heart's greatest trait—true Charity' (Ananda M 1918: 142). Using Buddhist narratives, he then encouraged his audience to see beyond the death toll and stressed that their very presence that day meant that, in former lives, they must have known Buddhism. With a quiet gentleness of expression, he pointed them to the Buddhist path, which involved realising the hard truth of suffering and finding the interior 'Heart's Kingdom,' where compassion and 'Love' had the capacity to embrace the whole world. Significantly, with typical humility, he placed himself on an equal plane with his listeners as among those 'who have even the earlier stages of the Holy Path still all before us,' with a gulf between the present and 'the final great Attainment' (Ananda M 1918: 145–147). Towards the end, with autobiographical vividness, perhaps betraying that he saw his own death as close, he stated:

> When, then, the dark clouds of the sad world's dreaming gather around us; when grief and pain assail us; when poverty fills our lives with squalid care; when the vast agony of life about us grips our hearts well-nigh to suffocation; even when death itself draws near; in each and every bitter circumstance of life we can find solace and new inspiration in the Law our Master left. (Ananda M 1918: 147)

When the talk was published in *The Buddhist Review*, the Editor, D. B. Jayatilaka, referred to Ananda M in a footnote as 'Thera Ananda Mettaya,' not as 'Ex-Thera,' evocatively implying that, although he wore lay clothes, he was still living the life of a *bhikkhu* and deserved the title, Thera, and his monastic name (Ananda M 1918: 141). Ananda M took over the editorship of the review from Jayatilaka at the end of 1918, his first editorial being in 1920, following a gap of two years in the publishing of the *Review* (Ananda M 1920a). It is significant that, again, this issue refers to Ananda M as 'Ananda Metteyya,' not Allan Bennett,[21] although a report in the same issue of a Buddhist meeting, at which Ananda M spoke about 'the inner vitalising flame' of Buddhism, cites him as 'Mr Allan Bennett, formerly the Thera Ananda Metteyya' (The Buddhist Review 1920a: 213–216). The journal *Light*, when advertising a talk on 'Kamma' to be given by Ananda M at the Buddhist Society's headquarters on 6 April, 1919, however, again refers to him as 'Ananda Metteyya' (Light 1919: iii).

Cassius Pereira states that Ananda M resumed 'his self-appointed work in London with the help of Clifford Bax' (Pereira 1923a: 6). Bax (1886–1962) was a playwright, journalist and free-thinker, with independent wealth, who, during the war, was working night shifts at Whitehall on news censorship (Bax 1933: e.g., 283). As a young man, he had played chess with Crowley in Switzerland and had joined the Theosophical Society (Evans 1927: 121; Bax 1933: 44–46, 120). During this phase, he had chaired one of Ananda M's meetings during his 1908 mission (Bax 1933: 271) and had joined the Buddhist Society of Great Britain and Ireland, having recently started a journal, *Orpheus*, which sought to revitalise the arts through Theosophy (Bax 1933: 146). He resigned from the Buddhist Society in October 1909.[22] He met Ananda M again through the Egyptologist Battiscombe Gunn (1883–1950), who had joined and left Theosophy, and his wife, Meena, who was a friend of Bax (Bax 1933 271–276; 1951: 164).[23] Ananda M's link with the Gunns could have been due to Battiscombe Gunn's former involvement both with Theosophy and the Golden Dawn. By 1905, for instance, Gunn was moving in 'circles associated with the former members of the order [Golden Dawn],' eventually becoming involved with a faction of the old movement, 'the Independent and Rectified Rite,' founded by Arthur Waite in 1903 (Vinson and Gunn 2014: 100–101). From 1912, Crowley was using him as a 'scholarly consultant' (Vinson and Gunn 2014: 103). By the time he met Ananda M, however, it is likely that he was losing interest in occultism, concentrating on his already considerable reputation as an Egyptologist.

Gunn invited Bax to meet Ananda M at Gunn's home in August 1918 and, from this point, Bax helped Ananda M find a voice beyond the Buddhist Society. Bax's description of Ananda M in 1918 sheds light on how he appeared then to persons such as Bax, eager to learn more about Buddhism, the context of the 1908 lecture forgotten. While they were shaking hands, he states that he felt 'as though something long-prepared had happened at last,' and continues:

> He was tall, but his constant ailments had left him with a stoop. His hands were long and were pleasant to touch. When he spoke, I remembered that a musical voice is said to be always an attribute of the *yogi*. In 1908, when I saw him first, he had worn his yellow robe and his head had been shaven. Now, in 1918, he was wearing European clothes, and his thick hair was so fine in texture and so intensely black that any one must have recognised its beauty.

> His face was the most significant that I have seen. Twenty years of physical suffering had twisted and scored it: a lifetime of meditation upon universal love had imparted to it an expression that was unmistakable. His colour was almost dusky, his mouth firm but in-sunken like that of an old man, and his eyes had the soft glow of dark amber. At first glance I realised that he never could have played at being a man of mystery. Indeed, he thought nothing of himself. He had passed, I believe, through experiences of more importance than those of any man in England, but he regarded them as early milestones on a road which all men, in the end, must travel. Above all, at the moment of meeting and always thereafter, I was conscious of a tender and far-shining emanation, an unvarying psychic sunlight, that environed his personality. (Bax 1933: 285)[24]

In this account, Bax calls Ananda M 'the Bhikkhu,' as the Gunns had done when they first mentioned him to Bax (Bax 1933: 271).[25] The conversation at the house of the Gunns focussed on *anattā* (non-self), with Bax and the Gunns struggling to understand Ananda M. It then moved to remembering past lives, or, as Ananda M put it, 'a life that has a special connection with the life in which you now find yourself involved' (Bax 1933: 289). Ananda M spoke about training the memory, as he had done in 'On the Culture of Mind' (Bax 1933: 289). When questioned further, he stressed that to remember in this way was a 'horrible' experience, 'like being forced to eat a banquet when you have already eaten your fill,' adding that it was 'one of the surest ways of realising—realising "in your bones"—that everything is impermanent, and that to exist is to suffer' (Bax 1933: 290; 1951: 164). Pressed further on *anattā*, Ananda M turned the traditional simile of a chariot into the simile of a car.[26] None of the parts of a car can be 'called the car.' Only when the parts are combined is it a car. Likewise, only when the different parts of a person are interconnected is there a person.

This description shows Ananda M gently explaining Buddhist doctrines in a personal, domestic context, within which he was evidently comfortable and relaxed. When Meena asked him to explain nirvana, he replied, 'Explain it, my dear? That is not possible' (Bax 1933: 294). Nevertheless, he used the simile that, for him, was now most useful, that of the splitting of a 'radio-active atom' (Bax 1933: 294–295). Then, he spoke of love, 'The great dissolvent [of the self] is love. True love is a union of the perceiver with the perceived.... and so it is that when our seeming selves are "blown out" ... something immeasurable and indescribable is released, as it were, and, as it were, takes their place' (Bax 1933: 294). This was core to his thought and experience at this point. Bax ends his description with this:

> Whenever he talked about Buddhism, whenever he "expounded the Dhamma," a great force took possession of his frail tortured body, and it was as though something mightier than the mind of any man were directed upon the thoughts of his collocutor. As a Buddhist, he was an alert and powerful personality; as a poor man, dwelling unknown in London, he was a sick creature prematurely old. "Lets go to the bus with him," said Gunn, and, while I was agreeing to do so, I saw Bennett putting on his overcoat, and heard Meena Gunn saying, "Why it's riddled with moths," and Bennett responding, "They're such pretty little things," and Meena continuing, "Some day we must get you a new one; this coat is too full of holes," and Bennett answering, shy of his pun, "But, you see, I'm supposed to be a holy man." (Bax 1933: 296)

At the bus stop, Ananda M invited Bax to visit him and Bax did so, once or twice a month at least until the winter of 1919. Through Bax's memoirs, a picture of him in Battersea emerges. His 'worldly goods' were 'two wicker chairs, a washing basin, a camp-bed, a number of books and reviews, neatly stacked on the floor, and a Burmese Buddha' on the mantelpiece. And the counterpane on his bed was moth-eaten (Bax 1933: 300). But generosity existed in his 'penury.' He always provided Bax with 'two fancy *gateaux*' (cakes) with his cup of tea (Bax 1933: 300). His one luxury, according to Bax, was 'an occasional packet of cigarettes' (Bax 1951: 164).

After many conversations about Buddhism, Bax persuaded Ananda M to give a series of lectures in his 'studio,' namely his apartment in Edwardes Square, Kensington, to an invited audience in the winter of 1919–1920. Ananda M later claims the lectures were written in the winter of 1917–1918 before being delivered in lecture form (Bennett 1923: vii) but Bax corrects this (Bax 1933: 300; 1951: 164) and indeed 1919–1920, for the delivery of the lectures, accords better with the timeline outlined above.

The audience would have consisted mainly of Bax's friends from the artistic world, steeped in but critical of Britain's Christian culture and perhaps proud of their interest in alternative spiritualities. Bax calls them 'an odd mixture' (Bax 1951: 165). Ananda M, therefore, included more references to Christianity than he would have done with Asian audiences, and more implicit references to Theosophy, particularly the soul concept. Although it is impossible to know whether Theosophists were present, it is highly likely that some were. This, together with the war, gave a new feel to his thought.

The first lecture was given on 4 November, 1919 at 9.00 p.m., with Ananda M reading his texts by candlelight. The effort needed for Ananda M to reach Bax's studio is glimpsed in Bax's description of his arrival:

> I heard the distressing sound of some one who had halted, half-way up the stairs, in a paroxysm of coughing. I went out. "It's all right," gasped the Bhikkhu, and caught my arm. "In there!" he groaned, staggering towards the kitchen. I switched the light on. I have never seen any man in a more lamentable condition. For two or three minutes he remained motionless, huddled up with closed eyes. Nothing less than his life-long devotion to Buddhism could have inspired him to make that journey. By degrees he recovered his equanimity. (Bax 1933: 313)

Later, Bax adds to this, saying that in the kitchen he restored himself 'by an injection of heroin,' adding 'no man wanted it less or needed it more' (Bax 1951: 165). By the time Bax's guests arrived, Ananda M was able to speak 'with the whole force and beauty of his personality' (Bax 1933: 317). He made the journey six times. Bax also records, using language familiar to Theosophists:

> While the Bhikku delivered his essays a mysterious sense of grandeur pervaded the room, making me understand how great a heightening of soul must have happened to those who spent some time with the noblest of all earth-visitants, the Christ and the Buddha. When I mentioned this experience to Ananda M., he answered, 'It is said to happen always if a priest is sincerely expounding the *Dhamma*. It has very little to do with the priest himself.' (Bax 1951: 165)

The lectures were published in 1923 before Ananda M's death, with an extensive introduction by Ananda M, inviting some publicity in the British press.[27] As we have already mentioned, Ananda M, almost immediately, on 2 February, sent a copy to Cassius Pereira, who logged it into his collection on 6 March. Pereira started to write comments in the margins, reaching page 20–the end of the first lecture. They include 'Rot,' 'gibberish' and 'pure Pantheism.'[28] Did this 'new feel' in his lectures warrant such a negative appraisal, from a friend who had supported him throughout his life and would continue to do so? The *Times Literary Supplement*'s verdict was also negative. After stating that Bennett sees Buddhism as the only cure for the West's individualism, the reviewer, Garnet Smith, makes his own judgement on Buddhism, stating that its 'code' is 'lacking in something,' verging towards a philosophy of despair (Smith 1923: 334).

THE CONTENT OF THE BAX STUDIO LECTURES, 1919–1920

The lectures were carefully but not unexpectedly sequenced, with Ananda M leaving until last the doctrines he believed were most difficult for Westerners. His method, though, was the same as he had used in the first issue of *Buddhism*, namely to challenge stereotypes. Ananda M's introduction to the later publication states that his anticipated audience were those who were 'weary of agnosticism' but could not accept Christianity (Bennett 1923: vii), which he describes as a failed, self-contradictory religion (Bennett 1923: xii-xv). Again, Buddhism is held out as the only force that can stop modern civilisation collapsing through individualism (Bennett 1923: vii-xii), as the Roman Empire had collapsed (Bennett 1923: xxii-xxiv). Drawing on evolutionary theory, he unsurprisingly stresses the need to understand 'Life as One,' arguing that 'this world system' has a future if its elements could realise this truth 'in one perfected symbiosis' (Bennett 1923: xxi-xxii). His hope, therefore, was that a 'mutation' in evolution was possible, if human beings really sought to transform their minds.

To pass to the lectures themselves, the Buddha came first ('The Source of the Teaching: The Buddha and his Attainment;' Bennett 1923: 1-20) and the stereotype contested was that Buddhism was simply a philosophy rather than 'a living, breathing Truth; a mighty power able to sweep whomsoever casts himself wholeheartedly into its great stream, far and beyond the life we know and live' (Bennett 1923: 7). To create a bridge with his audience and to evoke the difference he had frequently mentioned between textual and lived Buddhism, Ananda M began with an almost mystical experience. He invited his audience to imagine the 'Oneness' that could be felt when, alone at night 'beneath a moonless, star-lit sky,' one might realise that the whole cosmos is part 'of that same miracle of Life which throbs and surges in our own veins' and hear 'the murmur of the star's high silences, breathing at last the Word that answers all the mystery, that justifies all the awful suffering of life'—the 'unparalleled and impassionate *sacrifice* which pervades existence' (Bennett 1923: 1-3). His next step was to contrast this with the different quality of 'waking to the sunlight.' The Buddha, he argued, embodied a hundredfold the contrast between the two experiences. He had read books about Buddhism, he explained, but this for him had been the starlight. It was only when he went to Asia that he had experienced the 'Sun of the Teaching' (Bennett 1923: 6). In Ceylon and Burma, he had seen it penetrating everything as a 'vivid, potent living force'; 'the very air' had seemed 'vital with the urge of it' (Bennett 1923: 7). He stressed the difficulty of communicating this to the West, adding that he saw no 'greater work' than doing so. He then turned to his long-standing conviction that Buddhism was the 'culmination' of the long religious history of the 'Aryan race' (Bennett 1923: 9), and that Christianity was no longer suited for 'western peoples, save the least intelligent.' He sketched the history of this, drawing on the Theosophical concept of 'root-races'—'of all the various great root-races that have successively appeared on earth there can be no doubt as to the intellectual and moral supremacy of the Aryan race' (Bennett 1923:11). He then outlined the history of the Aryan 'race' and its two branches, Eastern and Western, until the time of the Buddha, echoing material he had used and would use again. The task he then set himself was to communicate 'the incomparable nature of His [the Buddha's] spiritual Attainment' and his 'personality,' pointing his readers to *The Light of Asia* for the biography (Bennett 1923: 16). There was a spiritual sacrifice, he stressed, but it was 'so great, so utterly beyond our ken, that we can only try to dimly represent it in terms of human life and thought and action.' The most important point, however, was that the Buddha 'after six hard years of wandering' discovered that the way of liberation from interminable suffering in repeated lives was not through 'ever-intensifying states of spiritual self-hood,' as in Brahmanism, but through seeing that 'Only *where Self is not*' can 'the Way' be found (Bennett 1923: 18–19).

This almost mystical beginning, Ananda M's rather romantic representation of the Buddha, and his stress on oneness and unity, might well have struck Cassius Pereira as extreme, in spite of Pereira's own defence of Buddhist devotion. Yet, it represents an important part of Ananda M's experience, both of Buddhism and Burma. In spite of U Dhammaloka's criticism that Ananda M 'recognised only the "Buddhism" created in European texts' (Turner, Cox and Bocking 2020: 143), this lecture sets Ananda M apart from those Western Buddhists who downplayed devotion and lived Buddhism, in the conviction that Buddhism was essentially a philosophy, embedded in texts.

The second lecture was entitled 'The Fundamental Principle: The Universal Reign of Law' (Bennett 1923: 21–41), a familiar theme for Ananda M since 'Animism and Law' in 1902 (Ananda Maitriya 1902a). It enabled him to balance the evocative and emotional nature of the first lecture with a stress on reason, science, and the dangers of some forms of mysticism and meditation. Yet, he again began with an illustration from nature, namely the cycle in lotus flowers from the decay of the seed to the growth of the flower, which mirrored the potential for human 'inner spiritual dawning,' after the death of 'our own cherished self-desires' (Bennett: 1923: 22). The heart of the lecture, however, was 'the nature of the Power' that the Buddha saw behind all phenomena and the 'spiritual universe'—'*Karma*—the Law ... of action' (Bennett 1923: 24). He prefaced this with a methodological note, namely that the Buddha had encouraged everyone to use their reason 'to investigate every statement,' even those that had been ascertained by insight, in order to prevent the drawing of false, egocentric conclusions from spiritual experiences such as attaining the first *jhāna*. He downplayed his own achievements in this field for similar reasons.[29] Yet, he did evoke his scientific experimentation in Burma, knowing that this would appeal to the Theosophists and freethinkers present, by suggesting that science would eventually be able to measure thought as vibration. As for the 'Law of Karma,' it was presented, as in his other writings, as compatible with science in its stress on causality, in contrast to systems that relied on 'some great *living Being or beings*' (Bennett 1923: 35). However, there was also a new thrust, in that he encouraged his listeners to see themselves as a 'manifestation' of karma and to grasp that understanding this was 'the most important thing in all the world for us to know' (Bennett 1923: 36–37).

The stereotype to be contested in this lecture was that Buddhism was selfish, an accusation beloved by Christians. So, he stressed that, although 'the Buddhist' is instructed in self-improvement, the ultimate aim of this was 'the betterment of life at large' (Bennett 1923: 37), which was reflected, for example, in the Asian Buddhist practice of transferring the merit of their actions to 'the whole universe of life' (Bennett 1923: 38).

The third lecture, 'The Buddhist World-View: The Three Signata' (Bennett 1923: 42–61), moved into a field Ananda M knew Western minds found difficult, namely *anicca* (impermanence), *dukkha* (unsatisfactoriness or pain) and *anattā* (non-self). Here, he gave one of his most complex, even tedious, explanations of his repeated statement, 'All life is One.' He appealed to scientific evidence for the indestructibility of force and a radical interdependence between all that exists, evoking Theosophical conviction: 'All the great universe thrills in answer to every movement of each living thing in each of all those countless islets of its life' (Bennett 1923: 47). Only then did he move to the three characteristics of existence, presenting them as '*conditions*' (italics: Ananda M's) of the Law of Karma and as so inherent within all existence that only a Latin word was appropriate—*Signatum* (that through which existence is signified; Bennett 1923: 50–51). They also represented truths that the human mind most resisted because of its craving for the permanent. Everything was impermanent, he stressed, even empires and the farthest stars and nebula (Bennett 1923: 53–54). When he reached *anattā*, he translated it as

'Unreality' (Bennett 1923: 57). It is worth quoting him in full, because it shows him most probably reaching out to the Theosophists in the audience. The result was that he gave his most Theosophist-friendly version, whilst at the same time offering a critique:

> I have preferred to translate it Unreality, for the idea is that there is not, as our inmost hopes would teach us, an ultimate and enduring Reality connected with this Self which we imagine to stand in the centre of our beings. The Buddhist idea is rather that so long as there remains even a vestige of that concept of the enduring self; so long as we look to any form of enselfed life whatsoever, howsoever subtle and exalted, we cannot reach that Further Shore of Life, which we Buddhists term Nirvāna. Self, and the thought of Self is, from the Buddhist point of view, the supreme obstacle to the attainment of Enfranchisement, Nirvāna, Arhanship, or Sainthood; and just as the Infinite can be said in no wise to have any part in the world of finite things, so we understand the Beyond of Life can have no part in any such life as this enselfed existence that we know. Rather we might put it that it is just our Selves—or the wrong concept of them, rather—which *because* they limit, stand between the life we ensoul, so to speak, and its enfranchisement in Nirvāna, in Sainthood, or Buddhahood. (Bennett 1923: 57)

The first part of this account would be used after his death to support a Theosophist reading of the self in a publication of the Buddhist Lodge in London, as described in the next chapter.

Only in the fourth lecture did Ananda M pass to the Four Noble Truths, in contrast to his 1901 Colombo lecture with its almost entirely Buddhist audience ('The Four Aryan Truths;' Bennett 1923: 62–81). Stressing that the Truths did not attempt to address the 'unanswerable Why—only the How of life' (Bennett 1923: 66), he suggested that they could seem 'trite' 'at first acquaintance.' His representation of them was uncontroversial and referred back to previous lectures. Yet, when explaining the first truth of *dukkha*, his main emphasis was the importance of compassion—'suffering by sympathy' and learning to live unselfishly 'for this piteous, suffering Life alone' (Bennett 1923: 70). He presented the second truth, that our suffering was caused by 'Self-desire,' as almost self-evident. When he reached the Eightfold Path, he sidestepped the normative contemporary classification of the path into morality, meditation and wisdom to focus on body, speech and thought. The components connected with the body, '*Right Action* and *Right Mode of Life*' were the first to be 'perfected,' followed by 'Right Speech' and then the rest, which were connected with thought (Bennett 1923: 74). *Sammāsati* and *sammāsamādhi* were translated respectively as 'Right Recollectedness' and, significantly, 'Right High Attainment,' with the qualification that there were no direct translations into English. He later translated *samādhi* more normatively as 'concentration' (Bennett 1923: 77). What came next went further than 'On the Culture of Mind' (Ananda Maitriya 1902b). '*Sati*,' he explained, implied a 'continued watchfulness' that was able to 'make the flame of the mind burn steadily' and *samādhi* was the intense 'interior concentration' that opened the gate to 'the inner, higher, mental realms' (Bennett 1923: 77).[30] In contrast to 'The Religion of Burma' (Ananda M 1910), he did not avoid what Buddhist mental culture involved: 'high attainment' within the field of consciousness.

The stereotype to be contested in this lecture was familiar: that the Truths were pessimistic.[31] So he argued that Buddhism should be styled 'the religion of ultra-optimism,' in that it looked life 'nobly and uncringingly in the face' and posited 'an incomparable goal beyond this mass of suffering'—'a State beyond all life' (Bennett 1923: 81).

The fifth lecture, 'The Path of Attainment,' began where the last ended, with 'mental culture' (Bennett 1923: 82–105). Ananda M started with ignorance, namely '*not understanding life*' and the cause of suffering (Bennett 1923: 83–84), asserting that 'attainment' was dependent on the realisation of *dukkha*. After that, it involved training the mind. Again using verse 183 of the *Dhammapada*, he stressed the importance of morality as the foundation of meditation practice—doing no harm to self and others and acting selflessly 'to overcome this illusion of the Self within us' (Bennett 1923: 92).[32] With the claim that the Pali Canon only provided difficult to translate 'set formulae' about meditation practices and the states to be attained, he took his material mainly from the *Visuddhimagga*, as he had done before. He explained that it classified meditation under 40 headings but that, before attempting any of them, '*Satipatthāna*,' 'recollectedness,' was necessary. Implicitly drawing on the *Satipaṭṭhāna Sutta* (The Foundations of Mindfulness) of the *Majjhima Nikāya*,[33] he explained this as 'noting accurately' what we are doing in the present with the following words at the back of our mind, '*This is not I; this is not Mine; there is no Self herein*' (Bennett 1923: 94).[34] In detail, he illustrated the difficulty of this, the '*patience*' it needed, particularly for Westerners, but the result was increased powers of observation and memory, together with protection against the megalomania that could enter the next stage of meditation, concentration, if the experience of the *jhānas* was interpreted solely in relation to 'Self.' He described the *jhānas* as 'states that we can only dimly conceive of by analogy with the immense difference between our memories of dreaming and of waking life,' through which the whole 'mental make-up becomes intensified beyond computation' (Bennett 1923: 96–97).

Personal experience and attainment are evident here. After this, he focussed on two practices: recovering the memory of past lives, as described in 'On the Culture of Mind,' to which he added reflection on what passes from life to life in the absence of a 'Self';[35] and the 'Four Sublime States,' translated as '*Love* to all beings,' '*Compassion* for the suffering of all creatures,' '*Joy*, or rather *Sympathy*, with the right happiness of all who are rightly happy' and '*Discrimination, or Aloofness* from the worldly life' (Bennett 1923: 104).[36] He again stressed that the aim of the practice of the first, recovering memory of past lives, was not to boost the 'Self' but to recognise the suffering of repeated rebirths. He presented the second as a daily discipline that involved summoning up the qualities 'till your whole being is pulsing and vital with them,' adding that the practice was the gateway to the *jhānas*, when the practitioner realises that 'all that here we know and love and hate and think so real. . . . is in truth but a little cloud, a tenuous film, as it were, upon the surface of that vast Consciousness in which then you function' (Bennett 1923: 104–105). This again demonstrated his personal experience, in a line that went back to his reference to 'Pure Consciousness' at his ordination address (Ananda Maitriya 1902e).

In the final lecture, 'The Three Refuges and Nirvana' (Bennett 1923: 106–129), Ananda M began with the Buddha's teaching method, namely meeting people where they were and leading them to take refuge in the Buddha, the *Dhamma* and the Sangha. Here, he presented the *Dhamma* not just as teaching or texts but as 'spiritual power' and Buddhahood as something beyond the personality of Prince Siddhartha, stating:

> Buddhahood consists not in His humanity, but rather in the fact that, through lives of incredible effort and endurance, He has attained to a spiritual evolution which renders Him as different from a human being as the Sun is different from one of its servient planets; which makes of Him, His personality whilst it endures; His Teaching, after that personality has passed away; a focal centre of spiritual power no less mighty in its sphere than that of the Sun in the material realm. (Bennett 1923: 111)

This spiritual power, he argued, could be accessed by anyone who took refuge in the Buddha and his teaching, the *Dhamma*. And here, Ananda M, whilst not straying seriously from mainstream Buddhism, nevertheless revealed the fruit of a spiritual practice that was always wider than

Buddhist texts and commentaries, and that had a feel that was very different from Buddhist modernism. His representation of *Dhamma* had a mystical element. Just as there was a power that made for change in the material realm of evolution, so there was a 'Power,' 'whereby we may enfranchise that droplet of Life's Ocean which we term ourselves' (Bennett 1923: 115). It was a power that had ultra-personal agency. It moved to good. It was manifested as a sense of oneness with all life and compassion, and was the 'spiritual energy making for perfection,' through which we are 'drawn upwards out of this life in which we live, towards the State Beyond—*Nirvāna*' (Bennett 1923: 118–119).

The Sangha, according to Ananda M, was 'the *Community of the Spiritually Attained*,' going beyond traditional Asian usage but nevertheless drawing on Pali sources. He claimed it was similar to the Christian concept of the Community of Saints and could be seen as 'a spiritual entity of a far higher order than the units which compose it'—a force acting for the betterment of 'Life' (Bennett 1923: 120–122). As for nirvana itself, Ananda M presented it as extinction of 'Desire, of Passion, of Self-delusion,' beyond 'all naming and describing' but 'nearer to us than our nearest consciousness,' 'dearer than the dearest hope that we can frame' (Bennett 1923: 122–125). Again, he stressed the framework of *anattā*: it was neither through 'successive subtilisations of the false idea of Selfhood' that nirvana was attained, nor through the 'States of Ecstacy,' the *jhāna*s, but when we 'though it be but for a moment—*forget our Self; and live, aspire and work for Life at large*' (Bennett 1923: 126). He then stressed, drawing on textual tradition, that a human birth was the best one in which to progress toward it. He added, 'Can you wonder that we smile, then, when those who have not understood His Teaching speak of it as a gloomy pessimism?' (Bennett 1923: 28).

In these lectures, Ananda M continued his dialogue with Theosophy, theism, science and Buddhist modernism. Nodding to the Theosophist stress on the existence of a 'false' sense of self, he continually challenged the Theosophical view that there was a true, individualised sense of self, while reaffirming a worldview Theosophists would have recognised. For each Buddhist concept, he attempted a scientific analogy, whether it was comparing the disintegration of the radioactive atom with nirvana, paralleling Darwin's concept of evolution with spiritual progress, or illustrating *dukkha* through the irritability of the amoeba. Throughout, he presented Buddhism as a way of life that transcended the reduced philosophy offered by some Buddhist modernists, whilst nevertheless revealing familiarity with the Pali Canon and the commentarial tradition present in the *Visuddhimagga*. Evidence of his attainment in meditation practice was also present. Additionally, he showed himself a forerunner of contemporary interest in mindfulness practice, which Ananda M correctly translated as 'recollectedness' and 'watchfulness.'

The publication that followed, entitled *The Wisdom of the Aryas*, also includes a chapter on rebirth, read at a meeting of the Buddhist Society for Great Britain and Ireland (The Scotsman 1923: 2). This continues his challenge to the Theosophical view that there is an unchanging substance or *atmā* that passes from life to life, arguing, in contrast, that both science and Buddhism prefer to speak of energies and force, whilst admitting that only those who are enlightened can fully explain what exactly passes over from life to life (Bennett 1923: 132-133).

In April 1921, a poem about Ananda M by the occultist and psychologist, Roland Meredith Starr (1890-1971)[37] appeared in a local London newspaper. It is possible that Starr had heard these lectures before writing this impassioned, retrospective response:

With eyes that looked immortal love
You gazed on men. I could not move,
Nor speak, nor think, but only gaze,
Lost in a deep delicious maze.
Some so sunny spell lay in your eyes
To draw me into ecstasy—
The pure delight in love, a wise
And luminous tranquillity.

O, I was nothing in that hour,
But love and Truth were all in all,
And the whole world was but a flower
That bloomed in Change's crannied wall:
While Love and Truth eternal stood
In bonds of silent brotherhood. (Starr 1921: 4)

BECOMING MORE ACTIVE: PROMOTING BUDDHISM IN BRITAIN

Whilst giving these lectures and preparing them for publication, Ananda M was also trying to re-organise the Buddhist Society and publish *The Buddhist Review*. In his first editorial for the *Review* in July 1920, he attempts to describe 'the present position of our movement' (Ananda M 1920a: 181). Beginning with the 'mental darkness and inertia' that had overtaken all such movements during the war, he suggests that the war itself had potentially made the minds of people in the West more open to Buddhism: 'no *period could possibly be more propitious to the fulfilment of our aims than that upon which we now have entered*' (italics are Ananda M's—Ananda M 1920a: 181).

Knowing that his readership lay both in Asia and the West, and that funding was needed from both, he then speaks of ambitious plans: purchasing land in London for a permanent headquarters;[38] the publication of 'a series of small books, each dealing with a different phase of Buddhist thought'; continuing a series of public lectures, the first of which had been held on 12 November, 1919; assisting in establishing a hostel for seamen from the East, particularly Buddhists; and founding a 'properly-endowed Buddhist monastery, where a duly-constituted chapter of *Bhikkhus* can live and teach and write that *Buddhist* literature of which we are so greatly in need' (Ananda M 1920a: 183). He stresses his continued belief that only through the 'exemplary lives' of a community of monks would Buddhism be spread in Britain. Ananda M then asks for donations from readers, giving different challenges to those in Asia and in the West. He also appeals for human resources. All of this is then placed against the crisis Ananda M sees in the West. Gone is his earlier optimism about science. The advance of 'physical science,' he now states, has not been matched by improved 'morality and self-restraint,' such that discoveries are being directed towards 'effecting the wholesale destruction of human life.' As for Christianity, it had failed to 'restrain the greed for world-empire' and this had led to the war. He continues:

> For stability it is essential that every advance in the conquest over nature should be accompanied by an equal advance in the conquest over *self*;—over the spirits of greed and passion and ambition, which have brought this late calamity upon our western world. (Ananda M 1920a: 186–187)

The only solution for Ananda M was, of course, Buddhism!

According to Pereira, financial help came from Burma and Ceylon, and Burmese and Ceylonese Buddhists resident in Britain, for instance, Wilmot Arthur de Silva and the brother of the Anagārika Dharmapāla, Dr. Charles Alwis Hewavitarne (1876–1929), who studied in Britain and visited regularly (Pereira 1923a: 6),[39] although the July 1920 issue reported the death of Cassius Pereira's father, J. E. Richard Pereira (The Buddhist Review 1920b). This pattern of help coming from Asians to Buddhists in Britain, particularly from Ceylonese and Burmese Buddhists, persisted, according to a key member of the later Buddhist Society, until the 1950s, due in no small part to Ananda M.[40] With this help, Ananda M continued to publish *The Buddhist Review*, the last issue appearing in Jan—Feb 1922, co-edited by Ananda M and John Ellam (Volume XII, No. 1).[41] The other plans voiced in 1920, however, were again doomed to failure, at least in Ananda M's lifetime.

In 1921, *The Buddhist Annual of Ceylon* published an article by Ananda M, 'Buddhism; The Religion of Compassion' (Ananda M 1921a).[42] Lying behind it was the question, 'Could anything have stopped the war?' Nothing in it is radically new, but it shows Ananda M's thought coming full circle. He revisits his views on 'race' with greater openness. Each 'race,' he argues, has its particular genius within a 'symphony' of races, with the proviso that the Indo-Aryan 'race' is supreme because its 'genius' is 'spiritual achievement.' What characterises this spiritual achievement is then reduced to one thing: compassion, 'the highest attribute of living creatures, even as it is the latest development of the human mind' (Ananda M 1921a: 32). Had it been developed in the West, he speculates, the war might not have happened. When he was a member of the Golden Dawn, he had invoked within the Ritual of the Talismans of Visions, 'Thou of Infinite Compassion.'[43] In July 1901, in Colombo, he had summarised Buddhism in one word—'Pity.' In 1921, 'compassion' replaced the more restricted connotations of 'pity,' but the theme was the same. The only response to *dukkha* (suffering and pain) was compassion.

After 1920, Ananda M may have gained help from Raphael Hurst (1898–1981), who, from the 1930s onwards, wrote under the name Paul Brunton. Hurst was not a Buddhist. He became more interested in Neo-Vedanta and is still revered as a promoter of Hinduism in the West. Nevertheless, he claims that he had assisted Ananda M in the evenings and on weekends, when he was a young man. Although we consider his claims to be dubious, we include this data in order to convey as full a picture as possible. In an article published long after Ananda M's death, Hurst describes Ananda M sitting in his room amidst 'heavy Victorian furniture, his table covered with books and palm-leaf classics, the floor around his chair littered with a miscellaneous assortment of manuscripts, letters, and scientific instruments' with Buddha images on the 'mantelshelf' (Brunton 1941). This does not seem to be the sparse and tidy room described by Bax in 1918. Bax, however, states that, between 1920 and 1922, '[s]omeone had enabled' Ananda M 'to rent a second room in the Battersea villa' where he could continue scientific experiments (Bax 1933: 320). It is possible but not verifiable that it was this second room that Hurst describes.

Hurst, however, gives what would appear to be an authentic description of Ananda M's appearance at this time:

> He was quite a tall man but he walked with a pronounced stoop, due partly to illness and partly to long hours bent over the palm-leaf

text or the laboratory table. His face constantly wore a tragic look, but it was frequently illuminated by fitful smiles. Its skin had turned quite yellow through tropical liver trouble. His hair was raven-black and was flung wild and unbrushed over his forehead. His eyes were set deep beneath heavy brows and their intensity evidenced the profound mind which dwelt behind them. (Brunton 1941)

He praises the balance Ananda M achieved between sitting for hours in meditation and busying himself with 'batteries, chemicals and instruments.' He also stresses that, for him, Ananda M is a 'yogi,' skilled in meditation. Hurst travelled to India in the 1930s and yet writes that he considers Ananda M far in advance of the 'Indian yogis' he had met, writing that few of them 'could hold a candle to him.' He calls Ananda M the 'white yogi' and judges him to be the most 'advanced Western Yogi' of the first part of the twentieth century. If Hurst's account is authentic, it confirms that Ananda M still practised some of the yogic practices he had learnt in Sri Lanka from Ramanathan and that he was skilled in *jhāna* practice, with Hurst writing: 'Years later I myself had personal evidence of this development [gaining 'extraordinary powers' through yoga practice] but was forbidden [by Ananda M] to talk about it, even as he himself would smilingly turn the subject or remain silent' (Brunton 1941).

Hurst's account of Ananda M, whether it is authentic or not, demonstrates the reverence that Ananda M could inspire in those interested in alternative spirituality in the last years of his life, as does Starr's poem and Bax's later judgement that Ananda M was 'the most beautiful person' he had known (Bax 1951: 161). Hurst's reference to palm-leaf manuscripts also suggests that Ananda M continued to work academically, testing his skills in Pali, no doubt with a dictionary beside him, although he had given his 1909 edition of Robert Childers's Pali-English Dictionary to the Youatts in Liverpool.[44]

Bax states that, throughout 1922, aided by a young man called Gray, Ananda M 'busied himself with the invention of a gramophone that should be able to play records of unlimited length' and was also devising 'an instrument that should record thought,' working with 'the zest of early youth' (Bax 1933: 320). However, again according to Bax, when Gray sought to take out a provisional patent for the former, they found that a similar device had been patented 20 years previously but never marketed (Bax 1933: 321; 1951: 163–164). With the publishing of his lectures at Bax's 'studio,' these scientific experiments and his work with the Buddhist Society, Ananda M, in spite of the energy he could sometimes summon, was stretching himself to his physical limits at this time, perhaps aware that he did not have long to live.

The Buddhist Review indicates that Ananda M was also seeking to build an international network similar to that which had surrounded the *Buddhasāsana Samāgama* in Burma. Vol XI of *The Buddhist Review* (1921) gives the names of five 'Honorary Correspondents' of the Society, representing Ceylon, Denmark, Germany, India (the Anagārika Dharmapāla) and Switzerland (C. T. Strauss), with Ananda M stating that he had written to 'Burma, China, France, Holland, Italy, Japan, Siam [Thailand] and the United States' to gain additional representatives, anticipating that they would be in place by the next issue of the Review (The Buddhist Review 1921: 144). The first issue of Vol XII (January–February 1922), however, is dedicated to something different, albeit compatible with Ananda M's vision—'the International Buddhist Union.' The issue is subtitled, *The Journal of the Buddhist Society of Great Britain and Ireland and of the International Buddhist Union*. The Anagārika Dharmapāla had inaugurated the Union at the consecration of the 'Sri Dharma Rajika Chaitya Vihara' in Calcutta in 1920 with the aim of networking individual Buddhists and Buddhist organisations globally, across different schools. By 1922, Buddhists in 24 countries were affiliated to it, including from Austria, British West Indies, Ceylon, Denmark, Honolulu, Japan, 'Siam' and Tibet. Individuals in support of it included D. T. Suzuki, C. T. Strauss, George Grimm, J. B. Jayatilaka and U Kyaw Yan. In January 1922, a meeting of the Buddhist Society agreed that 'immediate steps' should be taken for the 'establishment' of a joint headquarters for the two bodies in London, London being seen as the most effective location for the Union's work (The Buddhist Review 1922: 2–6).[45]

At this time, Ananda M was also writing prolifically. Vol XI contains three articles by him directed towards Westerners new to Buddhism. Each undermines not only Christianity but also other forms of spirituality contemporary to Ananda M, including his own yogic achievements, whilst affirming the existence of planes of consciousness beyond everyday thought. They also demonstrate his ongoing interest, and indeed competence, in the discipline of psychology.

The first of these, 'Buddhism and the Western World' (Ananda M 1921b)[46] offers again what Ananda M sees as the core of all forms of Buddhism, namely suffering and the cessation of suffering through the 'Law of Causation,' and reflects on spirituality in the West. 'It is not because the West is less, but because it is *more* religious that our churches are empty and our ministries the refuge of the intellectually incapable,' he declares (Ananda M 1921b: 54). In its place, he promotes a Buddhist '*gnosis*,' predicated on both scientific method and inner experience, speaking of a realm of consciousness that 'transcends our present waking life just as much as our waking life transcends a dream' (Ananda M 1921b: 56). In the second article, 'The Miraculous Element in Buddhism,' Ananda M first reminisces about the wonder and enchantment children experience as they encounter the world and replay some of the skills of their evolutionary ancestors, paralleling this with the 'imaginations of the peoples of the childhood of our race' (Ananda M 1921c: 128). After mentioning 'the utter miracle of consciousness,' he turns to what contemporary science is discovering about the 'Subliminal Self' with its perfect memory and 'perfect sense of the lapse of time' (Ananda M 1921c: 130), as seen in hypnotism. He then speculates that, in the past, this part of the mind was closer to the surface and that this could explain the frequent occurrence of miracles in Christianity, and the religions of India at the Buddha's time. Comparing these to contemporary 'spiritualist phenomena,' he argues that the error present then and now is one of interpretation—to believe that the phenomena are due to the gods, the spirits of the dead or 'spirit guides' (Ananda M 1921c: 133) and that miracle-working is a sign of truth.[47] Continuing, he points out that Buddhism recognises the 'so-called miraculous' but that miraculous powers prove nothing at all 'save a certain mastery over one's own mind, and over the forces of nature.' He then argues that Buddhism places these powers 'exactly in the place that the modern scientific and logical mind would put them,' as proving nothing about the nature of truth (Ananda M 1921c: 134–135). To strengthen his argument, he cites a discourse from the Pali Canon in which the Buddha demonstrated that the right understanding of *dhamma* was far preferable to the working of miracles: 'It is that great miracle of truth which here to-day has emptied and is emptying the churches which preach a creed whose very sanction lies in that old error that a miracle proves truth' (Ananda M 1921c: 136).[48]

'The Doctrine of the Aryas,' the third article, repeats Ananda M's racist views concerning the superiority of the two branches of the Aryan 'race,' the Indo-Aryan and the Western.[49] He contrasts materialists with idealists. The first is obsessed with the external world and the second is orientated towards inner consciousness. The first lives 'for Self alone' and the second has taken the first step 'towards realising his *oneness* with the whole of conscious life' (Ananda M 1921d: 151), which Ananda M then develops using the illustration of waves within the ocean (Ananda M 1921d: 153). Turning then to the Four Noble Truths and their use of the term 'Arya,' he again lauds the choice of the Indo-Aryans to explore the interior rather than the exterior world. As in the first lecture given in Bax's studio, he describes the long interior search involved, presenting the Buddha as its culmination. Here *sammāsamādhi* is translated as 'Right Concentration or Right Meditation' and his explanation concentrates in a familiar way on *samatha*, which, together with 'right recollectedness' (*sammāsati*), could lead to 'those successive "awakenings" into the interior spiritual realms of which mention has been made' (Ananda M 1921d: 161), a message that had been present since 'On the Culture of Mind' (Ananda Maitriya 1902b). He then returns to 'Right Views' and reiterates the importance of the three characteristics of existence, stressing that electron theory is proving the first (impermanence—*anicca*), and biology the second (pain—*dukkha*). This, the penultimate article that he wrote, returns to the basics of what he sees as the Buddhist worldview, with an implicit plea:

> And his own actual teaching [the Buddha's] was so simple, so obvious, that, like all that is really, greatly, true, one marvels, once one has understood, that one had not thought of it before. It is all summed up by the Great Teacher himself in one simple formula, to which he gave the style of the Four Aryan or Noble Truths. It is a formula which, like all such plain and simple things, seems at first sight to be obvious even to triteness, but which, as the more we study it, reveals ever greater and still vaster deeps, until the mind fails at their profundity; and yet there are deeps beyond. (Ananda M 1921d: 159)

The final article that Ananda M published appears in the last issue of *The Buddhist Review*. Entitled, 'A Scientific Analogy,' it shows that Ananda M was still writing with fluent intensity about parallels between Buddhism and science. The 'analogy' is between the splitting of the atom and 'the new science of radio-activity,' and breaking free from the imprisonment of birth and rebirth through the attainment of 'Nirvana' (Ananda M 1922: 19–20). This is not a new point for him but his argument brings in: planetary movements; the indestructibility of 'Kamma' both in world systems and the minds of persons; Abhidhamma; and 'Lokuttara-dhamma [lit. supramundane *dhamma*], the Law Beyond the Universe,' which gradually pushed humanity upwards through 'charity, love and self-sacrifice' (Ananda M 1922: 18). And he transforms his own former fascination with ceremonial magic into the 'magic' of spoken or written *dhamma*:

> But, reading the script of those dead signs, hearing the spoken sound, a miracle beyond all others that I know occurs. As at the touch of a magician's wand, the dead signs or sounds spring to new life in our hearts and minds, just as if a Pathway had been flung whereupon the thoughts could pass ... But those Scriptures, that Teaching, somehow, serves as the Vehicle of a Power greater than Kamma, greater even than Nescience [not-knowing]: able to enfranchise us, to cast out craving, hatred and self-delusion for ever. (Ananda M 1922: 18–19)

Towards the end, no doubt drawing on his own lessening attachment to human life, he writes: 'It is by the cessation of our own attraction to the things of earth, whereby we may find enfranchisement from the ever-whirling Wheel of Life' (Ananda M 1922: 20).

In addition to these activities, Ananda M was a mentor and helper to others. In March 1920, for instance, he wrote to Cassius Pereira about a Mr. W. Arnold Malabar, with words that illustrate his capacity for empathy and loving concern:

> But to you, dear Friend, I look to give him something more than mere support and medical aid should he unfortunately fall in need of this;—I would ask you to be his <u>friend</u>, remembering that he will be amongst strangers and therefore very lonely,—a friend to who[m] he can go with his troubles and difficulties with the certitude of finding loving helpfulness and sympathy.[50]

The Gunns also claimed that he settled quarrels between his landlady and her companion, and 'having some knowledge of medicine,' helped 'the destitute sick' (Bax 1933: 274). They shared with Bax a strange cameo about a soldier who visited them wanting to do something for 'the Bhikkhu,' because he had been helped by him two nights before. Ananda M had apparently scribbled down a doctor's name for the soldier on notepaper from the Gunns! The soldier had had a fever and was 'huddled up on the pavement.' Ananda M had gone out at about 10.00 p.m. 'to buy a packet of fags.' He had seen the soldier and taken him back to his room, whilst he sought the aid of a doctor. Failing in this, according to the Gunns, he 'sat up all night by the bedside. He put himself onto one of the higher levels of consciousness—jhānas, they call them: and toward morning the soldier woke up, and said, "Where am I? I've been in paradise."' (Bax 1933: 274-275; 1951: 164).

In spite of occupying two rooms, Ananda M was still in financial need at this time. In September 1921, he appealed directly to the Anagārika Dharmapāla and Dharmapāla gave a little.[51] Other well-wishers no doubt contributed what they could. The fact that the January—February 1922 edition of *The Buddhist Review* was the last that Ananda M edited and the last that was published may not solely have been due to Ananda M's physical inability to produce it. Money might have been the key problem, and hence his desperate search for a scientific device that could be patented. That he found energy for this would have been fuelled by his overriding concern that Buddhism should continue in the West. The failure of his patent application would have further affected his health, as no doubt it had done in Burma when he attempted the same tactic.

Ananda M sent Bax a copy of *The Wisdom of the Aryas* in early March 1923. Bax visited him the next day. When Bax praised the publication, Ananda M stated that, if people liked it, he 'would try to prepare a deeper book' (Bax 1933: 321). Again, this did not come to fruition. Shortly afterwards, Ananda M developed an intestinal obstruction and, five days later, died, on 9 March, 1923.[52] A touching cameo from his last day comes from the sister of F. E. Balls, who, according to Humphreys, writes, 'Though suffering terrible pain, he was still compassionately aware of a singing beggar in the road, and sent his landlady out with money within a few hours of his death' (Humphreys 1937: 44). Bax claims that Mrs. Green had told him a similar story about a person playing a penny whistle outside the house a few days before his death, with Ananda M sending her out with 'twopence' (Bax 1933: 325). It is possible that this was the same event.

Francis Payne was with Ananda M when he died and composed a Buddhist funeral for him. Bax claims that Mrs. Green told him that 'Mr P.,' whom they considered 'a horrid bouncing fellow,' took 'every scrap of what poor Mr Bennett had left,' leaving unpaid bills, which Bax probably met (Bax 1933: 326). This could have been Payne, and one of the things that we know he took away was Ananda M's Burmese Buddha *rūpa* (image), which Ananda M had probably donated to the Buddhist Society. Having been taken to see the body, laid out by Mrs. Green, Bax writes:

> I saw the dark-haired head of my friend, slightly back-tilted on the pillow, and the long hands folded on the breast. "He is not there at all," I felt. "How queer! He is simply not there." The figure, in its repose and dignity, looked like a waxen effigy: and to name that inert form "Alan Bennett" would have seemed to me as fantastic as to plant a waxen flower. (Bax 1933: 327)

News of his death reached Ceylon quickly. The money for the purchase of a grave plot was cabled from Ceylon by Charles Hewavitarne and Ananda M was buried in Morden cemetery on 14 March.[53] No gravestone was placed at the site.

An obituary was published in Ceylon on 28 April, 1923 by Cassius Pereira. It ends with:

> And now the worker has, for this life, laid aside his burden. One feels more glad than otherwise, for he was tired; his broken body could no longer keep pace with his soaring mind. The work he began, that of introducing Buddhism to the West, he pushed with enthusiastic vigour in pamphlet, journal and lecture, all masterly, all stimulating thought, all in his own inimitably graceful style. And the results are not disappointing, to those who know. (Pereira 1923a: 6)

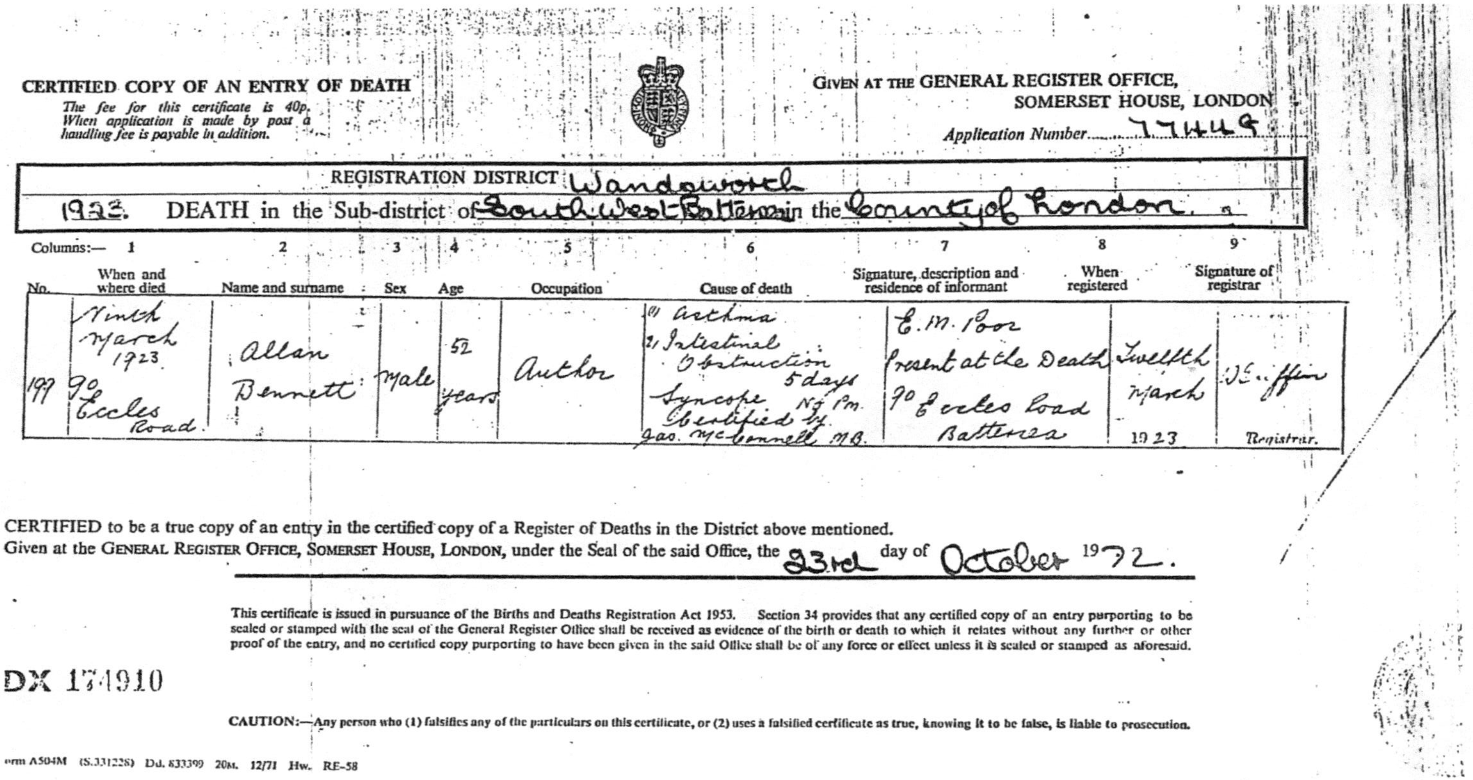
CERTIFIED COPY OF AN ENTRY OF DEATH

The fee for this certificate is 40p. When application is made by post a handling fee is payable in addition.

GIVEN AT THE GENERAL REGISTER OFFICE, SOMERSET HOUSE, LONDON

Application Number 77449

REGISTRATION DISTRICT Wandsworth

1923. DEATH in the Sub-district of South West Battersea in the County of London

Columns:— No.	1 When and where died	2 Name and surname	3 Sex	4 Age	5 Occupation	6 Cause of death	7 Signature, description and residence of informant	8 When registered	9 Signature of registrar
197	Ninth March 1923 90 Eccles Road	Allan Bennett	Male	52 years	Author	(1) Asthma 2) Intestinal Obstruction 5 days Syncope No P.M. Certified by Jas. McConnell M.B.	E. M. Poor Present at the Death 90 Eccles Road Battersea	Twelfth March 1923	[illegible] Registrar.

CERTIFIED to be a true copy of an entry in the certified copy of a Register of Deaths in the District above mentioned.
Given at the General Register Office, Somerset House, London, under the Seal of the said Office, the 23rd day of October 1972.

This certificate is issued in pursuance of the Births and Deaths Registration Act 1953. Section 34 provides that any certified copy of an entry purporting to be sealed or stamped with the seal of the General Register Office shall be received as evidence of the birth or death to which it relates without any further or other proof of the entry, and no certified copy purporting to have been given in the said Office shall be of any force or effect unless it is sealed or stamped as aforesaid.

DX 174910

CAUTION:—Any person who (1) falsifies any of the particulars on this certificate, or (2) uses a falsified certificate as true, knowing it to be false, is liable to prosecution.

orm A504M (S.331228) Dd. 833399 20M. 12/71 Hw. RE-58

***Figure* 5.2** *Ananda M's death certificate.*

Bax agreed with Pereira. After he heard the time of Ananda M's death, 5.00 p.m., he realised that, as he been writing at his desk, 'the man who had been least world-soiled of all whom I had known was encountering at last the most momentous of all experiences, the event which he had awaited with lifelong curiosity and, for many years, with a patient desire of release' (Bax 1933: 324).

Unlike the media interest that surrounded his mission to Britain in 1908, notices of his death do not seem to have appeared in the mainstream British media. Probably through Cassius Pereira or Charles Hewavitarne, however, the 1923 *Buddhist Annual of Ceylon* carried a picture of 'The Late Ananda Metteyya Thera (Allan Bennett)' in the middle of an article by Pereira on 'Anatta,' a fitting article for Ananda M to be found within in the year of his death (Pereira 1923b: 35).

Aleister Crowley learned of Ananda M's death while he was in Cefalu, Sicily, although who informed him and how is unclear. His death comes up in correspondence between Crowley and his magical student, Charles Stansfeld Jones, later in the year. In a letter dated 24 October 1923, Jones writes to Crowley:

> One further significance of the present Pass-word, perhaps unknown to you, is the Passing On of our Sainted and Honoured Frater I.A., which, I understand, occurred some two months ago. We both owe him a great debt and all reverence is due to his memory.[54]

Crowley's reply to this letter, written by his then secretary, Norman Mudd, dated 25 November, contains 'Concerning the death of Frater I.A., "666 [Crowley] wrote 777 [Jones] about this in March or April."' It would seem that this letter never reached Jones. Based on other statements made by Jones, this was not the first time this had happened.[55]

Both Buddhist and esoteric contacts of Ananda M, therefore, received news of his death fairly quickly. The subject of the next chapter is how these different interest groups kept the memory of Ananda M alive.

In Olcott's review of Ananda M's pamphlet describing his ordination and plan to spread Buddhism to the West, he ends with a wish that would ultimately come true. Olcott writes:

> Well, let the young man dream his dreams in peace and let us all hope that when his day of disillusionment comes, as it has to all of us his predecessors, he may have the pluck and perseverance to stand alone and fight his fight and, if it need be, die at his post, courageous and undaunted. (Olcott 1902: 688)

6

Ananda Metteyya's Legacy

Ananda M's death is not the end of our narrative. After he died, he was claimed and re-presented by both Buddhist and esoteric interest groups. Each projected onto Ananda M what they wanted him to be and signify, capitalising on Ananda M's vagueness about his own life history. On the one hand, there were Buddhists in Asia and the West who stressed his contribution to the global spread of Buddhism. On the other hand, occultists, such as devotees of Aleister Crowley, appropriated Ananda M as an icon of occultism. In both groups, some were loath to admit that Buddhism and the esoteric combined within Ananda M's life story. The result is that Ananda M has rarely been represented in his totality. This chapter does not attempt to be exhaustive but offers a flavour of the diverse representations of Ananda M that arose in the twentieth and early twenty-first centuries.

ALLAN BENNETT THROUGH THE EYES OF ALEISTER CROWLEY AND OTHER OCCULTISTS

This section concentrates on Aleister Crowley, those who were associated with him, and those who continue to be inspired by him. It demonstrates that this group of people rarely engaged with Ananda M's conversion to Buddhism. We begin, however, with an exception to this—a review of *The Wisdom of the Aryas* that appeared in *The Occult Review* in October 1923. The book is praised as a counterpoint to the ignorance surrounding Buddhism in England and Ananda M is described as 'a Buddhist convert of longstanding.' No hint is given in this review of his esoteric past (G. M. H. 1923: 256). As time passed, however, this was not how Ananda M was remembered by those involved in occultism. Yet, the fact that a book on Buddhism was reviewed in a journal focused on occultism in the 1920s demonstrates there was still an overlap between the two domains in the minds of many.

Crowley placed Allan Bennett on a pedestal and spoke of him with great reverence, both while Bennett was alive and after his death. He writes in his autobiography that one of his duties in writing his memoirs is to record as much as he can about the two men he admired most, one being Bennett (Crowley 1929: 210; 1989: 155).

In addition to his praise and story-telling about Bennett, Crowley published a picture of what he claimed was Allan, in which Bennett, wearing a robe, is standing under an arch with Egyptian Hieroglyphs. If the figure is Bennett, it is the only known photograph of him with a moustache. Nevertheless, some years later, someone took this picture and surrounded it with Bennett's names written in different ways. At the top is 'The Adeptus I.A.,' I.A. standing for Bennett's Golden Dawn motto, in Latinised Hebrew 'Iehi Aour.' Next to this are the initials, CHAB.A.M^{ac}G, which represent Bennett's name, Charles Henry Allan Bennett AKA MacGregor. Under this are the letters AC or AL, written unclearly, and the date 1896. This date may be an attempt to reference the year Bennett entered the Second Order of the Golden Dawn. If so, it is incorrect, as Bennett took this initiation in 1895. At the bottom of the image is 'Al Ayn ben Ayt,' which is Allan Bennett using Latinised phonetic Hebrew, and then, finally, his ordination name, Ananda Metteya. A portion of the Golden Dawn Requiem ritual is quoted under these. The original purpose of this construction may have been to provide a memorial of Bennett, thus the portion of the Requiem ritual. Regardless of its original intended use, many occultists today claim

Figure 6.1 *Fabricated certificate of Allan Bennett's initiation into the Second Order of the Golden Dawn.*

the image is Bennett's Golden Dawn initiation certificate into the Second Order. This claim, however, is simply not possible. First, as already noted, the date of 1896 is incorrect. Second, Bennett did not gain the name Ananda Metteyya until his ordination as a Buddhist monk in Burma, long after he had left the Golden Dawn. The whole image is obviously of later construction. Even with such clear evidence, occultists still believe that the evidence against it being his Golden Dawn ordination certificate is simply 'anachronistic.'

Crowley's autobiography is not the only work in which Crowley praises Bennett. References to Bennett are peppered through almost all of Crowley's writings. From 1912 to 1913, Crowley composed, with the assistance of others, his central text of ceremonial magic called, *Liber ABA*, or *Book Four*. Divided into four large sections, *Book Four* contains multiple references to Bennett's magical work and his relationship with Crowley, using his Golden Dawn motto, Frater I.A. For instance, when discussing evocation of entities, Crowley writes, 'Frater I.A., when a child, was told that he could invoke the Devil by repeating the "Lord's Prayer" backwards. He went into the garden and did so. The Devil appeared, and almost scared the life out of him' (Crowley 1997: 188). Crowley also dedicated published works to Bennett, such as his poem, 'The Sword of Song: Called by Christians the Book of the Beast' (Crowley 1904). Until his death in 1947, Crowley wrote letters to a variety of people regarding esoteric subjects. These letters were collected and posthumously published as *Magick Without Tears* in 1954. Within these letters, Crowley often mentions Bennett, speaking well of him and noting their relationship. For instance, in one letter, he writes, 'Bhikkhu Ananda Metteya, (Allan Bennett) the great English Adept, who was one of my earliest instructors in Magick, and joined the Sangha in Burma in 1902, gave me my first groundings in mystical theory and practice' (Crowley 1954: 157). When Crowley founded his own magical organisation and developed a curriculum of study for his students, he included works written by Bennett, including, as we have previously mentioned, 'Training of the Mind.' It is worth stressing again that Crowley came to the opposite conclusion from Ananda M concerning the remembrance of past lives. For Ananda M, the practice reinforced the pain of repeated rebirths and the need for liberation from suffering. For Crowley, it was a method of discovering who we really are, a reinforcing of personal identity, and this was the message that became linked with the memory of Ananda M in esoteric circles.

We have nothing from Ananda M regarding his feelings towards Crowley after a 1905 letter in which Ananda M refers to Crowley as a friend. The only indication in the following years comes through a single sentence in Clifford Bax's, *Some I Knew Well*, attributed to Ananda M: 'Crowley might have added much to the bettering of the world, but he took the wrong turning' (Bax 1951: 162). The context of these words is not given, the chronological narrative of Bax's recollections being disjointed, but it would have been after Ananda M's return to England in 1914, possibly when Bennett was presenting his lectures in Bax's studio in 1919. Regardless of when, Ananda M's words indicate disappointment with the life Crowley chose.

Because of the praise showered on Bennett by Crowley and other occultist writers, when there was renewed interest in Crowley and esoteric practice in the 1950s and 1960s, Bennett became somewhat of a mythical figure within esoteric circles. This impression of Bennett was enhanced when one of Crowley's former students, Israel Regardie, collected and published a significant portion of the Golden Dawn rituals, teachings and other internal documents. More Golden Dawn material was discovered and published in subsequent years, including Bennett's talisman ceremonies, copied from the notebooks he left with Crowley. These rituals became examples for future students to emulate. In addition to the ceremonial material, the history of the Golden Dawn became the subject of many books, and within them, Bennett is often noted for his magical abilities and for being Crowley's tutor in occultism. For instance, Francis King mentions the invocation of Taphthartharath in *Ritual Magic in England, 1887 to the Present Day* (King 1970). Both Bennett's magical prowess and his relationship to Crowley are prominent in Ellic Howe's *The Magicians of the Golden Dawn: A Documentary History of a Magical Order, 1887-1923* (Howe 1972), and Robert Gilbert references Bennett's use of his 'lustre' to blast a Theosophist unconscious in *The Golden Dawn: Twilight of the Magicians, The Rise and Fall of a Magical Order* (Gilbert 1983).

This published material became the basis of reconstructionist occultist groups, emulating the Golden Dawn or building upon Crowley's legacy. Within them, occultists of the past became role models to be revered and emulated. Because of his association with Crowley and his role in creating many Golden Dawn ceremonies, reconstructionist occultists viewed Bennett as a model occultist. His abandonment of occultism for Buddhism was frequently downplayed or rejected. Biographical accounts by occultists repeatedly claim that Bennett rejected Buddhism and embraced esotericism once more. For instance, Ithell Colquhoun describes, in a Golden Dawn history, Bennett's re-embrace of occultism on his return to England:

> Bennett did not remain permanently satisfied with the Orient as his spiritual home; by the 1920s he was again in England. According to Frater X., who knew and admired him at the time, he had outgrown his Buddhist phase, deep and prolonged though it had been, and

was seeking objective proof of the existence of the invisible world. He was no longer impressed by speculation on spiritual truth, nor dogmatic statement unsubstantiated by laboratory methods. He had reverted to a more Western attitude, involving occult experiment on a scientific basis which he believed to be the 'way' of the future. (Colquhoun 1975: 147–148)

These accounts of Bennett also claim that, when he died, among his few possessions was his 'blasting rod,' the term Crowley used to describe Bennett's Golden Dawn magical wand.

In 2001, Frater Petros Xristos, a member of a reconstructionist Golden Dawn group, the Mountain Temple, published a biography of Bennett on his website in which he, like Colquhoun, describes Bennett as not 'being satisfied with his life in the sangha' and as continuing 'his work in the Western magical tradition,' when he returned to England. This biography also mentions the 'blasting rod' being one of his few possessions, and that, at the time of his death, he was 'also dedicated to finding some means of communication with the astral world' (Petros Xristos 2001). Similar biographies are given on the websites of other Golden Dawn reconstructionist groups. For instance, The Golden Dawn Ancient Mystery School ends its biography by imagining the following:

> In Allan Bennett's last days, shortly before his death, he resigned from the Buddhist Lodge which he had formed. Allan Bennett was sick, tired, and realizing that his time on this earth was now at an end, he perhaps not in a formal way, but in a way that matters most, in his heart, he stood once again within the Hall of the Neophyte before the Banner of the East, and before an etheric figure of his late mentor, MacGregor Mathers. As his eyes may have glanced upward, he saw descending upon him, the Light of his own Higher Genius. (Golden Dawn Ancient Mystery School 2017)

The goal of these biographies is to reclaim Bennett as an occultist. To do so, the biographers have to explicitly state that Bennett rejected Buddhism and that he returned to his esoteric practice. These biographies are not focused on historical fact, but instead reinsert Bennett into the timeline of occultism. In contrast to Buddhists who ignore Bennett's involvement with esotericism, occultists ignore Bennett's conversion to Buddhism, or present it as a passing phase. Allan Bennett is used to legitimise occultism and to recapture a time in which the boundaries between science, magic and religion were porous, and occultism reached a pinnacle in practice and acceptance.

MYANMAR AND SRI LANKA

In both Myanmar and Sri Lanka, Ananda M entered colonial and post-colonial conversations to become a symbol of Buddhist confidence and independence under British imperialism, as interest in Buddhism grew in the West. With Christian missionary activity continuing to be seen by many Buddhists in both countries as a threat to their identity, Ananda M represented the counter movement, a reverse mission that effectively promoted Buddhism in the west.

In the period up to Ananda M's death, Daw Mya May remained in touch with the Buddhist Society of Great Britain and Ireland and offered financial aid at certain points, as we have shown, including to support a *bhikkhu* in London. Even after the Society was dissolved, Burmese support continued for the Buddhist organisations that replaced it.

In 1956, members of Daw Mya May's extended family revived the *Buddhasāsana Samāgama* and started a new Buddhist journal, *The Open Door*. The inspiration behind this was Tun Hla Oung, son of May Oung, Daw Mya May's nephew. After retirement from government service when he was 47, he devoted himself to Buddhist education in Ceylon and Burma. In addition to reviving the *Buddhasāsana Samāgama* and becoming its Honorary Secretary in 1956, he founded and directed the Buddhist World Mission, and edited a weekly Burmese Buddhist journal, *Buddha Dhamma Loka* (Sein Nyo Tun 1960: 15).

The new *Samāgama* saw itself as a direct heir to the one that was founded in 1902 by Ananda M. The first issue of *The Open Door* reprints the poem Edwin Arnold had written for the first issue of *Buddhism*, 'The Golden Temple' (Arnold 1903), and starts to serialise Ananda M's article in the fourth issue of *Buddhism*, 'The New Civilisation' (Ananda Metteyya 1904d). 'The Faith of the Future' (Ananda Metteyya 1903a) is also serialised in the first issues. The journal's aim was to give 'all possible aid toward the study, practice and propagation of the Buddha Dhamma as brought down in its purity and strength through the successive Six Buddhist Councils,' by publishing 'authentic works on the Buddha Dhamma' (Tun Hla Oung 1959: ii). Its representation of Buddhism combines a socially engaged emphasis and 'the path of inner culture' in a way that Ananda M would surely have approved. For instance, Tun Hla Oung states that the acceptance of Buddhist teaching:

> would involve the substitution [of] arbitration for punitive action, imprisonment for capital punishment, negotiation and co-existence for plunder and aggression and the abolition of cruelty and slaughter of animals—all practices being as degrading to the employer as it is cruel to the defenceless. (Tun Hla Oung 1959: ii)

By Volume II of *The Open Door*, 'The Religion of Burma' by Ananda M is listed as available from the Buddhist World Mission, together with several works by Sīlācāra. In addition, the journal: defends Theravada Buddhism;[1] retells suttas from the Pali Canon, using Sīlācāra's translations in a series entitled 'Sutta Stories Retold'; prints talks on Buddhism originally broadcast through the Burma Broadcasting Station, for example 'The Role of Buddhism under the Shadow of a Thermo-Nuclear War' (Sein Nyo Tun 1959); and commissions articles on general Buddhist themes. The journal's articles are generally short, except for the reprints of Ananda M's articles, catering to busy people. Tun Hla Oung died in May 1960, after a short illness. This seems to have put an end to both the journal and the revived *Buddhasāsana Samāgama*. Volume III No. 1 of *The Open Door*, which contains Hla Oung's obituary, was the last to be published.

After the demise of the second *Buddhasāsana Samāgama*, the memory of Ananda M did not fade completely. His time in Burma and his contribution to the spread of Buddhism has held an ongoing appeal for the people of contemporary Myanmar, as the following examples show. First, Ananda M has appeared in Dhamma School resources and in university courses. Min Yu Wai's work on Buddhist missionaries, including Ananda M, cited in Chapter Three (Min Yu Wai 2011), is now used in the Grade 7 reader within Myanmar's Dhamma Schools, often held on Sundays at Buddhist temples.[2] Material from Min Yu Wai's work is also recommended in postgraduate courses, for example in an MA course at Sasana University, Kabaraye, written by U KoKo Maing.

Second, Ananda M appears in resources that have been posted on the internet by Burmese scholars. In November 2013, U Tin Myint Moe posted an article entitled 'Buddhism and Foreign Scholars,' which mentions Ananda M briefly, alongside figures such as T. W. and Caroline Rhys Davids, Max Müller, Robert Caesar Childers, Christmas Humphreys and the Spanish scholar, Miguel de Unamuno. Only his time as a Buddhist monk, however, is described.[3] Later than this, a lengthy YouTube presentation in Burmese on Ananda M was posted under the account of Phay Zaw Gyi.[4] Citing the lack of knowledge about Ananda M, it includes references to Cassius Pereira, Sīlācāra and Ñāṇatiloka Thera. Significantly, it does not hide Ananda M's association with the Golden Dawn and its 'esotericism, mysticism and white magic.' Additionally, Ananda M is described as changing his name, when in Ceylon before becoming a Buddhist, 'into Swami Ananda Maitriya while learning yoga with Swami Paññānanda.'[5]

Third, Western sources on Ananda M have been translated into Burmese. For instance, Elizabeth Harris's 1998 booklet on Ananda M (Harris 1998) was translated and published by Sahajaata Publications in Burma in

2005. A second edition appeared in 2016. American scholar Alicia Turner told Elizabeth that she had seen it for sale on popular pavement book stalls.

In Ceylon, Cassius Pereira fulfilled his teenage commitment and was ordained as Bhikkhu Kassapa in 1947 at the temple patronised by his family, Vajirārāma Vihāraya. His writings keep the memory of Ananda M alive, including the piece he wrote as he became a *bhikkhu* (Pereira 1947). Over two decades before this, however, whilst still in medical practice, he helped to found the Servants of the Buddha, which re-invigorated Maitriya Hall and, therefore, the memory of Ananda M. Its first General Meeting was held on 16 April, 1921 and its first public talk, on the 23rd (Wijeyesekera 2021: 8). It met each Saturday at 5 p.m. at Maitriya Hall and continued the hall's original vision of encouraging life-long learning among Westernised, English-speaking Ceylonese Buddhists.[6] When Elizabeth Harris lived in Colombo in the late 1980s, lectures were still being held at Maitriya Hall every Saturday, the President being the previously mentioned Alec Robertson, who, as a young person, had known Cassius Pereira.[7] Robertson was able to share with Elizabeth what Pereira had told him about Ananda M, and we have used this in our biography.

The 2021 centenary publication of the Servants of the Buddha represents Ananda M as an honorary founder of the society. A biographical note about him from the editors states that he was 'a leading light in the formation of the Servants of the Buddha. Maitriya Hall is his namesake' (Ñānasīha and Senanayake 2021: 40). Wijesekera, in his history of the society, reinforces this, by quoting from Rudyard Kipling's poem, 'The Ballad of East and West,' and continuing:

> Such a meeting of East and West of "two strong men who came from the ends of the earth" [quote from Kipling] was the friendship that blossomed between Allan Bennett, (later Ven. Ananda Maitriya/Metteyya) one of the first Englishmen to be ordained as a Buddhist monk and Dr Cassius Pereira, LMS (Cey), LRCP (Lond), MRCS (Eng), a Sri Lankan medical doctor—the very first president of the Servants of the Buddha, who later ordained as Ven. Kassapa. The cement that bonded their friendship was their single-minded lifelong commitment to Buddhism. Its universal message of freedom and compassion, relevant to all mankind was the bridge that linked East and West and culminated in the formation of the Servants of the Buddha.
> [...]
> The Maitriya Hall and its architectural style is a monument to the universality of Buddhism ... While the two protagonists, Allan Bennett of England and Dr. Cassius Pereira of Ceylon devoted their

lives to Buddhism and its dissemination to Western audiences, the society they created in Ceylon survive[s] to this day. (Wijesekera 2021: 9–10)

Ananda M's friendship with Pereira thus became, in 2021, a symbol of the marriage of East and West that the Servants of the Buddha saw itself as embodying, the two of them being placed on an equal footing in the genesis of the society. Heavily selected extracts from 'The Faith of the Future' (Ananda Maitriya 1903a) are also included in the publication, the whole article being condensed into five pages. Ananda M's opening about the death of the gods in Western mythological literature and the imaginative illustrations he used to explain his points are omitted. What remains is in line with the positioning of the Servants of the Buddha, namely Ananda M's words about morality, and the West's need for a religion founded on reason, ethics and 'the reign of law' (Ananda Maithriya 1903a: 10–14; Ananda Maithriya 2021: 36). His description of the Four Noble Truths and the civilising value of Buddhism are also included. Ananda M's core message remains but his unique, rather wordy yet poetic, style is lost.

Before the death of Ananda M, Balangoda Ānanda Maitreya Mahayanake Thera (1896–1998), one of the most respected scholar monks in twentieth-century Sri Lanka, chose to be named after Ananda M at his ordination. He gained novice ordination in 1911 and higher ordination in 1916, within the Amarapura Nikāya (Bond 1988: 82). He told Gombrich and Obeyesekere that he made this choice after meeting the Buddhist monk, Ñāṇatiloka and hearing about Allan Bennett (Gombrich and Obeyesekere 1988: 299–300). He became known for his writings and his attainments in meditation[8] and remained deeply aware that he embodied the memory of Ananda M through his monastic name. Indeed, he followed in Ananda M's footsteps, learning about Theosophy and studying Hindu yoga when young (Gombrich and Obeyesekere 1988: 300–303). Elizabeth had the privilege of speaking to him in 1994, when, in his late nineties, he was visiting the Sri Saddhatissa International Buddhist Centre in Kingsbury, London. He was proud of the provenance of his monastic name and called Ananda M, Allan MacGregor, stressing that it was a Scottish name. He claimed that Ananda M had practised spiritualism before becoming a Buddhist and that one spirit had not been on good terms with him when he gave up the practice, causing him heart problems! In a later letter to Elizabeth, he writes, 'As regards Ananda Metteyya's using opium, I suppose it is a false rumour.'[9] Within the spirit-filled cosmology of Sri Lankan Buddhism and Maitriya's own investigations into Theosophy, Ananda M's namesake could tolerate Ananda M having been involved with spiritualism, but recognition that he could have taken opium, even medicinally, was more difficult for him.[10]

The memory of Ananda M cultivated by organisations such as the Servants of the Buddha and embodied in Balangoda Ānanda Maitreya meant that anniversaries connected with Ananda M's life were noticed by the Sri Lankan media. *The Daily News*, for instance, on 23 April, 1968, marks the 60th anniversary of Ananda M's mission to Britain. The mission is presented as 'the first Buddhist mission to a European country' and is romanticised through a picture of instant conversions on Ananda M's arrival: 'A shining figure in saffron robes he made a deep impression on those who sought his guidance on the truths of Buddhism and many were converted on this day' (Ratnajinendra 1968). The article cites the Buddhist centres in Britain as 'evidence' of 'Ananda Metteyya's indefatigable labours' and ends:

> As a sower of seeds, Ananda Metteyya deserves all praise. Were he alive today to see the harvest he would have good reason to rejoice. For Buddhism has gained a firm footing in Britain with many thousands of adherents who are steadily increasing in numbers from year to year. It is against this background that the mission Ananda Metteyya led to England sixty years ago acquires real significance. (Ratnajinendra 1968)

In 1973, William Peiris, a Sri Lankan journalist, broadcaster and writer, published thumbnail sketches of 89 westerners who had contributed to Buddhism, offering an early template for the understanding of Ananda M by Asians. Drawing on the writing of Christmas Humphreys, he presents Ananda M as the son of an engineer, the second Englishman to be ordained a Buddhist monk and the first to lead a Buddhist mission to the West. He dates his reading of *The Light of Asia* to 1890 [his 18th year] and claims, diverging from Humphreys, that his ordination was in Colombo. The Hope Lodge lecture is presented as 'his first sermon,' as if he had been already ordained (Pieris 2017: 63-64). The work was republished in 2017 by the Buddhist Cultural Centre in Dehiwela, south of the centre of Colombo, and so continues to influence Sri Lankan Buddhists.

In Asia, therefore, Ananda M has been largely represented after his death as a prime mover within the spread of Buddhism in the West. Neither his esoteric background nor his struggles with illness and the drugs prescribed to alleviate his symptoms are stressed, with the exception of the Phay Zaw Gyi clip in Myanmar. What is important is that Ananda M was an Englishman who wore the yellow robes of a Buddhist monk and had a passion for the spread of Buddhism to the West.

ENGLAND AND THE WEST

After Ananda M's death, the Buddhist Society of Great Britain and Ireland became weaker and was eventually dissolved in 1926 (Gethin 2000: 32), in spite of the 36 lectures on Buddhism that Francis Payne gave in 1923 and 1924 at the old Essex Hall in the Strand in central London in an attempt to keep the Society alive (Humphreys 1968: 16–17; 1985: 225).[11] By 1926, however, two other initiatives were continuing the vision of the original society, albeit in different ways. In 1924, British barrister and Theosophist, Travers Christmas Humphreys (1901–1983) founded a Buddhist Centre within the Theosophical Society, the first meeting being held on 24 July. He had been impressed by Payne's last lecture and a Vesak meeting held by the Buddhist Society and the London Buddhist League in 1924 (Humphreys 1968: 17–19). Humphreys's aim was 'to form a nucleus of persons ... as are prepared to study, disseminate and attempt to live the fundamental principles of Buddhism as viewed in the light of theosophy.'[12] Its first meeting attracted three Ceylonese, one Burmese and four people from Britain, including Humphreys and his future wife, Aileen Faulkner. The first meeting decided that the Centre would meet a need 'not at present supplied by the Buddhist League or Buddhist Society.'[13] In August of the same year, however, they decided to join the Buddhist League and made an effort to encourage members of what they saw as the dying Buddhist Society to join them (Humphreys 1968: 19).[14] According to Humphreys, many did, with the exception of Payne, who had a deep suspicion of Theosophy (Humphreys 1968: 20) and eventually moved toward the Anagārika Dharmapāla's initiatives. In November 1924, the Centre became a Buddhist Lodge, still within the Theosophical Society, and, at the beginning of 1925, it opened a Buddhist Shrine Room in London.

In May 1926, the first issue of the Lodge's journal, *Buddhism in England*, was released. It makes clear the link between the Lodge and Theosophy. In the second issue, for instance, Humphreys states, 'The cherished ideal of this Lodge is to re-establish in the East and West the recognition of the fundamental identity of Theosophy and Buddhism' (Humphreys 1926a: 29).

In October 1926, however, the Lodge became independent from the Theosophical Society, relationships having become strained due to differences concerning the nature of Theosophy (Humphreys 1968: 25).[15] Its object then changed: 'to form a nucleus of such persons as are prepared to study, disseminate, and endeavour to live the fundamental principles of Buddhism.'[16] Humphreys distinguishes the Lodge from the older Buddhist Society by stressing that the Lodge 'focused on producing Buddhists, unafraid to style themselves as such, rather than on making known the finer points of Buddhism' (Humphreys 1968: 21). Eventually, in 1943, the Lodge re-formed as The Buddhist Society (Humphreys 1985: 225).[17]

The second initiative began with the Anagārika Dharmapāla, who heard Humphreys speak at a special meeting of the Buddhist Lodge on 28 September, 1925, when he visited Britain on his way to America.[18] The next day, a meeting was held in Dharmapāla's bedroom 'to formulate plans for the future of Buddhism in London' with Dharmapāla, Raja Hewavitarne, E. E. Power, Aileen Faulkner, Payne and Humphreys among those present. Not unsurprisingly, Payne and Humphreys clashed. According to Humphreys, it was his own plan and not Payne's that was carried, namely, to begin with intellectuals and to rent a house rather than buy one.[19] At first, Dharmapāla and Humphreys seem to have worked together to acquire this house, but they soon diverged, Humphreys simply recording, 'We left the A. Dh to get his own house as he did not like the ones we suggested.'[20]

Dharmapāla bought a house at 86 Madeley Road, Ealing, in West London, which he named after Mary Foster, an American benefactress of Hawaiian origin who had funded some of his previous projects. At the same time, he formed the British Mahabodhi Society, which launched its own journal, *The British Buddhist*, with Francis Payne and McKechnie, who had disrobed by this time, on the editorial committee (Webb 2004: 2-3). Within the next two years, a further property was bought, 41 Gloucester Road, Regent's Park, to serve as a *vihāra* (monastery), financially supported by Ceylonese Buddhists (Buddhism in England 1928: 1-4). In July 1928, three *bhikkhus* from Ceylon arrived in Britain to take up residence, Paravahera Vajirañāna, Dehigaspe Paññāsāra and Hegoda Nandasāra (Webb 2004: 4-5). According to the report of this in *The British Buddhist*, 'One hundred British Buddhists and sympathisers and a score of Sinhalese Buddhists' gathered to welcome them and celebrate both a Buddhist festival and the second anniversary of the British Mahabodhi Society (The British Buddhist 1928: 12-13).[21] This marked the beginning of what would become the London Buddhist Vihara.

Initially, there was a close relationship between the Buddhist Lodge, with its Theosophical interest, and the British Mahabodhi Society and its *vihāra*. Asian Buddhists were involved with both initiatives, as the minutes of the Buddhist Lodge demonstrate. However, the two bodies did not merge. This may partly have been due to the influence of Francis Payne, and the tension between Payne and Humphreys.[22] Dharmapāla's initiative became rooted in Theravada Buddhism and developed a dislike for Theosophy, something Humphreys found difficult to understand, given Dharmapāla's initial involvement with the movement (Humphreys 1968: 26).[23] The Buddhist Lodge, on the other hand, in the words of Humphreys, 'would have found the tie to Theravada Buddhism embarrassing' (Humphreys 1968: 26). Humphreys was reported as saying at the welcome for the *bhikkhus* that he 'desired the formation of a new vehicle of Buddhism to suit the conditions prevailing in England' (The British Buddhist 1928: 13).

Ananda M's Buddha *rūpa* (image) also caused tension between these two initiatives. It was in the hands of Francis Payne and Humphreys evidently thought that it should belong to his Lodge if the Lodge was to gain its charter. Humphreys minutes, on 18 November, 1924, that 'A deputation was organised to descend upon Mr Payne and demand Metteyya's Buddha Rupa from him.'[24] An unclear entry suggests that Payne did hand it over.[25] In May 1926, it appeared 'covered with flowers on a platform' at the Wesak celebrations held by Buddhists in London.[26]

In addition to the conflict over Ananda M's Buddha image, the memory of Ananda M continued in both initiatives in a more positive way. By 1928, Ananda M's hope that a community of Buddhist monks would be established in the West as a role model for others was partly fulfilled through the Anagārika Dharmapāla, although the monks were not Western and, according to Webb, were, at first, 'totally unversed in Western ways' (Webb 2004: 5). Within the Buddhist Lodge, on the other hand, one of the first doctrinal issues discussed was *anattā* (not-self), the key point at which Ananda M diverged from Theosophy.[27] Then, in June 1925, the Lodge decided to study a book and chose Ananda M's, *The Wisdom of the Aryas* (Bennett 1923).[28] The Lodge also recorded their wish 'to get in touch with other Buddhist groups in Europe and form in time some form of International Alliance.'[29] We do not know whether this was done in awareness of the previously mentioned International Buddhist Union.

Christmas Humphreys, in addition, actively engaged with Ananda M's life, influencing, through his writing, early academic representations. His first account came in 1937 in *The Development of Buddhism in England* (Humphreys 1937: 13-37). A shortened version of this was submitted to the *Encyclopaedia of Buddhism* (Humphreys 1961), a magisterial government-sponsored project in newly independent Sri Lanka. His more extensive history, *Sixty Years of Buddhism in England 1907-1967*, begins with the formation of the Buddhist Society of Great Britain and Ireland, and Ananda M's mission (Humphreys 1968: 1-7). His accounts, which we have used in earlier chapters of this book, are based on personal encounters with those who had known Ananda M. The crayon drawing of Ananda M by Alexander Fisher, which can still be seen on the wall of the library at the present headquarters of The Buddhist Society in Eccleston Square, London, is included in each publication.[30] Humphreys does not hide Ananda M's struggle with drugs such as heroin, but hardly mentions his involvement with Theosophy, the Golden Dawn, or Aleister Crowley. Humphreys's Ananda M is purely a Buddhist monk and Buddhist missionary, who was hindered in his mission by drugs and chronic illness.

Myokyo-Ni (1921–2007), one of the early teachers of Zen in the United Kingdom, and a key voice at The Buddhist Society in the late-twentieth century,[31] in a letter to Elizabeth, remembers Christmas Humphreys often talking about Ananda M. She adds:

> Fact is that his arrival in this country had lasting effects—not only as a first attempt to proclaim the Buddha's teachings but resulting later in a most generous financial support and other gifts the Burmese Sangha accorded the nascent Buddhist Society well into the fifties I believe.[32]

It is interesting, however, that Ananda M is rarely mentioned in the first issues of *Buddhism in England*. A short history of Buddhism in Great Britain, published in 1929, briefly mentions his 1908 mission (Anon 1929b). Humphreys's response to Ananda M's letter concerning the worth of bringing a single *bhikkhu* to England, when it is reprinted in *The Buddhist Annual of Ceylon* of 1929 (Ananda Metteyya 1929), is also carried by the journal, gaining both critical and supportive responses (Humphreys 1929: 127; Buddhism in England 1930: 168–169). Then, when Humphreys appeals to Burmese Buddhists for ongoing financial support, the precedent of Ananda M is stressed (Humphreys 1930: 53).

In addition, *Buddhism in England* serialised, 'A Reasoned Exposition of Buddhism from a Western Standpoint,' which also engages with Ananda M.[33] It probably arose from conversations held during Lodge meetings. Immediately after the serialisation had finished, the whole was published as a book, *What is Buddhism? An Answer from the Western Point of View* (The Buddhist Society 1947). The first edition appeared in 1928, with a revised edition in 1931 and a war edition in 1942, reprinted in 1947, by which time the Buddhist Lodge had become The Buddhist Society. By 1968, it had sold almost 3,000 copies of these three editions (Humphreys 1968: 32). The publication uses a 'Question and Answer' format and draws on Theosophical, universalist and Buddhist sources, which are listed at the end. Two of these are by Ananda M: *The Wisdom of the Aryas* (Bennett 1923) and *The Religion of Burma* (Bennett 1929). Alongside these are works by Edwin Arnold, Blavatsky, Paul Carus, Ananda Coomaraswamy, Paul Dahlke, Walter Evans-Wentz, Max Müller, Olcott, T. W. Rhys Davids, Bhikkhu Sīlācāra and D. T. Suzuki (The Buddhist Society 1947: 217–221). In consequence, Buddhism is presented as a universalist religion. It expresses Humphreys's Theosophist identity, including his belief that Buddhism is 'the noblest and least defiled of the many branches of the undying parent tree' that Blavatsky spoke about (Humphreys 1968: 18). That 'All Life was One' is repeatedly stressed, with no reference to Ananda M's use of the term.

It was Ananda M's claim in his third Clifford Bax lecture that the Pali term *anattā* should not be translated as 'soullessness' that was seized on in *What is Buddhism?* (Bennett 1923: 57; The Buddhist Society 1947: 42), but the aim was to support the position of the Theosophist-inspired Buddhist Lodge rather than to promote Ananda M's thought. Admittedly, this section of Ananda M's lecture sought to reach out to the Theosophists in his audience, as indicated in the last chapter, but the Lodge uses it to go further than Ananda M would have desired. *What is Buddhism?* thus argues that the Buddha 'maintained a noble silence' on whether the soul existed and taught that *anattā* pointed towards the interconnectedness of everything (The Buddhist Society 1947: 44–45). It was the false, egoistic self, 'the fleeting personality,' that the Buddha condemned, not the true Self, which was 'nothing less than that Ultimate Reality of which each human being sooner or later comes to feel the need'—a 'Cosmic Principle,' the vehicle of which was '*Buddhi*, or *Bodhi*' (The Buddhist Society 1947: 74–75).[34] The book represents Ananda M as a pioneer of Buddhism in Britain, but he could not be seen as going against the principles underlying The Buddhist Lodge and so had to be reconstructed in its image. This may also explain why *Buddhism in England* did not publish Ananda M's articles.

The Anagārika Dharmapāla also rarely mentions Ananda M in *The British Buddhist*. In some lists of 'Buddhist Literature in English,' *The Wisdom of the Aryas* is mentioned but with his lay name misspelt as 'Allen Bennet.'[35] In 1927, however, the journal led with a short article by Ananda M, entitled 'Buddhist Psychology' (Ananda Metteyya 1927), which argues that *anattā* is 'the essence and foundation of Buddhism' (Ananda Metteyya 1927: 3). This could have held an implicit message for the Buddhist Lodge. Nothing, however, is said about Ananda M. The reason could be that the Anagārika Dharmapāla was, at this point, presenting himself as the leader of the first Buddhist mission to Britain. Volume One, Number 8 of *The British Buddhist* carries a photo of Dharmapāla on the front page, with the words 'The Ven'ble [Venerable] Anagarika Dharmapala, Director General of the First Buddhist Mission to England and founder of the Maha Bodhi Society.' This could be read as a supplanting of Ananda M's 1908 mission, although Dharmapāla had visited London twice before 1908, once in 1893 on the way to the World's Parliament of Religions in Chicago and once in 1904 (Kemper 2015: 453–460), when he did speak to English audiences. His diary states that he gave a lecture at the Unitarian Hall in Liverpool and then another at the Ruskin Society, adding that it was the first time he had spoken to an 'English audience.'[36] A few months later, in December 1927, Dharmapāla writes in the Maha-Bodhi Society's journal, 'I am the first Buddhist missionary to England and our Maha Bodhi Society intends to erect the first Temple in London shortly' (Guruge 1991: 446). Nevertheless, in a later volume of *The British Buddhist*, almost as a space-filler, a picture of Ananda M is included, with the statement that he 'brought the Message of Buddhism to the British people in 1907,' the date misremembered.[37]

In the years after the Buddhist Lodge became The Buddhist Society, there were further re-evaluations and reinventions of Buddhist identity in Britain, and these included the distancing of Buddhism from magic and occultism, and even from the Theosophical convictions of Humphreys. Francis Story, in the 1960s, for instance, published extracts from the early issues of *The Buddhist Review*. He stresses the commitment to and knowledge of Buddhism present in them, and uses them to draw a line between the former Buddhist Society and what had preceded it:

> It cannot be denied that there were some questionable personalities vaguely associated in the public mind with the early Buddhist movements, but the dabblers in the occult, make-believe magi[c]ians and other picturesque poseurs were not Buddhists in any sense, and most of them were not even on the fringe of genuine Buddhist activities. (Story 1981: 5)

Ananda M is not, however, included in this sweeping judgement, his involvement with the Golden Dawn forgotten or consciously ignored for the purpose of affirming affinity between *The Buddhist Review* and the new Buddhist Society. Story, therefore, represents Ananda M favourably at the end of his life, as engaged in 'a personal war against poverty and increasing sickness,' working 'on inventions that he hoped would bring much-needed money to the movement' and lecturing on the *Dhamma* 'when his health permitted, to a small group of earnest students' (Story 1981: 49). Later, Story states that together with Edward Greenly and J. E. Ellam, Ananda M had been 'gifted beyond the average in literary expression' (Story 1981: 65). Indeed, before Story wrote, *The Buddhist Review* reprinted Ananda M's 'Buddhist Self-Culture,' from 1914 (Ananda Metteyya 1954). As we show, however, magic and mystery continued to surround his memory, creating ambivalence and sometimes outright opposition to him among Buddhists in Britain.

FRIENDS AND ASSOCIATES OF ANANDA M

We have used posthumous accounts of Ananda M by his friends and associates in previous chapters in order to build up a picture of his life. These will not be repeated here. Crowley's representation of Ananda M has already been examined, as has Raphael Hurst's judgement that Ananda M was the most 'advanced Western Yogi' of the first part of the twentieth century (Brunton 1941: 1, 4).[38] As for Battiscombe and Meena Gunn, only speculations are possible. Spiritually, Battiscombe did not move further towards Buddhism, in spite of the undoubted influence of Ananda M. Rather, he and Meena became interested in Freudian psychoanalysis. Meena studied under Freud in Paris and practised in this field for over 40 years. Battiscombe became Professor of Egyptology at the University of Oxford in 1934. They divorced in 1940. Whether Ananda M's interest in the workings of the mind turned both towards Freud is not known, but it is a possibility.

In contrast to the Gunns, Clifford Bax continued to be influenced by Buddhism. For instance, he sent copies of *The Wisdom of the Aryas* to his close friends, including the playwright Gordon Bottomley. Bottomley replied with words that intimate what Buddhism and, by extension, Ananda M, continued to mean for Bax: 'I feel that in it is the core and intimacy of yourself, and that in sending it to me you are, as it were, trusting me in your sanctuary and treasure-house and with what is precious to you.' Although Bottomley cannot bring himself to sympathise with Ananda M's representation of Buddhism, he expresses his respect for 'Mr Bennett.'[39] In 1927, Eric Evans, assessing Bax's artistic output, suggests that, as he moved beyond Theosophy, 'he found himself nearer to a real mysticism, and nearer to Buddhism' and speculates, 'It must be to Allan Bennett that Mr. Bax owes much of the serenity which permeates some of his poems' (Evans 1927: 124).

The influence of Ananda M on Bax can be seen as late as 1947, when he wrote a radio play on the life of the Buddha that was broadcast on Sunday, 16 March of that year. Intimations of Edwin Arnold's *The Light of Asia* can be detected in it, but so also can Ananda M's views concerning *anattā* and the remembrance of past lives. Bax's Buddha, after his enlightenment, for example, is asked whether he will teach that there is no soul. The Buddha replies, 'I am. I must. For they think of the soul as though it were an indestructible diamond, ever the same' (Bax 1947: 43) Later, the Buddha says this:

> My ever-changing self is not separate from all other beings as my body is. That feeling of separateness is the great heresy. As I grew in meditation I began to transcend my personal self and to merge into the seeming selves of a thousand other entities. They became I and I became them. I am one with the beasts of the jungle, with the birds and insects, with the trees, with the round of earth itself and even with the gigantic stars of space. (Bax 1947: 44)

This could well have been influenced both by Ananda M's interpretation of *anattā* and by his insistence that 'All life is One.' Even closer to Ananda M's thought is the part in which Bax places in the Buddha's mouth the technique of remembering past lives through thinking backwards over one day and then over one's lifetime, until one begins 'to recall events that seem to pertain to some other person' but are 'both you and not you' (Bax 1947: 57–58). It is unlikely that Bax read the *Visuddhimagga* and more than likely that he was recalling conversations with Ananda M, or thinking of Ananda M's 'Training of the Mind,' published by Crowley, whom Bax knew (Ananda Metteya 1911).

THE SRI SADDHATISSA INTERNATIONAL BUDDHIST CENTRE

At the end of the twentieth century, the Sri Saddhatissa International Buddhist Centre/World Buddhist Foundation re-energised interest in Ananda M. Branding itself as a preserver of Sri Lankan Buddhist culture and a pioneer of outward-facing community relations, it was founded in 1989, in Kingsbury, north-west London, at a time of expansion for Theravada Buddhism in Greater London (Deegalle 2005: 177). Its Head Monk, Galayaye Piyadassi (d. 2022), when writing a dissertation on the role of the Sri Lankan Buddhist monk in the development of Theravada Buddhism in Great Britain, 'discovered' Ananda M's 1908 mission and, in conversation with Sri Lankan academic colleagues, decided that it should be given more recognition (Piyadassi 2008). So, in 1996, he started to hold annual United Kingdom Buddhist Days that were explicitly linked to Ananda M, as the founder of Buddhism in the United Kingdom. 'For the first time, Ananda Metteyya's work was recognised,' Piyadassi declares in 2008 (Piyadassi 2008). To take the 1997 event as an example, the promotional literature states:

> 'The United Kingdom Buddhist Day' commemorates the founding day of Buddhism in this land. The teaching was introduced 89 years ago by an Englishman named Charles Henry Allan Bennett who had been ordained as a Buddhist monk in Burma in 1902, taking the name of Ananda Metteyya. It was in 1908 that he returned to the United Kingdom to establish the Buddhist mission here.

The keynote speaker was Rupert Gethin of Bristol University, with the topic, 'The History and Development of Buddhism in the UK.' The mayors of Brent and Harrow, the Sri Lankan High Commissioner, representatives from other religions in Brent, and *bhikkhus* from other Sri Lankan Buddhist *vihāras* in London were invited, together with representatives from other Buddhist traditions. The programme was placed in a ritual setting with observation of the five precepts at the beginning and, after the vote of thanks, a *Buddhapūja* (devotion directed towards the Buddha) and *paritta* (the chanting of discourses from the Pali texts believed to bring blessing and protection).

In 1998, Elizabeth Harris gave a talk on Ananda M himself: 'The Power of Compassion: A Study of the Life and Thought of the Ven. Ananda Metteyya.'[40] By the seventh Buddhist Day, held on 2 June, 2003, the promotional words on the advocacy flyer had been reduced to, 'To commemorate the arrival of the first Buddhist Emissary Charles Henry Allan Bennett (Bhikkhu Ananda Metteyya) in 1908.' The speaker was the Sri Lankan scholar, Ananda Guruge, then attached to Hsi Lai University in Los Angeles. He spoke on 'Buddhism for the Western Society.' The civic nature of the event was by this time explicitly stressed: 'Participants will include members of the Maha Sangha; representatives of diplomatic corps, civic dignitaries; clergy of other faiths and distinguished laity.' In September 2005, Elizabeth Harris again spoke at the UK Buddhist Day Celebration, this time on the 'British Encounter with Buddhism in 19th Century Sri Lanka' using her 2006 monograph (see Harris 2006).

The 2008 commemoration, held on 28 September, 2008, had additional flair to mark the 'Centenary Celebrations of the Establishment of Buddhism in the UK.' Brent Town Hall was booked. Richard Gombrich and Ananda Guruge were enlisted as keynote speakers. Leaders of the monastic Sangha in Sri Lanka and Myanmar were invited to attend. A DVD on the life of Ananda Metteyya was produced and shown during the event, and an edited collection of 12 scholarly articles on Buddhism in the UK was published (Deegalle 2008). The authors of this biography each contributed a chapter to the volume (Crow 2008b; Harris 2008). In addition, all participants were handed a glossy brochure containing messages on behalf of the Queen and the Prince of Wales, together with congratulations from the President and Prime Minister of Sri Lanka, Sri Lankan Buddhist leaders, the Dalai Lama, and numerous other local and international religious and civic leaders. The formal proceedings were followed by a cultural concert of religious performances from different Buddhist countries, which lasted well into the evening.

The message of the brochure is encapsulated by the cover, which superimposes Alexander Fisher's crayon drawing of Ananda M onto an outline of Britain, together with the Buddhist flag and the flag of Britain. The implicit message is that Ananda M's mission, Buddhism and

Figure 6.2 Notices of UK Buddhist Day events, held by the Sri Saddhatissa International Buddhist Centre, courtesy Elizabeth Harris.

Figure 6.3 Cover of Dharma to the UK, *published by the Sri Saddhatissa International Buddhist Centre, London*

patriotism for Britain can go together. The Preface, written by Galayaye Piyadassi, justifies the focus on Ananda M with these words:

> According to Buddhist tradition recorded in Sri Lankan Chronicles, Buddhism is recognised to be established in a country only when a son of parents born in the country embrace[s] Buddhism, become[s] an ordained monk and teach[es] the doctrine in that country. The honour of being the first ordained Britisher to fulfil this criterion goes to Mr Charles Henry Bennett or Ven. Ananda Metteyya. Indeed not only in the United Kingdom, but for the whole Western World, he was the pioneer. (World Buddhist Foundation 2008: 3)

The separately printed programme gives a brief outline of Ananda M's life. Again, no mention is made of his esoteric background. His journey to Sri Lanka 'to study Buddhism further' is attributed to Sri Lankan Buddhists who were 'actively propagating the religion in the UK at the time.' He is also presented as giving 'a series of lectures on Buddhism at the Theosophical Society in Colombo.'

The beautifully illustrated DVD was produced by Tissa Madawela, a London-based Sri Lankan artist and photographer, and researched by Handupelpola Mahinda Nayaka Thera, who visited Divigalahena Devagiri Purāna Vihāraya at Kamburugamuwa, speaking to another informant from the one used by Elizabeth Harris—a Mr. Gunadasa, who confirmed

Figure 6.4 Cover of the brochure published by the World Buddhist Foundation/ Sri Saddhatissa International Buddhist Centre to mark the centenary of Ananda M's mission to Britain, 2008, courtesy Elizabeth Harris.

that Ananda M had been known as the 'slim, white gentleman.' The DVD makes no mention of Ananda M's Theosophist or esoteric involvements, stressing only that he had been influenced by *The Light of Asia*, had rejected the Roman Catholicism of his mother, and had turned to Hinduism before embracing Buddhism, all before he travelled to Sri Lanka. It was not Aleister Crowley who encouraged Ananda M to go to Sri Lanka but W. Arthur de Silva, who introduced him to Richard Pereira, who in turn took him to Kamburugamuwa. We have mentioned this possibility in Chapter Two. The myth that he was adopted by a Mr. McGregor, after his father died young, is repeated, and much is made of the fact that Ananda M created the first Buddhist temple in Britain, from his house in Barnes, when he returned in 1908. Some statements and dates are simply wrong, for example, that he returned from Burma to give his 1901 lecture on the Four Noble Truths in Colombo and that he moved to London in 1920, a date most probably taken from Mullen (Mullen 1989: 2). Nevertheless, the DVD fulfills its aim of presenting Ananda M as a pioneer, who believed that the deliverance of the West was possible through Buddhism. One of the last clips is of Galayaye Piyadassi and colleagues at Ananda M's unmarked grave in Morden Cemetery (Madawela 2008).

In 2009, it was John Crow who gave the keynote address, this time on 'Spreading the Light of Asia to Europe: Ananda Metteyya's Buddhist Message to the West' (Crow 2010). He focused on Ananda M's representation of Buddhism to Westerners, including his understanding of the Four Noble Truths, his view of Buddhism's compatibility with science, and his insistence that Buddhism was a total way of life, rather than something to be thought about occasionally.

By 2010, the celebration of the UK Buddhist Day had again shifted away from Ananda M to other topics. For instance, in 2010, Ananda Guruge's keynote lecture addressed the 'British Contribution to the Promotion of Buddhist Studies' (Guruge 2011).

ANANDA M'S GRAVE

Ananda M's grave remains unmarked, in an unconsecrated section of the cemetery reserved for non-Christians. There have been several attempts to have a gravestone erected. In the same decade as the Sri Saddhatissa International Buddhist Centre started its United Kingdom Buddhist Days, the 1990s, Ron Maddox, when he was General Secretary of The Buddhist Society, explored whether it would be possible to erect one. Another member of the Society found the grave and discovered that it would indeed be possible, if carried out by an organisation such as The Buddhist Society. However, when the idea was taken to the other office holders, there was opposition and no action was taken. When Elizabeth spoke to Maddox in 2023, he speculated that the probable reason was that Ananda M was such a mixture of 'darkness and light,' adding that he personally had been in favour of the Society doing something to mark the grave.[41] The Sri Saddhatissa Centre attempted the same thing, without success. Both Galayaye Piyadassi and Handupelpola Mahinda were keen to push this forward but ill health intervened for both of them, with the result that their hopes were not realised.[42] Complications regarding burial plot ownership and familial permission were also obstacles.

ACADEMIC REPRESENTATIONS OF ANANDA M

Academic representations of Ananda Metteyya in Britain and the West have been mentioned in the Introduction and throughout this biography. The writings of Christmas Humphreys have been a foundational resource. By the twenty-first century, a stereotype of Ananda M as a member of an uninteresting, educated elite had emerged, in contrast to the charisma of working class converts such as the Irish seaman, U Dhammaloka (e.g.,

Turner, Cox and Bocking 2020). Misrepresentations abounded, because of the lack of accurate information. He almost became a punchbag for those who wished to critique his perceived elitism or diminish his 1908 mission. Ian Oliver, one of the first academics to write on Buddhism in Britain, claims that 'Bennett' had turned to science because of his father's profession as an engineer and that his 1908 mission had been 'very successful,' with Ananda M returning to Burma 'delighted with his mission.' The reader, however, is confused with contradictory dates.[43] Oliver then intimates that, after 1908, Ananda M returned to Britain twice from Burma, once in 1914 and once in 1920 (Oliver 1979: 43–45). No mention is made by Oliver either of Theosophy or the esoteric in Ananda M's biography.

Stephen Batchelor, in 1995, presents a more accurate picture, stressing Ananda M's friendship with Crowley and his membership of the Golden Dawn, but buys into the half-truth that his 1908 mission was 'abandoned' because of failure (Batchelor 1995: 41). Specialist in Buddhism in Europe, Martin Baumann, writes in 2002 that 'Allan Bennett McGregor' was Scottish and states wrongly that he founded the Buddhist Society of Great Britain and Ireland in 1907 (Baumann 2002: 87), a point repeated by Jairam Ramesh in 2021 (Ramesh 2021: 230). J. Jeffrey Franklin, in his study of literature, Buddhism and Empire, gives Ananda M the name 'Charles Bennett,' states that he was 'the first British Buddhist monk,' and makes a direct causal link between his reading of *The Light of Asia* and his higher ordination as a *bhikkhu* (Franklin 2008: 25). Robert Bluck, in 2012, when writing a short account of Buddhism in the United Kingdom, mentions Ananda M only in the context of his 1908 mission, claiming that he 'was not a good speaker and, hampered by *Vinaya* restrictions on eating, sleeping and handling money, he returned disappointed to Burma after five months' (Bluck 2012: 396). All these representations are incomplete, based on paucity of data.

Twenty-first century academic representations of Ananda M include the theory that it was Ananda M who first used the term 'Theravada' to describe the religious culture and dispensation of Southern Buddhism, the form of Buddhism that is united by the Pali canonical texts. We have mentioned this in Chapter Four, citing the work of Todd LeRoy Perreira (LeRoy Perreira 2012).[44] LeRoy Perreira offers a detailed account of Ananda M's struggle to find a fitting term for what many people at the time were calling 'Hinayana'—the lesser vehicle. He cites an article that Ananda M published in advance of his 1908 mission in the *Bulletin de L'École française d'Extrême-Orient*, in which he mentions 'l'école Theravada' (Theravada school), not as a monastic community or a collection of texts but as modern, lived Buddhism in south and south-east Asia (LeRoy Perreira 2012: 549–550).

Perreira shows that Ananda M repeats this in his article 'Propaganda' (Ananda Metteyya 1908a), as well as in 'The Religion of Burma' (Ananda M 1910). The uncovering of this history was a turning point in Buddhist Studies, but has been contested. Bhikkhu Anālayo, for instance, argues that 'closer inspection shows the situation to be considerably more complex, as Asian antecedents to such usage can be identified' (Anālayo 2021: 108). Other aspects of his work, however, have been overlooked, particularly in the study of Buddhism in Burma and Ceylon, for instance, his contribution to the temperance movement in Ceylon, mentioned in Chapter Two, his sensitivity to lived religion, and his awareness of neuroscience.

As mentioned previously, historians of esotericism, particularly of the Golden Dawn, have focussed on Bennett's creation of magical ceremonies and his relationship with Crowley and Mathers. Other scholars of esotericism have looked at Bennett differently. Joscelyn Godwin's *The Theosophical Enlightenment*[45] is an intellectual history of esotericism that starts with the early Romantic period, tracing it to the beginning of the twentieth century. The last chapter, 'The Parting of East and West,' examines how Western esotericism embraced Eastern teaching, opening a completely new horizon at the end of the nineteenth century. In many ways, Bennett represents the culmination of the book. Godwin writes:

> Allan Bennett embodies the "enlightenment" of my title in both its meanings. He was a thoroughly modern man: converted to atheism by science; believing in evolution and progress; trusting in human reason and technology to bring about a Golden Age of peace and plenty. At the same time, he was a magician who commanded awed respect from his colleagues in the occult sciences, even the most ambitious and egotistic of them. (Godwin 1994: 374)

For Godwin, Bennett brings together both the nineteenth century's search for spiritual enlightenment, and the French Enlightenment's moral and philosophical quest. In the work of most other scholars of esotericism, Bennett is usually not mentioned.

The exception is scholarship related to Crowley, in which Bennett appears only through his interactions with Crowley. For instance, in a volume of collected essays on Crowley, Bennett is represented in ways similar to Golden Dawn histories. Bennett is Crowley's teacher of Golden Dawn magic, tutor of yoga and meditation in Ceylon, author of the Taphthartharath ritual, and the person who introduces Crowley to the use of drugs for spiritual and magical purposes (Bogdan and Starr 2012).

Bennett is mentioned briefly and in similar ways in most other Crowley scholarship, including the myriad biographies of Crowley. However, there are a couple of differences. First, the biographies include discussions of the Looking Glass trial, and thus mention Bennett in that context. Second, and more importantly, the authors occasionally include a commentary on the relationship between Crowley and Bennett. As most biographies of Crowley depend heavily on Crowley's own autobiography, and thus repeat the same information about Bennett, these commentaries shed more light on the author's view of Crowley or magic than on Bennett or his relationship with Crowley. For instance, Lawrence Sutin's biography claims that there was a distinct split between the two and, in evidence, he cites the review of Crowley's book, 777, in *The Buddhist Review*. Published in the third issue, in July 1909, the review ends by dismissing the volume, stating, 'No Buddhist would admit such correspondence, or consider it worth while to pass from the crystalline clearness of his own religion to this involved obscurity. Some of the language is extremely undignified' (The Buddhist Review 1909c: 222). From this unsigned review, Sutin surmises that Bennett now felt 'disdain' for Crowley, and that, when Crowley later tried to rekindle their relationship, Bennett was reluctant. As further evidence, Sutin cites a letter in which Crowley writes, 'I hope you're sitting down to the siege of Allan & picking his brains.' Sutin comments, 'The use of "siege" is telling; the friendship was now at an end' (Sutin 2000: 193–194). While this evidence seems conclusive to Sutin, and for Gary Lachman who repeats it in his biography (Lachman 2014: 169), Sutin's evidence is ambiguous, at best. Most importantly, the review of 777 is not signed by Bennett. At the time of the review's publication, the editor of *The Buddhist Review* was John E. Ellam, not Ananda M, and Ellam probably authored the review with the intention of distancing the Buddhist Society from Crowley. As for Sutin's claim that Crowley attempted to rekindle their relationship, there is no evidence for this as far as we are aware.[46]

Martin Booth's *A Magick Life: A Biography of Aleister Crowley* is the only work that picks up on Bennett's statement about Crowley as given by Bax: 'As Allan Bennett remarked to Clifford Bax some years on, Crowley could have brought much goodness to the world but took a wrong turning in his life instead' (Booth 2000: 243). Why no other biographers mention this statement is unclear.

In contrast, Israel Regardie writes in his biography of Crowley that 'Bennett had been a superb teacher. No wonder Crowley was thoroughly devoted to him, and spoke so glowingly of him for the rest of his life. Even when Allan became a Buddhist monk, no enmity sprang up between these two men' (Regardie 1982: 167). In a letter to John Symonds, an early Crowley biographer, Edward 'Ted' Bryant describes his impression of Crowley's feelings about Bennett when Crowley recalled Bennett-related stories in the early 1940s: 'Aleister always showed the deepest respect (reverence even) for Allan & it often struck me that in one corner of his mind, at least, he thought of himself as the Disciple to Allan's Master.'[47]

However, the most likely description of the relationship between Crowley and Bennett after Bennett's ordination is the one presented by Richard Kaczynski in his biography of Crowley. When examining the Looking Glass trial in 1910, Kaczynski notes, 'By this point the spiritual paths of Crowley and Metteya had diverged and they continued to drift apart' (Kaczynski 2010: 613n71). As noted in Chapter Four, there may have been a possibility of them meeting during Ananda M's mission in 1908, but if a meeting occurred, it is not mentioned by Ananda M and Crowley neglects to note it in his magical journals, which would be surprising, given Crowley's attitudes to his teacher.[48]

THE THEOSOPHICAL SOCIETY

Despite expelling Allan Bennett from the Theosophical Society in 1895 for supporting W. Q. Judge, Theosophists interpreted and engaged with Ananda M's writings and activities after his ordination. As we have shown, not only did he meet with significant leaders of the Society when they visited Rangoon, Theosophists frequently reviewed his published material, both positively and negatively, and reprinted a variety of his essays within Theosophical journals while he was alive. After his death, Theosophists had no qualms about consolidating and republishing his writings, always with an eye to re-contextualising what he said to better match Theosophical teachings. For instance, in 1929, the Theosophical Publishing House in Adyar, India, published *The Religion of Burma and Other Papers* by Allan Bennett. It contains nine of Ananda M's articles and two appendices: Cassius Pereira's obituary and a short piece by Ananda M, 'Buddha-Hood as an Office.' 'The Religion of Burma' from *Twentieth Century Impressions of Burma* (Wright 1910) comes first, followed by: The Three Signata; Right Understanding; The Culture of Mind; The Miraculous Element in Buddhism; The Rule of the Inner Kingdom; Devotion in Buddhism; Buddhist Self-Culture; and Kamma. The representation of Ananda M in the introduction is guarded. He is lauded as a poet and a 'remarkable man' (Bennett 1929: v-vi) and praised with the words, 'Ages have passed since the Dhamma has been set forth with such power, and who can tell when it will be so set forth again?' (Bennett 1929: vii). Yet, the reader is warned that Ananda M's sentences are 'often involved and hyperparenthetic' and that the essays combine 'ancient Pali Buddhism with certain ideas of modern origin' (Bennett 1929: vii-viii) and so could, therefore, be accused of lacking scholarly rigour.⁴⁹ The anonymous author, who signs as 'A Buddhist,' however, adds, 'But what if the need of the West to-day be just such a compound? Then, if it bring a fresh light into our lives, let us be grateful to the genius of Ananda Metteyya' (Bennett 1929: viii-ix). It is significant that this introduction, written not by a Theosophist but by someone who self-identifies as a Buddhist, calls Ananda M by his monastic name throughout.

The editors were not afraid to modify the articles, omitting parts that were deemed controversial or false. The version of 'The Religion of Burma' that is printed is Annie Besant's, published in *The Theosophist* in 1911. This is different from the version originally published in *Twentieth Century Impressions of Burma*, some of the edits driven by a Theosophist agenda.⁵⁰ For instance, when Ananda M is describing the Buddha's meditation attainments before enlightenment, he states that the Buddha-to-be reached 'that cosmic consciousness' which was 'Brahman or the Paramatman' (Ananda M 1910: 107). In Besant's version, this is changed to 'To that Supremest Cosmic Consciousness He won' (Ananda M 1911a:18). Ananda M uses the word 'supreme' a few lines before this, but the insertion subtly changes the meaning. Then, when Ananda M describes the night of the Buddha's enlightenment, Besant's version again changes the status ascribed to the experience of Brahman:

> ... the ancient saints said this was all; that beyond that Brahman was no further progress; and yet, even in that was still a bondage, even that heart of life was subject to the law of change, because still reigned in it desire. Desire! From height to depth of life desire was king; and the root of this desire was in the very citadel of selfhood. (Ananda M 1910: 108)

> ... the ancient saints said this was all; that beyond That Brahman was no further progress—*It, the Ultimate of Life*—and yet, even in *That* was still a bondage, even that *Heart of Being* still was subject to the *Law of Change, subject, since Desire still reigned in It.* Desire! From height to depth of life *Desire* was *King*; and the root of this *Desire lay hidden and protected* in the very citadel of *Self, of Life!* (Ananda M 1911a: 21; Besant's version, modifications have been emphasised)

Since this republication occurred during Ananda M's time in Burma, he was probably aware of these changes but could have been forced to accept them as the price for an accessible version of his article. There are several changes, however, that are only made in the Adyar publication. When Ananda M is describing the Noble Eightfold Path, he interprets the last step, *sammāsamādhi*, as 'Right Ecstacy' in the original (Ananda M 1910: 114) and this is retained in the Besant version (Ananda M 1911a: 42). In 1929, this is changed to the more normative 'Right Concentration' (Bennett 1929: 87), which Ananda M himself uses in the fourth lecture of *The Wisdom of the Aryas* (Bennett 1923: 77) and in 'The Doctrine of the Aryas' (Ananda M 1921d: 160–161).

'The Culture of Mind' is a reprint of 'On the Culture of Mind,' sent by Ananda M to Ceylon when he was in Akyab. However, in the Adyar publication, the section towards the end on remembering past births is entirely omitted. With a slight change of phrase, the editors resume the article when Ananda M moves to the practice of mindfulness, *sati* (Bennett 1929: 275–281). 'Devotion in Buddhism' is a modified reprint of the talk given by Ananda M to the Rangoon College Buddhist Association. Clear from these examples is that *The Religion of Burma and Other Papers* is not an exact reproduction of Ananda M's writings. The collection represents a Theosophical interpretation and appropriation of Ananda M's work.

Theosophists not only reinterpreted Ananda M's writings, but also included him within their own interpretation of history, recasting the parts of his life that related to the work of the Theosophical Society and ignoring his early ejection from the movement. Theosophist C. V. Agarwal, at the end of the twentieth century, in *The Buddhist and Theosophical Movements*, examines the ways Theosophy supported Buddhist revival in the nineteenth and twentieth centuries. Published by the Maha-Bodhi Society, the book nevertheless had the support of the Theosophical Society based in India. The International President of the Theosophical Society, Radha Burnier, contributed a foreword, the frontispiece features an icon of the Buddha from the Buddha Vihāra within the Theosophical Society headquarters in Adyar, and the book advertises that it can also be obtained through the Theosophical Publishing House in Chennai, India. Throughout the book, there is a conciliatory tone, linking both Buddhism and the Maha-Bodhi Society to the Theosophical Society. Venerable Dr. M. Wipulasara Mahathero, in his introduction on behalf of the Maha-Bodhi Society, writes, 'This book, written at our suggestion, is a result of the coming together of the two sister organisations, and is aimed at giving information in an interesting story-like style about their collaborative work, especially in the early days' (Agarwal 2001: 7). When the book comes to the involvement of Theosophy in the Buddhist revival in Burma, both Ananda M and the International Buddhist Society are included:

> Another Theosophist Bhikkhu, Ananda Metteya [sic], met Dr. Annie Besant and Mr. Leadbeater, when they toured Burma. He was the

founder of the International Buddhist Society, which aimed to carry Buddhism to the West.... His work for Buddhism in England is described in another Section. (Agarwal 2001: 45)

In the section, 'Buddhism in the West,' the creation of the Buddhist Society of Great Britain and Ireland is narrated, but Ananda M's involvement is not mentioned. Instead, the history stresses that over 20 members of the Theosophical Society were founding members of the Buddhist Society, including Dr. and Mrs. Rhys Davids, and C. Jinarajadasa, the fourth International President of the Theosophical Society. The next paragraph mentions Ananda M: 'The [Buddhist] Society derived much strength from a short visit from Burma led by Ven. Ananda Metteyya' (Agarwal 2001: 55). The rest of the paragraph gives a brief biography of Ananda M, citing as a source Humphreys's *Sixty Years of Buddhism in England* (Agarwal 2001: 103). While mentions of Ananda M and the Buddhist Society of Great Britain and Ireland are brief, each instance places them within a Theosophical depiction of events. In other words, whenever the book interprets and appropriates Ananda M's life, he is used to bolster the work of the Theosophical Society, although it is not hidden that he sought to spread the Buddha's teaching in the West.

Concluding Thoughts

The life of Ananda M provides a lens through which the spiritual seekership of the end of the nineteenth century and the early twentieth century, a period of dynamic change, can be viewed and assessed. To his search, Ananda M brought a fierce intelligence, a poetic sensitivity, an awareness of human suffering and a yearning for realms of consciousness beyond those experienced in every-day life.[1] Rejecting Christianity, he at first negotiated between science, esotericism and occultism, believing that the three could be mutually supportive. His eventual choice of Buddhism was informed not only by his personal experience of suffering and his scientific background, but also by esotericism, occultism and the yogic practices he learnt in Ceylon. For him, religion and science could be brought together through Buddhism and, even though he eventually rejected esotericism and occultism, his psyche remained influenced by them, and both influenced how he was remembered after his death.

Ananda M's life demonstrates that the past cannot be represented through clean categories. His life belongs to the histories of both Buddhism, and Western esotericism and occultism. Our narrative shows that the boundaries between science, esotericism, occultism and Buddhism were porous during Ananda M's lifetime, in spite of the resistance of some Western Buddhist converts to the very idea that Buddhism could be linked with esotericism and occultism. A study of Ananda M's life, therefore, offers an opportunity to break down further the orientalist boundaries that have been erected between Buddhist Studies and Western Esotericism Studies. It is significant, therefore, that one focus in contemporary Buddhist Studies is the presence of the esoteric and the magical in Asian Buddhism (e.g., Crosby 2020; Van Shaik 2020). We would argue that the same needs to be done in the narration of the histories of Buddhism and Esotericism in the West.

Ananda M can also be seen as a precursor of several trends within the development of Buddhism and Buddhist Studies after his death. He believed that the survival of the West depended on whether it could respond to Buddhism's message that individualism, competition and consumerism led not to prosperity but to war, social disruption and the death of civilisations. Foreshadowing contemporary secular Buddhism, he sought ways of communicating this without using the term Buddhism. Buddhist teaching was needed, rather than the label Buddhism. In his critique of Empire and the failings of Western society, he showed himself to be an engaged Buddhist before the term emerged. His search to apply Buddhist insights to contemporary issues, including the tragedy of World War I, places him within a line of Buddhists who continue to critically reflect on Buddhism's message for a world in crisis. Furthermore, his attempts to scientifically measure the human mind and what happens to it in meditation anticipated current interest by neuroscientists into the effect of meditation on the physiology of the mind.

A biography, however, is always a work in progress. This biography surpasses in accuracy and detail previous accounts of the life of Ananda M, but it leaves many questions unanswered. For instance, there are considerable gaps in the timeline of the early life of Allan Bennett, particularly after the death of his grandparents and his mother. For instance, who paid for his schooling, and did he retain contact with any of his maternal relatives? Who was his father and exactly how was his family linked to Bath and the south-west of Britain? When did he leave London to travel to Ceylon and what name did he use? We have reconstructed the periods he spent in Ceylon and Burma in broad terms through Sinhala and Burmese sources, but many of his activities passed under the radar of these sources and can only be touched through use of the imagination and the internal evidence of his writings, raising questions such as: How extensive were his travels in Burma from Rangoon before illness tied him to his monastery? How did the Looking Glass trial in 1910 impact his relationship with the Buddhist Society of Great Britain and Ireland and other Western Buddhists? What kind of mechanical and electrical equipment did he have in his monastic laboratory and what results did he obtain from all his research? How deeply did his relationship with Daw Mya May sour, as the drugs he took for his asthma and other physical pain impaired his judgement and threw him into states of paranoia? When he returned to Britain, we know, again from primary sources, that he moved from Liverpool to London during World War I, but the exact date remains unverified, as do the interactions he had with his sister when she was in Bath from 1916–1919. Lastly, whether Ananda M and Crowley interacted during his 1908 mission in London or later, when he returned to England, also remains unclear. We hope that these and other questions will be addressed by other researchers and that new discoveries are made to help fill in the missing pieces of Ananda M's fascinating but tragic life.

Selective Glossary

Priority is given to Pali, since this was the primary textual language used by Ananda M. Where Sanskrit (Skt.) was used first by Ananda M or Crowley, the Sanskrit term is placed first.

Lit: literal meaning

Abhidhamma (Skt. Abhidharma; lit: 'higher doctrine'): a scholastic analysis of teachings found in Buddhist discourses, particularly those relating to the mind. The third canonical 'basket' of teachings in the Theravada tradition is the Abhidhamma Pitaka.

Abhidhammatthasaṅgaha (lit: A Compendium of Abhidhamma): a summary of Abhidhamma, probably composed in the eleventh or twelfth century.

Ācariya (Pali and Skt.): spiritual teacher.

Adept: an individual who has attained a high level of mastery and knowledge in the practices and teachings of esotericism or occultism.

Anagārika (lit: homeless one): a status within Theravada Buddhism mid-way between a lay person and an ordained monastic.

Ānāpāna-sati (Skt. ānāpāna-smṛti): mindfulness of in and out breathing.

Anattā (Skt. anātman): non-self or not-self—that there is nothing permanent and unchanging within the human body or mind.

Arahant/arahat (Skt. arhat): one who has reached enlightenment through the teaching of the Buddha, used mainly in Theravada traditions.

Arūpa States (Skt. ārūpya; lit: formless): the formless states; states of higher consciousness reached after the 4th *jhāna*.

Aryan (lit: pure or noble): came to refer to groups of people who spoke Indo-European languages.

Āsana (Pali and Skt; lit. sitting, or seat/throne): a term referring to a physical posture, particularly during meditation, that fosters mental composure and mindfulness.

Avijjā (Skt. avidyā): ignorance or misconceptions about the nature of reality, in particular *anicca*, or impermanence, and *anattā*, or non-self. Synonymous with *moha* (delusion).

Ātman (Skt.): a self or individual essence.

Bhikkhu (Skt. bhikṣu): an ordained male member of the Buddhist monastic community.

Bhrāmaṇḍa Purāṇa: a Sanskrit Hindu narrative text, one of the major eighteen Purāṇas.

Borān kammaṭṭhāna: an old form of esoteric meditation present within Theravada Buddhist traditions before Buddhist modernism.
Brahmavihāras (Pali and Skt.; lit: divine abidings): four qualities that are promoted within Theravada Buddhism as meditation objects: loving kindness, compassion, sympathetic joy and equanimity.
Buddhapūja (Pali and Skt.): devotional act directed to the Buddha.
Buddha rūpa (Pali and Skt.): an image or statue of the Buddha.
Buddhi/Bodhi (Pali and Skt.; lit: awakening): enlightenment.
Ćakra: an energy centre in the body, a concept prominent in some forms of Hinduism and Tantric Buddhism.
Dāna (Pali and Skt.): giving, generosity.
Dhamma (Skt. Dharma; lit: that which supports): the universal law that holds together the cosmos; the teaching of the Buddha. A third meaning is present in Buddhist Abhidhamma to indicate the individual elements of existence, both mental and physical.
Dhammapada: a text within the *Khuddaka Nikāya* of the *Sutta Piṭaka* within the Pali Canon of Theravada Buddhism (Chinese versions also exist).
Dhāraṇa (Skt. *dhāraṇī*; lit: bearing in mind, remembrance): denotes the practice of concentration and focused mental retention within meditation.
Dukkha (Pali; Skt. *duḥkha*): pain, suffering, anguish, unsatisfactoriness. The first of the Four Noble Truths in Buddhism.
Esoteric: pertaining to hidden or secret knowledge, practices, or teachings that are typically reserved for a select group or initiated individuals.
Esotericism: the study of hidden or concealed spiritual and mystical truth, often involving secret or specialised knowledge and rituals.
Evocation/Invocation: the summoning or invoking of spiritual beings, deities, energies, or forces through ritual and incantation in occult practices.
Gematria: a numerological system that assigns numerical values to letters or words, used to reveal hidden meanings or connections in sacred texts. Commonly used in Kabbalah to find relationships between seemingly unconnected words, phrases and ideas.
Iddhi (Pali): power or potency; in Buddhist meditation mystical or psychic powers gained through the attainment of the *jhānas*.
Jhāna (Skt. *dhyāna*): states of higher consciousness gained through *samatha* meditation; four are itemised in the Theravada texts with a further 5 formless (*arūpa*) states.
Kabbalah: a Jewish mystical and esoteric teaching that sought to unravel the mystery of God's relationship with the world through the study of sacred texts, symbolism and numerology; used by occultists in the modern era.
Kamma (Skt. Karma; lit: action): the principle of kamma in Buddhism is that wholesome action produces wholesome consequences and unwholesome action produces unwholesome consequences.
Kasina bhāvanās: a set of Buddhist meditation practices that involve focusing the mind on a specific object to aid deep concentration; traditionally there are ten such objects, including the elements of earth and water, and colours such as blue and yellow.

Kośa (Skt.; Pali *kosa*): a container, sheath or covering; for instance, the five 'coverings' of the *ātman* in Hinduism.

Kyayouq Kyaung: used in Burmese Buddhism to refer to forest monasteries.

Lalitā Sahasranāma: a Sanskrit devotional text within the Bhrāmaṇḍa Purāṇa, dedicated to the Divine Mother, Lalitā Devi or Pārvatī.

Mahayana (lit: Great Vehicle): one of the two major branches of Buddhism; sometimes divided into Northern Buddhism (e.g., Bhutan, Mongolia, Nepal, Tibet) and Eastern Buddhism (e.g., China, Japan, Vietnam).

Maitriya (Skt.; Pali: *Metteyya*; lit: loving one): in Theravada Buddhist eschatology, the next Buddha, currently residing in the Tuśita Heaven.

Mettā (Pali; Skt.: *maitri*): loving kindness; the first of the four *brahmavihāra*s.

Milindapañha (lit: Milinda's Questions): a classical Pali text containing philosophical dialogues between the first century CE Bactrian king, Milinda or Menander, and a monk called Nāgasena. Probably originated in the first century CE. Influential in Sri Lanka and Myanmar.

Mokṣa (Skt.): release or liberation; the ultimate goal in Hinduism.

Moha (Pali): delusion or ignorance.

Neo-Vedānta: a modern philosophical movement that reinterprets and recontextualises the teachings of Hindu Vedānta (culmination of the Vedas).

Nibbāna (Skt. Nirvāṇa): enlightenment, liberation; the goal of the path in Theravada Buddhism.

Nikāya (Pali and Skt.; lit: assembly): used in Theravada Buddhism to denote the five collections of texts in the *Sutta Piṭaka* of the Pali Canon.

Occultism: a modern form of esotericism for the study, practice and exploration of hidden or concealed spiritual, mystical and supernatural phenomena, often involving secret or specialised knowledge, rituals, and beliefs; the term was first defined by Helena P. Blavatsky in 1875.

Pagoda: a structure in East Asian Buddhism that evolved from the *stūpa* (Skt.) of Indian Buddhism, which was essentially a funerary monument or relic-chamber.

Pali: the language of the Pali Canon, which unites Theravada Buddhist countries; a sister language to Sanskrit.

Parinibbāna (Skt. *parinirvāṇa*; lit: final or highest *nirvāṇa*): the final passing away of a fully enlightened being, the cessation of their existence in the realms of birth and rebirth.

Prāṇāyāma (Skt.): a technique of breath control practised within Hindu yoga to prepare the mind for one-pointed concentration.

Pavāraṇā Ceremony (Skt. *pravāraṇā*): an annual Theravada Buddhist ceremony that marks the end of the rains retreat.

Pratyāhāra (Skt.; lit: withdrawal): within Hindu yoga, the withdrawal of the mind from external sense experience in order to turn inwards and so achieve higher states of consciousness.

Saddhā (Pali; Skt. *śraddhā*): faith, trust or confidence in the Buddha and his teachings.

Śaivite: the practitioners of Śaivism, one of the major theistic traditions of Hinduism, which focusses on the worship of Śiva.

Samantapāsādikā: a fifth century C.E. commentary on the *Vinaya Piṭaka* (section of the Pali Canon dealing with monastic discipline) by Buddhaghosa.

Samatha (Skt. śamatha; lit: calm): an important meditation practice in Theravada Buddhism aimed at cultivating tranquility and concentration.

Samsāra (Pali and Skt.): the cyclical process of birth, death and rebirth within Buddhism.

Samma-samādhi (Skt. samyak-samādhi): right concentration or meditation, a component of the Noble Eightfold Path in Buddhism.

Samma-sati (Skt. samyak-smṛti): right mindfulness, a component of the Noble Eightfold Path.

Sangha (Skt. Saṃgha; lit: group or community): in Theravada Buddhism, the term usually refers to the monastic community of ordained monks.

Sankhāra (Skt. saṃskāra): a term that has different shades of meaning, most often signifying mental formations and volitional activities of body, speech or mind.

Sāsana (Skt. śāsana): the dispensation or religion of the Buddha, encompassing his teachings, monastic community and followers.

Sīla (Skt. śīla): moral conduct and ethical discipline in Buddhist practice.

Sīmā (lit: limit, boundary): the boundary formally drawn around monastic territory and monastic ritual practice in Theravada Buddhism.

Sinhala: pertaining to the Sinhala community of Sri Lanka; the language of the Sinhala community.

Sutta (Skt. sūtra; lit: thread): a discourse or teaching, usually of the Buddha.

Sutta Nipāta: a Theravada Buddhist text within the *Khuddaka Nikāya* of the *Sutta Piṭaka*, one of the three 'baskets' of the Pali Canon.

Sutta Piṭaka: one of the three divisions or 'baskets' within the Pali Canon, containing discourses, mainly given by the Buddha.

Talisman: an object, often inscribed or consecrated with esoteric symbols or words, believed to possess magical or protective properties and used in occult practices.

Thera: an honorific title for a senior monk in Theravada Buddhism; the seniority is determined not by age but by the length of time since the monk gained higher ordination—usually ten years is required before a monk can gain this title.

Theravada (lit: way of the elders): a school of Buddhism united by the Pali Canon, found mainly in Cambodia, Laos, Myanmar, Thailand and Sri Lanka.

Tipiṭaka (Skt. Tripiṭaka; lit: three baskets): the traditional name for the Pali Canon, comprising three collections.

Tiratna (Skt. Triratana; lit: three jewels or gems): the three 'jewels' revered by all Buddhists: the Buddha, the Dhamma and the Sangha.

Upajjhāya: a spiritual teacher or preceptor in Theravada Buddhism, who guides novice monks.

Upāsaka (lit: sitting close by): a male lay Buddhist devotee in the Theravada tradition.

Upasampadā: the higher ordination ceremony for novice monks in Theravada Buddhism.

SELECTIVE GLOSSARY

Uposatha: a day linked to the lunar calendar when Theravada monks recite the monastic rules contained in the Vinaya Pitaka; lay people may also follow extra moral precepts on this day.

Vassa (Skt. *varṣya*): the annual monastic rains retreat in Buddhism lasting three months, traditionally during the monsoon season from July to October.

Vesak/Wesak: the most important festival within Theravada Buddhism commemorating the birth, enlightenment and death of the Buddha; takes place on the full moon day in the western April–May.

Vihāraya/Vihāra (Pali and Skt; lit: living place): a Buddhist monastery or temple complex.

Vinaya: the monastic rules and disciplinary code in Theravada Buddhism.

Vipassanā (Skt. *vipaśyanā*; lit: seeing clearly): an important form of meditation in Buddhism that aims at insight into the nature of reality.

Viriya (Skt. *vīrya*): vigour, energy or perseverance directed towards gaining enlightenment.

Visuddhimagga (lit: the Path of Purification): one of the most influential Pali commentaries on the Buddha's teachings, written by Buddhaghosa in the fifth century C.E.; includes a systematic exposition of Buddhist meditation.

Vīthi (Pali and Skt.; lit: path or track): used in different contexts, including to denote the process of sense perception or cognition.

Yogi: an individual who engages in meditation practice and other spiritual disciplines in order to gain insight and liberation/enlightenment.

Notes

Introduction

1 A frequently repeated error, for instance, is that Bennett left England in 1898 (Humphreys 1972:133; Oliver 1979: 43; Batchelor 1995: 41), with the intention of becoming a Buddhist monk. Neither was true. See Chapter Six for a more detailed account of these misrepresentations.

2 Our use of 'liminal' follows Victor Turner's definition of the *liminal personae*, that is, people who elude or slip through the network of classifications that normally locate states and positions within cultural spaces. Turner writes, 'Liminal entities are neither here nor there; they are betwixt and between the positions assigned and arrayed by law, custom, convention, and ceremonial' (Turner 1969: 95).

3 Scholars debate the definition of occultism. Within this biography, we define occultism as a type of esotericism, developed in the late nineteenth century, which included the occult sciences of magic, alchemy and astrology, as well as aspects of modernism and orientalism, and which claimed to be compatible with science. While the term was initially defined by Blavatsky in 1875, it has come to encompass much more. For an examination of the term's history, see Hanegraaff 2006.

4 Letter from Ananda Metteyya to Charles Lanman, 14 December, 1903. From the personal papers of Charles Rockwell Lanman, Harvard University Archives, quoted in LeRoy Perreira 2012: 534.

1: The Formative Years

1 While the historical documentation, such as census records, are useful in detailing important facts about Bennett, they do a poor job describing what his childhood was like. Much of what we know about his childhood comes from his statements in a variety of correspondence, newspaper article interviews, and from his friends, Dr. Cassius Pereira, who became Venerable Kassapa Thera (1882-1963), and Aleister Crowley (1875-1947). Particularly important is Crowley's autobiography, *The Confessions of Aleister Crowley*. While these sources help develop a finer picture of what Bennett's life was like, they too are also less than reliable. Nevertheless, they are what is available and will contribute significantly to this chapter. Both the 1881 and 1891 English censuses have Notting Hill listed for Bennett's birthplace. As for Notting Hill, at this time, it was an area 'of extreme contrasts, fine houses and noxious slums existing in close proximity' (Weinreb and Hibbert 1983: 555).

2 Charlotte Louisa's birthplace of Brompton is the first of many locations in which she is listed as having been born. Within the 1871 census, Charlotte

Louisa is listed as 5 months old and born in Brompton. Within the 1881 English census, her birth location changes to Sussex, Brighton. The 1891 English census lists her as born in Battersea. Finally, the 1901 English census, the last in which she appears, again lists her as being born in Sussex, Brighton. With so many options, we are listing the first location from the 1871 census, as not only is it the first in the series, it also matches where her mother lived when Charlotte was less than a year old.

3   Sheridan married a widow, Therese Antoinette 'Angela' Boguille (b. 1852), originally from New Orleans, when he was 50 and she was 32. They had one daughter, Elmire Marie, born in Manhattan in 1887. She married Harry Gwinnell (1882–1986) in Richmond, New York in 1910 and they had two daughters, Elmire F. (1911–2003), and Angela Teresa (1912–2006). Like his father, Sherry Wardle represented a variety of performers and travelled extensively in North and South America, as well as Europe and Australia, promoting their entertainment. After he retired from promoting entertainment, he helped establish the Actor's Fund Home on Staten Island in 1902, acting as its first superintendent. The Actor's Fund Home still operates today, although it relocated to Englewood, New Jersey in 1928. For more information about the Actor's Fund Home, visit https://actorsfundhome.org/.

4   Katharine Alexandra, born in London, married Coventry Proctor Milnes Patmore (1848–1906). Milnes Patmore, as he was called, took up a mariner's life, becoming a captain of many ships, including private yachts. His father was Coventry Kearsey Deighton Patmore (1823–1896), well-known English poet, literary critic, and assistant at the British Museum. Milnes Patmore was one of the six children Coventry Patmore had with his first wife, Emily Augusta Andrews (1824–1862). A portrait of Emily, painted in oil by John Everett Millais in 1851, hangs in The Fitzwilliam Museum, Cambridge. Walter James Lionel Stewart was born in London and married Mary Georgiana Frances Roberts in 1905. They had two children, Marjorie Stewart (b. 1908) and Anthony Walter Stewart (1910–1977). Because Robert Walter Daysh Stewart died young, Josephine Madeleine remarried on 24 February, 1870, to a physician named John Stephenson Selwyn Harvey (b. 1849). The marriage took place in Paris but was also solemnised at St Saviour Paddington, according to the church register, ensuring the marriage was recognised by the Church of England. Despite the remarriage, Josephine's children, Katharine Alexandra, and Walter James Lionel retained the Stewart surname.

5   Clout (200: 102–103) suggests that Chelsea was an area where between 20–29% lived in comparative poverty. The Corbyn household, however, would not have fallen into this category. According to Booth's poverty maps of London, at the end of the nineteenth century, Chelsea contained some upper class and wealthy areas but also some lower middle-class and poor areas. Booth was an English industrialist and a social reformer who created poverty maps as part of his *Inquiry into Life and Labour in London* (1886–1903). He divided London into seven categories: (1) upper-middle and upper classes. Wealthy; (2) Middle class. Well-to-do; (3) Fairly comfortable. Good ordinary earnings; (4) Mixed. Some comfortable, others poor;

(5) Poor. 18s to 21s a week for a moderate family; (6) Very poor, casual. Chronic want; (7) Lowest class. Vicious, semi-criminal. See https://booth.lse.ac.uk/ and Booth 1889. Booth's methods have been criticised, as has his anti-semitism. Yet, his work provides an important tool.

6 Mick Brown also notes that Bennett and Charlotte were illegitimate, although he does not list the source of this claim. See Brown 2023: 73. In email correspondence with Mick Brown about the statement of illegitimacy, he states that he had attended Phil Baker's lecture at the Buddhist Society (email correspondence on 23 October, 2023 with Mick Brown).

7 At this time, Kensington was more affluent than Chelsea, with less than 10% in comparative poverty (Clout: 2000: 102–103). According to Booth's poverty maps, Fulham Road was 'middle-class, well-to-do' (Booth 1889). The whole of Brompton, according to Booth's poverty maps, was an affluent area of London, containing the well-to-do middle class and the wealthy upper class.

8 Notting Hill was an area where some very affluent housing was surrounded by more middle-class dwellings. See Booth 1889.

9 Booth's maps show this road to be in a mixed area with some residents comfortable and others poor. See Booth 1889.

10 Email correspondence between Alumni Relations Officer at Prior Park College, Emma-Louise Goymer, and Elizabeth Harris, 31 January, 2022. The records of the following schools and colleges were checked at the Bath Records Office or through the school archivists: King Edward's School, Bath Forum School, Weymouth House Boys' School, Bath College and Kingswood School. The admission registers of the Somerset Certified Industrial School in Bath (records held at the Somersetshire Heritage Centre, Taunton), which catered for boys in straitened circumstances, were also checked, without success. We have been unable to find the records of The Hermitage House School, which became the Preparatory School for Kingswood School in 1991.

11 See Chapter Five, endnote 16.

12 A list of people who attended the Speech Day of July 1890 includes the Secretary of State for the Colonies, the Agent-General for Victoria (Australia), a former Governor of Western Australia and numerous others with high positions, demonstrating the importance of the College from a state perspective.

13 By 1896, *The Times* reported that 30% of the Colonial College's graduates had gone to Canada, 18% to New Zealand, 12% to each of the United States, South Africa, and Australia, 8% to India and Ceylon, with the remaining graduates travelling to South America, the West Indies, and Tasmania (The Times 1896: 10).

14 While published in the *Journal of The Chemical Society, Transactions* in 1894, it was completed a few years prior, as indicated by the 1892 entry about Bennett in *Colonia*. It is also possible that the paper was published prior to 1894, although we have not been able to find any record of this. The 1894 paper is still referenced in modern scholarship. Semantic Scholar (https://www

.semanticscholar.org/), a website that tracks publication citations for hundreds of millions of papers, notes that 96 publications cite the Dyer paper, including scholarship as recent as 2022.

15   UK Equivalent determined by using the Bank of England inflation calculator which stated the inflation averaged 4.2% a year from 1904 to 2020. See www.bankofengland.co.uk/monetary-policy/inflation/inflation-calculator. The USD equivalent was calculated by multiplying 250 by 1.22, which was the conversion rate of British Pounds to US Dollars on 13 January, 2023.

16   At the time of their marriage, William L. B. Hill was a Lieutenant in the British Army, part of the Gloucestershire Regiment, 3rd Battalion. He began with the battalion and was commissioned as Second Lieutenant in 1892. The Gloucestershire Regiment was a line infantry regiment of the British Army formed in 1881. It was created by merging other units, including the 28th (North Gloucestershire) Regiment of Foot, which became the 3rd battalion, and the 61st (South Gloucestershire) Regiment of Foot, which became the 4th battalion. Lieutenant William L. B. Hill retired from the regiment in 1907, upon which he was granted half-pay. The Hills built their home on the shores of Clear Lake, at Konocti Bay, which gave them a beautiful view of the lake and mountains. During World War I, William Hill was reactivated by the British military. As a result, the Hills travelled to Glasgow, Scotland, in July 1916, where Hill was promoted, temporarily, to the rank of Captain of the Gloucestershire Regiment. He continued to serve with the army to the conclusion of the war. In the years leading up to World War II, Hill predicted that war was imminent, and when it began in 1939, he travelled to Canada to support the British war effort. However, due to his age, he was not able to assist and attempted to return home. To his surprise, he was unable to do so due to restrictions regarding immigration into America by English subjects, Hill never having become a U.S. citizen. It was only in January 1944 that he was able to return to his family in Lake County, California. Sadly, he died of a sudden heart attack on May 15th.

17   The Hill family fully participated in their community, becoming involved with numerous organisations and institutions. For instance, Charlotte became active in the Kelseyville Woman's Club, even helping found it in 1921. She was so active with the organisation that she served on the governing council for the California Federation of Women's Clubs, being the foreign relations and natural resources chairman. The women's club movement started on the East Coast of the United States in the 1880s–1890s as a social movement originating in churches in which middle-class white women initially focused on literary endeavours and self-improvement. As the organisations grew, the clubs took an active role in upholding the morality of the community while also attempting to shape social and public policy. By the beginning of the twentieth century, many clubs lobbied for women's suffrage, and once World War I began, supported the war effort. Charlotte was also a member of the Audubon Society, an organisation dedicated to protecting birds and their habitats, and the Anti-Steel Trap League,

an organisation promoting ethical hunting practices, including the banning of steel leg-clamping animal traps. Leslie Hill grew up in Kelseyville with her parents and attended Stanford University, in Palo Alto, California, joined Sigma Kappa sorority, and graduated in 1928. After graduating she continued to work at Stanford as a cashier in the employment office, renting a room from Kenneth and Alice Kelley, who owned a farm located at 499 Laqunita Drive in Palo Alto. In 1930 she married David Theodore McKeown (1900–1979), originally from Gresham, Oregon, whom she met at Stanford. They initially resided in Richmond, California where David worked as a salesman. By 1936 they were living at 83 Beaumont Avenue in San Francisco where David was a sales manager, and by 1937 they were in Sacramento. This is where they resided until they separated around 1938. David remained in Sacramento, and remarried, and Leslie returned to Lake County. Leslie remarried on 13 December, 1945, to William Edward Mullen (1927–2004) in San Benito County, California. They continued to live in Kelseyville. In 1966, Leslie divorced William Mullen. William Mullen quickly remarried after separating from Leslie. In fact, it seems he and his new wife, Jo Ann Hart (b. 1944), married in Carson City, Nevada on 29 March, 1966, four months before Leslie's and William's divorce was finalised in California. A little over a year after William and Jo Ann were married, they had a son, Mark Edward Upton Mullen (1967–2001). Despite being married twice, Leslie never had children. Since she remained close to William, she was also close to Mark. Despite being divorced, Leslie retained the Mullen name, and William and Leslie remained close with Leslie treating Mark like a son. After divorcing William, Leslie began working at Lakeport's Carnegie Library. When the Lake County Library formed in 1974 and incorporated the Lakeport Library into the county system, Leslie was hired to work for the county library system. She continued to work for the library until retirement. Not long after, Leslie died in 1984. Jan Cook, a Lake County Librarian and Historian, notes 'She was known for her gardening prowess and often took prizes at the county fair' (email correspondence between Jan Cook and John L. Crow, January 11, 2019). After Leslie's death, the library dedicated an indoor tree and planter in her honour.

18 See Introduction for information about the drugs Bennett took.
19 Between 1855 and 1900, 76,000 of the poorest Londoners were displaced to make way for new transport construction with the first underground railway opening in 1863 (Seaman 1973: 65). See also Clout 2000: 90.
20 The suspended particulate matter (SPM) of 1891 reached 623.38 micrograms per cubic metre. In comparison, the average SPM in London in 2016 was 16.0 micrograms per cubic metre. The air pollution caused numerous health issues, as well as increasing the death rate due to breathing diseases, such as bronchitis. Mortality from bronchitis increased from 25 deaths per 100,000 inhabitants in 1840 to 300 deaths per 100,000 in 1890. Average concentrations of SPM are measured in micrograms per cubic metre (Ritchie 2017). Those who used the underground railways were exposed to additional fumes and also acid gas (Seaman 1973: 68–69).

21 See Chapter Four, pp. 130–131.
22 Allan Bennett to F. L. Gardner, no date (Gerald Yorke Collection, Warburg Institute, University College London, NS10).
23 By 'Poggendorf,' Bennett could be discussing a number of inventions by Johann Christian Poggendorff (1796–1877), a German physicist and inventor. However, from the context of the letter, in which Bennett discusses disassembling an acid battery and using its parts, it seems Bennett is referring to either Poggendorff's potentiometer, which is a device that measures and balances electrical current, or a Poggendorff cell or element, which is a kind of battery. See Rutenberg 1939 and Greenslade 2005 for more on the potentiometer.
24 See Daily Telegraph 1908: 12; Humphreys 1953: 18; Malalasekara 1964: 539; Oliver 1979: 43; Harris 1998: 4; Jayatilleke 2006.
25 Crowley writes, 'Despite his ill-health, he was a tremendous worker. His knowledge of science, especially electricity, was vast, accurate and profound. In addition, he had studied the Hindu and Buddhist scriptures, not only as a scholar, but with the insight that comes from inborn sympathetic understanding' (Crowley 1989: 181).
26 Records indicate that an 'A. MacGregor' applied for a passport in February 1900. This may have been Bennett. No records have been found to indicate his actual departure date. In his 'Editorial Note' to the *Sepher Sephiroth*, Crowley states that Bennett departed for Ceylon in 1899 (Bennett and Crowley 1912).
27 Dassow 1994: plates 3 & 4. See Fletcher 2022 for an analysis of how the Egyptian Book of the Dead was incorporated into Bennett's rituals.
28 Alchemy, Bow Lodge, 22 Oct, 1893; Alchemy, Chiswick Lodge, 18 Nov, 1893; Astrology, Adelphi Lodge, 20 Nov, 1893; The Lore of Khem, Adelphi Lodge, 18 June, 1894; The Lore of Khem, Brixton Lodge, 29 June, 1894; The Lore of Khem, Chiswick Lodge, 16 July, 1894; The Lore of Khem, Bow Lodge, 9 Sep, 1894; The Lore of Khem, North London Lodge, 3 Oct, 1894; Medieval Magic, Adelphi Lodge, 31 Dec, 1894; Medieval Magic, Bow Lodge, 24 Mar, 1895; Medieval Magic, North London Lodge, 10 Apr, 1895.
29 For a full description of the Theosophical Society, see the Introduction.
30 See the Introduction for an explanation of Blavatsky's use of the term 'occultism.'
31 Coryn was also the president of the Lodge and a personal student of Blavatsky. He was a second generation Theosophist from a Theosophical family whose members were all in minor leadership positions throughout the organisation. This would be significant in the schism that split the society in 1895.
32 It is common within Theosophical literature that the section created by Blavatsky in 1888, initially called the Esoteric Section, was spoken of by its initials, ES. After Blavatsky's death, the Esoteric Section was extracted from the Theosophical Society and refounded as the Esoteric School. Although the name changed and the organisation became separate, in practice, access to the Esoteric School was only available to members of the Theosophical Society. Moreover, many prior members continued to call the Esoteric School by

its previous name. For simplicity, we will follow the Theosophical convention of calling the section or school the ES.
33 Howe 1972: 151; Owen 2004: 264n48.
34 The astral plane is a plane of existence postulated by esoteric philosophies and mystery religions in which the astral or ethereal part of a person can travel to both distant places, on earth or elsewhere, interact with spiritual beings, and transverse symbolic worlds related to esoteric correspondences. For more information, see Crow 2013.
35 The roster of the Golden Dawn lists Coryn as initiate number 178, having only taken the Neophyte initiation, and as 'resigned,' although it does not list when (Gilbert 1986b: 151).
36 Miss Jessie Louisa Horne, Soror Ave Atque Vale, was initiate number 127, participating from November 1891 to August 1892, when she resigned. She had completed three initiations, Neophyte, Zelator and Theoricus. Harold John Levett, Frater Sapere Aude, Incipe, took initiation into the Golden Dawn after Bennett, being initiate number 250. Levett took his Neophyte initiation on 18 June, 1895, and completed the first four grades, ending at Practicus. The roster also lists Levett as resigned, although it does not indicate a date. George Samuel Minson, Frater Equanimiter, also took initiation after Bennett on 18 December, 1894, and was admitted into the Inner Order on 14 February, 1896 (Gilbert 1986b: 148–154).
37 The six characteristics are: correspondences, living nature, imagination and mediations, experience of transmutation, the praxis of concordance, and transmission. Since its publication, other scholars of Western esotericism have critiqued the six-characteristics, developing other definitions of esotericism. Nevertheless, most scholars of Western esotericism recognise correspondences, or something similar to it in practice, as an important aspect of esotericism. For more information, see Faivre 1994: 10–15; Hanegraaff 1996; 2013; Hammer 2001; Stuckrad 2005; Albanese 2007; Goodrick-Clarke 2008.
38 'However, it does not seem necessary to deny altogether that some power may be present in the aforementioned objects [amulets], resulting from the power of celestial bodies—only it will be for those effects, of course, which any lower bodies are able to produce by the power of celestial bodies.'
39 Flashing, in the Golden Dawn, is the use of complementary colours to both create a strobe effect as well as to attract specific spiritual energies associated with the colours. In Bennett's case, he was adapting the Golden Dawn's system of 'Flashing Colours' to include sound, an innovation no one had previously tried.
40 Portions of Bennett's notebooks were transcribed and published in the 1970s within *The Monolith*, the magical journal of the Order of the Cubic Stone, Wolverhampton, England.
41 For a complete listing of all the sections of a Golden Dawn talismanic ritual, see Zalewski 2002: 225–29.
42 See Volume 2, *Excerpts from Allan Bennett's Esoteric Notebooks*, to read examples of the magical rituals Bennett composed.

43 The notebook containing the Ritual for Talisman of Vision is in the Gerald Yorke Collection, Warburg Institute, University of London, OS 71. For a transcribed version of the ritual, see Bennett 1976.

44 'RR et AC' is an abbreviation for Ordo Rosae Rubeae et Aureae Crucis (Order of Rose of Ruby and Cross of Gold), the non-public name of the Golden Dawn's inner order. Frequently, when Bennett writes the abbreviation for the inner order, he omits the punctuation. However, when the abbreviation is published, editors usually add the punctuation for each abbreviated word.

45 The Sleep of Siloam, within nineteenth-century occultism, is a trance or sleep state into which the person enters and through which they obtain a higher spiritual state and can communicate with higher beings. In *Isis Unveiled*, Blavatsky writes that, in the Sleep of Siloam, 'The body of the sleeper remains for several days in a condition resembling death, and by the power of the adept is purified of its earthliness and made fit to become the temporary receptacle of the brightness of the immortal Augoeides [higher spiritual beings]. In this state the torpid body is made to reflect the glory of the upper spheres, as a burnished mirror does the rays of the sun. The sleeper takes no note of the lapse of time, but upon awakening, after four or five days of trance, imagines he has slept but a few moments. What his lips utter he will never know; but as it is the spirit which directs them they can pronounce nothing but divine truth. For the time being the poor helpless clod is made the shrine of the sacred presence, and converted into an oracle a thousand times more infallible than the asphyxiated Pythoness of Delphi; and, unlike her mantic frenzy, which was exhibited before the multitude, this holy sleep is witnessed only within the sacred precinct by those few of the adepts who are worthy to stand in the presence of the ADONAI' (Blavatsky 1994: 357–58).

46 For a complete transcript of the ritual, see Zalewski 2002: 231–49. The word, YHShVH (יהשוה) or Yahshuah, is the Pentagrammaton, a constructed form of the Hebrew name of Jesus originally found in the works of late Renaissance esoteric sources. It is composed of the Tetragrammaton, יהוה, the Hebrew name of God transliterated in four letters as YHVH, articulated as Yahweh or Jehovah, with the Hebrew letter, shin ש, added in the middle. Kabbalists often equate the four letters of the Tetragrammaton to the four elements, Fire, Water, Air, and Earth. Christian Kabbalists equated the letter shin to spirit and thus by including it as the fifth element, the Pentagrammaton represents Jesus, the merger of spirit and matter in one being.

47 Zalewski 2002: 234. The name Thmaist, meaning the Double-Wanded One, refers to the Egyptian Goddess, Maat, the goddess or personification of truth, justice and the cosmic order. The Vault of the Adepts references the location in which the initiates of the Golden Dawn Inner Order took place. It is not a permanent location, but one magically constructed and deconstructed as needed. Zelator Adeptus Minor refers to an initiatory rank or grade within the inner order of the Golden Dawn. It is the initial grade within the inner order. Daath, sometimes called the 11th sefirot, or sphere, in the Kabbalistic

Tree of Life, and meaning 'knowledge,' represents the seven previous sefirot combined into a unity. The Kabbalistic Tree of Life is a symbolic representation of the universe in which the 10 sefirot are the manifestations of the first 10 statements of God as represented in the Book of Genesis. The Qlippoth is the name for the representation of impure spiritual forces in Kabbalah, the opposites of the holy sefirot. The word is often translated as 'shells,' as in the impure castoffs of the holy spheres.

48 Zalewski presents an ideal outline of the Golden Dawn talisman ritual, denoting each step. In practice, Bennett omits some steps and combines others. See Zalewski 2002: 225–29.

49 See Volume 2, which contains a typescript of Bennett's Taphthartharath ritual. See also Fletcher 2022 for an analysis of what Bennett referenced when constructing the ritual and how portions were subsequently incorporated into Crowley's *Liber Israfel*.

50 Gerald Yorke Collection, Warburg Institute, University College London, NS71. The name of Thoth is written in Coptic in the manuscript.

51 Gerald Yorke Collection, Warburg Institute, University College London, NS104. Spermaceti is a white waxy substance, produced by the sperm whale, used in candles and ointments. While these ingredients may seem strange, they are actually common within magical rituals found in multiple magical manuscripts, as denoted in *The Grimoire Encyclopedia*. For instance, the *Picatrix*, estimated to be a tenth-century magical text, denotes 'red snake blood' as an ingredient for incense used to invoke Mercury. The index of 'materia magica' or magical materials lists three manuscripts specifying snake fat as an ingredient for ceremonial use, nine manuscripts including snake skin, with one specifically stating its use in creating a candle, snake bodies, either whole, burned, cut up or live, mentioned in seven manuscripts, and spermaceti, mentioned in five manuscripts, with one denoting its use in creating incense for Hermes, the Greek god associated with the planet Mercury (Rankine 2023 1: 73; 2: 215, 312–314, 316–317).

52 Ammoniacum gum is a gum-resin exuded from the several perennial herbs in the genus *Ferula* of the umbel family. Although the context of the letter seems to indicate that the resin was for the hell broth, it was commonly used in Europe in the eighteenth and nineteenth centuries to treat asthma and other chronic illnesses of the lungs. William Lewis, in *The New Dispensatory*, writes that ammoniacum gum 'proves of considerable service in some kinds of *asthmas* where the lungs are oppressed by viscid phlegm; in this intention, a solution of gum ammoniacum in vinegar of squills proves a medicine of great efficacy, though not a little unpleasant' (Lewis 1799: 88), emphasis in original. In the same entry about ammoniacum gum, Lewis also calls it a useful *deobstruent*, or a drug which removes obstructions in the body by aiding the opening of ducts. Ammoniacum gum may have been one of the remedies Bennett used to treat his asthma.

53 Gerald Yorke Collection, Warburg Institute, University College London, NS104.

54 Although it is called an hour, the time of the performance was usually not 60 minutes. In ceremonial magic that incorporates astrological and zodiacal

influences, the day and night hours are calculated using the times of the sunrise and sunset, as well as the ruling planet of the day. In the Taphthartharath ritual, the ruling planet is Mercury, and the day of the week is Wednesday. In the following, Griffin explains how to calculate the planetary hour and determine planetary correspondence to perform a ceremony:

> One traditional Planet corresponds to each of the twelve hours of the day, beginning at sunrise with the Planet that rules the day. The planets then cycle downward according to the order that they correspond to the Sephiroth on the [Kabbalistic] Tree of Life (that is, in their order of their relative motion when viewed from Earth) as follows: Saturn, Jupiter, Mars, Sun, Venus, Mercury and the Moon. The next hour begins with Saturn again, and the cycles repeat until Sunrise the following day. The Planetary Hours are not usually sixty minutes long like normal hours are, however. To determine the duration of Planetary Hours on a given day, divide the number of minutes between Sunrise and Sunset into twelve equal parts. Each resultant is the duration of one Planetary Hour during daylight hours. Likewise, divide the hours between Sunset and Sunrise into twelve equal parts. Each of these parts is the duration of one nocturnal Planetary Hour. (Griffin 1999: 138)

Peter de Abano's *Magical Elements* contains tables denoting the names for the hours of the day and the Angel of the Hour. The eighth hour of the Hours of the Night is named Tafrac and lists the Archangel Michael as the Angel of the Hour (Abano 1655: 105).

55 Sorror S.S.D.D. or *Sapientia Sapienti Dono Data*, meaning, 'Wisdom is a Gift Given to the Wise,' was the magical name of Florence Farr (1860–1917), a British West End leading actress, composer, director and activist.

56 Greer writes, 'The traditional lore of the Golden Dawn maintains that Taphthartharath actually did appear (probably to the astonishment of all involved) on this occasion.' (Greer 1995: 173)

57 The Goetia is a general name for a group of 72 spirits, or demons, that have varying abilities and command legions of demons which can be evoked and commanded to complete tasks for the magician. The name comes from the magical text, *Ars Goetia, The Lesser Key of Solomon the King*.

58 Sidney Colvin was a British literary and art critic and is primarily remembered for association with Robert Louis Stevenson.

59 For claims of adoption, see Brunton 1941; Harris 1998: 4; Jayatilleke 2006. Formal adoption laws in England were not instituted until 1926. Until these laws were established, no parent could relinquish rights and responsibilities for a child nor could another adult assume them. Most of the adoptions at this time were informal and consisted of those with financial means supporting and raising children who were orphaned or were poor. See Walker 2006.

60 Ithell Colquhoun claims that Bennett stayed with the Matherses when they lived in Paris. Howe notes that Bennett was planning on visiting the Matherses in Paris with Gardner, but the trip was cancelled. Also, Bennett

was in Paris with the Matherses when MacGregor Mathers signed a publishing contract in 1897. See Howe 1972: 155, 187; Colquhoun 1975.
61. Patent number: GB189916357, 11 Aug, 1899. The European patent office also lists Bennett as owning patent GB189919758, although details of this patent could not be located by the authors or the British Intellectual Property Office.
62. Buer is a demonic entity described as 'a Great President. He appeareth in Sagittary [a centaur], and that is his shape when the Sun is there. [He can only be evoked when the sun is in Sagittarius, from around November 22nd to December 21st.] He teaches Philosophy, both Moral and Natural, and the Logic Arts, and also the Virtues of all Herbs and Plants. He healeth all distempers in man, and giveth good familiars. He governeth 50 legions of spirits, and his Character of obedience in this [his seal or sigil], which thou must wear when thou callest him forth unto appearance' (Hymenaeus Beta 1997: 33). George Cecil Jones would be the plaintiff in the 1910 court case that seriously hurt Ananda M's reputation in London. See Chapter Four, pp. 163–164 for additional details.
63. See Volume 2, which contains Bennett's essay, *A Note on Genesis*.
64. *The Clavicula Salomonis* is the *Key of Solomon the King*. Elohim (אלהים) is a Hebrew name for God. In the King James translation of the Bible, Jehovah Elohim is translated as Lord God. Ain Soph (אין סוף) is Hebrew which can be translated as infinite, limitlessness, infinity, or nothingness. In Kabbalah, *Ain Soph* is understood to be God prior to any self-manifestation. Kether (כתר), meaning crown, is the first sphere of manifestation on the Kabalistic Tree of Life. It is the first step in creation, that is, being emerging from nothing.
65. See endnote 26, in this chapter, which also discusses Bennett's departure from Britain.
66. See Chapter Four, pp. 164–165.
67. See Chapter Two, p. 63, where we mention a letter written by Ananda M to Cassius Pereira in 1905 that mentions contact with Crowley.

2: Allan Bennett in Ceylon

1. See Volume 2, which contains Bennett's essay, *The Four Noble Truths*.
2. Theosophy in Ceylon at this time was an arm of the Buddhist Revival. Western Theosophists came to Sri Lanka to aid Buddhists in their defensive actions against Christian missionaries rather than to propagate Theosophy. Only a few Sri Lankans actually became Theosophists.
3. The *Times of Ceylon*, the premier English language newspaper in Sri Lanka at the time, for instance, does not mention Bennett/MacGregor's Hope Lodge lecture either before or after its delivery.
4. It is worth noting Crowley's comment, 'Allan never knew joy; he disdained and distrusted pleasure from the womb' (Crowley 1989: 234).
5. Edwin Arnold also stresses the oneness and 'continuity of all life,' for instance, when speaking in Japan in 1889 (Ramesh 2021: 177). It is not impossible that Arnold may have influenced Bennett here.

6 For example, see the typescript of the Taphthartharath ceremony in Volume 2 for words within this ritual that describe submission to the 'Lord of the Universe' and finding one's self through this Lord: 'In myself I am nothing; in Thee I am All Self; and live in Thy Self Hood from Nothing! Live Thou in Me and bring me unto That self wh [which] is in Thee.' These words are not Bennett's. They are similar to other Golden Dawn rituals and were inspired by Kabbalah, but Bennett at this time believed them to be sacred.

7 Technical terms in this chapter are given in Pali, the language of the texts of Theravada Buddhism, except when quoting from the notebook that Crowley and Bennett wrote when in Kandy. Sanskrit equivalents can be found in the Glossary.

8 See Chapter One, p. 23.

9 That opium had beneficial medical applications is not denied, although the arguments of the 'Anti-Opium Association' are noted (West Ridgeway 1903: 115).

10 Revivalist Buddhists, for instance, were convinced that the Department of Public Instruction was more sympathetic to missionary than to Buddhist aspirations, citing 'the Quarter-mile clause' as evidence. Introduced in 1892 with retrospective effect, it prevented 'the registration and building of a Buddhist school within a quarter of a mile from a Christian one,' thus challenging one aspect of Buddhist revivalist strategy, namely that Buddhist schools should be located in close proximity to Christian institutions to draw Buddhist children away from missionary influence (Harris 2018: 61). As the Buddhist revivalist A. E. Buultjens writes in 1893, 'The injustice is so palpable, so gross, so shameless that every Buddhist will feel great indignation at the attempt to bring rules to bear on schools opened before 1892 simply to aid Christians' (Buultjens 1893: 188; Harris 2018: 61). On the Christian side, Church Missionary Society worker Helen Phillips's view that 'The Buddhist relations are harsher [or harder—handwriting unclear] than ever now in this District' is typical of the mood—see Helen P. Phillips to Baring Gould (London), 17 July, 1901 (CMS Archives: Ceylon Mission G2 CF/01 1901 Nos 131 to end). Phillips worked in Dodanduwa, in the Buddhist south of the country. By 1900, Christian condemnation of Buddhism was not as blatantly polemic as in earlier decades. See, for instance, from the Methodist Church in Ceylon, *Minutes of the Annual Meeting of the Galle District Synod*, 6–10 January, 1899, under Question 29 (Can any means be adopted for the promotion of the work of God?): 'that we should ever remember that our aim is not so much to confute Buddhism as to convince our congregations of sin and their need for a Saviour' (WMMS Archives, SOAS, London).

11 Under the category of murder and homicide, there were 146 cases in 1900 and 160 in 1901. Under the category of robbery, there were 289 cases in 1900 and 382 in 1901. Cases of burglary numbered 1,245 in 1900 and 1,384 in 1901. Cases of arson reached 98 in 1900 and 148 in 1901. As for rioting, three were charged in 1900 and 10 in 1901. In 1900 there were 328 convictions in the Supreme Court but in 1901, there were 468, compared to 646 in District Courts (Administration Report 1902: B1 Part III).

12 Ceylonese Buddhists have always had a strong link with Thai Buddhists, and so the presence of a Thai monk in Colombo is not surprising. To discover which temple he actually visited is almost impossible.
13 Letter from H. H. Beamish, 19 May, 1899. *Colonia* 5, April 1898–December 1899: 275–276.
14 Mahindaratne was the son of Peter Singho, who had been the principal lay devotee at the temple and an expert in its history, including the period when Bennett had stayed.
15 Formed in 1803 from Sri Lanka's coastal regions, the Amarapura Nikāya, inaugurated from Amarapura, Burma, had aimed for a caste-free monastic fraternity in contrast to the dominant Siyam Nikāya, which had been inaugurated from Thailand and accepted novices only from the highest caste in Sri Lanka, the Goyigama (See Malalgoda 1976: 87–105).
16 Personal conversation with Dilkushi Pereira, the niece of Cassius Pereira, in January 2019.
17 Now Sri Sambuddhathwa Jayanthi Mawatha (Street).
18 Email correspondence in May 2022 with Professor Manouri Senanayaka, Board Member of The Servants of the Buddha (see Chapter Six).
19 He is not examined, for instance, by Guruge, in his seminal work on the correspondence between Western orientalists and Sri Lankan Buddhist monks (Guruge 1984).
20 Email correspondence between Elizabeth Harris and Professor Manouri Senanayake, May 2022.
21 Ven. Mahinda Nayake Thera told Elizabeth Harris in March 2023, in a private conversation, that he had gained this information from conversations with the Buddhist monks at Vajirarāma Vihāraya, during the course of his research prior to 2008.
22 See Chapter Three, pp. 86 and 97–100.
23 The *Jātaka* is a book within the Pali Canon of Theravada Buddhism, which describes the previous lives of the historical Buddha.
24 Robert Chalmers translated this birth story in 1895 (Chalmers 1895), and Bennett most probably used it.
25 Bennett, handwritten notebook, held by the Harry Ransom Centre, University of Texas, Austin, U.S.A.
26 Traditionally, Mātara was a centre for Buddhism, although its power as *the* Buddhist centre in the south waned in the nineteenth century (Malalgoda 1976: 186).
27 Buddhist monks in Sri Lanka can be placed within two general groups: those living in the 'forest' and those living in towns and villages. Those within the forest tradition focus on meditation whereas those residing among the people tend to place more emphasis on scholarship and providing services for the laity. See Carrithers 1983 for a study of the forest monastic tradition.
28 See pp. 66–68 in this chapter for further information about Maitriya Hall.
29 Letter written to Alice Major, 19 August 1900, stating that he would leave 'the monks' to follow Ramanathan: cited in Gould, Kelly and Toomey 1997: 551, footnote 3.

30 Crowley was an associate of Coomaraswamy in 1916—more correctly, with his wife, Alice Ethel Coomaraswamy, née Richardson (1885–1958), with whom Crowley had an affair. Ananda Coomaraswamy was aware of the relationship as Crowley assisted him in locating his own mistress. The arrangement came to an end when Alice became pregnant with Crowley's child. For more details, see Crowley 1989: 773–774; Kaczynski 2010: 298–301.

31 His proficiency in yoga was developed in the 1890s through a Hindu teacher, Arulparananda Swamigal from Tanjore in India, who stayed several years in Ceylon (Vythilingam 1971: 327–331). After this, Ramanathan took the religious name of Sri Parānanda when in the role of Śaivite guru, for instance, when writing on the Christian gospels of Matthew and John (Parānanda 1898; 1902). R. L. Harrison, who became Ramanathan's second wife, after having been his disciple, edited these books.

32 Vythilingam adds, 'They were both the geniuses behind the agitation for making the Wesak Day a public holiday, for safe-guarding the Buddhist temporalities [land-holdings] against speculation and fraud and for the revival and rehabilitation of Buddhist institutions.' See also Vythilingam 1971: 478–483 for a reprint of Ramanathan's talk at Ananda College (Colombo) on the 'Denationalisation of the Singhalese,' in which he criticised his audience for not using the Sinhala language and for becoming materialistic through Western influence.

33 *The Vahan*, the theosophist journal mentioned in Chapter One, makes no mention of Ramanathan's visits, suggesting that he gave no formal presentations to Theosophists at these times. Greer claims that Bennett introduced Ramanathan to Florence Farr, a key member of the Golden Dawn, who travelled to Sri Lanka in 1911 to work at a school founded by Ramanathan in the north of the country (Greer 1995: 343). No date is given but it is possible that this was during the 1897 Diamond Jubilee visit or after Bennett had left Sri Lanka.

34 On a visit to Kandy, Elizabeth was able to discover 'Marlborough' through personal contacts, although it no longer retains this name and would be difficult for anyone to find independently. The current owners told Elizabeth that they do not want any visitors coming to the property because of its former use by Bennett and Crowley.

35 Aleister Crowley Notebook, named on the cover 'Nama Shivá-ya Namaha AUM: the Beginning and End of Udghâta.' Gerald Yorke Collection, Warburg Institute, University College London: (OS) 42. Crowley built on what he learned from Bennett during the following decades to develop a complete esoteric system combining yoga and meditation. See Crowley 1991.

36 Gerald York Collection, Warburg Institute, University College London, (OS) 42.

37 The first *jhāna* is characterised by joy and happiness together with thought. In the second, thought disappears but joy and happiness remain. The third is characterised by a happiness that is distinct from joy and, in the fourth, happiness is replaced by equanimity and mindfulness. The *arūpa* states are sometimes seen as modes of the fourth *jhāna* and include: boundless space;

boundless consciousness; nothingness; and a state of neither perception nor non-perception (Shaw 2006: 19).

38 See, for instance, the *Sāmaññaphala Sutta* (The Fruits of the Homeless Life), *Dīgha Nikāya* i 77–80.

39 An alternative reading would be that Bennett had come into contact with what Kate Crosby has identified as *borān kammaṭṭhāna*, an esoteric form of Theravada meditation, transmitted 'in closed teacher-pupil lineages' in Ceylon and other Theravada countries. It was being suppressed when Bennett was in Asia, as Buddhist modernism developed (Crosby 2013: 14). Crosby argues that this form of meditation was once the dominant form within Theravada cultures and that it offered a graduated path towards the realisation of Buddhahood, through which practitioners changed, through meditative practices, the very fabric of their bodies, 're-creating themselves as Buddhas' (Crosby 2013: 16; 2020: 33, 43–48). It included breath control and used 'the energy bases in the body' to internalise meditative experiences within the body's physicality. Although Crosby did not find the term *cakra* used in traditional *borān kammaṭṭhāna* manuals and argues that the method built on traditional Abhidhamma concepts (Crosby 2020: 48–65), its methods touched those of Hindu yoga. Because it was an orally transmitted tradition, from teacher to pupil, it is unlikely but not impossible that Bennett could have been exposed to it.

40 The Anagārika Dharmapāla, for instance, writes in his personal diary on 7 April, 1891, 'The Burmese are as a rule more pure and consistent than the Ceylon priests. The former have more ascetic habits.' *Diary of the Late Anagarika Dharmapala typed from the original diary by order of the Board of Management, Anagarika Dharmapala Trust*, held in Colombo at the Mahabodhi Society. Hereafter *Diary*.

41 These are now held by The Buddhist Society in London, accompanied by a list compiled during Ananda M's lifetime. The collection holds 36 slides of Ceylon, 27 of which are of Anuradhapura.

42 See Ananda Maitriya 1903f: 149, in which Ananda M reports a riot in Anuradhapura and the failure of the British to protect Buddhism there, and Ananda Metteyya 1908e: 346–348, where he reviews a book by Ceylonese revivalist, Harischandra, which asked for a commission of inquiry to address the 'desecration' of the city through archaeological excavations (Harishchandra 1908). See Harris 2018: 116–141 for an examination of Anuradhapura during the British period. For an account of the riot on 9 June, 1903, see Harris 2018: 136–137, plus A. E. Dibben to Baring Gould, 18 June, 1903, quoting Major Mathison (Church Missionary Society Archives, Ceylon Mission G2 CE/0 1903).

43 Except when separately referenced, the following information was gained in a conversation between Elizabeth and Cassius Pereira's niece, Dilkushi Pereira, in January 2019. Cassius was one of seven siblings, four girls and three boys. Of the boys, he was in the middle, with Richard Lionel being the elder and Merrille Wilson the younger. Of the three brothers, Cassius, or Cash for short—Bennett used this in his letters to Pereira—had the lightest colour skin, a witness to his dual heritage. Pereira trained as a medical

doctor, married and had a son and daughter, although the daughter died when she was young. According to Dirilakuru, he served in government hospitals for two years and then started his own medical practice (Dirilakuru 1978: 223–224). Pereira himself states that he resigned from government service when he was in charge of the Government Infectious Diseases Hospital and the Municipal Enteric Hospital (Pereira 1947: 68). His wife died in 1925, but it was only after his son became independent that he honoured the vow he made at Bennett's Hope Lodge lecture that one day he would become a Buddhist monk (Pereira 1947: 67). Cassius and his wife had been very close. The son, Ananda, became Assistant Solicitor General. Cassius was ordained with the name Kassapa through the Vajirarāma Vihāraya, the temple his family had patronised, receiving novice (*sāmaṇera*) ordination and higher ordination (*upasampadā*) on the same day in 1947, at the age of 65. Alec Robertson would come to know him from 1948 (Ratnayake 1992: ii).

44 Personal conversation between Elizabeth Harris and Alec Robertson, 26 August, 1995.
45 This letter was discovered by Sr Nyanasiri (Helen Wilder), interleaved in a publication at The Buddhist Publication Society in Kandy. Elizabeth Harris gained a photocopy of it from her in 1995.
46 Personal conversation between Elizabeth Harris and Alec Robertson, 26 August, 1995.
47 When Elizabeth visited the Vajirarāma Vihāraya in August 2018, she was shown a handwritten draft by Cassius Pereira for a booklet entitled '*Ānāpāna Sati*' (Pereira 1922), which was first published in 1927—3rd edition 1962. The booklet differentiates concentration on the breath from 'breathing gymnastics' such as *prāṇāyāma* (Kassapa Thera 1962: 5) and stresses that the breath is to be noted at the 'nose door' or 'lips.' Pereira locates it within *kammaṭṭhāna* practice (traditional meditation practices outlined in the *Visuddhimagga*) and attainment of the *jhānas*, leading to the goal of the path. Although the practitioner is called the *Yogāvacara*, evoking the Pali-Sinhala text, the *Yogāvacara's Manual*, which expresses the tradition of *borān kammaṭṭhāna* (Crosby 2013: 4), Pereira's booklet does not lie in this tradition. His aim was to contest Hindu forms of meditation and also *vipassanā*, by championing a traditional form of *samatha*, a form that Bennett also promoted after his novice ordination.
48 See Chapter Three, p. 121.
49 In a communication between Sr Nyanasiri (Helen Wilder) and Elizabeth Harris on 3 October, 1995, Nyanasiri shared that Cassius Pereira's copy of *The Wisdom of the Aryas* had been given to her. Bennett had sent it to Pereira on 2 February, 1923, and it bore his inscription. We investigate this further in Chapter Five.
50 See, for instance, Pereira 1923b, an article on *anattā*, which contains a photograph of 'The Late Ananda Metteyya Thera' as a monk, taken by the Colombo Apothecaries in Kandy, suggesting 1903 as a date. The inclusion of the photograph implies influence from him. The article surveys what theistic religions had misunderstood and then describes the Buddha's discovery of *anattā* as 'the silken net that holds us to Samsāra' (Pereira 1923b: 37).

51 Personal conversation between Balangoda Ananda Maitriya (1896–1998), who was named after Ananda Metteyya, and Elizabeth Harris in 1994, on a visit of Maitriya to the Sri Saddhatissa International Buddhist Centre in Kingsbury, north-west London. See Chapter Six for further information about this monk.
52 We are thankful to Alicia Turner for confirming this in June 2020.
53 See Ananda M 1920b: 223, wherein Ananda M announces the death of Richard Pereira, stating, 'he it was who assisted the present writer to enter the Buddhist Order at Akyab, and later acted as his principal Dayaka [donor] when in Colombo' to open Maitriya Hall.
54 An American, Charles F. Powell, for instance, declared in Colombo's Theosophical Hall just over 10 years before Bennett arrived, 'But you must remember one fact, and that is that the Buddhism they [Westerners] are so eagerly accepting is not the mere popular Buddhism of Ceylon; it is a Buddhism purified—cleansed from the excrescences that *must* in time gather upon every faith' (Powell 1889: 311; Harris 2006: 139). Powell, interestingly, appears in the Anagārika Dharmapāla's diaries. He arrived in Ceylon from India in August 1889. Dharmapāla describes him as 'an elderly gentleman' and 'an earnest theosophist' (Anagārika Dharmapāla, *Diary*, 5 August, 1889). He travelled extensively around the island to speak to groups, including Hindus. But in November a decision was taken not to publish three articles by him because they were 'very vehemently written against the whole Priesthood, and the whole Buddhist Nation' (Anagārika Dharmapāla, *Diary*, 19 November, 1889).
55 See Volume 2, which contains both essays, 'Animism and Law' and 'On the Culture of Mind'; the content of both essays are examined in Chapter Three.
56 Ananda M, in 1918, claims the hall is in Maradana (Ananda M 1920b: 223). We consider this to be a mistake. Records of his visit in *Sarasavi Sandaresa* place the hall in Bambalapitiya: e.g., *Sarasavi Sandaresa* 1903f: 1.
57 Personal conversation with Dilrukshi Pereira, January 2019.
58 For reference to the sponsorship, see endnote 53 in this chapter.
59 The contribution of Robertson to Ananda M's legacy in Ceylon is examined in Chapter Six.
60 Each synod report within the Wesleyan Methodist mission from at least the 1890s includes temperance returns: e.g., Synod of the Galle District for 1898, held in January 1899, reports that there are four Temperance Societies with 149 members and 22 Bands of Hope with 889 members. *Wesleyan Methodist Missionary Society Ceylon Synod Minutes* WMMS Archives, School of Oriental and African Studies, London.
61 The *Visuddhimagga* (lit: path of purification) is a compendium of Buddhist belief and practice, in Pali, drawn from the *Tipiṭaka*, attributed to Bhadantācariya Buddhaghosa, an Indian scholar of Pali, who worked in Sri Lanka in the fifth century CE. It is largely seen as normative for Theravada Buddhism. See Ñāṇamoli 1991.
62 Anagarika Dharmapāla, *Diary*, 30 March, 1904, when he visited the Hall and found 'signs of decay, the Hall not having been swept.' It gained new

life after The Servants of the Buddha was founded by Cassius Pereira, Ven. Narada Thera and H. H. Basnayake in 1921.

3: Ananda Metteyya in Burma

1 See Strong 2001: 122–123 for reference to the tradition that the Buddha visited an area that is now part of Myanmar, and Leider 2009 for an examination of an apocryphal text in which the Buddha refers to relics linked to his previous lives in Arakan.
2 See Smart 1957: 37: 'There are a few modern temples in Akyab which are interesting, inasmuch as their architectural style is a mixture of the Burmese turreted pagoda and the Mahomedan four-cornered minaret structure surmounted by a hemispherical cupola. The worship, too, is mixed; both temples are visited by Mahomedans and Buddhists, and the Buddermokan has also its Hindu votaries.' Porous boundaries, therefore, existed between religions, meaning that citizens might identify with more than one tradition.
3 See Harvey 1946: 69–72 for a colonial critique of the effects of this migration: 'They [Indian migrants] constituted an acute problem, and it was our doing' (p. 69).
4 The Buddhists involved in these associations sought to create a 'moral community' aimed at rescuing Buddhism from perceived moral decline in the context of colonialism (Turner 2014).
5 In Pali, *ānanda* means joy or pleasure. *Metteyya* means friendliness and *sāsanajotika* means illumination of the Buddhist religion. See the Introduction for information about the changes Ananda M made to his name throughout his life.
6 See Volume 2, which contains the full text of Ananda Metteyya's *The Foundation of the Sangha of the West: Being an Account of the Upasampada Ordination of Bhikkhu Ananda Maitriya*.
7 See Volume 2, which contains both 'Animism and Law' and 'On the Culture of Mind.'
8 See, for example, Ananda Metteyya 1904a, 'The Law of Righteousness,' where Metteyya writes of 'an evolution ever reaching further towards the goal of selflessness' in which belief in a punishing being or god is placed at the lowest point—humanity's 'nursery-days' (Ananda Metteyya 1904a: 354–355). Ananda Metteyya 1910a offers an evolution from the Age of Faith (i.e., blind faith as seen in theistic religions) through the 'Age of Investigation,' which he sees in Western science, to The Age of Understanding, namely Buddhism.
9 Literally 'the state of being firmly fixed or concentrated.'
10 The compatibility of Buddhism and science became an important part of what is now known as Buddhist modernism. See McMahan 2008: 89–116.
11 The complete verse in Pali is: *sabbapāpassa akaraṇaṁ kusalassa upasampadā, sacittapariyodapanaṁ etaṁ buddhāna sāsanaṁ*. A contemporary translation is: 'Not to do any evil, to cultivate the good, to purify one's mind,—this is the Teaching of the Buddhas' (Roebuck 2010: 37).

12 Tranquillity/serenity and insight meditation are normatively considered to be the two main forms of meditation in Buddhism.
13 The teaching of *vipassanā* meditation increased in importance during Ananda M's period in Burma. Ledi Sayadaw (1846–1923) and Mingun Sayadaw (1868–1955) were the pioneers. Houtman suggests that the first *vipassanā* meditation centre that could cater for lay people was founded in 1911 (Houtman 1990: 43).
14 In contemporary discourses, the Pali word *sati* is usually translated as mindfulness, but it is more accurately translated as recollection or remembrance. See Bodhi 2011 for an excellent account of 'mindfulness' in the Pali Canon.
15 See Chapter Two, endnote 60 for a description of the *Visuddhimagga*.
16 More usually translated as loving kindness, compassion, sympathetic joy and equanimity.
17 *Visuddhimagga* XIII 13–71 (Nāṇamoli and Bodhi 1995: 406–418). The *Vimuttimagga* was probably written in Sri Lanka. It was subsequently translated into Chinese, from where it was re-discovered in the twentieth century and translated into English. Remembering past births is outlined in a section on 'Subjects of Meditation.' See Ehara, Soma and Kheminda 1995: 22–224.
18 For example, in the Golden Dawn Second Order ceremony called The Consecration Ceremony of the Vault of the Adepti With Watch-Tower Ceremony, the 'Chief' overseeing the ceremony goes to each of the altars in the cardinal directions, calling out divine names and then invoking the Watchtower of that direction. In the east the Chief states, 'ORO IBAH AOZPI. In the Names and Letters of the Great Eastern Quadrangle, I invoke ye, ye Angels of the Watch Tower of the East.' Upon completing each direction, the Chief goes to the western altar, faces east and says, 'In the Names and Letters of the Mystical Tablet of Union, I invoke ye, ye Divine Forces of the Spirits of Life. I invoke ye, ye Angels of the Celestial Spheres whose dwelling is in the invisible. Ye are the Guardians of the Gate of the Universe! Be ye also the Watchers of the Mystic Vault. Keep far removed the Evil; strengthen and inspire the Initiates, that so we may persevere unsullied this abode of the Mysteries of the Eternal Gods. Let this place be pure and holy, so that we may enter in and become partakers of the Secrets of the Divine Light' (Regardie 1995: 259). It should be noted, however, that 'light' is also present as an important motif in the visual experiences associated with meditation in Buddhist traditions.
19 Liber Thisharb is the Latinisation of the text's title, which is written in Hebrew. The full title of the text is 'Liber תישארב Viæ Memoriæ Sub Figurâ CMXIII.'
20 Charles Stansfeld Jones had multiple magical names. For this diary entry, he used the magical name Frater V.I.O., which is the abbreviation of VNVS IN OMNIBVS, meaning 'all for one' in Latin. For most of his writings he used the name Frater Achad. Achad in Hebrew translates to 'one' or 'to unify.'
21 For examples of contemporary occultists referencing Liber Thisharb, see Cornelius 2018; Cornelius 2019.
22 A stretch of water such as a natural lake or the sea, according to the Commentary on the *Vinaya*, the *Samantapāsādikā*, was particularly suitable for the performance of monastic acts, since it required 'no further legislation

to exclude aliens' (Dhirasekera 1982: 173, citing *Samantapāsādikā* V. 1052). See also Turner, Cox and Bocking 2020: 139.

23 See Volume 2, which contains the full text of Ananda Metteyya's 'Akyab Plan,' contained in, *The Foundation of the Sangha of the West: Being an Account of the Upasampada Ordination of Bhikkhu Ananda Maitriya*.

24 See also Chapter One, p. 22.

25 The Buddha is recorded as laying down a rule that a newly ordained monk should live 10 years under the guidance of his teacher and should have been 10 years a monk before teaching others. Modifications were made to this but it became the traditional practice in Theravada monasticism, with monks becoming eligible for the honorific title 'Thera' after 10 years. See *Vinaya* I 60 and Dhirasekera 1982: 132–133.

26 Golden Dawn rituals continually spoke of moving from darkness to the light. One of the things said to the new initiate in the first Golden Dawn ritual, the Neophyte ritual, was 'Wanderer in the Wild Darkness, we call thee to the Gentle Light' (Regardie 1995: 125). See also: 'On the altar is the White Triangle to be in the Image of Immortal Light, that Triune Light which moved in Darkness and formed the World out of Darkness and out of Darkness. There are two contending Forces and One always uniting them. And these Three have their Image in the three-fold wave of the sensual world' (Regardie 1995: 128).

27 For instance, Part One of *The Burma Gazette* gives a quarterly catalogue of books published. During Ananda M's most productive time in Burma between 1902 and 1906, nothing by him appears in it, although Burmese Buddhist authors such as Ledi Sayadaw are well represented. He did not write for this readership and the pamphlets published by the *Buddhasāsana Samāgama* are not included.

28 Elizabeth is grateful to Dr. Pyi Phyo Kyaw for giving her this information in December 2018, in Myanmar.

29 This should be seen in light of the criticism that had been levelled against other Westerners who had gained *upasampadā*. U Dhammaloka will be mentioned later in the chapter. Gordon Douglas, an educationalist in Sri Lanka, was ordained on 20 January, 1899, as Ven. Asoka, by a Burmese *bhikkhu* visiting the country. A letter from 'A Buddhist' in the Sinhala newspaper, *Lanka Pradipaya*, only days later, implies that the people had not been happy with his behaviour and that he should leave for Burma (Lanka Pradipaya 1899: 2). See Turner, Cox and Bocking 2020: 131–155 for an examination of who the first Western Buddhist monk was.

30 See Chapter Four, pp. 141–142.

31 Mānitasirī and Nandamālābhivaṁsa were appointed to write Sankin Sayadaw's biography by the Mahāvisuddharama Monastery whilst Sankin was still alive. They used interviews with him and also interviews with elderly disciples from his village (Mānitasirī and Nandamālābhivaṁsa 1972: 14–26).

32 An interesting light is thrown on this by Wesleyan Methodist missionary Arthur Bestall, who, in July 1900, refers to a new journal in Mandalay, 'The Newspaper of the Buddhist Missionary Church—the Society for Promoting Buddhism,' which stimulates 'rich Buddhists to join the Crusade of

Gautama' by frightening them with the numbers of Christian missionary converts. Arthur Bestall to Hartley, 13 July, 1900. *WMMS Burma Correspondence 1886-1919*. WMMS Archives, SOAS, London.

33 Mendelson refers to the reliable historian, Payapyu Sayadaw, to suggest that the Head of the Shwegyin Nikāya was Ingan Mahawithudayon Sayadaw when Ananda M was in Mandalay. We are grateful to Alicia Turner for pointing us to this.

34 When Elizabeth visited the Visuddharama West Monastery in December 2018, the elderly monk in charge of the monastery's archives was adamant both that they contained nothing that related to Ananda M and also that Ananda M had not stayed there but at the Visuddharama East Monastery. When she then visited Visuddharama East Monastery, she spoke to an elderly monk, who pointed to an old building within the monastery and said with authority that that was where Ananda M had resided. The building obviously predated 1900 and is now superseded by more modern monastic accommodation. When we asked him if he knew anything more about Ananda M, he said that he did not. We are very grateful to Aung Myint Oo, the librarian at the Ludu U Hla Library, for accompanying Elizabeth on these visits.

35 Unlike in Sri Lanka, where places of Buddhist devotion are also monasteries (*vihāra*s), in Myanmar, monasteries and 'pagodas' are separate. If Ananda M had been given a room at Shwekyimyin Pagoda, he would not have been within a monastic community, but it is likely that lay people would have supported him there.

36 In 2023, this would be over £8,000.

37 Arthur Bestall to Findlay, 24 May, 1901. *WMMS Burma Correspondence 1886-1919*. WMMS Archives, SOAS, London.

38 See also Ananda Metteyya 1904e, as further evidence that the meditation methods used by Ananda M fell within *samatha* meditation and included the *jhāna*s (meditative absorptions or altered states of consciousness).

39 See Angell 1998; Harris 2018: 101–107.

40 See, for example, the civil servant Harold Fielding-Hall, who was sympathetic to Buddhism but similarly saw the Burmese as a 'young race' in its 'childhood' (Fielding Hall 1913: 26–27). Within the Theosophical view of races, also called root-races, the Burmese were descendants of the 4th root-race, while South Asian Indians and Europeans were from the 5th root-race, the Aryans. As a result, Theosophists saw South Asia as the home of Eastern wisdom and believed that South-East Asians should follow both Britain's and India's lead in terms of spiritual evolution. The 7th sub-race of the 4th root-race, the Mongolian, evolved around the yellow river and came to be known as the Chinese. Other East and South-East Asians, including the Japanese, Vietnamese, Cambodians, Burmese, Malay, etc. were the results of different sub-races of the 4th root-race mixing. C. Jinarajadasa, 5th International President of the Theosophical Society, gives an example of the ways Theosophists saw groups of Asians in the early twentieth century when he writes about the Japanese: 'With the Japanese especially, it is as though they are the final ebullition of the whole [4th] Root-race, as a

crowning effort, before the energies of the race begin their slow decline; hence they possess many qualities which differentiate them from the seventh sub-race, the Chinese' (Jinarajadasa 1938: 52).
41 Anagārika Dharmapāla, *Diary*, 21 August, 1904.
42 Ananda Metteyya to Cassius Pereira, 10 February, 1905, from the offices of the Buddhasāsana Samāgama, I Pagoda Road.
43 Anagārika Dharmapāla, *Diary*, 14 April, 1907.
44 Letter dated 23 March, 1911, Shwe Z. Aung to Caroline Rhys Davids (Peradeniya University Library Special Collections, Sri Lanka). See also endnote 60 in this chapter.
45 See the Introduction for a description of what was prescribed for asthma in Ananda M's time.
46 Pearn gives the exact Census returns for 1911: 90,153 Burmese, Karens and other indigenous groups; 165,495 Hindus and Muslims, mainly from India; 16,055 Chinese; 5,732 Europeans, 5,831 Anglo-Indians; 219 Armenians and 750 Jews (Pearn 1939: 287).
47 Pearn places this in a chapter on 'Modern Rangoon: 1898–1938.' His implication is that nothing changed in the living conditions of the poor within the period covered by the chapter.
48 'Notifications of the Lieutenant-Governor of Burma' in Part One of *The Burma Gazette* reveal that numerous regulations and bylaws were laid down in connection with public health during these years. To take 1903 as an example, on 25 July, rules restricting activities in markets and bazaars were laid down. No person could 'cook or have any fire in the bazaars.' There was to be no sub-letting and no meat could be sold unless covered by permission from the slaughterhouse (The Burma Gazette 1903: 493). Further restrictions on public markets were laid down on 26 September (The Burma Gazette 1903: 558–659 and 671–674). On 29 August, lodging houses were targeted: 'Every keeper of a common lodging-house shall cause the floor of every room or passage and every stair to be thoroughly swept once at least in every day before the hour of ten in the forenoon.' 'Filth and refuse' had to be removed at least once a day, again before 10.00 a.m., and the Health Officer had to be informed if a lodger was ill from an infectious disease (The Burma Gazette 1903: 583). Some of the downtown, colonial buildings were also falling into disrepair. The old Town Hall was unsafe during Ananda M's time in the city and would not be rebuilt until the 1920s (Pearn 1939: 284).
49 Johnston, in his overturning of racial stereotypes about the Burmese, leads up to the statement that the Burman 'has discovered how to make life happy without selfishness, and to combine an adequate power of hard work with a corresponding ability to enjoy himself gracefully,' which is contrasted positively with British values (Johnston 1908: 344). He is also positive about Buddhism; see Johnston 1908: 348–355.
50 Fielding Hall uses the term 'All Life is One' to describe the Buddhist world view in Myanmar (Fielding Hall 1898: 248–271), a term that Bennett also used in his 1901 Hope Lodge lecture, although it is probable that Ananda M drew on Theosophy rather than Fielding Hall. See Crow 2008a. With

reference to colonialism, Fielding Hall describes the annexation of Upper Burma and comments critically on the effects of British rule, e.g., 'For the Anglo-saxon, a great coloniser, is a hopelessly bad ruler of subject people' (Fielding Hall 1913: 139).

51 Elizabeth is thankful to Joanna Hodgkin for supplying this information during a conversation in November 2023.

52 For instance, 'Did not he by this enlightenment become something more than man? Not at all. He had learned nothing of God, not even that such a being existed. He entertained no thought that he himself had acquired any supernatural character or power. And so he died. Even the common people of the jungle villages know all this, and yet they prostrate themselves before these images of brass, wood and stone' (Cochrane 1904: 114–115). See Harris 2006 for an examination of missionary representations of Buddhism in nineteenth-century Ceylon.

53 See also McGuire, another Baptist missionary, who dismisses Buddhist ethics as unworkable, Buddhist philosophy as pessimistic and the whole religion as 'out of harmony with the conditions which environ it in Burma,' making revival impossible (McGuire 1912: 33), and Frederickson 1914: 61–62, who stresses the inability of Buddhism to give hope to its devotees.

54 See, for instance: (1) Arthur M. Knight (Bishop of Rangoon) to SPG Headquarters, 22 August, 1903, which suggests that a revival of Buddhism was coming and mentions two organisations established 'for the maintenance and spread of Buddhism': the Maha-Bodhi Society and 'The Buddha Sana Samagama, or international Buddhist Society' with its headquarters in Rangoon, adding 'There are two or three men of English tongue actively Buddhist here' (SPG CLR 67 Copies of Letters received from Rangoon 1898–1905). The letter has been republished as Knight 1903; (2) Purser 1911: 225–230, in which he argues that on questions such as God and the salvation of the soul, Buddhism and Christianity diverge utterly.

55 D. A. W. Smith, in his opening address at the centennial celebrations of the American Baptist mission in Burma, said of the majority of Burmese: 'the many still "without God and without hope,"—those millions who, if reached at all, must be reached by us *at once*' (Smith 1914: 54). The theology underlying this statement was that these 'millions' were 'dying,' destined for eternal hell unless they converted (Smith 1914: 57).

56 See Arthur M. Knight to SPG Headquarters, 26 July, 1903, speaking of education: 'No children who enter as heathen leave as Xtians—& apparently none show any enquiring disposition' (SPG CLR 67 Copies of Letters received from Rangoon 1898–1905). Arthur Edward Taylor's report to SPG Headquarters, March 1908, states that there are very few Burmese men in the Rangoon Town congregation, only Burmese women who had married Christian men 'generally of some other race than their own' (SPG Missionary Reports 1908 E 63 [C] SPG Archives Oxford). See also Wesleyan Methodist missionary Arthur Bestall to Findlay, 4 December, 1906, stating that at Kyankse, he had 'baptized six Buddhists, the largest number at one time in our history' (*WMMS Burma Correspondence 1886–1919*. Wesleyan Methodist

Missionary Society [WMMS] Archives, SOAS, London). See Arthur Bestall and Alfred Woodward to WMMS, *General Letter from Wesleyan Mission, Mandalay*, 11 January, 1901, which states that 44 Buddhists had been baptised in the last year (Wesleyan Methodist Missionary Society Burma Synod Minutes 1889–1918/1919. WMMS Archives, SOAS, London).

57 Bestall, for instance, writes that the Burmese 'are as yet a superficial people, fond of a life of pleasure, willing to listen to anyone that entertains them for a moment, and losing interest in it when once the novelty wears off,' demonstrating a complete failure to understand Burmese Buddhists (Bestall 1905: 44).

58 Anagārika Dharmapāla, *Diary*, 14 October, 1909. Dhammaloka was invited to Sri Lanka by the Anagārika Dharmapāla, who praised him at first for his vigorous anti-Christian preaching. However, the relationship soured because of his unconventional behaviour, his mercenary nature and his attitude towards Ananda M. See, for instance, diary entry for 16 October, 1909, where Dharmapāla accuses him of having a 'revengeful temper,' and 18 October, when Dharmapāla writes, 'He is ignorant of Buddhism; is very unclean and is easily provoked to anger.' Yet, successful lectures followed this. For an account of the whole visit, see diary entries between 27 August and 5 November, 1909. See Sirisena 2017 for a postcolonial studies perspective on Dhammaloka's tour of Ceylon, and Turner, Cox and Bocking 2020: 197–221.

59 Reinhold Rost, although born in Germany, spent most of his life in Britain, becoming Head Librarian of the India Office Library.

60 He translated with Caroline Rhys Davids the *Abhidhammatthasaṅgaha*, a manual of Abhidhamma, under the title 'The Compendium of Philosophy' (Shwe Zan Aung 1910) and authored articles in the journal of the Burma Research Society (Harcourt Butler 1927: 11) and Ananda M's journal, *Buddhism*, e.g., Shwe San Aung 1903.

61 *The Burma Gazette Part One: Notifications of the Lieutenant Governor of Burma 1903*: 75, when this appointment was confirmed.

62 Email correspondence with U May Oung's great granddaughter, Myadali, in December 2018.

63 Correspondence between Ethel Powell-Brown and Gerald Yorke, undated (Gerald Yorke Collection, Warburg Institute, University College London, NS 104).

64 This family history was aided by email correspondence between Elizabeth and May Oung's great granddaughter, Myadali, in December 2018.

65 *The Burma Gazette Part One: Notifications of the Lieutenant Governor of Burma 1906*: 17. A 'pandol' is a free-standing display using colour, light and possibly flowers. If created in a Buddhist setting, its panels often focus on Buddhist textual narratives.

66 See also the advertisements for the schools that appeared in *Buddhism*, e.g., 1904. 'Advertisements.' *Buddhism* 1.4: 5.

67 According to *The Buddhist Review* 1917b: 74, Mrs Hla Oung lived at Elgindale, 2A Pagoda Road, Rangoon. Pagoda Road led from Rangoon College to the Shwedagon Pagoda, according to colonial maps, and was just outside the crowded commercial centre (Bird 1897: 145).

68 Ananda Metteyya to Charles Lanman, 22 July, 1907, HUL.

69 See Ethel Powell-Brown to John Symonds, 13 February, 1952 (Gerald Yorke Collection, Warburg Institute, University College London, NS 96).

70 There are discrepancies in dates regarding the building and availability of Ananda M's monastery and laboratory. In February 1906, noted Theosophist, Charles W. Leadbeater, visited Rangoon. He was accompanied by other Theosophists, including the young Fritz Kunz and Basil Hodgson Smith. Smith's journal entry for Saturday, 10 February, records a visit to Ananda M: 'At 1.30 [Leadbeater] called to take us to see the white monk Ananda Mitriya. He is an interesting man and has a good laboratory & in fact he seems much more of a scientist than a monk. He wanted L. to test his experiments. He is looked upon with some doubt because of all this, but he is trying to work for Buddhism along his own line.' Personal diary, Basil Hodgson Smith, 10 February 1906. The statement about Leadbeater testing Ananda M's experiments indicates that Leadbeater was asked to test the experiments using his clairvoyance. If the monastery and laboratory mentioned by Smith are the same as mentioned by Ananda M in his July 1907 letter to Lanman, where he writes, 'Now I have just moved in to the first Monastery of my own which I have yet possessed out here' or the one that Dharmapāla refers to (see endnote 67), the monastery and laboratory could have been available as early as the beginning of 1906. Another possibility is that Smith was referring to the living quarters occupied by Ananda M prior to the first monastery of his own, accommodation in which he also had some sort of laboratory.

71 Anagārika Dharmapāla, *Diary*, Saturday 19 October, 1907.

72 See Ananda Metteya-Thera to Mrs E. Powell-Brown, 24 May, 1913 (Gerald Yorke Collection, Warburg Institute, University College London, NS 104).

73 May Oung's legal studies were sponsored by Ethel Powell-Brown's uncle. Ethel met May Oung through this when she became engaged to Captain Powell-Brown. May Oung wrote to his aunt, Mrs. Hla Oung, who befriended the young couple and introduced them to Ananda M. Ethel's account suggests this was after Ananda M's mission to Britain when he was 'very ill and wanted to get away from the Burmese climate.' See undated typed account of Ananda M sent to Gerald Yorke, entitled 'About the two letters which I have. . . . from the Bhikkhu Ananda Maitreya' (Gerald Yorke Collection, Warburg Institute, University College London, NS104).

74 She describes the wood as teak in Ethel Powell-Brown to John Symonds, 13 February, 1952 (Gerald Yorke Collection, Warburg Institute, University College London, NS 96.)

75 Rhona Galley (Mrs. E. P. Brown), 'A Buddhist Mystic.' Article sent by Powell-Brown to Gerald Yorke and typed by Yorke with the words 'Mrs Brown thinks the above was published in the Westminster Gazette' (Gerald Yorke Collection, Warburg Institute, University College London, NS104). We have not been able to find the published article.

76 See also Ethel Powell-Brown to John Symonds, 13 February, 1952 (Gerald Yorke Collection, Warburg Institute, University College London, NS 96), in which she writes that the meals were sent up by Mrs. Hla Oung.

77 W. B. Yeats to Florence Farr, 7 October, 1907, written from Dublin, in Bax 1946: 58–59. Yeats had received this information from his dentist, who told Yeats of a friend of his, who had gone to 'Burma' and become a Buddhist monk, working with Ananda M. This was probably McKechnie, and Yeats would have shared this with Farr, because both had been friends of Bennett through their mutual membership of the Golden Dawn in London in the 1890s.

78 P Monin was his lay name. It was traditional in Burma for some people to retain their lay names even if ordained.

79 See Chapter Two, p. 63.

80 The 'discovery' by Prosper-René Blondiot of these rays, linked to radiation, was eventually discredited.

81 See also Chapter Four, p. 152.

82 Ted Bryant to John Symonds, undated (Gerald Yorke Collection, Warburg Institute, University College London: Scrap Book Volume One, p. 324a). It is possible that Crowley conflated or confused the Kandy experience and this one, although the separate instance recorded by Ethel Powell-Brown suggests that Crowley could indeed have seen Ananda M levitating twice.

83 Undated typed account of Ananda M by Ethel Powell-Brown sent to Gerald Yorke, entitled 'About the two letters which I have. . . . from the Bhikkhu Ananda Maitreya' (Gerald Yorke Collection, Warburg Institute, University College London, NS104).

84 Rhona Galley (Mrs. E. P. Brown), 'A Buddhist Mystic' (Gerald Yorke Collection, Warburg Institute, University College London, NS104). This description of going up while meditating is also similar to the Golden Dawn practice of 'Rising in the Planes,' which was one of many practices of astral projection and clairvoyance: 'Rising in the Planes is a spiritual process after spiritual conceptions, and higher aims; by concentration and contemplation of the Divine, you formulate a Tree of Life passing you to the spiritual realm above and beyond you. Picture yourself that you stand in Malkuth—then by use of the Divine Names and aspirations you strive upward on the path of Tau to Yesod, neglecting the crossing rays which attract you as you pass up. Look upwards to the Divine Light shining down from Kether upon you' (Frater D.D.C.F. 1987: 80).

85 See Volume 2, which includes four of the six pamphlets, including: *The Foundation of the Sangha of the West: Being an Account of the Upasampada Ordination of Bhikkhu Ananda Maitriya*; *Revised Prospectus of the Buddhasāsana Samāgama or the International Buddhist Society*; *The Four Noble Truths*; and *Animism and Law*.

86 See also the reprint of a letter written by Ananda M in April 1909 to a friend in England, in which he explains that anger and hatred are evil in the context of people assuming a 'spiritual monopoly' for Christianity (Ananda Metteyya 1931: 59).

87 See Chapter Two, pp. 53–54, 63–64 for Ananda M's links with de Silva and the Pereiras.

88 In addition, there are shorter articles: De Lorenzo 1903; Neumann 1903; Taw Sein 1903—the *sutta* he translated is usually now presented as No. 62, the *Mahārāhulavāda Sutta*. The end of the issue includes: 'The Awakening'

(Ananda Maitriya 1903e—a piece probably written by Ananda M inviting news of Buddhist activities); 'News and Notes' (Ananda Maitriya 1903f); 'Ourselves' (Ananda Maitriya 1903g) and 'Buddhist Activities' (Ananda Maitriya 1903h), which describes the activities of a selection of Buddhist organisations in Asia. At the very end is a poem by Ananda M, which sends the Buddha's message to the West with lines such as: 'His Light go with thee to the waiting West' (p. 175).

89 See Volume 2, which contains the essay, 'The Faith of the Future.'
90 Throughout Ananda M's writings, Mahayana Buddhism and Tibetan Buddhism are presented in negative terms as distortions of the teaching of the Buddha, although he includes articles on these Buddhist cultures in *Buddhism*, e.g., De Grey-Downing 1904.
91 Although a number of the British in Myanmar remarked with surprise at the responsibilities undertaken by Burmese women (e.g., Bidwell 1911: 113; Fielding Hall 2013: 23–24; Purser and Saunders 1914: 63), one accusation made by some Christian missionaries in Asia was that Buddhism oppressed women (e.g., Harris 2006: 70, 108).
92 The article continues in *Buddhism* 1.2: 267–288; 1.3: 462–472; 1.4: 631–645 (Ananda Metteyya 1904e). See Volume 2, which contains the full essay, 'In the Shadow of Shwe Dagon.'
93 Childers (1838–1876), who served in Ceylon as a civil servant, compiled one of the first authoritative Pali-English dictionaries, published in two volumes in 1872 and 1875. In an attempt to release the concept of *nibbāna* from dispute, he argues for a two-tier model: 'namely that the word Nirvána is used to designate two different things, the state of blissful sanctification called Arhatship, and the annihilation of existence in which Arhatship ends' (Childers 1909: 266; Harris 2006: 121).
94 See, for example: Rhys Davids 1903a; 1903b; 1904; Carus 1904.
95 See Ananda Maitriya 1903e: 149; 1903l: 48, Ananda Metteyya 1904e: 517; 1908e: 346–348, for news items about Sri Lanka, and Perera 1904 for an article about Buddhist antiquarian remains in Ceylon. For an analysis of the British imperial presence in Anuradhapura and the Buddhist response, see Harris 2018: 116–141.
96 See *The Burma Gazette* Part One: Notifications of the Lieutenant Governor of Burma 1904, which in addition states that any Burmese who broke this neutrality did so 'at their Peril.'
97 See also Ananda Metteyya 1905: 120, where Ananda M, at the end of the war, praises Japan for showing herself greater in peace than in warfare, and for being able to teach the West about peace.
98 See also Ananda Metteyya 1904g: 677, when Ananda M passed around 'a small exhibit of radium' at a meeting of the *Buddhasāsana Samāgama*.
99 See Volume 2 for the text of Ananda M's obituary of Olcott.
100 See Volume 2, which contains the essay, 'The Faith of the Future.'
101 See Volume 2 for the full text of this presentation.
102 Fritz Kunz also briefly mentions meeting Ananda Metteyya in a letter to his sister dated February 27th, 1906. He writes, 'We were pleased with our stay in Burma, and felt there is so much work to be done there; I hope we may

soon be able to return and do it! . . . We also went to see Ananda Maitreya, the English Buddhist monk who edits the magazine "Buddhism."' Fritz Family Collection, Box 1, folder 24. Theosophical Society in America Archives.

103   In addition, see Turner, Cox and Bocking 2020: 146, for a list of 'seven to ten' possible names of other Westerners, some already working in Asia, who were ordained by or on behalf of U Dhammaloka.

104   Ananda Metteyya to Cash Pereira, 10 February, 1905. He speaks very highly of Ñāṇatiloka: 'He is a very good Monk, and since he has been in Burma has made as deep a study of Buddhism as is possible thro' the medium of translation. . . . he is an easily-contented mortal, with a very gentle and considerate nature.'

105   See endnote 25 in this chapter. See also Burma Echo 1907: 9, which claims that Sīlācāra was ordained a novice in an unorthodox way at the Buddhist Girls' School by Daw Mya May (quoted in Turner, Cox and Bocking 2021: 148). It is possible that the newspaper saw Ñāṇatiloka's involvement as irrelevant.

106   Elizabeth is grateful to John Randall for this information and for permission to use Kelly's portrait, which is owned by Randall.

107   Introduced to Crowley through her brother, they were married in 1903. She became a significant occult muse for Crowley, helping him with his occult practice and writing.

108   See, for example, Sinhala Bauddhaya 1908a: 12.

109   See, for example, Sinhala Bauddhaya 1908b: 9, which praises the appearance of *The Buddhist Review*, the journal of the Buddhist Society of Great Britain and Ireland, mentioning its stance on non-violence. The formation of the Society is given in the next chapter.

110   From 1892–1900, the journal was called *Journal of the Maha-Bodhi Society*. It changed its name from 1901.

111   Other articles followed in subsequent years, e.g., Ananda Metteyya 1913. This contribution was praised as 'learned and illuminating.'

112   Anagārika Dharmapāla, *Diary*, 17 and 19 May, 1904.

113   Anagārika Dharmapāla, *Diary*, 21 August, 1904.

114   See Anagārika Dharmapāla, *Diary*, 7 December, 1921, in which Dharmapāla states that he had sent £10 to Ananda M in response to a letter from him asking for help, and that he had sent the same amount the previous month.

115   See, for example, Anagārika Dharmapāla, *Diary*, 2 August, 1906, and 8 May, 1909.

116   Anagārika Dharmapāla, *Diary*, 14 May, 1908.

117   Anagārika Dharmapāla, *Diary*, 19 May, 1908.

118   Anagārika Dharmapāla, *Diary*, 12 July, 1909.

119   Anagārika Dharmapāla, *Diary*, 6 & 7 January, 1907, 18 February, 1907, and 9 & 10 March, 1907.

120   Anagārika Dharmapāla, *Diary*, 15 March, 1907.

121   See Anagārika Dharmapāla, *Diary*, 19 March, 1907, wherein he criticises the 'Inter Buddhist Society' in Rangoon—Ananda M's International Buddhist Association—for claiming that it was the only Buddhist Society 'propagating the Dhamma in the West.'

122 Anagārika Dharmapāla, *Diary*, 12 April, 1907.
123 Anagārika Dharmapāla, *Diary*, 14 April, 1907.
124 Anagārika Dharmapāla, *Diary*, 17 April, 1907.
125 The second issue of *Buddhism* includes information about the Thathanabaing and a full report of the installation, including the Lieutenant Governor's speech: Ananda Maitriya 1903i: 177–208. The Thathanabaing was traditionally head of only one of the monastic lineages in Burma, the Thudhamma, but the British government sought to make him akin to an 'archbishop' with oversight of all monastic lineages in the country. See Turner 2014: 10–15.
126 See also Ananda Metteyya 1905b: 7, where he mentions that his visit to Tavoy (Dawai) and Mergui had brought in much financial help.
127 Mention is made of the 'new Rangoon College building' in Report on Public Instruction in Burma for the Year 1900–1901 1901: 12. According to later maps, however, this did not entail shifting the College's location. It remained opposite the Anglican Cathedral.
128 See Second Quinquennial Report on Public Instruction in Burma for the Years 1897–98 to 1901–2 1901: 36. By 1911, numbers had risen to 268–see Report on Public Instruction in Burma for the Year 1910–11 1911: 2. The College was placed under the Educational Syndicate in 1885 and transferred to direct government control in 1904. In 1920, together with the American Baptist Mission College, it became the University of Rangoon and in the years following moved to buildings north of the city (Pearn 1939: 242, 282).
129 In 1914, U Kin, speaking to the Annual General Meeting (AGM) as President, praised one student for speaking to the AGM in 'his mother tongue,' demonstrating the rarity of this (Rangoon College Magazine 1914: 75). By the 1920s, when the College became a University College, a Burmese section had evolved.
130 See Volume 2 for the complete text of 'Devotion in Buddhism.'
131 This was probably the talk that was advertised in *Thuriya* the day before: Thuriya 1911: 13.
132 Ananda M praises Zan Aung's ability to mediate between the West and Asian traditions, and the lucidity of his introductory essay on Buddhist philosophy and Abhidhamma, in which Zan Aung judges Abhidhamma to be 'the final and greatest product of generations immemorial of Indo-Aryan philosophic thought' (Ananda M 1911c: 134). See endnote 60 in this chapter for Zan Aung's collaboration with Caroline Rhys Davids.
133 When introducing the second book review, the author, Professor Ross (Rangoon College) states that a review that 'is not looked upon from the point of view of religious partisanship' will please the public, referring implicitly to Ananda M's review. He then proceeds to judge that Buddhist philosophy had been 'eviscerated in this work' (Ross 1911: 60–61). He praises the author's English expression but suspects 'a tendency to force an identity between Buddhist and western ideas' (Ross 1911: 65).
134 The Members of the Council in 1910 consisted of 15 people, only five of whom were Burmese, including Shwe Zan Aung and May Oung. Of the Western members, four were ordained Christian clergy.

135 The full text of Ananda Metteyya's contribution to *Twentieth Century Impressions of Burma* is given in Volume 2.
136 Besant reports that she left for Rangoon on 12 January but visited numerous places on the way, arriving on the 28th (Besant 1911: 870). The Burmese Theosophical journal gives the arrival as 16 January. See Lat 1911.
137 Maung Lat's report demonstrates that she spoke on a wide variety of topics, including 'Prevention of Cruelty to Animals,' 'Theosophy in Relation to Modern Science,' 'Noble Eightfold Path,' 'Zoroastrianism,' 'Islam in the Light of Theosophy,' 'Temperance,' 'Teacher of Gods and Men' and 'The Law of Action and Reaction' (at a Buddhist School in Mandalay; Lat 1911).
138 The foundation stone of the boys' school was laid during Annie Besant's visit in 1911 (Lat 1911: 234) and, by that time, the girls' school was already constructed, maintained under the patronage of B. Cowasji, President of the Burma Lodge (Lat 1911: 232).
139 Arthur M. Knight to SPG (Society for the Propagation of the Gospel) Headquarters, 22 August, 1903 (SPG CLR 67 Copies of Letters received from Rangoon 1898–1905).
140 In the mid-nineteenth century, the British had attempted to transform the excellent education provided by monasteries into a system of primary schooling that would be consistent with the aims of the colonial administration. This attempt failed, because the British failed to understand the purposes of monastic schools (Turner 2014: 53–54). Ananda M also comments on the failings of Anglo-Vernacular Schools in Ananda Maitriay 1903l: 46–48.
141 At this time, Ledi was beginning to formulate methods of meditation that could be taught on a mass scale, bypassing the *jhānas* (Braun 2013: 44). In addition, in 1901, he published the *Paramatthadīpanī*, a commentary on a twelfth-century handbook on Abhidhamma from Sri Lanka, the *Abhidhammatthasaṅgaha*, which caused controversy because it challenged another authoritative commentary used by the monastic Sangha in Burma (Braun 2013: 45–76). His books feature regularly in the 'Quarterly Catalogue of Books' published in *The Burma Gazette*. For instance, Ledi Sayadaw 1903 appears in the *Gazette* of 11 June, 1904. See also *The Burma Gazette*, 18 February, 3 June and 2 December, 1905, when further books by Ledi Sayadaw, mainly on Abhidhamma, are listed.
142 One of his most popular writings for the broader population was *Summary of the Ultimates* (*Paramattha saṃ khip*), a traditional poem that made the *Abhidhammatthasaṅgaha* accessible to lay people (see Braun 2013: 102–121).
143 See White 1913: 198: 'Never for a moment did the Ledi Sayadaw fall under a shadow of suspicion as to the purity of his motives and conduct, or the good intention of his pilgrimage [travels through the country for preaching].'
144 Personal conversation with Elizabeth Harris, December 2018. Professor Khammai Dhammasami is the founder and rector of Shan State Buddhist University in Myanmar.
145 Ādiccavamsa became a controversial figure through his support of higher ordination for women. He was put on monastic trial in 1935 because of this, and disrobed in 1941 (Janaka 2016: 108).

146 For a photograph of U. Titthila with Christmas Humphreys, see Humphreys 1985: opposite p. 129.
147 According to Major Ba Thaung, Sayā U Pyé became a novice monk at the age of 13 and then took higher ordination. He became known for his Pali expertise. He disrobed after his 14th rains' retreat and, after teaching Burmese and Pali at a government high school in Yangon [Rangoon College], turned to editing and translating at the Hanthawaddy Press and the Pyi Gye Mandai Press. His work includes the Pali commentaries. He was the first Burmese layman to receive the title *Aggamahapandita* (foremost, great learned one; Major Ba Thaung 2002: 293–295).
148 For instance, Lanman mentions that U Pyé had published a work by Buddhaghosa in Pali (Lanman 1913: 149). Ananda M had sent Lanman U Pyé's *Visuddhimagga*. Lanman's response was that he had found only two minor errors in the first two thirds (Ananda Metteyya 1908b: 331).
149 See Colston 1904, in which Colston, a British civil servant, demonstrates sensitivity to Buddhism and knowledge of the work of Shwe Zan Aung. An E. J. Colston I. C. S. is also mentioned in the Minutes of the Buddhist Society in London as one of their contacts in Burma: e.g., The Buddhist Society of Great Britain and Ireland Minute Book, Council Meeting, 12 April, 1910.
150 See Chapter Two, p. 50.
151 Ananda Metteyya to Charles Lanman, 22 July, 1907, quoted in LeRoy Perreira 2012: 546–547.
152 Volume 2 contains the full text of Ananda M's article, 'Propaganda.'

4: Ananda M's Mission to Britain and Return to Burma

1 See Chapter One, endnote 5.
2 As our photo demonstrates, the Bury Street Headquarters announced itself as 'The Buddhist Society of England.' The reason might have been pragmatic, namely that there was no room for the complete title. It is more likely that it represents a point before the Society took over these premises.
3 According to a Ceylonese journal, Ananda M reported at the 5th AGM of the *Buddhasāsana Samāgama* that about 200 had attended the inaugural meeting. See Sinhala Bauddhaya 1908a: 12.
4 See for instance 6 February 1908 to Ven. Seelakkhandha in Ceylon, reprinted in Guruge 1984: 412.
5 Westminster Gazette 1908a: 3—'There is, no doubt, a great deal in Buddhism worth learning, but life must be a difficult thing to live with so many restrictions.'
6 E.g., Belper News 1908: 7; Daily Mail 1908b: 5; Daily Mirror 1908: 13; Homeward Mail from India, China and the East 1908: 528; London and China Express 1908a: 311; Ross-shire Journal 1908: 3; The Bystander 1908b: 422; The Sphere 1908: 16. The Maha-Bodhi and the United Buddhist World 1908: 88 also repeats this, calling him Allan Bennett MacGregor.
7 E.g., Irish Independent 1908: 8; The Evening Telegraph and Post, Dundee 1908: 4; Warminster and Westbury Journal 1908: 2.

8   E.g., Belper News 1908: 7, followed by The Courier 1908: 11.
9   See also Sevenoaks Chronicle and Kentish Advertiser 1908: 2.
10 E.g., Sheffield Evening Telegraph 1908: 3; Wharfedale and Airdale Observer 1908: 7.
11 Cyrus West Field (1819–1892) was an American businessman who co-created the Atlantic Telegraph Company and laid the first trans-Atlantic telegraph cable in 1858, spanning from Newfoundland to Ireland.
12 See also Morning Post 1908b: 9.
13 The transactions of the Congress lists a paper on 'Religious Experience in Buddhism' but states that it was 'not printed' (Anon 1908: 455). Ananda M mentions a paper of this name as a priority for publication when writing to MacGregor Reid on his return journey to Burma and asks him to send a copy to Dr Estlin Carpenter (Oxford University), President of the Congress. Given that the paper was not published in the transactions, MacGregor Reid probably failed Ananda M here. See Ananda M to W. MacGregor Reid 15 November, 1908 (Gerald Yorke Collection, Warburg Institute, University College London, NS10).
14 The first Congress took place in Paris in 1901 (*Le Premier Congres International d'Historie des Religions*) at the time of *L'Exposition Universelle* and the second was held in Basel in 1904. After World War II, an official body was formed: The International Association for the Study of the History of Religions (Braybrooke 1992: 282). See Anon 1908 for the transactions of the third congress relating to Indian religions.
15 Ananda Metteyya to Dr Watson MacGregor-Reid, 2 September, 1908 (Yorke Collection, Warburg Institute, University College London, NS10).
16 See Yorke Collection, Warburg Institute, University College London, NS101 pp. 15–17. The letter from Ananda M to Watson MacGregor Reid, 2 September, 1908 (endnote 15) mentions a weekly Sunday evening lecture at the 'Fisher's,' namely the home of Alexander Fisher, an early supporter of the Buddhist Society.
17 This could have been at the invitation of the person whom Ananda M called 'a religious and very liberal-minded person ... who invited me to give a sermon on Buddhism in his Church one Sunday afternoon' (Ananda Metteyya 1909b: 13).
18 Walter Basil Hodgson Smith (1887–1929), diary entry for Wednesday, 10 June, 1908 (Theosophical Society in America Archives, Wheaton, Illinois).
19 Letters from Ananda M to Dr. W. MacGregor-Reid dated 31 July, 1908 and 1 August, 1908 (Yorke Collection, Warburg Institute, University College London, NS10).
20 Letters from Ananda M. to Dr. W. MacGregor-Reid dated 1 August and 2(?) September, 1908 (Yorke Collection, Warburg Institute, University College London, NS10).
21 See, for instance, Ananda M to Dr. Watson MacGregor Reid, dated I August, 1908, in which his reliance on MacGregor Reid for the publication of his message is evident. He speaks of reviewing his lecture on 'Kamma' and states that no others who see the value of the 'Dhamma' have 'the ability, the training or the organisation that are at your disposal' (Yorke Collection, Warburg Institute, University College London, NS10).

22 For an assessment of Copleston's book, see Harris 2006: 125–138.
23 The third lecture, for instance, mounts an attack on the Buddhist concept of 'merit' as 'self-regarding,' failing as 'a leading motive' for action: 'The pessimism of those who seek for merit has no place in Christianity' (Fyffe 1908: 337). The last critiques 'theoretical' Buddhism's concept of *anattā*, argues for fundamental difference between the Christian heaven and 'the Buddhist Nirvana,' claims transmigration mitigated against moral effort and represents Buddhism as offering no hope (Fyffe 1908: 452–460).
24 Some of this data is repeated in: The Aberdeen Daily Journal 2nd Edition 1908: 5, which adds, 'Buddhism, he maintains, is not antagonistic to any religion, and he holds that it is the only means by which Christian ideals can be restored'; Somerset and West of England Advertiser 1908: 6; and Motherwell Times 1908: 7, which also reports that Ananda M hopes to return to Britain in 'two and a half years' time, and celebrate the 2500th anniversary of the attainment of Buddhahood by building a monastery, and placing in permanent residence there five Buddhist monks.'
25 Letter to members of the Buddhist Society from Alex. Fisher, 21 September, 1908. The meeting was to be held at the Studio, 12 St Mary Abbot's Place, Kensington at 7.00 p.m. on 26 September (Gerald Yorke Collection, Warburg Institute, University College London, NS101).
26 Ananda M. to W. MacGregor Reid, 2 September, 1908 (Gerald Yorke Collection, Warburg Institute, University College London, NS10).
27 See, for instance, Civil and Military Gazette Lahore 1908: 9, which quotes from an interview given by Ananda M in *The Daily Chronicle*: 'Our fathers have sown the dragon's teeth of Individualism, our children are nigh to reaping its harvest, of wars, civil, and national.'
28 Ananda Metteyya to Dr. Watson MacGregor-Reid, September 1908, day unclear (Gerald Yorke Collection, Warburg Institute, University College London, NS10).
29 Ananda Metteyya to Dr. Watson MacGregor-Reid, September 1908, day unclear (Gerald Yorke Collection, Warburg Institute, University College London, NS10).
30 See also Daily Record (Lanarkshire) 1908; 3; Motherwell Times 1908: 7.
31 Ananda M to Dr. Watson MacGregor Reid, 2(?) September, 1908 (Gerald Yorke Collection, Warburg Institute, University College London, NS10).
32 See also the 'Report of the Second Annual Meeting of the Buddhist Society of Great Britain and Ireland' held on 9 June, 1909, when Mr. Greenly is credited with mounting a special appeal to defray the debts of the society and contributing £30 himself (The Buddhist Review 1909d: 291).
33 See Rost's description of Ananda M's lecture in Clapham, quoted earlier.
34 Ananda Metteyya to Dr. Watson MacGregor-Reid, 2 September, 1908 (Gerald Yorke Collection, Warburg Institute, University College London, NS10).
35 Francis Payne to the Anagārika Dharmapāla, 1 December, 1908, translated and reprinted in *Sinhala Bauddhaya* 3.14, 16 January, 1909: 16 and in *The Maha-Bodhi and the United Buddhist World* XVII.1, February 1909: 31.

36 See Ananda M to Watson MacGregor Reid, 15 November, 1908, for a reference to asthma during his return voyage (Gerald Yorke Collection, Warburg Institute, University College London, NS10).
37 The other two were 'The Coming Religion' and 'Self-Renunciation.' See Letter from Ananda M to Dr. W. MacGregor-Reid, dated 15 November, 1908, from S.S. *Ava* (Gerald Yorke Collection, Warburg Institute, University College London, NS10)
38 See Volume 2 for the full text of 'Right Understanding.'
39 Ananda M to W. MacGregor Reid, 17 April, 1909 (Gerald Yorke Collection, Warburg Institute, University College London, NS10).
40 According to Ellam, some members were critical of the Society becoming 'booksellers.' The meetings of the Society were transferred to a room in Kensington belonging to a member (12 St Mary Abbot's Place) and the Orient Press in Great Russell Street became the Society's Headquarters and Book Depot (Ellam 1909: 2–3). When some found Kensington 'too remote,' new rooms for the Society's weekly lectures were found at 11 Hart Street, in Bloomsbury (The Buddhist Review 1909d: 292).
41 See Volume 2 for the full text of this presentation: 'Extension of the Empire of Righteousness to Western Lands.'
42 See the beginning of this chapter.
43 We have not found a copy of this, but it is mentioned in The Buddhist Review 1909b: 227–230, with the words 'As the Bhikkhu says, the amount of Buddhism that exists here in a kind of latent state, is most surprising; and he is disposed to find the explanation of this in the belief that, "for the past few decades in England there have been taking birth men and women, who in their past lives were Buddhists."'
44 See Volume 2 for the version of this letter that was reprinted in 1930: 'Excerpts from the Buddhist Correspondence of Ananda Metteyya: An Open Letter to the Buddhists of London.'
45 Ananda Metteyya to Dr. Watson MacGregor-Reid, 2 September, 1908 (Gerald Yorke Collection, Warburg Institute, University College London, NS10). See also Crow 2008b.
46 Ananda Metteyya to Dr. Watson MacGregor-Reid, 2 September, 1908, (Gerald Yorke Collection, Warburg Institute, University College London, NS10).
47 Ananda Metteyya to Dr. Watson MacGregor-Reid, 17 April, 1909 (Gerald Yorke Collection, Warburg Institute, University College London, NS10).
48 Ethel Powell-Brown to Gerald Yorke, 18 November, 1952 (Gerald Yorke Collection, Warburg Institute, University of London, NS104).
49 See Chapter Three, p. 96.
50 See, for instance, Grossman and Van Dam 2011; Ricard and Singer 2017.
51 Minutes of The Buddhist Society of Great Britain and Ireland, Council Meeting, 18 June, 1909.
52 Minutes of The Buddhist Society of Great Britain and Ireland, Council Meeting, 23 July, 1909.
53 Francis Payne to the Anagārika Dharmapāla, 1 December, 1908, translated and reprinted in *Sinhala Bauddhaya* 1909: 16, and in The Maha-Bodhi and the

United Buddhist World 1909: 31. In the latter, the date of the letter is given wrongly as 1 December, 1909.
54 E. H. Stevenson was ordained Sāsana Dhaja in 1908 in Sagaing in Burma, sponsored by U Kyaw Yan, and was highly regarded by Ananda M. See letter from Ananda M to representatives of the *Buddhasāsana Samāgama* and the Buddhist laity in general, 30 December, 1908 (Gerald Yorke Collection, Warburg Institute, University College London, NS 104).
55 Minutes of The Buddhist Society of Great Britain and Ireland, Council Meeting, 18 June, 1909. See also Dharmapāla 1909a: 11, wherein Dharmapāla adds an appeal to the Ceylonese for money to his words concerning the potential of Ananda M's mission.
56 Anagārika Dharmapāla, *Diary*, 29 August, 1909.
57 Minutes of The Buddhist Society of Great Britain and Ireland, Council Meeting, 16 March, 1909. She promised 1000 rupees. This had not been received by June 1909 (Minutes for 18 June, 1909). Another donation is mentioned later in this chapter.
58 Minutes of The Buddhist Society of Great Britain and Ireland, Council Meeting, 19 January, 1910.
59 E.g., Minutes of The Buddhist Society of Great Britain and Ireland, Council Meeting, 3 May, 1910, when £53 was held and 19 June, 1910, when £65.2.8 was held.
60 Minutes of The Buddhist Society of Great Britain and Ireland, Council Meeting, 26 May, 1911.
61 Minutes of The Buddhist Society of Great Britain and Ireland, Annual Meeting, 30 April, 1912.
62 Minutes of The Buddhist Society of Great Britain and Ireland, Annual Meeting, 30 April, 1912. See also endnote 40 in this chapter.
63 Minutes of The Buddhist Society of Great Britain and Ireland, Council Meeting, 4 April, 1913.
64 See Bhikkhu U Sāsana-Dhaja to W. MacGregor Reid, 28 January, 1909, expressing a wish 'to accompany my friend Ananda Metteyya on his next mission to England.' By January 1910, however, he was leaving Burma for Melbourne, Australia—see letter from Bhikkhu Sāsana Dhaja to W. MacGregor-Reid, 27 January, 1910 (Gerald Yorke Collection, Warburg Institute, University College London, NS104).
65 Minutes of The Buddhist Society of Great Britain and Ireland, Council Meeting, 3 September, 1909, and the minutes of 19 November, 1909, when the Council was told that it was doubtful whether a *bhikkhu* could be spared from Burma.
66 Minutes of The Buddhist Society of Great Britain and Ireland, Council Meeting, 28 June, 1910.
67 Minutes of The Buddhist Society of Great Britain and Ireland, Council Meeting, 27 January, 1911.
68 Minutes of The Buddhist Society of Great Britain and Ireland, Council Meeting, 12 May, 1911.
69 See Minutes of The Buddhist Society of Great Britain and Ireland, Council Meeting, 8 December, 1911, and 26 July, 1912.

70 See also Bruce Herald 1913: 3; The Civil and Military Gazette (Lahore) 1913, which adds extended commentary about the life of a Buddhist monk; and The Cheltenham Looker-On 1913, which claims that the great [Christian] missionary societies would be 'lacerated' by the advertisement.
71 Minutes of The Buddhist Society of Great Britain and Ireland, Council Meeting, 23 January, 1914.
72 Minutes of The Buddhist Society of Great Britain and Ireland, Council Meeting, 18 December, 1913.
73 Minutes of The Buddhist Society of Great Britain and Ireland, Council Meeting, 9 January, 1914.
74 *The Maha-Bodhi and the United Buddhist World* XXI.10, October 1913: 225–226; XXI.11, November 1913: 253–254. Due to inflation in India not being measured until 1958, and in Sri Lanka until 1960, it is difficult to calculate the equivalent in today's currencies. Nevertheless, it was a considerable amount.
75 Extracts from letters written by Ananda Metteyya to a friend in England, published by The Buddhist Annual of Ceylon 1931 (Ananda Metteyya 1931). We have not been able to find the originals. A date of 25 April, 1909 is given at the beginning but several letters are amalgamated, including one written on 24 January, 1910 (Ananda Metteyya 1931). See Volume Two for the complete text of the reprint of these letters.
76 See also Ananda M to W. MacGregor Reid, 17 April, 1909, in which he states that he has done nothing since he last wrote because he had 'been much troubled' by asthma (Gerald Yorke Collection, Warburg Institute, University of London, NS10).
77 Minutes of The Buddhist Society of Great Britain and Ireland, Council Meeting, 3 December, 1909, with reference to the *Rangoon Gazette* of 1 November (The Buddhist Society, London).
78 See Paper dated 27 April, 1910, from the Office of Public Instruction (National Archives Yangon AG 1/15E Accession 3339 2E-6). The conditions for Religious Education being taught was that it should be requested by parents and guardians and that 'facilities shall be provided for such instruction only out of school hours.' If instruction in more than one religion was requested, the classes for each should be in different classrooms and at different times, the teacher being selected by the parents and guardians, unless the Inspector of Schools judged the choice undesirable 'for disciplinary reasons.' Schools were mandated to submit a report of this activity, listing the number of religions taught and the pupils in each.
79 The 1911 Census results calculated that there were between 16 and 17 thousand private educational institutions in Burma, of which nearly 16,000 were kept by Buddhists, over 15,900 belonging to the monastic order (Webb 1911: 173), leaving less than 100 additional Buddhist schools.
80 See Chapter Three p. 93. See also Volume Two for the complete text of 'The Religion of Burma.'
81 In this context, he laments that, in the nineteenth century, scholars first translated Sanskrit, Chinese and Tibetan texts rather than the Pali texts,

a phenomenon he compares to scholars seeking to understand Christianity but first accessing 'the later, garbled and miracle-teeming writings of medieval monks' (Ananda M 1910: 102). Todd LeRoy Perreira argues that Ananda Metteyya was the first person to use the term 'Theravada' to unite the Buddhist traditions of South and South-East Asia, in opposition to the term 'Hinayana' (LeRoy Perreira 2012: 532–561). See Chapter Six for an examination of this claim.

82 See Chapter Three, endnote 11, for the Pali text and translation.
83 See Ananda M 1921a: 32, for the assertion that 'The measure, indeed, of the civilisation of a race may properly be meted by the extent to which it manifests Compassion; or as we rightly term it, the highest attribute of the human mind,—Humanity.'
84 Explaining it, he refers back to his explanation of *sammāsamādhi*: it is 'the intent contemplation of some object with a view to the attainment of one or other of those higher states of consciousness of which mention has been made, and which form a very large subject by themselves, impossible to deal with' (Ananda M 1910: 115).
85 Fielding Hall makes the same point, again suggesting that Ananda M and Fielding Hall not only had many views in common but shared conversation with each other. See Fielding Hall 1913: 180. See Chapter Three, endnote 40 and pp. 89–90.
86 Francis Payne's 1911 review of the book published (Payne 1911) states that it was available in Rangoon and through Luzac and Co. in London.
87 Minutes of The Buddhist Society of Great Britain and Ireland, Council Meeting, 30 April, 1912. See Council Minutes of 20 October, 1911, which record that the Society had paid Luzac for the carriage of 1000 copies.
88 Minutes of The Buddhist Society of Great Britain and Ireland, 31 March, 1911.
89 Minutes of The Buddhist Society of Great Britain and Ireland, 2 May, 1913.
90 See Chapter Four, p. 156 for evidence of this.
91 The transcript of the trial was republished in two newspapers: *The Times* on 27 April, 1911 and *The Looking Glass* on 6 May, 1911. George Cecil Jones was being questioned by Mr. Schiller, who represented the publisher. When asked about the letters in *Truth* and if the claims by Dhammaloka were true, Jones replied, 'No, but in a number of *Truth* I am told they published a letter written by Bennett in reply. You would not bring that with you.' Schiller ignored this reply and continued questioning Jones. Soon the questioning shifted to Crowley but then came back to Bennett. When Schiller asked why Bennett had not taken any action against *Truth* for the claims of Dhammaloka, Jones replied, 'I was told that Allan Bennett wrote a letter which was published; that is exactly what I was told. You would not look.' This, again, was ignored by Schiller. Quotations from a reprint of the transcript in Kaczynski 2005: 113–136.
92 The Gerald Yorke collection contains a letter from Edward 'Ted' Bryant to John Symonds, an early Crowley biographer, relating stories Crowley told about Bennett to Bryant in the early 1940s. Within the letter, Bryant states, 'When Allan returned to England to lead his Buddhist mission, A. C. did not

see so much of him as during their Golden Dawn days, partly because Aleister had kept his spiritual exercises almost confined to magic(k), where as Allan had switched over completely to Buddhist meditation & also because Allan tended to acquire a circle of woolly sisters whom Aleister loathed.' While on the surface this would seem to be a strong indication they met, in the context of the letter, it becomes apparent quickly that Bryant has his timelines frequently confused. For instance, Bryant wonders why Crowley was excluded from participation in Bennett's Golden Dawn Taphthartharath ritual, not understanding that it took place years prior to Bennett and Crowley meeting in 1899. Similarly, Bryant claims that Crowley was with Bennett near his death in 1923, when Crowley was in Sicily, and had been there for some time, when Bennett died. While it is likely that Bryant is correctly relating what he was told by Crowley, the unreliableness in the narratives seems to come from Crowley misremembering the stories told decades later. Bryant explicitly states Crowley's memories about Bennett were 'vague.' Bryant writes, 'He [Crowley] wanted me to write a biography of Allan (I think as a memorial to him) but his references to the dates & accessory material that would be needed were so vague that I soon gave up.' Thus, it may be that Crowley and Ananda M met during his mission. But this letter from Bryant is not a reliable source to make a definitive claim one way or the other. Gerald Yorke Collection, Warburg Institute, University College London, OS EE1 324a.

93 As a postscript to a letter written to Frank Bennett, Crowley adds, 'Are you any relation of Allan Bennett afterwards Allan McGregor and now Bhikkhu Ananda Metteya? He was my guru for years. The 'Note on Genesis' in No. 2 (of the Equinox) is by him, and No. 3 will be full of his magical rituals.' Correspondence, Aleister Crowley to Frank Bennett, 9 February, 1910, Ordo Templi Orientis Archives.

94 The index of the book denotes seven pages in which Bennett or Ananda M are mentioned.

95 According to Kenneth Grant, who knew Crowley at the end of his life, Crowley described Bennett as a 'White Knight.' Grant quotes Crowley as writing, 'We called him the White Knight from Alice through the Looking Glass—so lovable, so harmless, so unpractical! But he was a Knight, too! And white—there never walked a whiter man on earth. He never did walk on earth, either! A genius, a flawless genius! But a most terribly frustrated genius' (Grant 1972: 82).

96 As mentioned previously, Daw Mya May also lost her son in July 1910. See The Buddhist Review 1910: 318–319.

97 Clifford Bax to Aleister Crowley, 17 July, 1944 (Gerald Yorke Collection, Warburg Institute, University College London, Scrap Book Volume 2 OSEE2).

98 Rhona Galley (Mrs. E. P. Brown), 'A Buddhist Mystic' (Gerald Yorke Collection, Warburg Institute, University College London, NS 96).

99 Clifford Bax to Aleister Crowley, 17 July, 1944. See also Bennett 1923: viii, where Ananda M, writing his Introduction in the third person, states that he had to leave the Order because of 'the complete break-down of his health.'

100 Ethel Powell-Brown to John Symonds, 13 February, 1944 (Gerald Yorke Collection, Warburg Institute, University College London, NS 93 p. 3).
101 Ethel Powell-Brown to Gerald Yorke, 30 October, 1952 (Gerald York Collection, Warburg Institute, University College London, NS 104).
102 See undated typed account of Ananda M by Ethel Powell-Brown sent to Gerald Yorke, entitled 'About the two letters which I have. . . . from the Bhikkhu Ananda Maitreya' (Gerald Yorke Collection, Warburg Institute, University College London, NS104).
103 From Ananda Metteyya Thera to Mrs. E. M. Powell-Brown, 24 May, 1913, and Ananda Metteyya Thera to Capt. J. Powell-Brown, 24 May, 1913. Typed versions of the originals, Gerald Yorke Collection, Warburg Institute, University College London, NS194.
104 Ethel Powell-Brown to Gerald Yorke, 30 October, 1952 (Gerald Yorke Collection, Warburg Institute, University College London, NS104). For the reference to Mrs. Hla Oung, see 'About the two letters which I have. . . . from the Bhikkhu Ananda Maitreya' (Gerald Yorke Collection, Warburg Institute, University College London, NS104).
105 Ibid.
106 Ethel Powell-Brown to John Symonds, 13 February, 1952 (Gerald Yorke Collection, Warburg Institute, University College London, NS 96 p. 3); Ethel Powell-Brown to Gerald Yorke, 30 October, 1952 (Gerald Yorke Collection, Warburg Institute, University College London, NS104). 'About the two letters which I have. . . . from the Bhikkhu Ananda Maitreya' (Gerald Yorke Collection, Warburg Institute, University College London Yorke Collection, NS104).
107 Ibid. She mentions this in all the above accounts.

5: In Britain

1 The friend was probably Dr. Edward Greenly. Humphreys writes that Greenly is 'one of the few men living who knows the facts,' and that he had described to him 'the wretched drama in all its sad simplicity' (Humphreys 1937: 35).
2 Ethel Powell-Brown to Gerald Yorke, 30 October, 1952 (Gerald Yorke Collection, Warburg Institute, University College London, NS104).
3 The Liverpool Branch was the first to be formed after the London-based Society. In July 1909, Mrs. Beatrice Avery, Secretary of the Branch, told the London branch that she could only count on seven members in Liverpool: The Buddhist Society of Great Britain and Ireland Minute Book, General Meeting, 2 July, 1909. A Miss. Deaken was mentioned as an 'Associate' in Liverpool in November 1911: The Buddhist Society of Great Britain and Ireland Minute Book, General Meeting, 17 November, 1911. At the 1917 AGM, there were 'about 11' members: The Buddhist Review 1917d: 109–110.
4 The Buddhist Society of Great Britain and Ireland Minute Book, Council Meeting, 24 July, 1914.
5 The Buddhist Society of Great Britain and Ireland Minute Book, Council Meeting, 2 October, 1914.

6 See, for instance, Ananda M 1918: 148.
7 The war had begun on 28 July, when the Austro-Hungarian Empire declared war on Serbia in response to the assassination of the Austrian Archduke Franz Ferdinand, after which Russia mobilised in support of Serbia, prompting Germany, an ally of Austria, to declare war on Russia and France (Russell 2018: 20–23).
8 Particularly impressive were St George's Hall, the Walker Art Gallery and the William Brown Library and Museum. On the waterfront, since Ananda M had left Britain in 1908, the Royal Liver Building had been built, its two towers topped by massive copper birds, inspiring the legend that, if they left, 'Liverpool would cease to exist' (Lees 2011: 105). The Cunard Building was begun in 1914.
9 When Germany declared war, it demanded access to France through Belgium and attacked Belgium. When this was refused, 'enormous numbers' came to Britain as refugees (Russell 2018: 23).
10 'Constitution of the Association, approved by the Committee on 9th December, 1891.' In 1914, it received financial contributions from 50 bodies, according to its Twenty-Fourth Annual Report for the year ending December 1914 (file for the Association held by the Liverpool Records Office and Archives).
11 The passenger manifest for the S.S. *St. Paul* denotes that Charlotte Louisa Hill and Alexandra Leslie Hill arrived in New York, coming from Liverpool, England, on the 21 September, 1914.
12 Handwritten note in Ananda M's Dictionary, given to Jean Pemberton by the daughter of Dr. Youatt. This is now in the possession of David Evans.
13 Personal letter to Elizabeth Harris from Mr. T. Pemberton, 26 October, 1994. Jean Margaret Pemberton was a practising artist, who taught at what is now Leeds Arts University. She was a vegetarian and a Buddhist, who felt an affinity with Ananda M because she also suffered from asthma. Email correspondence between Elizabeth Harris and Julia Williams, Jean's niece, 1 February, 2023.
14 Personal letter to Elizabeth Harris from Mr. T. Pemberton, 26 October, 1994.
15 An 'A. M. Fund' was established. A total of 55 pounds and 17 shillings were sent to 'the doctor' first, comprising 12 donations mainly from British supporters, followed by a further amount, mainly from well-wishers in Sri Lanka, including Cassius Pereira. See The Buddhist Review 1917a; 1917c.
16 Charlotte, her husband, W. L. B. Hill, and daughter, Alexandra Leslie, arrived in Liverpool, England on the Tuscania of the Anchor Line, travelling from New York to Glasgow, Scotland, via Liverpool. The manifest notes the Tuscania arrived in Glasgow on 25 July, 1916. Its stop at Liverpool was likely only a day or two prior. An additional passenger manifest lists Charlotte, W. A. Hill [sic], and Alexandra Leslie returning to the United States on the ship, Northland, travelling from Liverpool, on 13 May, 1919, to Philadelphia, Pennsylvania, arriving on 25 May, 1919. Significantly, the manifest lists Bath as the permanent residence of Charlotte and her daughter while W. L. B. Hill was active with the British Army.

17 See Minutes of the Buddhist Society of Great Britain and Ireland, Council Meetings for 10 July, 17 July, 24 July, 7 August, 24 August, and 18 September, 1914. Possession of the house began in September 2014 and the first public lecture there was on 20 September (Council Meeting, 14 September, 1914).
18 Minutes of the Buddhist Society of Great Britain and Ireland, Council Meeting, 2 October, 1914, in which Duffus reports that he had received a wire from Upper Burma saying, 'Ready to send Silacara, any hindrance.' The agreed response was 'Council welcomes Silacara.'
19 In 1917, the Society managed 40 pages (e.g., Vol IX.1, January–June 1917). In 1918, Volume X, the issues reached only 19 pages. For this reason, the 1920 issue was considered part of Volume X, with the pagination running on from 1918.
20 See, for instance, Chelsea News and General Advertiser 1915 (unpaginated), which advertises a meeting at the Society's Headquarters (43 Penywern Road, Earls Court) on 28 May with four speakers, including E. J. Mills and the Bengali scholar B. M. Barua (1888–1948; Saint Pancras Gazette 1915: 2). The notice was republished in other local papers. In 1917, several London papers advertised a Buddha Day meeting on 7 May, again at Penywern Road, with D. B. Jayatilleke in the chair and additional speakers: B. M. Barua, Reginald Farrar, Wm Loftus Hare and Francis Payne—see Chelsea News and General Advertiser 1917: 2.
21 See front cover of *The Buddhist Review* XI, July 1920.
22 Minutes of the Buddhist Society of Great Britain and Ireland, Council Meeting, 29 October, 1909.
23 'Meena' was her nickname. She had been born Lillian Meacham and, after Ananda M's death, would study psychoanalytic technique with Sigmund Freud.
24 An edited version of this account was published as Bax 1968: 23.
25 In this conversation, recorded by Bax, Battiscombe Gunn also calls him a Scotsman, suggesting that Ananda M at this time perpetuated this myth or did nothing to prevent it (Bax 1933: 271).
26 In the non-canonical text, the *Milindapañha*, Venerable Nāgasena explains the concept of *anattā* to King Milinda using the simile of a chariot. See Mendis 1993: 29–31.
27 For instance, Westminster Gazette 1922: 1, which states that *The Wisdom of the Aryas* is 'in the press with Messrs. Kegan Paul,' and The Scotsman 1923: 2, which notes the book's publication, declaring that the lectures 'are interesting and instructive as skillful and readable expositions of an ancient mystical doctrine, that looks to Nirvana as an ultimate goal.' See Volume 2 for the complete text of the 1923 publication, *The Wisdom of the Aryas*.
28 Letter from Sr. Ñyānasirī to Elizabeth Harris, 3 October, 1995, after she had been given Cassius Pereira's copy of *The Wisdom of the Aryas*. We have been unable to trace this copy after Sr. Ñyānasirī's death.
29 The Gunns, when first speaking to Bax about Ananda M, referred to his view that 'anyone who perseveres can attain to the higher states of consciousness.' They then asserted their conviction that Ananda M had achieved this,

adding, 'but apparently all Buddhist monks are under a vow to say nothing upon their own authority. So he won't tell of his experiences' (Bax 1933: 272). Ananda M might also have been respecting the Vinaya, where claiming to have attained a spiritual state that one has not attained is one of four *pārājikā* (defeat) offences that demand expulsion from the Order. However, see Chapter Three, p. 97 for a description of a meditative experience that he shared with Ethel Powell-Brown.

30 See Chapter Three, p. 75.
31 See Harris 2006: 101–109, for an account of the Christian missionary representation of the Truths as nihilistic.
32 See Trainor 2012, for an examination of the significance of this verse in Buddhist modernism and orientalist representations.
33 *Majjhima Nikāya* i 55–69.
34 These phrases are taken directly from the Pali Canon, e.g., *Alagaddūpama Sutta* (The Simile of the Snake), *Majjhima Nikāya* i 136, where the Buddha is recorded as saying that the 'well-taught noble disciple' regards body, feelings, perception, consciousness etc. as 'This is not mine, this I am not, this is not my self' (Ñāṇamoli and Bodhi 1995: 136).
35 Ananda M's theory was that 'our mental make-up' or karma passes from life to life and that this is kept intact and bound together by continued thoughts of 'Self.' For the person who has reached enlightenment, this does not happen—the 'mental complex' dissipates into general space (Bennett 1923: 99–101).
36 These are more normatively translated as: loving kindness (*mettā*); compassion (*karunā*); sympathetic joy (*muditā*) and equanimity (*upekkhā*).
37 Born with the name Herbert Close, Starr wrote for Aleister Crowley's journal, *The Equinox*, and knew Florence Farr. He later aligned with the nature cure movement. Starr's poem demonstrates that occultists continued to interact with Ananda M.
38 In 1919, the Society's lease of 43 Penywern Road, Earl's Court, expired, in line with the five-year break that the Society had negotiated in 1914. When Ananda M wrote, the Society was meeting at the Emerson Club, 19 Buckingham Street, the Strand, and had held, on 12 November, 1919, the first of what was hoped to be a series of public meetings at the Caxton Hall.
39 See also the short obituary of Dr. Hewavitarne that appeared in *Buddhism in England*: Buddhism in England 1929: 20.
40 Personal letter from Myo Kyo Ni to Elizabeth Harris, 2 December, 1994.
41 Most bibliographic entries for *The Buddhist Review* list the journal as only having 11 volumes, ignoring the last issue, which began volume 12.
42 See Volume Two for the complete text of 'Buddhism: A Religion of Compassion.'
43 Ritual of the Talismans of Visions (Gerald Yorke Collection, Warburg Institute, University College London, NS71 Volume 6).
44 Jean Pemberton was given Ananda M's dictionary by the daughter of Dr. Youatt and it was passed to David Evans, who conducted Jean's Buddhist funeral. See Childers 1909.

45 See also Humphreys 1937: 42–43.
46 See Volume Two for the full text of 'Buddhism and the Western World.'
47 Ananda M had said something similar in a 1908 interview published in the Spiritualist journal, *Light*. See Wright 1908: 225. Wright later quoted frequently from his Ananda M interview in his book, *A Manual of Buddhism* (Wright 1912). Ananda M's critique of Spiritualism has parallels with the Theosophical critique of Spiritualism. Theosophists claimed that there is an astral world where the remnants of a person's astral or emotional body might persist after death for a limited time, called a 'shell,' but that the spirit or soul of the person, called a 'monad' in Theosophical parlance, had moved on after death and would reincarnate according to their karma. Theosophists argued that Spiritualists were mistaking the astral remnants of the deceased to be the persistence of the person's spirit after death. See Blavatsky 1966.
48 The discourse is not named. The *Kevaddha Sutta* (Dīgha Nikāya i 211–223) and the *Saṅgārava Sutta* (Aṅguttara Nikāya Book of the Threes, 60) both show the Buddha giving primacy to the 'miracle' of teaching or instruction.
49 See Volume Two for the full text of 'The Doctrine of the Aryas.'
50 Ananda M to Cassius Pereira, 18 March, 1920, quoted in Sr. Ñyānasirī to Elizabeth Harris, 3 October, 1995. Ñyānasirī commented 'What a sensitive man. What a gentleman. The letter shows humility, gratitude, concern, mettā.' After Ñyānasirī's death, we have not been able to find the original.
51 See Anagārika Dharmapāla, *Diary*, 7 September, 1921: 'Read letter from Ananda M. asking for help as he is in distress. Sent him draft through the Bk: for £10/-/-. Last month sent him £10/-/-.'
52 Death certificate for 'Allan Bennett,' dated 12 March, 1923 (General Register Office, Somerset House, London). Bax claims that Ananda M died at the end of March, but he must have misremembered.
53 Three grave plots were purchased in unconsecrated ground that was set aside for non-Christians. The cemetery plot numbers are FL1588 to FL1590, with FL1590 being adjacent to the cemetery section's road, and the specific plot in which Bennett was buried.
54 CS Jones Papers, Private Collection. Jones's mention of a password relates to Crowley's magical order, called the A∴A∴, of which Jones was a member. Jones getting the time period of Bennett's death wrong may indicate that he learned about it indirectly through a network of correspondence.
55 Earlier in his 24 October letter, Jones writes that correspondence from another of Crowley's students mentions a letter from Mudd to Jones on behalf of Crowley. Jones writes, 'So far his letter is not in hand, so yours remains unanswered.' At the time, Jones was living in Chicago, but Crowley had relocated to Tunisia in North Africa. With Crowley relocating frequently, and mail travelling long distances to multiple countries, that letters were lost is not surprising.

6: Ananda Metteyya's Legacy

1. See, for instance, Ohn Ghine 1959, which argues that Theravada Buddhism is not incomplete, as some Mahayana Buddhists claim.
2. Dhamma School Grade 7 reader: page 69–71. The Dhamma School Foundation was established in Myanmar in March 2012, based in Yangon. It organises Dhamma schools in most towns and villages and also trains Dhamma school teachers. It has trained over 90,000 teachers as of 2022. Although most Dhamma schools are held on Sundays, there is flexibility in this, but one day a week is normative. The syllabus contains 10 grades, with a completion certificate given for each. Information gained through Swe Swe Mon, from the Secretary of the Dhamma School Foundation.
3. Buddha Vada Hnit Bhathacha Pin Nya Shin Myar (Buddhist and Religious Scholars): https://utinmyintmoe.wordpress.com/2013/11/26/. The Burmese has been translated by our research assistant Swe Swe Mon as, 'Venerable Ananda Metteyya was extraordinary. First, he became a monk with the help of Myanmar Buddhists in Sittwe Town, having Shwe Pyar Sayadaw as his teacher. It is said that Dr. Tha Nu supported him. Later, he moved to Yangon and resided in a monastery which was two miles away [from where is not stated]. This Venerable Ananda Metteyya had a strong faith in Buddhism and he accepted *nibbāna*. He also admitted that even though we study hard and learn Buddhism, we cannot know more than Burmese monks.'
4. Phay Zaw Gyi was founded in 2020 to share knowledge about Buddhism (information from Swe Swe Mon).
5. Ahnaut Kaba Ko Buddhabhatha Pyantpwasete Htoochate Pokko Ashin Ananda Metteyya (Venerable Ananda Metteyya, a unique person who spread Buddhism to the Western world): www.youtube.com/watch?v=GwBCyruKKxg. (Translations from the clip made by Swe Swe Mon.)
6. Its 'Rules and Constitution' state that its object was 'the search for Enlightenment (*Bodhi*)' (The Servants of the Buddha 1921: 1). Monks and novices could become Honorary Members, with five initially opting for this. Lay people could either become Active Members, who had voting rights, or Associate Members. Sixty-five within the former group were named in 1921 (The Servants of the Buddha 1921: 11–13). A journal entitled *The Blessing* began in 1925. Edited by Cassius Pereira, it at first contained translations into English of Pali texts by two erudite Buddhist monks, Nārada and Mahinda. Nārada and Cassius Pereira, after he was ordained, also produced *The Mirror of the Dhamma*, a resource for lay Buddhists, containing devotional chants and popular discourses from the Pali Canon in English and Pali (Narada and Kassapa undated). In the years before independence, the organisation made representation to the Legislative Council on causes such as Buddhist holidays and accommodation for monks on trains (Wijesekera 2021: 16). After independence in 1948, it reverted to its role as educator.
7. Robertson, after having been Secretary of the organisation, became President in 1968, continuing until 1998. See Robertson 1990, for an example of his writing on Buddhism.

8 See, for instance, Anandamaitreya 1993, which draws together talks he had given in Europe and America on topics ranging from 'Development of Divine States' to Abhidhamma.
9 Balangoda Ananda Maitreya to Elizabeth Harris, 1 December, 1993, written from Sri Nandārāmaya, Udumulle, Balangoda. See also Chapter Two, p. 64 for the first mention of this monk.
10 See Trainor 1997: 194, where one of his informants describes Maitreya as 'not being close-minded like some monks,' with Trainor adding 'presumably referring here to his willingness to consider such psychic phenomena [magical rituals connected with relics].'
11 They were held in three series. The first ran from 8 January to 28 May, 1923, the second between October 1923 to March 1924. These were followed by seven more, ending on 26 May, 1924 (Humphreys 1968: 16–17).
12 Minutes of The Buddhist Centre of the Theosophical Society in England, 14 July, 1924 (The Buddhist Society, London), hereafter Minutes of The Buddhist Centre of the Theosophical Society.
13 Minutes of The Buddhist Centre of the Theosophical Society, 14 July, 1924.
14 Minutes of The Buddhist Centre of the Theosophical Society, 15 August, 1924.
15 See also Buddhism in England 1926b: 1. Tensions seem to have been present since the end of 1925. Humphreys states in December 1925, 'I told them [those present for a meeting of the Lodge] of the rude card from A. E. Powell virtually telling us to leave H.Q. We decided to move ourselves first' (The Minutes of The Buddhist Centre of the Theosophical Society, 7 December, 1925).
16 *Buddhism in England* 1.6, December 1926, the inner back cover.
17 The Buddhist Society continues to exist, seeking 'to publish and make known the principles of Buddhism and to encourage the study and practice of those principles.'
18 Forty-two were present from the different Buddhist organisations in London at a meeting addressed by Humphreys on the 'position of Buddhism in London today.' Dharmapāla also spoke. See Minutes of The Buddhist Centre of the Theosophical Society, 28 September, 1925; Webb 2004: 1–2.
19 Minutes of The Buddhist Centre of the Theosophical Society, 29 September, 1924.
20 Minutes of The Buddhist Centre of the Theosophical Society, 25 January, 1924.
21 *Buddhism in England* also carried a description, which declared that Payne had forcefully disagreed with most of the points made by Humphreys: Humphreys 1928: 77.
22 It is obvious from the minutes of the meetings of the Buddhist Lodge that Humphreys did not think much of the Buddhist Society that Payne tried so hard to keep going, e.g., 'We heard with approval that there was some talk of dissolving the moribund Buddhist Society of Great Britain and Ireland' (Minutes of The Buddhist Centre of the Theosophical Society, 15 August, 1924). He admitted that Payne had done 'splendid work for Buddhism' (Minutes of The Buddhist Centre of the Theosophical Society in England,

30 October, 1924) but was evidently hurt that Payne had a low opinion of Theosophy. Yet, Humphreys also expressed delight when Payne positively responded to plans to honour Buddha Day in 1925: 'All very friendly. Payne was so touched at my interest in Buddha Day that he became positively affable, it would appear that whatever our intellectual differences may be, in the heart-side of things, we are at one' (Minutes of The Buddhist Centre of the Theosophical Society, 23 April, 1925).

23 If Humphreys had read Dharmapāla's journal, *The Maha-Bodhi and the United Buddhist World*, he might have been more prepared. See for example Dharmapāla 1907, which carries uncompromising condemnation of Theosophy under Annie Besant, predominantly because she ignored difference between religions and did not recognise the supremacy of Buddhism. Antagonism to Theosophy is evident in Dharmapāla's diaries at an earlier date. See Anagārika Dharmapāla, *Diary*, 19 January, 1903: 'Theosophy is counterfeit Buddhism.'

24 See Minutes of The Buddhist Centre of the Theosophical Society, 4 and 18 November, 1924.

25 Minutes of The Buddhist Centre of the Theosophical Society, 19 November, 1924.

26 Minutes of The Buddhist Centre of the Theosophical Society, 27 May, 1926. A Wesak celebration was held at Holborn Hall, with the Anagārika Dharmapāla speaking, alongside others.

27 See Minutes of The Buddhist Centre of the Theosophical Society, 9 September, 1924, and 2 December, 1924.

28 Minutes of The Buddhist Centre of the Theosophical Society, 22 June, 1925.

29 Minutes of The Buddhist Centre of the Theosophical Society, 15 August, 1924.

30 Fisher was a sculptor who had been one of the first supporters of Dr. Rost, as he worked with others to form the first Buddhist Society of Great Britain and Ireland to welcome Ananda M (Humphreys 1968: 4). See Chapter Four, p. 139.

31 Myokyo-ni was born Irmgard Schloegl, in Austria. She attended Zen classes led by Christian Humphreys and then took formal Zen training in Japan in the Rinzai school. She returned to Britain in the early 1970s, became ordained in 1984 as Myokyo-ni and taught Zen at The Buddhist Society. Christopher Humphreys left his house to her when he died in 1982. It was renamed *Shoboan* (Hermitage of the True Dharma; Waterhouse 1997: 44; 2004: 60–61).

32 Letter from Myokyo-ni to Elizabeth Harris, 2 December, 1994, sent from the Zen Centre, 58 Marlborough Place, London NW8.

33 The serialisation began in Vol. 1, No. 8, November 1927, and continued in almost monthly instalments until Vol. 3 No 3, July 1928.

34 See also a two-part article by Humphreys (1926b and 1926c), which argues that Theosophy and Buddhism are united in their views of the soul.

35 e.g., *The British Buddhist* 1.2, November 1926.

36 Anagārika Dharmapāla, *Diary*, 15 February, 1904.

37 *The British Buddhist* 4.8–9, May–June 1930: 143.

38 See Chapter Five, pp. 188–189.
39 Gordon Bottomley to Clifford Bax, 13 March, 1923 (British Library mss collection, Ms 88957/1/30).
40 This was published by the Sri Saddhatissa International Buddhist Centre in a book to mark the new millennium. See Harris 2000, in Perera 2000.
41 Private conversations between Elizabeth Harris and Ron Maddox in 1995 and February 2023.
42 Private conversation between Elizabeth Harris and Ven. Handupelpola Mahinda at the Sri Saddhatissa International Buddhist Centre in March 2023.
43 The Buddhist Society of Great Britain and Ireland was founded in 1907, as we have shown. Oliver states, 'On 23 April 1907, the Mission from Burma arrived with Ananda Metteyya announcing himself as the Secretary-General of the International Buddhist Society of Rangoon' (Oliver 1979: 49–50). A few pages prior, Oliver writes, 'In April of 1908, at the age of thirty-six, Ananda Metteyya set foot in England, welcomed by members of the Buddhist Society of Great Britain and Ireland' (Oliver 1979: 44).
44 See Chapter Four, endnote 81.
45 The term 'Theosophical' in the title is not a reference to the Theosophical Society but refers 'to the tradition of religious illumination' (Godwin 1994: xii). The term 'Enlightenment' has two meanings for Godwin. The first comes from the French Enlightenment, referring to those who 'sought a universal view of history, mythology, and world religions without being bounded by biblical fundamentalism or Christaian supremacy' (Godwin 1994: xi). The second is the 'nineteenth century's search for new modes of spiritual enlightenment' (Godwin 1994: 24).
46 Tobias Churton comes to a similar conclusion about Sutin's claim in one of his biographies of Crowley. See Churton 2019: 401–402.
47 Gerald Yorke Collection, Warburg Institute, University College London, OS EE1 324a.
48 See Chapter Four, pp. 164–165.
49 See, for instance: 'Indeed, it is difficult to avoid a suspicion that some of the compilers of the *Pitakas* would be mightily astonished, could they see the towering structures which he, with a chemistry and physics whereof they never dreamed, with a literary power which they rarely wielded, and a poetic imagination to which they seldom if ever rose, has built up around their phrases' (Bennett 1929: viii).
50 This version changes the capitalisation, inserting sub-headings and amending terminology. For instance, Ananda M's 'wisdom' in one line (Ananda M 1910: 107) is changed to 'Insight' in Besant's publication (Bhikkhu Ananda M 1911a: 18). More clearly driven by a Theosophist agenda are those we have put in the main body of the text.

Concluding Thoughts

1 In addition to his general writing having a poetic character, he occasionally wrote poems, one of which, 'The Word of the Buddha,' is printed in Volume 2.

Bibliography

Abano, Peter de, 1655. 'Heptameron or Magical Elements of Peter de Abano, Philosopher.' Robert Turner (trans). In Henry Cornelius Agrippa, *Henry Cornelius Agrippa, His Fourth Book of Occult Philosophy. Of Geomancy. Magical Elements of Peter de Abano. Astronomical Geomancy. The Nature of Spirits. Arbatel of Magick*. London: John Harrison: 73–107. https://www.loc.gov/item/11031418/.

Adam, James, 1913. *Asthma and its Radical Treatment*. London: Henry Kimpton.

Administration Report, 1902. *Administration Reports—Ceylon–1902. Judicial—Police B1-Part III*. Colombo: George J. A. Skeen (Government Printer).

Agarwal, C. V., 2001. *The Buddhist and Theosophical Movements 1873-2001*. 2nd Revised Ed. Varanasi: Maha-Bodhi Society of India.

Albanese, Catherine L., 2007. *A Republic of Mind: A Cultural History of American Metaphysical Religion*. New Haven, CT: Yale University Press.

Almond, Philip C., 1988. *The British Discovery of Buddhism*. Cambridge: Cambridge University Press.

Amunugama, Sarath, 2016. *The Lion's Roar: Anagarika Dharmapala & the Making of Modern Buddhism*. Colombo: Vijitha Yapa.

Anālayo, Bhikkhu, 2021. *Superiority Conceit in Buddhist Traditions: A Historical Perspective*. Somerville, MA: Wisdom.

Ananda M, 1908. 'A Letter from Bhikkhu Ananda Metteyya Written to a Friend in Colombo, Dated 28 November 1908.' *The Maha-Bodhi and the United Buddhist World* XVI.11–12, November–December: 180–182.

Ananda M, Bhikkhu, 1910. 'The Religion of Burma.' In Arnold Wright (ed), *Twentieth Century Impressions of Burma: Its History, People, Commerce, Industries and Resources*. London, Durban, Perth, Colombo, etc.: Lloyds Greater Britain Publishing Company: 102–116.

Ananda M, 1911a. 'The Religion of Burma.' *The Message of Theosophy* VII.1, April: 9–16; VII.2, May: 26–37; VII.3, June: 49–55; VII.5, September: 123–129; VII.7, October: 157–160.

Ananda M, Bhikkhu, 1911b. *An Outline of Buddhism or Religion of Burma. Reprinted with Introductory Notes from "The Theosophist" April and May 1911, C.E.* Rangoon: International Buddhist Society.

Ananda M, 1911c. 'The Compendium of Philosophy.' *Journal of the Burma Research Society* 1.1: 131–136.

Ananda M, 1918. 'Realisation.' *The Buddhist Review* X.2, July–September: 141–148.

Ananda M, 1920a. 'To Our Readers.' *The Buddhist Review* X.4, July: 181–187. (Original issue has a typo on its cover wrongly identifying it as Vol XI.)

Ananda M, 1920b. 'Notes and News.' *The Buddhist Review* X.4, July: 222–224. (Original issue has a typo on its cover wrongly identifying it as Vol XI.)

Ananda M, 1921a. 'Buddhism: The Religion of Compassion.' In S. W. Wijayatileke (ed), *The Buddhist Annual of Ceylon* 1.2. Colombo: E. W. Bastian & Co.: 31–33.
Ananda M, 1921b. 'Buddhism and the Western World.' *The Buddhist Review* XI: 49–60.
Ananda M, 1921c. 'The Miraculous Element in Buddhism.' *The Buddhist Review* XI: 127–136.
Ananda M, 1921d. 'The Doctrine of the Aryas.' *The Buddhist Review* XI: 149–163.
Ananda M, 1922. 'A Scientific Analogy.' *The Buddhist Review* XII.1: 11–20.
Ananda Maitriya (Allan MacGregor), 1902a. 'Animism and Law.' *The Buddhist* XII.2, May: 29–41.
Ananda Maitriya, 1902b. 'On the Culture of Mind.' *The Buddhist* XII.3, June: 53–68.
Ananda Maitriya, 1902c. *On the Culture of Mind*. Colombo: Ceylon Examiner Press.
Ananda Maitriya, 1902d. 'The Ordination Address of Bhikshu Ananda Maitriya.' *The Buddhist* XIII.4, July–August: 77–86.
Ananda Maitriya, 1902e. 'The Address.' In Anon 1902b: 5–18.
Ananda Maitriya, 1902f. 'Beyond the Graves.' *The Buddhist* XII.5, September–October: 115–117.
Ananda Maitriya, 1903a. 'The Faith of the Future.' *Buddhism* I.I: 6–38.
Ananda Maitriya, 1903b. 'In the Shadow of Shwe Dagon.' Prologue. *Buddhism* I.I: 101–112.
Ananda Maitriya, 1903c. 'Nibbāna.' *Buddhism* I.I: 113–134.
Ananda Maitriya, Bhikkhu, 1903d. 'Nibbana.' *The Maha-Bodhi and the United Buddhist World* XII.1–2, November–December: 8–16.
Ananda Maitriya, 1903e. 'The Awakening.' *Buddhism* I.I: 140–144.
Ananda Maitriya, 1903f. 'News and Notes.' *Buddhism* 1.1: 145–162.
Ananda Maitriya, 1903g 'Ourselves.' *Buddhism* 1.1: 163–167.
Ananda Maitriya, 1903h. 'Buddhist Activities.' *Buddhism* I.I: 169–174.
Ananda Maitriya (ed), 1903i. 'The Thathanabaing.' *Buddhism* 1.2: 177–208.
Ananda Maitriya, 1903j. 'Ourselves.' *Buddhism* 1.2: 313–319.
Ananda Maitriya, 1903k. 'As Others See Us.' *Buddhism* 1.2: 320–332.
Ananda Maitriya, 1903l. 'News and Notes.' *Buddhism* 1.2: 339–350.
Ananda Maitriya, 1903m. *On Religious Education in Burma*. Publications of the Buddhasāsana Samāgama 2. Rangoon: Hanthawaddy Press.
Ananda Maitriya, 1903n. 'Western Education for Buddhist Bhikshus: Address of the Bhikkhu Ananda Maitriya Delivered at the Opening of the Maitriya Temple at Colombo, on the 25th April, 1903.' *The Buddhist* XII.8, May–June: 181–187; XII.9, August–September: 199–203.
Anandamaitreya, Balangoda, 1993. *Buddhism: Speeches and Essays on Buddhism*. First Series. Colombo: Samayawardhana.
Ananda Maithriya, Bhikkhu (a.k.a. Bhikkhu Ananda Metteyya), 2021. 'The Faith of the Future: Excerpted & Edited from 'Buddhism: Illustrated Quarterly Review' 1903 Vol 1. (No.1).' In Ñānasīha and Senanayake (eds) 2021: 36–40.
Ananda Metteya, 1909. 'The Extension of the Empire of Righteousness in Westernlands.' *The Theosophist* 30.9: 302–309.
Ananda Metteya, 1911. 'The Training of the Mind.' *The Equinox* 1.5: 28–59.
Ananda Metteyya, 1904a. 'The Law of Righteousness.' *Buddhism* I.3: 353–376.

Ananda Metteyya, 1904b. 'Ourselves.' *Buddhism* 1.3: 473–479.
Ananda Metteyya, 1904c. 'News and Notes.' *Buddhism* 1.3: 497–520.
Ananda Metteyya, 1904d. 'The New Civilisation.' *Buddhism* 1.4: 529–560.
Ananda Metteyya, 1904e. 'In the Shadow of Shwe Dagon.' 4th Installment. *Buddhism* 1.4: 631–645.
Ananda Metteyya, 1904f. 'News and Notes.' *Buddhism* 1.4: 649–656.
Ananda Metteyya, 1904g. 'Ourselves.' *Buddhism* 1.4: 673–680.
Ananda Metteyya, 1905a 'News and Notes.' *Buddhism* 2.1, October: 119–125.
Ananda Metteyya, 1905b. 'Director's Address.' In Anon 1905: 7–18.
Ananda Metteyya, 1906. *A Lecture on Anatta*. Rangoon: The Rangoon College Buddhist Association.
Ananda Metteyya, 1908a. 'Propaganda.' *Buddhism* 2.2: 169–192.
Ananda Metteyya, 1908b. 'A Burmese Pali Scholar.' *Buddhism* 2.2: 329–332.
Ananda Metteyya, 1908c. 'Obituary.' *Buddhism* 2.2: 333–338.
Ananda Metteyya, 1908d. 'Buddhist Activities.' *Buddhism* 2.2: 338–342.
Ananda Metteyya, 1908e. 'News and Notes.' *Buddhism* 2.2: 343–348.
Ananda Metteyya, 1908f. *An Outline of Buddhism: Delivered at the Rooms of the Royal Asiatic Society, May 6th, 1908*. London: The Buddhist Society of Great Britain and Ireland.
Ananda Metteyya, 1908g. 'Buddhist Gratitude to Henry Steel Olcott.' *The Theosophical Review* XLII.250, June: 363–367.
Ananda Metteyya, 1908h. 'Entre Nous: Letter to the Editor by Ananda Metteyya Dated 8 July, 1908.' *Truth*, 15 July 1908: 130.
Ananda Metteyya, 1909a. 'Followers of the Buddha.' *The Buddhist Review* 1.1: 7–12.
Ananda Metteyya, 1909b. *Extension of the Empire of Righteousness to Western Lands: Address of Bhikkhu Ananda Metteyya, Director of the Buddhasasana Samagama at the Sixth Annual Convention of the International Buddhist Society, December 27, 1908*. Mandalay: Chanea Press.
Ananda Metteyya, 1909c. *The Mahā-Maṅgala and Vasala Suttas. With Bhikkhu Ananda Metteyya's Discourse on the Four Noble Truths*. Printed for Free Distribution by J. D. Fernando. Colombo: Lankabhinawa Vissruta Press.
Ananda Metteyya, the Rev. Bhikkhu, 1910a. *Devotion in Buddhism*. Rangoon: Burma Buddhist Mission Press.
Ananda Metteyya, 1910b. 'On Devotion in Buddhism.' *The Buddhist Review* II.1: 11–30.
Ananda Metteyya, 1910c. 'On Devotion in Buddhism.' *The Maha-Bodhi and the United Buddhist World* XVIII.6, June: 531–539.
Ananda Metteyya, 1913a. 'Right Understanding.' *The Buddhist Review* V.2: 85–108.
Ananda Metteyya, Rev. Bhikkhu, 1913b. 'Right Understanding.' *The Maha-Bodhi and the United Buddhist World* XXI.6, June: 102–126.
Ananda Metteyya, 1914. 'Buddhist Self-Culture.' *The Buddhist Review* 6.2, April–June: 133–146.
Ananda Metteyya, 1927. 'Buddhist Psychology.' *The British Buddhist* 2.3, December: 1–3.
Ananda Metteyya, 1929. 'The Order in the West: From a Letter to a Friend in England, December 8, 1910 by the Late Ananda Metteyya.' *The Buddhist Annual of Ceylon 1929*: 171–178.

Ananda Metteyya, 1930. 'An Open Letter to the Buddhists of London by the Late Bhikkhu Ananda Metteyya, Rangoon, 28 December 1908.' *The Buddhist Annual of Ceylon 1930*: 269–270.

Ananda Metteyya, 1931. 'Extracts from Letters to a Friend in England by Ananda Metteyya.' *The Buddhist Annual of Ceylon 1931*: 59–65.

Ananda Metteyya, 1954. 'Buddhist Self-Culture.' *The Middle Way* 29.3, November: 125–130 (Part One); *The Middle Way* 29.4, February 1955: 187–191 (Part Two). Reprint of Ananda Metteyya 1914.

Angell, Marisa, 1998. 'Understanding the Aryan Theory.' In Mithran Tiruchelvam and C. S. Dattathreya (eds). *Culture and Politics of Identity in Sri Lanka*. Colombo: International Centre for Ethnic Studies: 41–71.

Anon, 1902a. 'The Upasampada Ordination of Bhikshu Ananda Maitriya.' *The Buddhist* XIII.4, July–August: 91–93.

Anon, 1902b. *The Foundation of the Sangha of the West: Being an Account of the Upasampada Ordination of the Bhikkhu Ananda Maitriya (Allan Bennett Macgregor) At Akyab, Burma on the Full-moon day of Vesakha 2446 (May 21st 1902)*. Rangoon: Hanthawaddy Press.

Anon, 1904. 'Education in Burma.' *Buddhism* I.3, March: 393–410.

Anon, 1905. *Account of the Third Annual Convention of the International Buddhist Society, Held on 29th October, 1905*. Publications of the Buddhasāsana Samāgama 7. Rangoon: Hanthawaddy Press.

Anon, 1908. *Transactions of the Third International Congress for the History of Religions, Vol. 2*. Oxford: Clarendon Press.

Anon, 1912. 'Review of *The Three Signata* by the Ven. Bhikkhu Ananda Metteyya. Rangoon, Rangoon College Buddhists Association, 1911.' *The Open Court* (Chicago) XXVI: 382.

Anon, 1929a. *Select Speeches of Ponnambalam Ramanathan Delivered in the Legislative Council of Ceylon, Vol. I 1879–1894*. Colombo: Daily News Press.

Anon, 1929b. 'History of the Buddhist Movement in Great Britain.' *Buddhism in England* 4.2, June: 41–43; 4.3, July: 62–68.

Aquinas, St. Thomas, 1956. *Summa Contra Gentiles, Book Three. Providence, Part II*. Reprint. London: Notre Dame Press.

Arnold, Edwin, 1903. 'The Golden Temple.' *Buddhism* 1.1: 1–5.

Baker, Phil, 2017. 'Allan Bennett AKA Ananda Metteyya.' *The Middle Way* 19.1, May: 11–34.

Baker, Phil, 2022. *City of the Beast: The London of Aleister Crowley*. London: Strange Attractor Press.

Baptist Missionary Magazine, 1904. 'A Recent Buddhist Convention.' *Baptist Missionary Magazine* 84.12, December: 779–780.

Barker, Felix, 1995. *Edwardian London*. London: Lawrence King.

Batchelor, Stephen, 1995 [1994]. *The Awakening of the West: The Encounter of Buddhism and Western Culture 543 BCE–1992*. London and San Francisco: Thorsons.

Baumann, Martin, 2002. 'Buddhism in Europe: Past, Present, Prospects.' In Charles S. Prebish and Martin Baumann (eds). *Westward Dharma: Buddhism Beyond Asia*. Berkeley and Los Angeles: University of California Press: 85–105.

Bax, Clifford, 1933 [1925]. *Inland Far: A Book of Thoughts and Impressions*. London: Lovat Dickson.

Bax, Clifford (ed), 1946. *Florence Farr, Bernard Shaw, W. B. Yeats: Letters*. London: Home & Van Thal.
Bax, Clifford, 1947. *The Buddha: A Radio Version of his Life and Ideas*. London: Victor Gollancz.
Bax, Clifford, 1951. *Some I Knew Well*. London: Phoenix House Ltd.
Bax, Clifford, 1968. 'Ananda Metteyya.' *The Middle Way* 43.1: 23–27.
Bell, Sandra, 1994. 'British Buddhism and the Negotiation of Tradition.' Paper Given at a Symposium on 'The Invention and Reinvention of Tradition,' St Mary's College, 22–24 September 1994. Text made available by the author.
Belper News, 1908. 'A Scottish Buddhist.' *Belper News*, 1 May: 7.
Bennett, Allan, 1923. *The Wisdom of the Aryas*. London: Kegan Paul, Trench, Trubner and Co. Ltd.
Bennett, Allan, 1929. *The Religion of Burma and Other Papers*. Adyar: Theosophical Publishing House.
Bennett, Allan, 1976. 'Ritual for a Talisman of Visions (From a Notebook in the Hand of Allan Bennett. Date about 1899)—From the Gerald York Collection.' David Edwards (intro). *The Monolith* 1.10, Winter Solstice: 11–20.
Bennett, Allan, 1977. 'Of Flashing Sounds (From a G.D. Notebook of Frater Iehi Aour—Allan Bennett)—From the Gerald York Collection.' David Edwards (intro). *The Monolith* 2.1, Summer Solstice: 5–11.
Bennett, Allan and Aleister Crowley, 1912. 'Sepher Sephiroth.' *The Equinox* 1.8 [Supplement]: i-xvi, 1–101.
Besant, Annie (ed), 1909. 'Reviews.' *The Theosophist* 30.10: 524.
Besant, Annie, 1911. 'On the Watch-Tower.' *The Theosophist* 32.5: 867–874.
Bestall, Arthur H., 1905. 'From the Bank to Mandalay: A Chat with Rev Arthur H. Bestall.' *The Foreign Field* I 1904–1905: 43–46.
Biddulph, Desmond, 2014. 'Planting the Seeds of Buddhism in Britain: Anagarika Dharmapala 1864–1933.' *The Middle Way* 89.2: 75–82.
Bidwell, David D., 1911. *As Far as the East is from The West: Tales of a Traveler who Toured the World Toward the Rising Sun*. 3rd Ed. Hartford: The S. S. Scranton Company.
Bird, G. W., 1897. *Wanderings in Burma with Illustrations and Maps*. Bournemouth: F. J. Bright and Son; London: Simpkin, Marshall, Hamilton, Kent & Co.
Birkenhead News, 1908, 'Buddhism.' *Birkenhead News*, 26 September: 1.
Birmingham Daily Gazette, 1908. 'Buddhist Missionaries for London.' *Birmingham Daily Gazette*, 20 April: 3.
Blackburn, Anne, 2010. *Locations of Buddhism: Colonialism and Modernity in Sri Lanka*. Chicago, IL and London: Chicago University Press.
Blavatsky, Helena Petrovna, 1966 [1874]. 'Marvellous Spirit Manifestations.' In *H. P. Blavatsky Collected Writings, 1874–1878, Vol. 1*. Wheaton, IL: Theosophical Publishing House: 30–36.
Blavatsky, Helena Petrovna, 1993a [1888], Boris de Zirkoff (ed). *The Secret Doctrine: Cosmogenesis, Vol. 1*. The Complete Works of H. P. Blavatsky. Facsimile ed. Wheaton, IL: Quest Books.
Blavatsky, Helena Petrovna, 1993b [1888], Boris de Zirkoff (ed). *The Secret Doctrine: Anthropogenesis, Vol. 2*. The Complete Works of H. P. Blavatsky. Facsimile ed. Wheaton, IL: Quest Books.

Blavatsky, Helena Petrovna, 1994 [1877], Boris de Zirkoff (ed). *Isis Unveiled: A Master-Key of The Mysteries of Ancient and Modern Science and Theology: Science.* The Complete Works of H. P. Blavatsky. 2 Vols. Facsimile ed. Wheaton, IL: Quest Books.

Bluck, Robert, 2012. 'Buddhism in the United Kingdom.' In Oliver Abenayake and Asanga Tilakaratne (eds), *2600 Years of Sambuddhatva: Global Journey of Awakening.* Colombo: Ministry of Buddhasasana and Religious Affairs, Government of Sri Lanka: 395–407.

Bodhi, Bhikkhu, 2011. 'What does Mindfulness Really Mean? A Canonical Perspective.' *Contemporary Buddhism* 12.1: 19–39.

Bogdan, Henrik, and Martin P. Starr (eds), 2012. *Aleister Crowley and Western Esotericism.* Oxford: Oxford University Press.

Bond, George, 1988. *The Buddhist Revival in Sri Lanka: Religious Tradition, Reinterpretation and Response.* Columbia, SC: University of South Carolina Press.

Booth, Charles James (ed), 1889. *Labour and Life of the People of London.* London: Williams and Norgate.

Booth, Martin, 2000. *A Magick Life: A Biography of Aleister Crowley.* London: Hodder and Stoughton.

Boyle, Richard, 1996. 'The Yogic Quest: Encountering Aleister Crowley.' *The Sunday Times Plus*, 27 October: 1; 3 November: 3, 6; 10 November: 2.

Braun, Erik, 2013. *The Birth of Insight: Meditation, Modern Buddhism and the Burmese Monk Ledi Sayadaw.* Chicago and London: University of Chicago Press.

Braybrooke, Marcus, 1992. *Pilgrimage of Hope: One Hundred Years of Global Interfaith Dialogue.* London: SCM.

Brown, Mick, 2023. *The Nirvana Express: How the Search for Enlightenment went West.* London: Hurst.

Bruce Herald, 1913. 'Search for a "Bhikkhu."' *Bruce Herald* XLIX.29, 10 April: 3.

Brunton, Paul, 1941. 'A Pioneer Western Buddhist.' *Ceylon Daily News Vesak Number* May. Reprinted by the Paul Brunton Philosophic Foundation as 'Bhikkhu Ananda Metteyya: A Pioneer Western Buddhist by Paul Brunton' https://web.archive.org/web/20230204154845/https://www.paulbrunton.org/bhikku-ananda-metteya.php. Retrieved January 2023.

Buddhasāsana Samāgama or International Buddhist Society, 1903a. 'Supplement to *Buddhism*: Includes Constitution and Rules of the Buddhasāsana Samāgama.' *Buddhism* 1.1: ii-xii.

Buddhasāsana Samāgama or International Buddhist Society, 1903b. *The Revised Prospectus of the Buddhasāsana Samāgama or the International Buddhist Society.* Rangoon: Hanthawaddy Press.

Buddhism, 1903. 'Books Received.' *Buddhism* 1.2: 337–338.

Buddhism, 1904. 'Books Received.' *Buddhism* 1.4: 696.

Buddhism in England, 1926a. 'Editorial.' *Buddhism in England* 1.1, May: 1–5.

Buddhism in England 1926b. 'Editorial.' *Buddhism in England* 1.6, December: 121–123.

Buddhism in England, 1928. 'Decision to send Three Priests: London Temple Project.' *Buddhism in England* 2.7, April: 1–4.

Buddhism in England, 1929. 'Obituary.' *Buddhism in England* 4.1, May: 20.

Buddhism in England, 1930. 'Correspondence.' *Buddhism in England* 4.7: 168–169.

Buddhist Studies Review, 1997. 'U Thittila 10 July 1986–3 January 1997.' Obituary. *Buddhist Studies Review* 14.1: 57–60.

Buultjens, A. E., 1893. 'The Quarter-Mile Clause: An Appeal to Buddhists.' *The Buddhist* V.24, 30 June: 188.

Burma Echo, 1907. 'Buddhism.' *Burma Echo*, 27 July: 9.

Cadwell, David H. and Henk J. Spierenburg, 1995. 'A Historical Introduction.' In Henk J. Spierenburg (ed), *The Inner Group Teaching of H. P. Blavatsky*. 2nd Revised Ed. San Diego: Point Loma Publications: vii-xxviii.

Caine, W. S., 1898. *Picturesque India: A Handbook for European Travellers*. London and New York: George Routledge and Sons.

Carrithers, M., 1983. *The Forest Monks of Sri Lanka: An Anthropological and Historical Study*. Calcutta: Oxford University Press.

Carus, Paul, 1904. 'The Philosophy of Buddhism.' *Buddhism* 1.4: 561–574.

Cave, Henry, 1894. *Picturesque Ceylon: Kandy and Peradeniya*. London: Sampson Low, Marston & Co., Ltd.

Cave, Henry, 1908. *The Book of Ceylon*. London, Paris, New York, Toronto and Melbourne: Cassell.

Century Path, 1908. 'The Real Buddhism.' *Century Path: A Magazine Devoted to the Brotherhood of Humanity, the Promulgation of Theosophy and the Study of Ancient and Modern Ethics, Philosophy, Science and Art* XI.32, 14 June: 3.

Chalmers, Robert (trans), 1895. *The Jataka: Stories of the Buddha's Former Births, Vol. 1*. Cambridge: Cambridge University Press.

Chattopadhyaya, J. C., 1908. 'The Persistence of the Individual According to the Pali Pitakas—Did the Buddha Deny It?' *The Message of Theosophy* IV.7, October: 161–163; IV.8, November: 182–189.

Chelsea News and General Advertiser, 1915. Advertisement. *Chelsea News and General Advertiser*, 21 May: (unpaginated).

Chelsea News and General Advertiser, 1917. Advertisement. *Chelsea News and General Advertiser*, 4 May: 2.

Childers, Robert, 1909 (1875). *Dictionary of the Pali Language*. 4th Impression. London: Kegan Paul, Trench, Trubner and Co.

Churton, Tobias, 2019. *Aleister Crowley in India: The Secret Influence of Eastern Mysticism on Magic and the Occult*. Rochester, VT: Inner Traditions.

Civil and Military Gazette Lahore, 1908. 'Buddhism: Its Mission in the West.' *Civil and Military Gazette Lahore*, 2 June: 9.

Clout, Hugh (ed), 2000 [1991]. *The Times History of London*. London: Times Books.

Cochrane, Henry Park, 1904. *Among the Burmans: A Record of Fifteen Years of Work and its Fruitage*. New York, Chicago, Toronto, London and Edinburgh: Fleming H. Revell Co.

Colonia, 1890a. 'Speech Day, July 16th, 1890.' *Colonia: The Colonial College Magazine* 1.3: 163–165.

Colonia, 1890b. 'The Following Freshmen Entered this Term.' *Colonia: The Colonial College Magazine* 1.4, Winter Session: 266.

Colonia, 1892. 'News of Alumni.' *Colonia: The Colonial College Magazine* 2.2, Summer Session: 134.

Colquhoun, Ithell, 1975. *Sword of Wisdom: MacGregor Mathers and 'The Golden Dawn.'* London: Neville Spearman.

Colston, E. J., 1904. *A Monograph on Tanning and Working in Leather in the Province of Burma.* Rangoon: Office of the Superintendent (Government Printer).

Cooke, Alistair, 1995. 'Introduction.' In Barker 1995: 9–13.

Copleston, R. S., *Buddhism Primitive and Present in Magadha and Ceylon.* London: Longman, Green and Co.

Cornelius, Erica M., 2019. 'On Getting Nothing from Something: The Importance of ThIShARB.' In *Essays: Volume Eight.* Berkeley, CA: Privately Published: 149–154.

Cornelius, J. Edward, 2018. 'On Thinking Backwards, Magical Memory and Cause and Effect.' In *Essays: Volume Seven.* Berkeley, CA: Privately Published: 68–78.

Cornish and Devon Post, 1908. 'Church Notes.' *Cornish and Devon Post*, 29 August: 3.

Coryn, Herbert A. W., 1895a. 'Brixton Lodge.' *The Vâhan* 4.6, January: 15.

Coryn, Herbert A. W., 1895b. 'Brixton Lodge.' *The Vâhan* 4.8, March: 8.

Cousins, L. S., 2022, Sarah Shaw (ed). *Meditations of the Pali Tradition: Illuminating Buddhist Doctrine, History and Practice.* Boulder, CO: Shambhala.

Crosby, Kate, 2013. *Traditional Theravada Meditation and its Modern-Era Suppression.* Hong Kong: Buddha Dharma Centre of Hong Kong.

Crosby, Kate, 2020. *Esoteric Theravada: The Story of the Forgotten Meditation Tradition of Southeast Asia.* Boulder, CO: Shambala.

Crow, John L., 2008a. 'The Unity of All Life: Ananda Metteyya's View of Nature.' *The Middle Way: The Journal of the Buddhist Society* 83.3, November: 131–137; 83.4, February 2009: 195–202.

Crow, John L., 2008b. 'Venerable Ananda Metteyya's Buddhist Mission to the UK.' In Deegalle 2008: 14–36.

Crow, John L., 2009. 'The White Knight in the Yellow Robe: Allan Bennett's Search for Truth.' MA Thesis, University of Amsterdam, Amsterdam.

Crow, John L., 2017. 'Occult Bodies: The Corporal Construction of the Theosophical Society, 1875–1935.' PhD Dissertation, Florida State University, Tallahassee. http://purl.flvc.org/fsu/fd/FSU_2017SP_Crow_fsu_0071E_13796.

Crow, John L., 2012. 'Taming the Astral Body: The Theosophical Society's Ongoing Problem of Emotion and Control.' *Journal of the American Academy of Religion* 80.3, September: 691–717. https://doi.org/10.1093/jaarel/lfs042.

Crow, John L., 2013. 'Accessing the Astral with a Monitor and Mouse: Esoteric Religion and the Astral in Three Dimensional Virtual Realms.' In K. Granholm and Egil Asprem (eds), *Contemporary Esotericism.* London: Acumen Publishing: 159–180.

Crow, John L., 2010. 'Spreading the Light of Asia to Europe: Ananda Metteyya's Buddhist Message to the West.' *Budumaga: The Buddha's Way* 20.1: 6–9.

Crowley, Aleister, 1904. 'The Sword of the Song Called by Christians the Book of the Beast.' In *The Works of Aleister Crowley, Vol. 2.* 1906. Foyers: Society for the Propagation of Religious Truth: 140–211.

Crowley, Aleister [Perdurabo], 1908. 'The Man in the Yellow Robe. An Intimate Study.' *What's On*, 13 June 1908: 17.

Crowley, Aleister, 1910. 'The Temple of Solomon the King [Book II Continued].' *The Equinox* 1.3: 133–280.
Crowley, Aleister, 1912. 'Liber תישארב Viæ Memoriæ Sub Figurâ CMXIII.' *The Equinox* 1.7: 105–116.
Crowley, Aleister, 1929. *The Spirit of Solitude: An Autohagiography, Subsequently Re-Antichristened, The Confessions of Aleister Crowley, Vol. 1.* London: Mandrake Press.
Crowley, Aleister, 1935. 'In Search of the Absolute.' *The Sunday Referee*, 5 March: 9.
Crowley, Aleister, 1954. *Magick Without Tears.* Hampton, NJ: Thelema Publishing Company.
Crowley, Aleister, 1989, John Symonds and Kenneth Grant (eds). *The Confessions of Aleister Crowley: An Autohagiography.* Harmondsworth: Penguin (Arkana).
Crowley, Aleister, 1991 [1939]. *Eight Lectures on Yoga.* 2nd Revised Ed. Phoenix: New Falcon Publications.
Crowley, Aleister, 1996, Israel Regardie (ed). *777 and Other Qabalistic Writings of Aleister Crowley: Including Gematria & Sepher Sephiroth.* York Beach, ME: Samuel Weiser.
Crowley, Aleister, 1997, Hymenaeus Beta (ed). *Magick, Liber ABA, Book Four, Parts I-IV.* 2nd Revised Ed. York Beach, ME: Samuel Weiser.
Crowley, Aleister, 1998 [1918]. 'The Revival of Magick.' In *The Revival of Magick and Other Essays, Oriflamme 2.* Temple, AZ: New Falcon Publications: 21–26.
Daily Express, 1908. 'Wee Macgregor with the Bowl. Life on the Lines of Least Resistance: Very Humble.' *Daily Express London*, 24 April: 5.
Daily Mail, 1908a. 'The Scottish Buddhist: Penniless Buddhist Monk: His Reception in England Today.' *Daily Mail*, 22 April: 3.
Daily Mail 1908b. 'The Scottish Buddhist: Arrival in London: Objects of his Visit.' *Daily Mail*, 23 April: 5.
Daily Mail, 1908c. 'Temple in Bedroom: Buddhist Monk First Day in England.' *Daily Mail*, 24 April: 6.
Daily Mirror, 1908. 'Scotsman as Buddhist Priest.' *Daily Mirror*, 23 April: 13.
Daily Record (Lanarkshire), 1908. 'Buddhist Monk A MacGregor: Mission to Spread Ideas. British Converts.' *Daily Record (Lanarkshire)*, 29 September: 3.
Daily Telegraph, 1908. 'Ananda Metteyya: Buddhism in England.' *Daily Telegraph*, 29 September: 12.
Dassow, Eva Von (ed), 1994. *The Egyptian Book of the Dead: The Book of Going Forth by Day.* San Francisco, CA: Chronicle Books.
De Grey-Downing, John, 1904. 'The Lama Prayer Wheel.' *Buddhism* 1.4: 613–620.
De Lorenzo, Guiseppe, 1903. 'Buddhist Ideas in Shakespeare.' *Buddhism* 1.1: 54–56.
Deegalle, Mahinda, 2005. 'Theravada Buddhist Missions in London: The Legacy of Sri Saddhatissa International Buddhist Centre.' In Galayaye Piyadassi, Lakshman Perera and Ratna Wijetunge (eds), *Buddhism in the West.* London: World Buddhist Foundation: 171–195.
Deegalle, Mahinda (ed), 2008. *Dharma to the UK: A Centennial Celebration of Buddhist Legacy.* London: World Buddhist Foundation.
Dhammaloka, 1908. 'Entre Nous.' *Truth*, 8 July: 65.
Dhammasami, Khammai, 2018. *Buddhism, Education and Politics in Burma and Thailand: From the Seventeenth Century to the Present.* London, Oxford and New York: Bloomsbury.

Dharmapala, Anagarika, 1907. 'Mrs Besant's Bastard Theosophy and Buddhism.' *The Maha-Bodhi and the United Buddhist World* XV.12, December: 184–186.

Dharmapala, Anagarika, 1909a. 'Buddhism in England.' *The Maha-Bodhi and the United Buddhist World* XVII.1, January: 8–11.

Dharmapala, Anagarika, 1909b, 'The Gift of the Truth to the West.' *The Maha-Bodhi and the United Buddhist World* XVII.4–5, April–May: 103–104.

Dhirasekera, Jotiya, 1982. *Buddhist Monastic Discipline: A Study of its origins and development in relation to the Sutta and Vinaya Pitaka*. Colombo: Ministry of Education.

Dirilakuru, Thangalle, 1978. *Siri Damreki Sangha Parapura* (Sinhalese). Colombo: Sri Dharmarakshita Sangha Sabhava.

Dublin Daily Express, 1908. 'Buddhist Mission to Great Britain.' *Dublin Daily Express*, 21 April: 2.

Duncan, James S., 1990. *The City as Text: The Politics of Landscape Interpretation in the Kandyan Kingdom*. Cambridge: Cambridge University Press.

Dyer, Bernard Shirley, 1894. 'XV.—On the Analytical Determination of Probably Available "Mineral" Plant Food in Soils.' *Journal of The Chemical Society, Transactions* 65: 115–167. https://doi.org/10.1039/CT8946500115.

Ehara, N. R. M., Soma Thera and Kheminda Thera (trans), 1995 [1961]. *The Path of Freedom* (Vimuttimagga) *by the Arahant Upatissa*. Kandy: Buddhist Publication Society.

Ellam, J. E., 1909. 'Editorial.' *The Buddhist Review* 1.1, January: 1–5.

Evans, Eric, 1927. 'Clifford Bax.' *The Bookman*, May: 121–124.

Faivre, Antoine, 1994. *Access to Western Esotericism*. Albany, NY: State University of New York Press.

Fielding Hall, Harold, 1898. *The Soul of a People*. London: MacMillan & Co.

Fielding Hall, Harold, 1913 [1906]. *A People at School*. London: MacMillan & Co.

Fletcher, Matthew, 2022. 'Inventing a Modern Ritual Magic Text: Assembling and Dis(a)ssembling Liber Israfel.' *Magic, Ritual, and Witchcraft* 17.2, Fall: 297–333.

Franklin, J. Jeffrey, 2008. *The Lotus and the Lion: Buddhism and the British Empire*. Ithaca and London: Cornell University Press.

Frater D.D.C.F. [S.L. MacGregor Mathers], 1987. 'Flying Roll No XI: Clairvoyance.' In Francis King (ed), *Astral Projection, Ritual Magic, and Alchemy: Golden Dawn Material by S.L. MacGregor Mathers and Others*. Rochester, VT: Destiny Books: 75–83.

Frater I.A. [Allan Bennett], 1909. 'A Note on Genesis.' *The Equinox* 1.2: 165–185.

Frater V.I.O. [Charles Stansfeld Jones], 1919. 'Liber CLXV: A Master of the Temple, Being an Account of the Attainment of Frater Unus in Omnibus, Abridged from his Magical Record.' *The Equinox* 3.1: 127–170.

Frederickson, Miss, 1914. 'Address to the Judson Centennial Celebrations.' In Phinney 1914: 58–63.

Furnivall, John S., 1948. *Colonial Policy and Practice: A Comparative Study of Burma and Netherlands India*. Cambridge: Cambridge University Press.

Fyffe, Rollestone Sterrit, 1908. 'Christianity and Buddhism.' *The Rangoon Diocesan Magazine* XII.6, June: 232–237; XII.7, July: 268–276; XII.9, September: 331–338; XII.12, December: 452–460.

G. M. H., 1923. 'Review of *The Wisdom of the Aryas*.' *The Occult Review*, October: 256.

Gethin, Rupert, 2000. 'Buddhism in Britain: A Brief Sketch of its History and Development.' In Lakshman S. Perera (ed), *Buddhism for The New Millennium*. London: World Buddhist Foundation: 26–41.

Gilbert, R. A., 1983. *The Golden Dawn: Twilight of the Magicians, The Rise and Fall of a Magical Order*. Wellingborough: Aquarian Press.

Gilbert, R. A., 1986a. *The Golden Dawn and the Esoteric Section*. London: Theosophical History Centre.

Gilbert, R. A. (ed), 1986b. *The Golden Dawn Companion: A Guide to the History, Structure, and Workings of the Hermetic Order of the Golden Dawn*. Wellingborough: Aquarian Press.

Gisborne Times, 1913. 'Search for a "Bhikkhu."' *Gisborne Times* XXXIV.3787, 26 March: 7.

Godwin, Joscelyn, 1994. *The Theosophical Enlightenment*. Albany, NY: State University of New York Press.

Golden Dawn Ancient Mystery School, 2017. 'Golden Dawn Biographies: Allan Bennett 1872–1923.' https://goldendawnancientmysteryschool.com/golden-dawn-magical-tradition/golden-dawn-biographies-personalities/allan-bennett/. Retrieved September 2022.

Gombrich, Richard and Gananath Obeyeskere, 1988. *Buddhism Transformed: Religious Change in Sri Lanka*. Princeton, NJ: Princeton University Press.

Goodrick-Clarke, Nicholas, 2008. *The Western Esoteric Traditions: A Historical Introduction*. Oxford: Oxford University Press.

Gould, Warwick, John Kelly and Deirdre Toomey, 1997. *The Collected Letters of W. B. Yeats Vol. Two 1896–1900*. Oxford: Clarendon Press.

Grant, Kenneth, 1972. *The Magical Revival*. London: Frederick Muller.

Green, Thomas, 1895. 'Additional Signatures to the Dublin Lodge Circular.' *The Vâhan* 4.7, February: 12–13.

Greenly, Edward, 1945. 'Ananda Metteyya: Some Reminiscences.' *The Middle Way*, November–December: 84–87.

Greenslade, Thomas B., Jr., 2005. 'The Potentiometer.' *The Physics Teacher* 43: 232–235. https://doi.org/10.1119/1.1888084.

Greer, Mary K., 1995. *Women of the Golden Dawn: Rebels and Priestesses*. Rochester, VT: Park Street Press.

Griffin, David, 1999. *The Ritual Magic Manual: A Complete Course in Practical Magic*. Beverly Hills, CA: Golden Dawn Publishing.

Grossman, Paul and Nicholas T. Van Dam, 2011. 'Mindfulness by Any Other Name . . . : Trials and Tribulations of *Sati* in Western Psychology and Science.' *Contemporary Buddhism* 12.1, May: 219–239.

Gunewardene, D. H., 1973. *F. L. Woodward: Out of his Life and Thought*. Colombo: D. H. Gunewardene (printed by Wesley Press).

Guruge, Ananda, 1984. *From the Living Fountains of Buddhism: Sri Lankan Support to Pioneering Western Orientalists*. Colombo: Ministry of Cultural Affairs.

Guruge, Ananda, 1991. *Return to Righteousness: A Collection of Speeches, Essays and Letters of the Anagarika Dharmapala*. Colombo: Department of Cultural Affairs.

Guruge, Ananda, 2011. 'British Contribution to the Promotion of Buddhist Studies.' *Budumaga: The Buddha's Way* 21.1: 6–7.

Hackmann, H., 1910. *Buddhism as a Religion: Its Historical Development and its Present Conditions* (from the German, revised and enlarged by the author). London: Probsthain & Co.

Hammer, Olav, 2001. *Claiming Knowledge: Strategies of Epistemology from Theosophy to the New Age.* Leiden: Brill.

Hammer, Olav and Mikael Rothstein (eds), 2013. *Handbook of the Theosophical Current.* Brill Handbooks on Contemporary Religion. Leiden: Brill.

Hanegraaff, Wouter J., 1996. *New Age Religion and Western Culture: Esotericism in the Mirror of Secular Thought.* Leiden: Brill.

Hanegraaff, Wouter J., 2006. 'Occult/Occultism.' In W. J. Hanegraaff, R. van den Broek and J. P. Brach (eds), *Dictionary of Gnosis & Western Esotericism.* Leiden: Brill: 884–889.

Hanegraaff, Wouter J., 2013. *Western Esotericism: A Guide for the Perplexed.* London: Bloomsbury.

Hanthawaddy Bi-Weekly Review, 1905. 'Dawei Myoe Thadin: Britisha Phone Gyi Ananda Metteyya Yauk Shi La Chin' (Dawei Township News: The Arrival of British Monk, Ananda Metteyya). *Hanthawaddy Bi-Weekly Review*, 19 April: 945; 'Britisha Phone Gyi Ananda Metteyya Ahkyaung' (About the British Monk Ananda Metteyya). *Hanthawaddy Bi-Weekly Review*, 19 April: 946.

Harcourt Butler, H. E. (patron), 1927. *Who's Who in Burma 1926 under the Distinguished Patronage of H. E. Sir Harcourt Butler, Governor of Burma: A Biographical Record of Prominent Residents of Burma with Photographs & Illustrations.* Calcutta and Rangoon: Indo-Burma Publishing Agency.

Harishchandra, Walasinha, 1908. *The Sacred City of Anuradhapura.* Colombo: Colombo Apothecaries.

Harris, Elizabeth J., 1993. 'Crisis, Competition and Conversion: The British Encounter with Buddhism in Nineteenth Century Sri Lanka.' Unpublished Doctoral Dissertation, Postgraduate Institute of Pali and Buddhist Studies, University of Kelaniya, Colombo.

Harris, Elizabeth J., 1998. *Ananda Metteyya: The First British Emissary of Buddhism.* Kandy: Buddhist Publication Society.

Harris, Elizabeth J., 2000. 'The Power of Compassion: A Study of the Life and Thought of Venerable Ananda Metteyya.' In Perera 2000: 42–62.

Harris, Elizabeth J., 2006. *Theravāda Buddhism and the British Encounter: Religious, Missionary and Colonial Experience in Nineteenth-Century Sri Lanka.* London and New York: Routledge.

Harris, Elizabeth J., 2008. 'Ananda Metteyya: Contester of Misinterpretations of Buddhism.' In Deegalle 2008: 37–52.

Harris, Elizabeth J., 2018. *Religion, Space and Conflict: Colonial and Postcolonial Contexts.* London and New York: Routledge.

Harris, Elizabeth J., 2019. 'Buddhist Meditation and the British Colonial Gaze in Nineteenth-Century Sri Lanka.' *Contemporary Buddhism* 20.1-2, May–November: 200–222.

Harvey, G. E., 1946. *British Rule in Burma 1824-1942.* London: Faber and Faber.

Headlam, Cecil, 1903. *Ten Thousand Miles through India and Burma: An Account of the Oxford University Authentics' Cricket Tour with Mr. K. J. Key in the year of the Coronation Durbar*. London: J. M. Dent.
Hecker, Hellmuth and Bhikkhu Ñāṇatusita (eds), 2008. *The Life of Ñāṇatiloka Thera: The Biography of a Western Buddhist Pioneer*. Kandy: Buddhist Publication Society.
Hindley, Katherine Storm, 2019. 'The Power of Not Reading: Amulet Rolls in Medieval England.' In *The Roll in England and France in the Late Middle Ages*. Vol. 28. Berlin and Boston: De Gruyter: 289–306.
Hla Oung, M. M., 1903. 'The Women of Burma.' *Buddhism* I.I: 61–82.
Homeward Mail from India, China and the East, 1908. 'Buddhist Mission to Britain.' *Homeward Mail from India, China and the East*, 25 April: 528.
Houtman, Gustaaf, 1990. 'The Tradition of Practice among Burmese Buddhists.' Unpublished PhD Thesis, School of Oriental and African Studies, London University, London.
Howard Moore, Elizabeth, 2013. 'The Sacred Geography of Dawei: Buddhism in Peninsular Myanmar (Burma). *Contemporary Buddhism* 14.2: 298–319.
Howe, Ellic, 1972. *The Magicians of the Golden Dawn: A Documentary History of a Magical Order, 1887-1923*. Wellingborough: Aquarian Press.
Humphreys, Christmas, 1926a. 'Ourselves and the T.S. And Explanation.' *Buddhism in England* 1.2, June: 29.
Humphreys, Christmas, 1926b. 'The Doctrine of Anatta 1: The Metaphysical Standpoint.' *Buddhism in England* 1.2, June: 32–33.
Humphreys, Christmas, 1926c 'The Doctrine of Anatta 2: The Logical Standpoint.' *Buddhism in England* 1.3, July: 47–48.
Humphreys, Christmas, 1928. 'British Maha-Bodhi Society; The Coming of the Bhikkhus.' *Buddhism in England* 3.4, October: 77–82.
Humphreys, Christmas, 1929. 'The Order in the West.' *Buddhism in England* 4.6, December: 127–129.
Humphreys, Christmas, 1930. 'To Our Friends in Burma: A Message from the President.' *Buddhism in England* 5.2, June: 53.
Humphreys, Christmas, 1937. *The Development of Buddhism in England: Being a History of the Buddhist Movement in London and the Provinces*. London: The Buddhist Lodge.
Humphreys, Christmas, 1953. 'Obituary—Ven. Ananda Metteyya: The First English Bhikkhu.' *The Middle Way* XXVIII.1: 18–19.
Humphreys, Christmas, 1961. 'Ānanda Metteyya.' In G. P. Malalasekera (ed), *Encyclopaedia of Buddhism*. Fascicle One. Colombo: Government of Ceylon: 539–542.
Humphreys, Christmas, 1968. *Sixty Years of Buddhism in England 1907-1967*. London: The Buddhist Society.
Humphreys, Christmas, 1972. 'Ananda Metteyya: With some Observations on the English Sangha.' *The Middle Way*, November: 133–135.
Humphreys, Christmas, 1985 [1951]. *Buddhism: An Introduction and Guide*. Harmondsworth: Penguin.
Hull Daily Mail, 1908. 'A First Appearance.' *Hull Daily Mail*, 8 May: 3.
Hymenaeus Beta (ed), 1997, *The Goetia, The Lesser Key of Solomon the King*. 2nd Ed. Samuel Liddell MacGregor Mathers (trans). York Beach, ME: Samuel Weiser.

Ikeya, Chie, 2011. *Refiguring Women, Colonialism, and Modernity in Burma*. Honolulu, HI: University of Hawaii Press.

Irish Independent, 1908. 'To "Convert" England: Buddhist Monk's Mission.' *Irish Independent*, 27 April: 8.

Jackson, Mark, 2010. '"Divine stramonium": The Rise and Fall of Smoking for Asthma.' *Medical History* 54.2: 171–94. https://doi.org/10.1017/s0025727300000235.

Janaka, Ashin, 2016. 'Die-Human, Born-Human. The Life and Posthumous Trial of Shin Ukkattha, a Pioneering Monk during a Tumultuous Period in a Nation's History.' Unpublished Doctoral Dissertation, King's College, London.

Jayasundara. A. D., 1920. 'Frank Lee Woodward: A Buddhist Idealist.' *The Buddhist Annual of Ceylon* 1.1: 10.

Jayatilleke, R. 2006. 'Ven. Ananda Metteyya Thera The First Western Buddhist Monk.' Parts 1–3, *Budusarana*. https://web.archive.org/web/20160706060000/http://www.lakehouse.lk/budusarana/2006/02/12/Budu19.pdf; https://web.archive.org/web/20140802015924/http://www.lakehouse.lk/budusarana/2006/02/27/Budu12.pdf.

Jinarajadasa, C., 1938. *First Principles of Theosophy*. 5th Revised Ed. Adyar: Theosophical Publishing House.

Johnston, R. F., 1908. *From Peking to Mandalay: A Journey from North China to Burma through Tibetan Such'uan and Yunnan*. London: John Murray.

Journal of the Burma Research Society, 1911. 'Account of the First General Meeting.' *Journal of the Burma Research Society* 1.1: 10–14.

Kaczynski, Richard, 2005. *Perdurabo Outtakes*. Blue Equinox Journal 1.

Kaczynski, Richard, 2010. *Perdurabo: The Life of Aleister Crowley*. Revised Ed. Berkeley: North Atlantic Books.

Kassapa Thera, 1962 [1927]. *Ānāpāna Sati*. 3rd Ed. Colombo: M. D. Gunasena.

Keck, Stephen L., 2015. *British Burma in the New Century, 1895-1918*. Basingstoke: Palgrave Macmillan.

Kelly, John and Ronald Schuchard, 2005. *The Collected Letters of W. B. Yeats Vol. Four 1905-1907*. Oxford: Oxford University Press.

Kelly, R. Talbot, 1905. *Burma Painted and Described*. London: Adam and Charles Black.

Kemper, Steven, 2015. *Rescued from the Nation: Anagarika Dharmapala and the Buddhist World*. Chicago and London: University of Chicago Press.

King, Francis, 1970. *Ritual Magic in England, 1887 to the Present Day*. London: Neville Spearman.

King, Richard, 1999. *Orientalism and Religion: Postcolonial Theory, India and 'The Mystic East.'* London and New York: Routledge.

Knight, Arthur M., 1903. 'Revival of Buddhism in Burma.' *The Mission Field: A Monthly Record of the Proceedings of the Society for the Propagation of the Gospel at Home and Abroad* XLVIII, December: 355–361.

Kramer, Heirich and James Sprenger, 1928. *The Malleus Maleficarum*. Reprint. New York, NY: Dover Publications.

Lachman, Gary, 2014. *Aleister Crowley: Magick, Rock and Roll, and the Wickedest Man in the World*. New York, NY: Tarcher/Penguin.

Lanka Pradipaya, 1899. 'Bawuddayakugen Liyumak' (Letter from a Buddhist). *Lanka Pradipaya*, 4.27, 28 January: 2.

Lanman, Charles Rockwell, 1913. 'Buddhaghosa's Treatise on Buddhism, Entitled "The Way of Salvation." Analysis of Part 1, on Morality.' *Proceedings of the American Academy of Arts and Sciences* 49.3, August: 149–169.

Lat, Maung, 1911. 'Mrs Besant's Visit to Burma.' *The Message of Theosophy* VI.10–12, January–March: 225–240.

Lees, Andrew, 2011. *The Hurricane Port: a Social History of Liverpool.* Edinburgh: Mainstream Publishing Company.

Ledi Sayadaw, 1903. *Paramatta Thankeik Kyan* (Digest of Abhidhamma Sangaha). Mandalay: Zabumyethman Press.

Leider, Jacques P., 2009. 'Relics, Statues and Predictions: Interpreting an Apocryphal Sermon of Lord Buddha in Arakan.' *Asian Ethnology* 68.2: 333–363.

Leigh, Michael, D., 2011. *Conflict, Politics and Proselytism: Methodist Missionaries in Colonial and Postcolonial Burma 1886-1966.* Manchester and New York: Manchester University Press.

LeRoy Perreira, Todd, 2012. 'Whence Theravāda? The Modern Genealogy of an Ancient Term.' In Peter Skilling, Jason A. Carbine, Claudio Cicuzza and Santi Pakdeekham (eds), *How Theravāda is Theravāda? Exploring Buddhist Identities.* Chaing Mai: Silkworm: 443–561.

Lewis, Frederick, 1926. *Sixty-Four Years in Ceylon: Reminiscences of Life and Adventure.* Ceylon: The Colombo Apothecaries Company Ltd.

Lewis, William, 1799 *The New Dispensatory: The Whole Interspersed with Practical Cautions and Observations.* 6th Ed. London: J. Nourse.

Light, 1914. 'Notice of Meetings at the Buddhist Society of Great Britain and Ireland.' *Light*, 29 March: ii.

Light, 1919. Advertisement. *Light*, 15 April: iii.

Lloyds Weekly Newspaper, 1908. 'England's first Buddhist Monk.' *Lloyds Weekly Newspaper*, 26 April: 5.

London and China Express, 1908a. 'Miscellaneous.' *London and China Express*, 24 April: 311.

London and China Express, 1908b. 'Miscellaneous.' *London and China Express*, 14 August: 603.

London Daily News, 1908. 'Buddhist Missionaries.' *London Daily News*, 21 April: 7.

MacGregor, Allan, 1902. 'The Four Noble Truths.' *The Buddhist* XII.1, April: 9–20.

Madawela, Tissa (producer), 2008. *Bhikkhu Ananda Metteyya and His Legacy: 100 Years of Buddhism in the UK.* DVD. Script written by Wimal de Silva. Researched by Handupelpola Mahinda Nayake Thera. London: World Buddhist Foundation/Sri Saddhatissa International Buddhist Centre.

Madras Weekly Mail, 1903. 'A Scottish Buddhist Priest interviewed in Rangoon.' *Madras Weekly Mail*, 2 July 1903: 20.

Maeder, Clara Fisher, 1897, Douglas Taylor (ed). *Autobiography of Clara Fisher Maeder.* New York, NY: The Dunlap Society.

Mahinda, Ven. Dr. Handupelpola, 2008. 'Some Research on Ananda Metteyya's Legacy.' In *The Buddhist Legacy of United Kingdom: 100 Years of Buddhism in the UK.* London: World Buddhist Foundation: 46–52.

Major Ba Thaung, 2002. *Sarsotawmyar Atthuppatti* (Biographies of Authors). Yangon: Yarpyae Publishing.

Malalasekera, Gunapala Piyasena (ed), 1964. 'Ananda Metteyya.' In *Encyclopaedia of Buddhism*. Colombo: Government. of Ceylon: 539–542.

Malalgoda, Kitsiri, 1976. *Buddhism in Sinhalese Society, 1759-1990*. Berkeley and Los Angeles, CA: University of California Press.

Mānitasirī, U and U Nandamālābhivaṁsa, 1972. *Sankin Sayadaw Guruppattikathā* (Biography of Sankin Sayadaw). Mandalay: Daw Hla Khin & Sons.

Marks, John Ebenezer, 1917. *Forty Years in Burma*. New York, NY: E. P. Dutton.

May Oung, Maung, 1910. 'Manners and Customs.' In Arnold Wright (ed), *Twentieth Century Impressions of Burma: Its History, People, Commerce, Industries and Resources*. London, Durban, Perth, Colombo, etc.: Lloyds Greater Britain Publishing Company: 76–89.

May Oung, Maung, 1911. 'Inaugural Address.' *The Journal of the Burma Research Society* 1.1: 2–9.

May Oung, Maung 1916. *A Selection of Leading Cases on Buddhist Law with Dissertations. Part II: Adoption, Pre-emption, Gift and Religious Usage*. Rangoon: British Burma Press.

McGuire, John, 1912. 'The Buddhism of the Buddha and the Buddhism of Burma.' In *Buddha, Buddhism, and Burma*. Rangoon: American Baptist Mission Press: 5–34.

McKechnie, John, 1904. 'The Aim of Religion.' *Buddhism* 1.4: 604–612.

McKechnie, John, 1905. 'Buddhism and Pessimism.' *Buddhism* 2.1: 33–47.

McMahan, David L., 2008. *The Making of Buddhist Modernism*. Oxford: Oxford University Press.

Mead, G. R. S. (ed), 1893. 'Brixton Lodge.' *The Vâhan* 2.12, July: 7.

Mead, G. R. S., 1895. 'Secession of Mr. Judge's Supporters.' *The Vâhan* 5.1, August: 1–2.

Mead, G. R. S. (ed), 1903. 'On the Watch-Tower.' *The Theosophical Review* 33.195: 193–200, 276–277.

Mendelson, Michael E., 1975, John P. Ferguson (ed). *Sangha and State in Burma: A Study of Monastic Sectarianism and Leadership*. Ithaca, NY: Cornell University Press.

Mendis, N. K. G. (ed), 1993. *The Questions of King Milinda: An Abridgement of the Milindapañha*. Kandy: Buddhist Publication Society.

Min Yu Wai, 2011. *Naigangya Buddhasāsanapyumyar Atthuppatti: Atthuppatti Htoo* (Biographies of Missionary People). 3rd Ed. Yangon: Seik Ku Cho Cho Publishing.

Morning Post, 1908a. Notice. *Morning Post*, 18 April: 6.

Morning Post, 1908b. 'Arrangements: Sunday.' *Morning Post*, 30 May: 9.

Morning Post, 1908c. 'The Congress of Religions at Oxford: Subjects and Speakers.' *Morning Post*, 15 September: 7.

Motherwell Times, 1908. 'Buddhist Monk a Macgregor: Mission to Spread Ideas.' *Motherwell Times*, 2 October: 7.

Mullen, Kenneth, 1989. 'Ananda Metteyya: Buddhist Pioneer.' *The Middle Way* 64.1 (January): 91–94.

Myint Swe, 2017. *Ashin Adiccavamsa Kyaung Tike Thamine Hnit Ashin Adiccavamsa Atthupatti* (History of Adiccavamsa Monastery and Biography of Ven. Adiccavamsa). 2nd Ed. Internal Publication of the Monastery.

Ñāṇamoli, Bhikkhu (trans), 1991 [1956]. *The Path of Purification* (Visuddhimagga) *by Bhadantacariya Buddhaghosa*. Kandy: Buddhist Publication Society.

Ñāṇamoli, Bhikkhu and Bhikkhu Bodhi (trans), 1995. *The Middle Discourses of the Buddha: A New Translation of the Majjhima Nikāya*. Boston, MA: Wisdom.

Ñāṇasīha, Vajirārāmaye Thera and Manouri Senanayake (eds), 2021. *Dhamma Gems: 2565/2021 Centenary Publication of The Servants of the Buddha*. Private Publication by Servants of the Buddha.

Narada Maha Thera and Bhikkhu Kassapa, undated. *The Mirror of the Dhamma*. Moratuwa: Thisara Printers.

Nature, 1908. 'Third International Congress for the History of Religions.' *Nature* 78.2031, 1 October: 552–533.

Neumann, Karl E., 1903. 'Translation. The Instruction of Rāhulo (Majjhima Nikaya, 63).' *Buddhism* 1.1: 135–139.

Ngwe Gaing, 1910. *The Report of the Rangoon College Buddhist Association 1909-10*. Appended to Silacara 1910.

Nyanaponika Mahathera (ed), 1978. *Nyanatiloka Centenary Volume on the Occasion of the 100th Birth Anniversary of the Venerable Nyanatiloka Mahathera*. Kandy: Buddhist Publication Society.

Occasional Correspondent, 1907. 'Buddhism in England: Formation of a Branch Society in London.' *Pall Mall Gazette*, 15 November 1907: 10.

Ohn Ghine, Maung, 1959. 'Not So, Brother!' *The Open Door* II.1, 19 July: 11–13.

Olcott, Henry S., 1902. 'The Ordination of Allan MacGregor.' *The Theosophist* 23.11, August: 683–688.

Olcott, Henry S., 1903. 'Reviews.' *The Theosophist* 24.1, October: 56–59.

Olcott, Henry S., 1904a. 'A Buddhist Quarterly.' *The Theosophist* 25.6, March: 374–375.

Olcott, Henry S., 1904b. 'Reviews.' *The Theosophist* 25.9, June: 571–572.

Oliver, Ian P., 1979. *Buddhism in Britain*. London: Rider.

Oman, John Campbell, 1908. *Cults, Customs and Superstitions of India*. London: T. Fisher Unwin.

Oxfordshire Weekly News, 1908. 'Our London Letter (From Our Special Correspondent).' *Oxfordshire Weekly News*, 6 May: 2.

Overland China Mail, 1913. 'Buddhism in England.' *Overland China Mail*, 8 March: 38.

Owen, Alex, 2004. *The Place of Enchantment: British Occultism and the Culture of the Modern*. Chicago, IL: University of Chicago Press.

P Monin, 2009. *Pi Monin Ei Pi Monin* (P Monin's P Monin). Yangon: Moe Kyaw Publishing House.

Payne, Francis, 1911. Review of 'An Outline of Buddhism or The Religion of Burma.' *The Buddhist Review* III.4: 313–316.

Parānanda, Sri, 1898. *The Gospel of Jesus According to Matthew as Interpreted to R. L. Harrison by the Light of the Godly Experience of Sri Parānanda*. London: Kegan Paul, Trench, Trubner.

Parānanda, Sri, 1902, R. L. Harrison (ed). *An Eastern Exposition of The Gospel of Jesus According to St. John being an Interpretation thereof by Sri Parānanda by the Light of Jnāna Yoga*. London: William Hutchinson & Co.

Patterson, Bryan, 1999. 'Wickedest Man in the World.' *The Sunday Leader* (Sri Lanka), 17 January: 27. Reprinted from *Sunday Herald*.

Pearn, B. R., 1939. *A History of Rangoon*. Rangoon: American Baptist Mission Press.

Pelletier, Ernest E., 2004. *The Judge Case: A Conspiracy which Ruined the Theosophical Cause*. Edmonton: Edmonton Theosophical Society.

Pereira, Cassius, 1905. 'News from Ceylon: From Our Own Correspondent.' *Buddhism* 2.1, October: 126–127.

Pereira, Cassius, 1918. 'The Decline of the Modern Sangha.' *Journal of the Maha-Bodhi Society* XXVI.10–12, October–December: 119–121.

Pereira, Cassius, 1922. *Ānāpāna Sati*. Handwritten Booklet.

Pereira, Cassius, 1923a. 'The Late Mr Alan Bennett.' *The Buddhist*, 28 April 2466–1923: 6.

Pereira, Cassius, 1923b. 'Anatta.' In Silacara Thera and S. W. Wikayatilake (eds), *The Buddhist Annual of Ceylon B.E. 2467*. Colombo: W. E. Bastian & Co.: 34–37, 40–43.

Pereira, Cassius A., 1945. *The Simpler Side of Buddhist Doctrine, being the Sixth Lecture under the Dona Alpina Ratnayake Trust Delivered by Dr. Cassius A. Pereira, L.R.C.P. (Lond), M.R.C.S. (Eng) at The University of Ceylon on 15th June, 1945*. Pamphlet. Colombo: The Public Trustee of Ceylon.

Pereira, Cassius A., 1947. 'Why Do I Renounce the World.' *Ceylon Daily News Vesak Number* 2491: 66–68.

Perera, Arthur R., 'The Stone Antiquities of Ceylon.' *Buddhism* 1.4: 621–630.

Perera, Lakshman (ed), 2000. *Buddhism for The New Millennium*. London: World Buddhist Foundation.

Petros Xristos, Frater, 2001. *Allan Bennett. The Mountain Temple & Order of the Golden Dawn*. https://web.archive.org/web/20071229064646/http://home.earthlink.net:80/~xristos/GoldenDawn/biobennett.htm. Retrieved April 2007.

Phinney, P. D. (ed), 1914. *The Judson Centennial Celebrations in Burma 1813-1913*. Rangoon: American Baptist Mission Press.

Pieris, William, 2017 [1973]. *The Western Contribution to Buddhism*. Dehiwela: Buddhist Cultural Centre.

Pike, Albert, 1871. *Morals and Dogma of the Ancient and Accepted Scottish Rite of Freemasonry*. Charleston, SC: A∴M∴.

Piyadassi, Galayaye, 2008. Introduction to Madawela 2008.

Po Lat, U, 2012. 'When and How Theosophy came to Burma.' In *Centennial Commemoration Burmese Section of the Theosophical Society*. Yangon: Yangon Theosophical Society: 69.

Po Me, Moung, 1903. 'Animism and Agnosticism.' *Buddhism* 1.1: 83–100.

Powell, Charles F., 1889. 'The Progress of Buddhism in the West: A Lecture given in the Theosophical Hall.' *The Buddhist* I.42, 4 October: 329–332.

Powell-Brown, Ethel M., 1911. *A Year on the Irrawaddy*. Rangoon: Myles Standish.

Prothero, Stephen, 1996. *The White Buddhist: The Asian Odyssey of Henry Steel Olcott*. Bloomington, IN: Indiana University Press.

Prothero, Stephen, 2001. *Purified by Fire: a History of Cremation in America*. Berkeley, CA: University of California Press.

Purser, W. C. B., 1911. *Christian Missions in Burma*. Westminster: Society for the Propagation of the Gospel in Foreign Parts.

Purser, W. C. B., 1912. 'Buddhist Ideals: Kenneth Saunders, Christian Lit: Soc:.' *The Rangoon Diocesan Magazine* XVI.10, October: 322–324.

Purser, W. C. B. and K. J. Saunders, 1914. *Modern Buddhism in Burma: Being an Epitome of Information Received from Missionaries, Officials and Others*. Rangoon: Christian Literature Society Burma Branch.

Ramanathan, Ponnambalam, 1905. 'The Spirit of the East contrasted with the Spirit of the West: Being a Lecture delivered by P. Ramanathan K.C., C.M.G. (Solicitor General of Ceylon) before the Brooklyn Institute of Arts and Sciences at its Opening Meeting of the Season of 1905-6.' New York, NY: Copyright of the Author.

Ramanathan, Ponnambalam, 1907, Myron H. Phelps (ed). *The Culture of the Soul Among Western Nations*. New York, NY: G. P. Putnam & Sons; London: The Knickerbocker Press.

Ramesh, Jairam, 2021. *The Light of Asia: The Poem that Defined The Buddha*. Gurugram: Penguin Random House India.

Rangoon College Magazine, 1914. 'The Rangoon Buddhist Association.' *Rangoon College Magazine* I, April: 71–75.

Rankine, David, 2023. *The Grimoire Encyclopedia: A Convocation of Spirits, Texts, Materials, and Practices*. 2 Vols. West Yorkshire: Hadean Press.

Ratnajinendra, M., 1968. 'First Buddhist Mission to England.' *Daily News*, 23 April: 13 (page not clear).

Ratnayake, Premil, 1992. 'A Church of the Buddha?' *The Island, Saturday Magazine*, 9 May: i–ii.

Regardie, Israel, 1982 [1970]. *The Eye in the Triangle: An Interpretation of Aleister Crowley*. 2nd Ed. Tempe, AZ: New Falcon Publications.

Regardie, Israel, 1995. *The Golden Dawn: A Complete Course in Practical Ceremonial Magic, Four Volumes in One*. St. Paul, MN: Llewellyn Publishing.

Regardie, Israel, 2003. *The Complete Golden Dawn System of Magic*. 2nd Revised Limited Ed. Tempe, AZ: New Falcon Publications.

Report on Public Instruction in Burma for the Year 1900–1901, 1901. Rangoon: Government Printing Press.

Report on Public Instruction in Burma for the year 1910–11, 1911. Rangoon: Government Printing Press.

Resident Director, 1891. 'The Origin of the Colonial College.' *Colonia: The Colonial College Magazine* 1.1, 1889–1891: 4–7.

Rhys Davids, C. A. F., 1903a. 'The Threshold of Buddhist Ethics.' *Buddhism* I.I: 39–53.

Rhys Davids, C. A. F., 1903b. 'On the Pali and Sanskrit Texts.' *Buddhism* 1.2: 249–258.

Rhys Davids, C. A. F., 1904. 'Seeing Things as They Are.' *Buddhism* I.3: 378–392.

Ricard, Matthieu and Wolf Singer, 2017. *Beyond the Self: Conversations between Buddhism and Neuroscience*. Cambridge and London: MIT Press.

Ritchie, Hannah, 2017. *What the History of London's Air Pollution Can Tell us about the Future of Today's Growing Megacities*. https://ourworldindata.org/london-air-pollution. Retrieved June 2025.

Robertson, Alec, 1990. *Buddha: The Healer Incomparable*. Colombo: State Printing Corporation.

Roebuck, Valerie (ed/trans), 2010. *The Dhammapada*. London: Penguin.

Rogers, John D., 1989. 'Cultural Nationalism and Cultural Reform: The 1904 Temperance Movement in Sri Lanka.' *The Indian Economic and Social Review* 26.3: 319–341.

Ross, G. R. T., 1911. Review of 'Compendium of Philosophy.' *The Journal of the Burma Research Society* 1.2: 60–65.

Ross-shire Journal, 1908. 'Our London Letter.' *Ross-shire Journal*, 1 May: 3.

Rost, E. R., 1930. 'A Sangha for the West.' *The Buddhist Annual of Ceylon 1930*: 272–275.

Russell, Pamela, 2018. *Liverpool: Remembering 1914-18*. Great War Britain Series. Stroud: The History Press.

Rutenberg, D., 1939. 'The Early History of the Potentiometer System of Electrical Measurement.' *Annals of Science*, 4:2, 212–243. https://doi.org/10.1080/00033793900201221.

Saddhatissa, H. (trans), 1985. *The Sutta-Nipāta*. London: Curzon.

Saint Pancras Gazette, 1915. Advertisement. *Saint Pancras Gazette*, 21 May: 2.

Sarasavi Sandaresa, 1903a. 'Ingreesi bhikshunwahanse namak' (An English Bhikkhu). *Sarasavi Sandaresa* 16.90, 7 April: 1.

Sarasavi Sandaresa, 1903b. 'Abhidarmaya.' *Sarasavi Sandaresa* 12.2, 19 April: 3.

Sarasavi Sandaresa, 1903c. 'Aluth Denweemak.' News Notice. *Sarasavi Sandaresa* 16.94, 28 April: 5.

Sarasavi Sandaresa, 1903d. 'Bambalapitiye Maithri Dharma Shalawa saha Bhikshunwahanselage Patashalawa' (Maithri Dhamma Hall of Bambalapitiya and the School for the Bhikkhus). *Sarasavi Sandaresa* 17.2, 19 May: 7.

Sarasavi Sandaresa, 1903e. 'Aluth Denweemak.' News Notice. *Sarasavi Sandaresa* 7.4, 26 May: 5.

Sarasavi Sandaresa, 1903f. 'Ananda Maithriya' (Bhikkhu Ananda Maithriya). *Sarasavi Sandaresa* 17.7, 5 June: 1.

Sarasavi Sandaresa, 1903g. 'Ananda Maithriya Bhikshunwahansege Awasana Dharma Deshanawa' (The Last Dhamma Sermon of the Ven. Ananda Maithriya). *Sarasavi Sandaresa* 17.7, 12 June: 1.

Sarasavi Sandaresa, 1903h. 'Senkadagala Dharmadeshana' (Dhamma Sermons of Senkadagala). *Sarasavi Sandaresa* 17.7, 12 June 1903: 2.

Schober, Julianne, 2011. *Modern Buddhist Conjunctures in Myanmar: Cultural Narratives, Colonial Legacies, and Civil Society*. Honolulu, HI: University of Hawai'i Press.

Seaman, L. C. B., 1973. *Life in Victorian London*. London: B. T. Batsford.

Second Quinquennial Report on Public Instruction in Burma for the Years 1897–98 to 1901–2, 1901. Rangoon. Government Printing.

Sein Nyo Tun, 1959. 'The Role of Buddhism under the Shadow of a Thermo-Nuclear War: A Broadcast talk for the Burma Broadcasting Studio by U Sein Nyo Tun on 25th July 1959.' *The Open Door* II.2, 15 October: 17–19.

Sein Nyo Tun, 1960. 'Obituary.' *The Open Door* III.1, 15 July: 15.

Sevenoaks Chronicle and Kentish Advertiser, 1908. 'The Scottish Buddhist.' *Sevenoaks Chronicle and Kentish Advertiser*, 1 May: 2.

Shaw, Sarah, 2006. *Buddhist Meditation: An Anthology of Texts from the Pāli Canon.* Abingdon, Oxon and New York: Routledge.

Sheffield Evening Telegraph, 1908. 'The Buddhist Missionary Arrives.' *Sheffield Evening Telegraph*, 23 April: 3.

Shwe Zan Aung, 1903. 'On the Processes of Thought.' *Buddhism* 1.2: 259–266.

Shwe Zan Aung, 1910, Caroline Rhys Davids (ed). *Compendium of Philosophy, being a Translation now Made for the First Time from the Original Pali of the Abhidhammattha—Sangaha, with Introductory Essay and Notes.* London: Henry Froude.

Sinnett, Alfred P., 1883. *Esoteric Buddhism.* London and Benares: Theosophical Publishing House.

Sīlācāra, Bhikkhu, 1908a. 'Perseverance.' *The Message of Theosophy* IV.6, September: 124–128.

Sīlācāra, Bhikkhu, 1908b. 'The Foolish and the Wise.' Translation from the *Majjhima Nikāya*. *The Message of Theosophy* IV.7, October: 149–153.

Sīlācāra, Bhikkhu, 1908c. 'Anatta.' *The Message of Theosophy* IV.8, November: 172–176.

Sīlācāra, Bhikkhu, 1908d. 'The Meditation on Loving Kindness and of Compassion.' *The Message of Theosophy* IV.9, December: 197–201.

Sīlācāra, Bhikkhu, 1910. *A Discourse on Viriya.* Rangoon: Burma Mission Press on Behalf of the Rangoon College Buddhist Association.

Sinhala Bauddhaya, 1908a. 'Burumaye Bawuddha Sangamaya: Paswana Warshika Maha Sabha Resweema' (The Buddhist Society of Burma: the Fifth Annual General Meeting). *Sinhala Bauddhaya* 2.88. January: 12.

Sinhala Bauddhaya 1908b. 'Maha Brithanyaye Baudhdhagama' (Buddhism in Great Britain). *Sinhala Bauddhaya* 3.134, 3 September: 9.

Sinhala Bauddhaya, 1909. 'Wedagath Liyumak.' Reprint and Translation of Letter from Francis Payne to Anagārika Dharmapāla, Written on 1 December, 1908. *Sinhala Bauddhaya* 3.14, 16 January: 16.

Sirisena, Mihirini, 2017. 'The Dissident Orientalist: An Interpretation of U Dhammaloka's 1909 Tour of Ceylon.' *Interventions* 19.1: 126–143.

Smart, R. B., 1957 [1917]. *Burma Gazetteer: Akyab District Volume A.* Rangoon: Government Printing Press.

Smith, D. A. W., 1914. 'The Look Forward.' In Phinney 1914: 54–57.

Smith, Garnet, 1923. 'A Call to Buddhism—the Wisdom of the Aryas by Allen Bennett.' *The Times Literary Supplement*, 17 May, Issue 1113: 334.

Spence Hardy, Robert, 1850. *Eastern Monachism: An Account of the Origin, Laws, Discipline, Sacred Writings, Mysterious Rites, Religious Ceremonies and Present Circumstances of the Order of Mendicants Founded by Gotama Buddha.* London: Partridge & Oakley.

Somerset and West of England Advertiser, 1908. 'England Ready for the Reception of Buddhism.' *Somerset and West of England Advertiser*, 8 October: 6.

South Wales Daily Post, 1908. 'To Convert England: Buddhist Missionary from Rangoon.' *South Wales Daily Post*, 21 April: 6.

Starr, Meredith, 1921. 'To Ananda Metteyya.' *The Pall Mall and Globe*, April 13: 4.

Story, Francis, 1981 [1961]. *Early Western Buddhists: Extracts from Articles Published in "The Buddhist Review," 1909-1914, Selected and Presented by Francis Story.* Kandy: Buddhist Publication Society.

Stout, Adam, 2011. *Universal Majesty, Verity and Love Infinite—A Life of George Watson Macgregor Reid.* The Fifth Mount Haemus Lecture, The Order of Bards Ovates & Druids. https://web.archive.org/web/20160403093444/https://druidry.org/events-projects/mount-haemus-award/fifth-mount-haemus-lecture. Retrieved March 2018.

Straits Times, 1908. 'Buddhist Mission. Rangoon Lady Bears cost of Monk's English Tour. Efforts to Convert Britain.' *Straits Times* (Singapore), 19 May: 5.

Strong, John S., 2001. *The Buddha: A Short Biography.* Oxford: Oneworld.

Stuckrad, Kocku von, 2005. *Western Esotericism: A Brief History of Secret Knowledge.* London: Equinox Publishing.

Sutin, Lawrence, 2000. *Do What Thou Wilt: A Life of Aleister Crowley.* New York, NY: St. Martin's Griffin.

Taw Sein, 1903. 'Pali Examinations in Burma.' *Buddhism* 1.1: 58–60.

Than Aung, Maung, 1978. *Index to the Journal of the Burma Research Society 1911-1977.* Submitted as Part of a Postgraduate Diploma in Librarianship. Rangoon: Arts and Science University.

The Aberdeen Daily Journal 2nd Edition, 1908. 'Our London Letter.' *The Aberdeen Daily Journal*, 29 September: 5.

The British Buddhist, 1928. 'Dhammachakka Festival and Welcome to the Ven. Bhikkhus.' *The British Buddhist* 2.2, August: 12–13.

The Buddhist Annual of Ceylon, 1923. 'News and Notes. Ananda Metteyya.' *The Buddhist Annual of Ceylon B.E. 2467*: 69.

The Buddhist Review 1909a. 'News and Notes.' *The Buddhist Review* 1.2, April: 142–150.

The Buddhist Review 1909b. 'News and Notes.' *The Buddhist Review* 1.3: 227–230.

The Buddhist Review, 1909c. 'Reviews and Notices.' *The Buddhist Review* 1.3: 221–224.

The Buddhist Review 1909d. 'Report of the Second Annual Meeting of the Buddhist Society of Great Britain and Ireland.' *The Buddhist Review* 1.4, October: 289–300.

The Buddhist Review, 1910. 'Notes and News: Obituary Notice Ba Hlā Oung.' *The Buddhist Review* II.4, October–December: 318–319.

The Buddhist Review, 1911. 'Reviews and Notices: The Compendium of Philosophy.' *The Buddhist Review* III.3, July–September: 225–230.

The Buddhist Review, 1912. 'Special Notices.' *The Buddhist Review* IV.1, January–March: 80.

The Buddhist Review, 1917a. 'Donations to the A. M. Fund.' *The Buddhist Review* IX.1: 40.

The Buddhist Review, 1917b. 'Shall the Sangha be represented in England: An Appeal?' *The Buddhist Review* IX.2: 73–74.

The Buddhist Review, 1917c. 'Donations: A. M. Fund.' *The Buddhist Review* IX.2: 100.

The Buddhist Review, 1917d. 'Report of the Annual General Meeting 1917.' *The Buddhist Review* IX.3: 109–110.
The Buddhist Review, 1920a. 'Caxton Hall Meeting.' *The Buddhist Review* X, July: 198–220.
The Buddhist Review, 1920b. 'News and Notes.' *The Buddhist Review* X, July: 222.
The Buddhist Review 1921. 'Notes and News.' *The Buddhist Review* XI: 144–148.
The Buddhist Review 1922. 'The International Buddhist Union.' *The Buddhist Review* XII.1: 2–7.
The Buddhist Society, 1947. *What is Buddhism? An Answer from the Western Point of View*. London: The Buddhist Society.
The Burma Gazette Part One: Notifications of the Lieutenant Governor of Burma 1903. Burma: Government Printer.
The Burma Gazette Part One: Notifications of the Lieutenant Governor of Burma 1904. Burma: Government Printer.
The Burma Gazette Part One: Notifications of the Lieutenant Governor of Burma 1906. Burma: Government Printer.
The Bystander, 1908a. 'Bhikkhu Ananda Metteyya.' *The Bystander*, 29 April: 213.
The Bystander, 1908b. 'John Macgregor (alias Bhikkhu Ananda Metteyya). *The Bystander*, 27 May: 422.
The Cheltenham Looker-On, 1913. 'Looking on.' *The Cheltenham Looker-On*, 1 February 1913: 21–22.
The Church Times, 1908a. 'Central London Mission: The Bishop at St. James', Clerkenwell.' *The Church Times*, 27 March: 401.
The Church Times, 1908b. 'H. Fielding Hall's New Book on Buddhism.' *The Church Times* LIX.2,363, 1 May: 569.
The Church Times, 1908c. Advertisement. *The Church Times*, 9 October: 476.
The Church Times, 1908d. Review of John Campbell Oman 'Cults, Customs and Superstitions of India.' *The Church Times*, 20 November: 691.
The Civil and Military Gazette (Lahore), 1913. 'Buddhism in England: A Missionary Movement.' *The Civil and Military Gazette*, 23 February: 7.
The Clarion, 1908. 'General.' *The Clarion*, 28 August: 7.
The Courier, 1908. 'A Scottish Buddhist.' *The Courier*, 2 May: 11.
The Daily Telegraph, 1908. 'Ananda Metteyya: Buddhism in England.' *The Daily Telegraph*, 29 September: 12.
The Evening Telegraph and Post, Dundee, 1908. 'English Buddhist: A Macgregor who is not a Scot: A Strange Incident.' *The Evening Telegraph and Post*, 23 April: 4.
The Falkirk Herald, 1908. 'Our London Letter: From Our Special Correspondent.' *The Falkirk Herald*, 29 April: 5.
The Kansas City Star, 1908. 'This Buddhist Priest Would Convert "Heathen" America.' *The Kansas City Star*, 7 June: 8C.
The Londonderry Sentinel, 1913. 'British Buddhists: Propagation in London. Wanted a Bhikkhu.' *The Londonderry Sentinel*, 1 February: 8.
The Looking Glass, 1910a. 'An Amazing Sect.' *The Looking Glass*, 29 October: 140–142.
The Looking Glass, 1910b. 'An Amazing Sect No. 2. *The Looking Glass*, 12 November: 203–5.

The Maha-Bodhi and the United Buddhist World, 1902. 'The Upasampada Ordination of Bhikkhu Ananda Maitriya.' *The Maha-Bodhi and the United Buddhist World* XI.3, July: 60–64; XI.4, August: 81–84; XI.5, September: 100–101.

The Maha-Bodhi and the United Buddhist World, 1908. 'Britain's First Buddhist Temple.' *The Maha-Bodhi and the United Buddhist World*, June: 88–90.

The Maha-Bodhi and the United Buddhist World, 1909. Reprint of Letter from Francis Payne to Anagārika Dharmapāla, Written on 1 December, 1908. *The Maha-Bodhi and the United Buddhist World* XVII.1, February: 31.

The Maha-Bodhi and the United Buddhist World, 1913. 'The Rangoon College Buddhist Association.' *The Maha-Bodhi and the United Buddhist World* XXI.10, October: 211–212.

The Maha-Bodhi and the United Buddhist World, 1924. 'Buddha Gaya and the Burmese Buddhists.' *The Maha-Bodhi and the United Buddhist World* XXXII.5: 217–222.

The Missionary Review of the World, 1909. 'England Invaded by Buddhists.' *The Missionary Review of the World* XXII.1, January: 66–67.

The Montgomery Advertiser, 1908. 'Religious News of Montgomery.' *The Montgomery Advertiser*, 10 May: 24.

The Open Court, 1908. 'Miscellaneous: Bhikku Ananda Metteyya.' *The Open Court* XXII, 9, September: 573–574.

The Rangoon Times, 1908a. 'Temple in Bedroom: Buddhist Monk's First Day in England.' *The Rangoon Times*, 23 May: 12.

The Rangoon Times, 1908b. 'Proposed Buddhist Association.' *The Rangoon Times*, 15 August: 10.

The Scotsman, 1923. Notice. *The Scotsman*, 19 February: 2.

The Servants of the Buddha, 1921. *The Servants of the Buddha: Rules and Constitution.* Colombo: Oriental Press.

The Sketch, 1908. 'The Scottish Buddhist who has been Seeking Converts in this Country, the Rev. Bhikkhu Ananda Metteyya.' *The Sketch*, 14 October: 8.

The Spectator, 1908. Advertisement. *The Spectator*, 3 June: 876.

The Sphere, 1908. 'A Buddhist Missionary to England.' *The Sphere*, 2 May:16.

The Telegraph, 1912. 'Buddhists in England, Establishing a Monastery.' *The Telegraph* (Brisbane, Queensland), 23 October: 13.

The Times, 1896. 'The Colonial College.' *The Times*, 27 July: 10.

The Times, 1913. 'Personal: Buddhism—Wanted.' *The Times*, 25 January 1913: 1.

Tike Soe, 2018. *Sarthamar Ei Sar Poung Choke Dutiya Twe* (Collection of a Bookworm). Vol. 2. Yangon: Seik Ku Cho Cho Publishing House.

Thorowgood, John C., 1894. *Asthma and Chronic Bronchitis.* London: Baillierre Tindall & Cox.

Thuriya, 1911. 'Yangon College Buddhabhatha Ahthin' (Rangoon College Buddhist Association). *Thuriya*, 9 September: 13.

Trainor, Kevin, 1997. *Relics, Ritual and Representation in Buddhism; Rematerializing the Sri Lankan Theravāda Tradition.* Cambridge: Cambridge University Press.

Trainor, Kevin, 2012. 'Buddhism in a Nutshell: The Uses of *Dhammapada* 183.' In Carol Anderson, Susanne Mrozik and R. M. W. Rajapakse (eds), *Embedded Religions: Essays in Honor of W. S. Karunatillake.* Colombo: S. Godage: 109–146.

Trotman, Francis E., 1908. 'The Buddhist Propaganda.' *The Rangoon Diocesan Magazine* XII.4, April: 141–147.

Trotman, Francis E., 1909. 'The Church's Message to Buddhists.' *The Mission Field* LIV: 269–275.

Tun Hla Oung, 1959. 'Buddha Sāsana Samāgama: Information for Enquirers.' *The Open Door* II.2, 15 October: ii.

Turner, Alicia, 2011. 'Narratives of Nation, Questions of Community: Examining Burmese Sources without the Lens of Nation.' *The Journal of Burma Studies* 15.2: 263–282.

Turner, Alicia, 2013. 'The Bible, the Bottle and the Knife: Religion as a Mode of Resisting Colonialism for U Dhammaloka.' *Contemporary Buddhism* 14.1: 66–77.

Turner, Alicia, 2014. *Saving Buddhism: The Impermanence of Religion in Colonial Burma*. Honolulu, HI: University of Hawai'i Press.

Turner, Alicia, Laurence Cox and Brian Bocking, 2020. *The Irish Buddhist: The Forgotten Monk Who Faced Down the British Empire*. Oxford: Oxford University Press.

Turner, Victor, 1969. *The Ritual Process: Structure and Anti-Structure*. Chicago, IL: Aldine Publishing.

Tweed, Thomas A., 1992. *The American Encounter with Buddhism 1844–1912*. Bloomington, IN: Indiana University Press.

Van Schaik, Sam, 2020. *Buddhist Magic: Divination, Healing and Enchantment through the Ages*. Boulder, CO: Shambhala.

Vijja Mg Nyan Shin, 1962. 'Rangoon Takkatho Buddhabhatha Athingi Thamine' (History of Rangoon University Buddhist Association). *The Rangoon University Association Magazine*: 46.

Vinson, Steve and Janet Gunn, 2014. 'Studies in Esoteric Syntax: The Enigmatic Friendship of Aleister Crowley and Battiscombe Gunn.' In William Carruthers (ed), *Histories of Egyptology: Interdisciplinary Measures*. London and New York: Routledge: 96–111.

Vythilingam, M., 1971. *The Life of Sir Ponnambalam Ramanathan*. Vol. 1. Colombo: Ramanathan Commemoration Society.

W. A. P., 1946. 'Dr MacGregor-Reid.' *The Occult Review* LXXXIII.1, January: 3–6.

Walker, Pamela J., 2006. 'Adoption and Victorian Culture.' *The History of the Family: An International Quarterly* 11: 211–221.

Warminster and Westbury Journal, 1908. 'Our London Letter: From Our Special Correspondent.' *Warminster and Westbury Journal*, 2 May: 2.

Waterhouse, Helen, 1997. *Buddhism in Bath: Adaptation and Authority*. Community Religions Project Monograph Series. Leeds: University of Leeds.

Waterhouse, Helen, 2004. 'Buddhism in Britain: A Brief Overview.' In Elizabeth J. Harris and Ramona Kauth (eds), *Meeting Buddhists*. Leicester: Christians Aware: 53–66.

Webb, C. Morgan, 1911. *Census of India 1911 Vol IX Burma Part 1*. Rangoon: Government Printing.

Webb, Russell, 2004. *London Buddhist Vihara: A Chronicle*. London: Linh-So'n Buddhist Association.

Weinreb, Ben and Christopher Hibbert (eds), 1983. *The London Encyclopaedia*. London: Book Club Associates.

Westminster Gazette, 1908a. 'Notes of the Day.' *Westminster Gazette*, 23 April: 3.

Westminster Gazette, 1908b. 'Buddhism in the West End.' *Westminster Gazette*, 1 June: 5.

Westminster Gazette 1922. Notice. *Westminster Gazette*, 23 November: 1.

West Ridgeway, Joseph, 1903. *Administration of the Affairs of Ceylon, 1896-1903: A Review*. Colombo: George J. A. Skeen (Government Printer).

Western Chronicle, 1908. 'Notes on News.' *Western Chronicle*, 7 February: 5.

Wharfedale and Airdale Observer, 1908. 'Our London Letter.' *Wharfedale and Airdale Observer*, 1 May: 7.

White, Herbert Thirkell, 1913. *A Civil Servant in Burma*. London: Edward Arnold.

Wijeyesekera, Anoji, 2021. 'One Hundred Years.' In Ñānasīha and Senanayake 2021: 8–23.

Wootton, A. C., 1910. *Chronicles of Pharmacy*. London: MacMillan.

World Buddhist Foundation, 2008. '100 Years of Buddhism in the UK: The Buddhist Legacy of the United Kingdom.' Brochure for an Event held at Brent Town Hall, 28 September 1908. London: World Buddhist Foundation.

Wright, Arnold (ed), 1907. *Twentieth Century Impressions of Ceylon: Its History, People, Commerce, Industries and Resources*. London, Durban, Colombo, Perth, Singapore and Hong Kong: Lloyds Greater Britain Publishing Company.

Wright, Arnold (ed), 1910. *Twentieth Century Impressions of Burma: Its History, People, Commerce, Industries and Resources*. London, Durban, Perth, Colombo, etc.: Lloyds Greater Britain Publishing Company.

Wright, Dudley, 1908. 'Spiritualism and Buddhism: Interview with the Bhikku Ananda Metteya,' *Light: A Journal of Psychical, Occult, and Mystical Research* XXVIII.1,426, 9 May: 225.

Wright, Dudley, 1912. *A Manual of Buddhism*. London: Paul, Trench, Trübner & Company.

X. Y. Z., 1916. 'The Ex-Thera Ananda Metteyya.' *The Buddhist Review* VIII.4, November–December: 217–219.

Zalewski, Pat, 2002. *Talismans and Evocations of the Golden Dawn*. Loughborough: Thoth Publishing.

Zay Yar, Maung, 2010. *Myanmar Lukyaw Taya Pathama Twe* (One Hundred Famous People in Myanmar). Vol. 1. Yangon: Colour Tone Publishing.

Zion's Herald, 1908. 'Our English Letter "Alafia."' *Zion's Herald* 86.37, 2 September: 1131.

Index

Numbers in bold refer to figures.

Abhidhamma, 64, 73, 83, 86, 87, 94, 96, 192, 258n60, 263n132, 264n141
Abhidhammatthasaṅgaha, 258n60, 264nn141–142
Adelphi Lodge [of the Theosophical Society], 24
Ādiccavaṃsa, Ven., 126, 264n145
Adyar, 4, 25, 106, 223–225
Agarwal, C. V., 225–226
Akyab: Bennett arrives in, 62, 65; Bennett leaves, 83; Bennett ordains in, 11, 65, 73–74, 80–81, 83, 92, 141, 251n53; British in, 72–73; cosmopolitanism of, 64–65, 72–73; Crowley in, 73–74; Rangoon compared to, 88–89; temples in, 252n2
Akyab Plan, 81–82, 86, 94, 96, 98, 101, 112, 118, 129
alchemy, 4, 24, 26, 31, 235n3
alcohol, 56, 64, 68, 161
Almond, Philip, 8
Amarapura Nikāya, 53, 55, 247n15
ammoniacum gum, 39, 243n52
amulets. *See* talismans
Anālayo, Bhikkhu, 221
Ananda M [Ananda Metteya]: academic representations of, 219–220; arrives in Liverpool (1914), 178; arrives in London (1908), 133; Buddhist education of, 86; commemorations of, 214–218; death of, 194, **195**; descriptions of, 135–137, 145, 168, 175–177, 188–189; diet of, 95, 134; disrobing of, 11–12, 167, 168–169, 174, 272n99; as educational pioneer, 124–125; final years of, 11–12; finances of, 12, 65, 66, 82, 112, 114–115, 116–117, 119, 129, 146, 168–169, 171–172, 177, 187, 193, 274n15; grave of, 218–219, 277n53; health of, 11–12, 85, 87, 96, 109–110, 116–117, 119, 121, 141, 152, 154, 156, 157, 165–167, 168, 176, 178, 189, 272n99; importance or legacy of, 3, 9, 12, 206, 214–218; interviews with, 22, 134, 138, 145, 148, 149, 267n27, 277n47; as inventor, 96, 189, 193; as liminal figure, 5, 6, 104, 227, 235n2; meditation practice of (*see under* meditation); as mentor, 193; as missionary, 11–12, 82, 111, 117, 129, 130–146, 202, 206; monastic rules and, 136, 146, 147, 149, 155, 167, 220; ordinations of (*see under* ordination); *pavāraṇā* ceremony of, 85; photos, drawings, or paintings of, **68, 99, 100, 116, 120**, 135, **140**, 198, 209, 212, 215, 250n50; as public speaker, 67, 139, 141, 147–148, **154**, 163, 220; refused passage to US, 170; reputation of, 11, 92, 106–111, 127, 141–142, 146, 163–164, 189; returns to London (1918), 172; as scientist, 95–96, 105–106, 112, 127, 148, 152, 181, 185, 188–189, 191, 259n70, 261n98; works by, 5–6, 9–11, 12, 65–66, 98, 188, 223, 254n27 (*see also individual titles*); as yogi, 1, 10, 57, 86, 169, 175, 189–190, 213, 227. *See also* Bennett, Allan; Frater I.A.; MacGregor, Allan

Ānanda Maitreya Mahayanake Thera, Balangoda, 64, 205–206, 251n51
anattā, 61, 104, 107, 120, 147, 158, 160, 162, 201, 209, 213–214, 250n50, 267n23; Bax studio lectures on, 181–182, 185–186, 211; chariot analogy for, 176, 275n26; C. Pereira on, 64, 196, 250n50; Theosophists and, 49, 102, 111, 123, 185–186, 211; translation of, 211
Anglo-Vernacular Schools, 124–125, 264n140
'Animism and Law', 65, 74–75, 76, 98, 101, 159, 180
Anuradhapura, 62, 71, 80, 105, 249nn41–42, 261n95
Aquinas, Thomas, 32
Arakan, 64–65, 83, 252n1; British in, 72–73
Arnold, Sir Edwin, 100, 160, 166, 202, 210, 245n5; *Light of Asia* by, 23, 128, 136, 143, 145, 180, 206, 213, 218, 220
Aryans, 2, 19, 87, 159, 180, 188, 191, 255n40
Äsala Perahära, 61–62
asthma, 96, 136, 168, 268n36, 274n13; in Burma, 11, 63, 74, 85, 87–88, 116, 141, 156–157, 165; in Ceylon, 50, 87; cigarettes for, 148; in Liverpool, 171; in London, 21, 141, 270n76; treatments for, 2–3, 21, 167, 228, 243n52
astral plane or travel, 60, 70, 241n34, 260n84, 277n47
astrology: Bennett's use of, 24, 32; in Burma, 84; Golden Dawn or magic and, 26, 70, 163, 165, 243–244n54; occultism and, 4, 31–32, 235n3
atmā. *See* soul/self
audiences: for Bax studio lectures, 177–179; Burmese, 82–83, 118, 254n27; Ceylonese, 48, 67–68, 76, 182, 248n32; mixed, 12, 66–67; Theosophist, 49, 182, 185, 211; Western, 12, 83, 118, 141, 157, 161–162, 177, 179, 182, 190, 205, 211–212

Ba Cho, Maung, 119
Baker, Phil, 16, 237n6
Balls, Frank E., 173, 194
Bambalapitiya, 53, 251n56
Ba Myan, 94
Batchelor, Stephen, 220
Bath, 17–18, 172, 228, 237n10, 274n16
Baumann, Martin, 220
Bax, Clifford, 147, 175–177, 189, 193–194, 196, 199, 213. *See also* Bax studio lectures
Bax studio lectures, 177–180, 189, 199; *anattā* in, 181–182, 185–186, 211; Buddha in, 179–180; 'Buddhist World-View', 181–182; 'Four Aryan Truths', 182–183; 'Fundamental Principle', 180–181; 'Path of Attainment', 183–184; responses to, 178; 'Three Refuges', 184
Beamish, L. H. and H. H., 18, 52
Bell, Sandra, 149
Bengalis, 72
Bennett, Allan: as anthropologist, 2; aunts and uncles of, 14–17, 19; birth and childhood of, 13–14, 17; Buddhist Day commemorations of, 214–215; in Burma, 62, 64–65; as Catholic, 22; ceremonial magician (*see* ceremonial magicians: Bennett as); in Ceylon (*see under* Ceylon); death of, 194, **195**; early spiritual interests of, 18, 22–23; education of, 14, 17–19, 22; father of, 13–14, 16, 19, 43, 218, 237n6; finances of, 1, 10, 13, 41, 44, 46; formative years of, 7, 10, 13–47; as Golden Dawn member (*see* Golden Dawn, Hermetic Order of the: Bennett as member of); grandparents of, 10, 13–17, 19, 228; health of, 2, 10, 20–21, 44, 58, 74; importance of, 9, 46; as inventor, 43–45, 245n61; as liminal figure, 1–2, 5; 'lustre' or blasting rod of, 41, 200, 201;

meditation practice of (*see* meditation); mother of (*see* Bennett, Mary Ann); *Note on Genesis* by, 46; notebooks of, 31–35, 40, 44, 50, 55, 200, 241n40, 246n7; as public speaker, 48, 54; racial views of, 2; as scientist, 2, 14, 18–19, 22, 31, 34, 43, 63, 237–238n14, 240n25; sister of (*see* Bennett, Charlotte Louisa; Hill, Charlotte Louisa; Johnson, Charlotte Louisa); sources for life of, 7, 13, 54; as Theosophist, 1, 8, 10, 23–24, 29, 30–31, 43, 223; views about, 1–2, 197; as writer, 14, 48. *See also* Ananda M [Ananda Metteya]; Frater I.A.; MacGregor, Allan

Bennett, Charlotte Louisa, 10, 13, 16–17, 19, 235–236n2. *See also* Hill, Charlotte Louisa; Johnson, Charlotte Louisa

Bennett, Mary Ann [Charlotte P. Corbyn], 5, 10, 13–14, 16–17, 19

Besant, Annie, 27–30, 224, 280n23; Ananda M and, 111–112, 122, 151, 159, 162, 281n50; in Burma, 122–123, 225, 264nn136–138

Bestall, Arthur, 91, 254–255n32, 257–258n56

bhikkhus, 65–67, 84, 154–155; in Ceylon/Sri Lanka, 64, 114, 247n15, 247n27; conventions for, 254n25; names or titles for, 254n25, 260n78; use of Pali by, 54, 246n7. *See also* ordination; Western bhikkhus

Blavatsky, Helena Petrovna, 24–29, 142, 210–211, 235n3, 240n31; death of, 28; Esoteric Buddhism of, 8, 109; Esoteric Section of, 4, 25, 240n32; *Isis Unveiled* by, 242n45; practical occultism and, 4, 25; scandal involving, 24–25; *Secret Doctrine* by, 24, 28; Theosophical Society founded by, 3

Bluck, Robert, 220

Bocking, Brian, 65, 92, 254n29, 262n103

Bodh Gaya, 117–118

Böhme, Edwin, 113

Booth, Martin, 222

Bottomley, Gordon, 213

Bradford, Edgar, 50, 127

British Buddhist, The, 208, 211–212

British Empire, 1, 72–73, 87, 169, 228

British Mahabodhi Society, 208

Brixton Lodge [of the Theosophical Society], 24, 29–31

Brown, Mick, 172, 237n6

Brunton, Paul [Raphael Hurst], 188–189, 213

Bryant, Edward 'Ted', 96–97, 222–223, 271–272n92

Buddha, the, 49–50, 63, 64, 111, 192; Bax studio lectures on, 179–180, 184; biography of, 160; images or *rūpa* of, 102, 114, 117, 194, 209; radio play about, 213; Theosophists on, 224

Buddha Day, 173, 275n20, 280n22

Buddhaghosa, Bhadantācariya, 70, 251n61. See also *Visuddhimagga*

Buddhasāsana Samāgama (International Buddhist Society), 11, 71, 86, 89, 110, 150, 153, 158, 225, 254n27, 262n121; Ananda M's 1908 address to, 111; Christian response to, 143, 257n54; effectiveness of, 142; meetings of, 118, 261n98, 265n3; members of, 98–100; objectives of, 97–98; regional representatives in, 118, 158; revival of, 202–203

Buddhism: Ananda M on 'Dhamma' vs., 157, 160; Bennett's introduction to, 10, 14, 18, 23; misconceptions about, 6, 101–102, 104, 179; occultism and, 3–4, 8–9, 197, 212, 227–228; secular, 227; spread to West of, 3, 9, 149, 154, 156–157, 205; Theosophy and, 3, 8–10, 52, 102, 107–111, 162, 182, 185, 207, 224–225

Buddhism (periodical), 71, 94, 98, 129, 202; contributors to, 101, 105, 116, 125; distribution of, 106, 110, 112, 118; first issue of, 100–105, 179, 260–261n88; last issue of, 157; reviews of, 107–109; second issue of, 263n125; third issue of, 116; Trotman's use of, 158
'Buddhism and the Western World', 190
Buddhism in England, 207, 210–211, 279n21
Buddhist Centre [within the Theosophical Society], 207
Buddhist League, 207
Buddhist Lodge, 182, 207–212, 279n15
Buddhist modernism, 2, 3, 185, 249n39, 252n10
Buddhist Publication Society (Kandy), 5–6
Buddhist Review, The, 143, 148, 173, 212, 262n109; on Ananda M, 146–147, 157, 164, 169, 170, 174; Ananda M's articles in, 186, 190–192; cost of publishing, 153, 173; Ellam and, 187, 222; Honorary Correspondents listed in, 190; last issue of, 187, 192–193, 276n41; lectures published in, 150; new Buddhist Society and, 212; reviews in, 164, 222; Sīlācāra's contributions to, 162
'Buddhist Self-Culture', 169, 212, 223
Buddhist Society, The, 16, 208–212, 219, 249n41, 279n17
Buddhist Society of Great Britain and Ireland, 8, 133, 146, 148, 150–153, 157–158, 161, 162, 222, 265n2; Ananda M's lectures for, 137, 139, 150, 167, 173, 186; Ananda M's letter to, 145; Ananda M's reputation with, 163–165, 228; Ceylonese or Burmese support for, 153, 187, 202; Christian response to, 143; dissolved, 207, 279n22; finances of, 11–12, 146, 150–154, 156, 172, 187, 267n32; founding of, 8, 115, 131–133, 209, 220, 226, 280n30, 281n43; International Buddhist Union and, 190; Liverpool Branch of, 12, 168, 170–172, 273n3; meetings of, 139, 145, 173; members of, 17, 148, 150, 164, 175, 226, 266n16; publications of, 162, 173 (see also *Buddhist Review, The*); Theosophists and, 8, 162, 226, 279n22; World War I–era, 172–173, 186
Buddhist Theosophical Society, 65
Buddhist World Mission, 202–203
Bullock, Percy, 25
Burghers, 66
Burma: Americans in, 90; Ananda M's decision to leave, 166–167; Ananda M's health in, 87, 157, 166; Ananda M's impact on, 118–128, 203–204; Ananda M's ordinations in, 11, 64–65, 71, 73–74, 80–84, 199, 214; Ananda M's residences in, 94–96, 114, 255n35; Ananda M's return to, 5, 11, 71, 146, 150, 218, 220; Ananda M's sponsors in, 7, 65, 73–74, 82–86, 93–94, 98, 118, 123, 129, 151, 158–159, 187; Ananda M's travels in, 119, 228, 263n126; Ananda M's view of, 103–104, 128, 159 (see also 'Religion of Burma'); Bennett arrives in, 72; British in, 50, 72–73, 89–90, 125–126, 159, 256nn48–49, 257n50, 260n91, 261n91; Buddhist sites in, 119, 255n35; Ceylon compared to, 62, 64, 249n40; Chinese or Indians in, 82–83, 88–89, 157, 252n3, 256n46; Crowley's visit to, 47, 62, 73–77, 96; education in (*see* schools: in Burma/Myanmar); missionaries in (*see* missionaries, Christian: in Burma); organizations in, 54, 73, 84–85, 89, 158, 252n4, 278n2 (*see* also *Buddhasāsana Samāgama*);

religious education in, 86, 119, 123–124, 158, 202, 270n78; Theosophists in, 87, 89, 111, 122–123, 223, 225, 264n136; view of Ananda M in, 202–203, 278n3; Westerners in, 87, 101, 112–115, 256n46 (*see also* Dhammaloka, U); women in, 93–94, 103, 257n56, 260n91. *See also* Myanmar

Burma Research Society, 119, 120, 121–122, 258n60, 263n134

Burmese Buddhists: Ananda M's relations with, 125–127, 133, 141, 146, 159; Bodh Gaya cases and, 117; devotional practices of, 2, 63, 103, 121, 160, 180; English-speaking, 11, 83, 96, 117–120, 124, 125–126, 128; fundraising appeals to, 106, 151; lay practices of, 76, 160; in London, 133–134, 150, 187; Mandalay for, 83; ordinations of (*see* ordination: in Burma); reformist, 126; revivalist, 161, 225; scholars, 127; as sponsors, 202 (*see also* Burma: Ananda M's sponsors in); views about, 64, 89–90

Burmese language, 7, 11, 82, 96, 118, 128, 158, 263n129

Burnier, Radha, 225

Buultjens, A. E., 246n10

Bya Sayadaw Khemālaṅkāra Mahāthera, Ven. Shwe, 80

Carus, Paul, 100, 105, 115, 142

caste, 64–65, 247n15

Cave, Henry, 58

census records, 13, 15, 16, 18, 72, 88–89, 235nn1–2, 236n2, 256n46, 270n79

ceremonial magicians: Bennett as, 1, 10, 27, 31, 34–41, 55, 192, 200–201, 221, 241n42; in Golden Dawn, 4, 26–27, 34–35, 203, 221; ingredients used by, 39, 243nn51–52; occultism and, 201, 235n3; rituals of, 35–37, 50; time for, 243–244n54; tools or weapons of, 34–36, 39, 41–42. *See also* Crowley, Aleister: magical system of

Ceylon: Ananda M in, 55–56, 65–71, 87, 89, 104, 125, 164, 179, 228; Ananda M's links to, 115–116; anti-imperialist activities in, 71; Bennett in, 11, 23, 48–59, 189, 218, 221, 227; Bennett leaves for, 7, 10, 44, 46–47, 235n1, 240n26; British in, 1, 5, 18, 50–52, 62, 66, 87, 150, 237n13; *Buddhasāsana Samāgama* in, 115; Buddhist sites in, 61–62, 80, 255n35; caste in, 64; Christian converts in, 48; crime in, 52, 246n11; education in, 51–52, 56, 66–67, 246n10; 'quarter-mile clause' in, 246n10; religious milieu in, 51; Thai Buddhists in, 52, 247n12; Theosophists in, 11, 48–49, 52, 56, 89, 123, 245n2, 251n54; Western *bhikkhus* in, 112–114, 156

Ceylonese/Sri Lankan Buddhists, 1, 50–52, 100, 190; Ananda M's articles published by, 73, 74, 77, 188; Buddhist education in, 246n10; Burmese Buddhists compared to, 62, 64, 249n40; devotional practices of, 2, 63, 65, 255n35, 278n6; English-speaking, 48, 55, 58, 66–67, 113, 115, 204; lay practices of, 61, 76; in London, 54, 153, 187, 207, 208, 214; monastic practices of, 64, 147; ordination of (*see* ordination: in Ceylon/Sri Lanka); Pali studies and, 54–55, 64, 113; revivalists, 65, 71, 105, 110–111, 153, 245n2, 246n10, 249n42; sects or orders of, 55, 64, 247n15; as sponsors, 54, 65, 153, 187, 194, 208, 251n53; Thai Buddhists and, 247n12; views about, 55–56, 62, 64, 65, 87; Westernised, 66, 204

Chalmers, Robert, 247n24
Chennai, 4, 25, 225. *See also* Adyar; Madras
Childers, Robert Caesar, 203, 260n93
Chinese Buddhism, 270n81
Chinese people, 72, 83, 88, 255–256n40
Christians or Christianity, 1, 6, 11, 48, 50, 51, 55–56, 66, 67, 74, 78, 81, 90–91, 187, 227; Bax studio lectures on, 179–180; *Buddhist Review* articles on, 190–191; in Burma, 159, 257–258n56; in Ceylon, 48; criticism of, 91, 114–115, 127. *See also* missionaries, Christian
Churton, Tobias, 281n46
Clapham lecture, 139, 142, 148, 157
Cochrane, Henry Park, 90–92, 257n52
Colombo: Ananda Metteyya in, 65–66, 68–69, 182, 188, 206, 218, 250n50, 251n53; Bennett in, 10–11, 48, 50, 52–53, 55, 57–58; Ramanathan's talk in, 248n32; Theosophical Society in, 48, 217. *See also* Hope Lodge lecture; Maitriya Hall
colonialism, 90, 104, 252n4, 257n50, 264n140; Buddhism under, 11, 67–68, 73–74, 120, 202, 252n4
Colquhoun, Ithell, 200, 244n60
Colston, E. J., 127, 265n149
Colvin, Sidney, 42, 244n58
compassion: Ananda M on, 75, 103, 137, 139, 160–162, 182, 184, 194, 215, 271n83; Buddhism as religion of, 188; Powell-Brown on, 115
Coomaraswamy, Ananda, 56, 138, 210, 248n30
Copleston, Bishop Reginald, 143
Corbyn, Charlotte P. *See* Bennett, Mary Ann
Corbyn, Harry Wardle, 14, 15
Corbyn, Katherine 'Kate' Blandford, 14, 15–17
Corbyn, Louisa, 14–15, 17, 19
Corbyn, Roland, 14, 15

Corbyn, Rosa, 14–15, 17
Corbyn, Sheridan 'Sherry', 14, 15, 19, 236n3
Corbyn, Wardle, 14–17
correspondences, 31–36, 70
Coryn, Herbert, 24, 27, 29–30, 240n31, 241n35
Cox, Laurence, 65, 92, 254n29, 262n103
Crosby, Kate, 249n39
Crow, John L., 6–7, 219
Crowley, Aleister, 196, 210, 218, 245n4, 277n55; autobiography of, 41–42, 165, 222, 235n1; Bax as friend of, 175; Bennett admired by, 165, 197–199, 272n95; Bennett as friend of, 1, 11, 163–165, 199, 271–272n92; Bennett as teacher of, 6, 7, 9, 10, 23, 41, 46, 79, 165, 199, 221–223, 248n35, 272n93; on Bennett's childhood or youth, 22–23, 235n1; Bennett's first meeting with, 41–42; on Bennett's health, 2–3, 50, 58, 240n25; biographies of, 222–223; Bryant letter on, 271–272n92; Burma visited by, 73–77, 89, 96; Ceylon visited by, 47, 50, 52, 55, 58–61, 64; children of, 115; *The Equinox* journal of, 40, 46, 77–79, 164, 276n37; *Key of Solomon* by, 38; levitation stories of, 97, 260n82; *Liber ABA* or *Book Four* by, 199; *Liber Israfel* by, 243n49; *Liber Thisharb* by, 78–79, 253n19, 253n21; *Looking Glass* case and, 163–164, 222–223, 271n91; on 'lustre', 41–42; magical system of, 77–80, 199–200; *Magick Without Tears* by, 199; notoriety of, 11, 47, 163; as To Mega Therion, 9; 'Training the Mind' and, 77–79, 164, 199, 214 (*see also* 'On the Culture of Mind')

Dahlke, Paul, 155, 210
Daḷadā Māligāva, 61

Daw Mya May. *See* Hla Oung, May
demons, 24, 74, 244n57, 245n62
de Silva, P. A., 69
de Silva, Wilmot Arthur, 54, 100, 153, 155, 187, 218
de Unamuno, Miguel, 203
devotion, 2, 63, 103, 121, 160, 180, 225
Dhamma, 157, 160, 184–185, 192. See also *tiratana*
Dhammaloka, U, 1, 98, 121, 180, 219, 262n103; Anagārika Dharmapāla and, 92, 258n58; as anti-imperialist, 1, 92; criticism of Christians by, 91, 127; letters to press from, 91–92, 141–142, 164, 271n91; *Truth* accusations of, 164
Dhammānusārī, Ven. [Walter Markgraf], 112–114
Dhammapada, 55, 75, 114, 160, 183, 252n11
Dhammasami, Ven. Dr. Khammai, 126, 264n144
dhāraṇā, 59
Dharmapāla, Anagārika: Ananda M and, 71, 87, 95, 105, 116–118, 149, 153, 211, 277n51; Ananda M meets, 116, 118; Bodh Gaya campaign of, 117–118; brother of (*see* Hewavitarne, Charles); correspondence of, 87, 150; Dhammaloka and (*see under* Dhammaloka, U); diaries of, 71, 92, 117, 153, 249n40, 251n54, 251n62, 262n114, 262n121, 277n51, 280n23; financial help from, 117, 153, 193, 262n114, 269n55, 277n51; in India, 190; journals of (see *British Buddhist, The*; Maha-Bodhi Society: journal of); in London, 131, 208–209, 211–212, 279n18, 280n26; on London mission, 149; Theosophy and, 208, 280n23. *See also* Maha-Bodhi Society
dhyāna, 59–60. *See also* meditation
Dias, Mrs. Jeremias, 153

Divigalahēna Dēvāgiri Purāna Vihāraya, 52–53, 217
Douglas, Gordon, 254n29
drugs, 2–3, 50, 166–167, 206, 209–210, 221, 228; heroin, 88, 178, 209; opium, 2, 51, 88, 204–205, 246n9
Dublin Lodge Circular [of the Theosophical Society], 29–30
Dyer, Bernard, 18–19, 134, 238n14

Egypt or Egyptians, 4, 23–24, 26, 38, 198, 240n27, 242n47
Eightfold Path, 75, 133, 161, 182–183, 224, 264n137
Ellam, John E., 131, 146–147, 212
Enlightenment, French, 221, 281n45
enlightenment, spiritual, 50, 61, 115, 221, 224, 257n52, 276n35, 281n45. See also *nibbāna*
Esoteric Buddhists, 8, 108–109
Esoteric Section or School, 4, 25, 27–29, 240–241n32
esotericism, 26, 241n34, 242n46; Ananda M/Bennett and, 1, 14, 31–35, 57, 77, 86, 197, 199–201, 203, 206, 217–218, 220–221, 227; Blavatsky's, 25–26, 235n3; Buddhism and, 3–4, 6, 8–9, 102, 108–109, 147, 227; characteristics of, 31–32, 241n37; Crowley's, 248n35; occultism and, 4, 9, 235n3. *See also* occultists; Western Esotericism
Evans, Eric, 213
Evans-Wentz, Walter, 210
'Extension of the Empire of Righteousness . . .', 111

'Faith of the Future', 101, 105, 111, 123, 159, 202, 205; review of, 107–108
Faivre, Antoine, 31
Farr, Florence, 39, 41, 95–96, 244n55, 248n33, 259–260n77, 276n37
Faulkner, Aileen, 207, 208
Felkin, Robert Wlilliam, 37–38
Fernando, J. D., 74, 153

Field, Cyrus, 136, 266n11
Fielding Hall, Harold, 89, 127, 143, 158, 255n40, 256–257n50, 271n85
Fisher, Alexander, 139, 154, 209, 215, 266n16, 280n30
Foster, Mary, 208
Four Noble Truths, 102, 205, 219, 276n31; Bax Studio lecture on, 179, 182; Colombo lecture on, 10, 48–49, 70, 98, 182, 218; 'Doctrine of the Aryas' on, 191–192; 'Faith of the Future' on, 102; 'Four Aryan Truths' on, 182; *Mahā-Maṅgala* and, 153; pamphlet on, 98, 260n85; 'Religion of Burma' on, 160
Franklin, J. Jeffrey, 220
Frater Finem Respie. *See* Felkin, Robert Willliam
Frater I.A., 9, 27, 36–37, 40, 46, 196, 198–199
Frater Petros Xristos, 201
Freemasons, 4, 24, 26, 27
funerals, 4, 90, 194, 276n44
Furnivall, J. S., 121
Fyffe, Rollestone, 143, 267n23

Gardner, Frederick Leigh, 19, 22, 25, 39, 244n60
Gematria, 35
Gethin, Rupert, 214
Gilbert, Robert, 200
goddesses, 59–60
Godwin, Joscelyn, 6, 221, 281n45
Goetia, 41, 44, 244n57
Golden Dawn, Hermetic Order of the: astral travel in, 60, 260n84; Bennett as member of, 1, 5, 6, 10, 23, 27, 31–32, 36–38, 43, 165, 188, 198–199, 203, 208, 210, 212, 220–221, 272n92 (*see also* Frater I.A.); ceremonial magic and, 26–27, 31, 34–37, 40; colours in, 32, 39, 69, 241n39; founding of, 4, 26; Inner or Outer orders of, 26, 27, 35, 242n44, 242n47; leadership of, 26, 43; *Looking Glass* on, 163; meditation in, 69–70; members of, 4, 5, 26–27, 30, 44, 175, 241nn35–36, 248n33, 254n26, 260n77; Ramanathan and, 56–57; reconstructed, 46, 201; scholarship on, 40–41, 200, 221; Secret Chiefs of, 26; theism of, 75; Theosophical Society and, 4–5, 10, 25–26, 175. *See also* rituals: Golden Dawn
Gombrich, Richard, 205, 215
Grant, Kenneth, 272n95
'Great White Brotherhood', 26
Greenly, Annie, 146
Greenly, Edward, 96, 146–147, 149, 152, 168–169, 212, 267n32, 273n1
Greer, Mary, 41, 244n56
Grimm, George, 190
Gueth, Anton, 112. *See also* Ñāṇatiloka, Ven./Thera
Gunn, Battiscombe and Meena, 175–177, 193, 213, 275n23, 275n25, 275–276n29
Guruge, Ananda, 215, 219, 247n19

Hanegraaff, Wouter, 6
Hardy, Robert Spence, 64
Harris, Elizabeth, 5–6, 203–204, 215
Harrison, R. L., 248n31
Hebrew, 32, 35, 36
Hermes, 38–39, 243n51
heroin, 88, 209
Hewavitarne, Charles, 153, 155–156, 187, 194, 196, 208, 276n39
Hewavitarne, Raja, 208
Hill, Alexandria Leslie, 21, 170, 239n17, 274n11, 274n16
Hill, Charlotte Louisa, 12, 21, 168, 170, 172, 228, 238n17, 274n11, 274n16. *See also* Bennett, Charlotte Louisa; Johnson, Charlotte Louisa
Hill, William Leonard Bertram 'W. L. B.', 21, 238n16, 274n16
Hindus or Hinduism, 104, 117, 138, 188, 205, 218; Bennett's knowledge of, 14, 23, 44, 240n25; in

Burma, 72, 88, 103, 123, 159, 252n2, 256n46; in Ceylon, 1, 10–11, 51, 56, 62, 248n31, 251n54; meditation in, 11, 57, 59, 61, 249n39, 250n47; Theosophists and, 4, 44, 122–123
Hla Oung, Ba, 93–94, 133, 158–159
Hla Oung, May (Daw Mya May), 73, 87, 113, 129, 151, 155, 158, 167, 171, 202, 258n67, 259n73, 272n96; accomplishments of, 93–94; article by, 101, 103; in London, 133; monastery built by, 95–96, 114, 119; 'pandol' erected by, 94, 258n65; photos of, **93**, 98, **99**; schools of, 123, 262n105, 264n138
Hla Oung, Tun, 202–203
Hla Oung, U, 93–94
Hodgson-Smith, Basil, 111–112, 139, 259n70
Hollesley Bay Colonial College, 18–20, 22, 50, 52, 237nn12–13
Hope Lodge lecture, 10, 48, 55, 57, 63, 102, 121, 206, 245n3, 250n43, 256n50; publication of, 65
Horne, Jessie Louisa, 30, 241n36
Howe, Ellic, 200, 244n60
Humphreys, Christmas, 64, 147, 149, 166–167, 168, 173, 194, 203, 206, 219, 226, 273n1; on Ananda M, 210; Buddhist Centre/League/Lodge of, 207–209, 279n15, 279nn17–18; Dharmapāla and, 207–208, 280n23; Myokyo-ni and, 280n31; Payne and, 207, 279n21, 279–280n22; as Theosophist, 207, 208, 210, 212, 280n23, 280n34; works by, 209
Hurst, Raphael, 188–189, 213

iddhi, 60–61
imperialism, 1, 3, 74, 153, 159, 202; resistance against, 66, 71, 118, 126
India: British, 72; Buddhist sites in, 117–118, 190; Theosophical Society in, 4, 25

Ingan Mahāwithudayon Sayadaw, 84–85, 255n33
initiations, 24, 26–27, 41, 198–199, 241nn35–36
Inner Group [within Blavatsky's Esoteric Section], 25, 28, 29
insomnia, invention to cure, 43–45
International Buddhist Society. See *Buddhasāsana Samāgama*
International Buddhist Union, 190

Jackson, Mark, 2
Jackson, R. J., 131
Janaka, Ashin, 83, 118
Japan or Japanese, 105–106, 117, 160, 255n40, 261n97
Jayasundara, A. D., 82
Jayatilaka, D. B., 174, 275n20
Jayatilaka, J. B., 190
*jhāna*s, 60, 69, 76, 181, 183–184, 189, 193, 248–249n37, 255n38, 264n141
Jinarajadasa, C., 226, 255n40
Johnson, Charlotte Louisa, 19–21, 172, 218, 228. *See also* Bennett, Charlotte Louisa; Hill, Charlotte Louisa
Johnson, Godfrey Barrington, 19–20
Johnston, R. F., 89, 256n49
Jones, Charles Standsfeld, 79; as Frater V.I.O., 80, 253n20
Jones Jr., George Cecil, 44, 142, 163–164, 245n62, 271n91, 277nn54–55
Judge, William Quan, 27–31, 223
Jupiter, 36, 38, 163, 244n54

Kabbalah or Kabbalists, 26, 32, 35, 39, 46, 242n46, 242–243n47, 245n64, 246n6
Kaczynski, Richard, 223
Kamburugamuwa, 10, 52–56, 64, 217–218
kammaṭṭhāna, 75, 86, 250n47
Kandy, 58–61, 68; 'Marlborough' bungalow in, 58–59, 248n34

karma/kamma, 4, 75, 81, 141, 159, 181, 192, 266n21, 276n35, 277n47
*kasina*s, 69
Kelly, Gerald Festus, 115, **116**
Kelly, Rose Edith, 115
Kelly, Talbot, 83, 88
King, Francis, 200
KoKo Maing, U, 203
Kramer, Heinrich, 32
Krishnamurti, 122
Kumāra Mahāthera, U, 113
Kunz, Fritz, 111, 259n70, 261–262n102
Kyarook Sayadaw, 73
Kyaw Yan, U, 84–86, 190
Kyayouq Kyaung, 73–74

Lachman, Gary, 222
Lanman, Charles, 5, 94, 129, 138, 265n148
Lat, Maung, 122, 264n137
'Law of Righteousness', 116, 252n8
lay people: Burmese, 76, 160; Ceylonese, 61, 76; Western, 114
Leadbeater, Charles Webster, 111–112, 122, 225, 259n70
Ledi Sayadaw, 121, 125–126, 158, 253n13, 254n27, 264nn141–143
Levett, Harold John, 30, 241n36
light, 27, 44, 77, 82, 137–138, 253n18, 254n26, 260n84
Light of Asia, The. See Arnold, Sir Edwin
Lindsay, William, 24
Liverpool, 167, 274n8; Ananda M in, 12, 146, 168–169, 170–172; Ananda M leaves, 172, 228; Buddhist Society in, 12, 168, 170–172, 273n3; Dharmapāla in, 211; as port, 86, 146, 167, 169, 274n11, 274n16; World War I–era, 169–171
London: air quality or climate in, 21, 38, 44, 130, 239n20; Ananda M's final years in, 12, 64, 117, 172, 175, 177, 218, 228; Ananda M's lodgings in, ix, 132, 169, 172, 177; Ananda M's mission to, 1, 47, 52, 117, 130–139, 141–143, 145–147, 164, 228; Ananda M's reputation in, 163–164, 245n62; Bennett's birth in, 13, 17, 136, 235n1; Bennett's employment in, 18–19, 22; Bennett's family in, 13, 15–17; *bhikkhu* for, 154–156, 202; Booth's poverty maps of, 236–237n5, 237nn7–9; *Buddhasāsana Samāgama* in, 100, 131, 133; Buddhist organizations in, 279n18 (*see also* Buddhist Centre; Buddhist League; Buddhist Lodge; Buddhist Society, The; Buddhist Society of Great Britain and Ireland; International Buddhist Union; Sri Saddhatissa International Buddhist Centre); Buddhist Shrine Room in, 207; Buddhists in, 153, 209, 211, 214; Burmese in, 126; Ceylonese/Sri Lankans in, 54, 153, 214–215, 217; changes in, 130–131, 239n19; monastery in, 153–154, 187; occultists or Golden Dawn in, 4, 10, 37; Theosophists in, 24–25, 106–107, 177, 181; *vihāra*s in, 208, 215; 'wettest summer' in, 38; World War II–era, 126
Looking Glass, 142, 163–164, 222–223, 228, 271n91

MacGregor, Allan, 5, 10, 43–44, 134, 198, 205, 220, 240n26, 265n6; in Ceylon, 48–50, 53, 245n3 (*see also* Hope Lodge lecture); Olcott on, 106–107, 109. *See also* Ananda M [Ananda Metteya]; Bennett, Allan; Frater I.A.
MacGregor Mathers, Samuel Liddell. *See* Mathers, Samuel Liddell MacGregor
MacGregor Reid, George Watson, 141, 146, 148, 150, 152, 266n13, 266n21
Madawela, Tissa, 217
Maddox, Ron, 219
Madras, 73, 91–92, 94. *See also* Adyar; Chennai
Maeder, Clara Fisher, 14

magic. *See* ceremonial magicians
magic lantern slides, **61**, **62**, **71**, 80, **119**
Maha-Bodhi Society, 65, 114, 116, 118, 208, 211–212, 225; journal of, 116, 121, 135, 150, 153, 156, 212, 262n110, 280n23
Mahayana Buddhism, 102, 109, 155, 261n90
Mahinda Nayaka Thera, Handupelpola, 54, 217, 219
Mahindaratne, Hewadiddenige, 53–54, 247n14
Maitriya Hall, 55–56, 66, 68–69, 71, 204, 251n53
Ma Mra Nyo, 73, 74
Mandalay, 118, 254–255n32, 258n56; Ananda M in, 83–85, 119, 126, 255n33; Besant in, 124, 264n137; Ledi Sayadaw in, 125–126, 158; reformist fraternity or Shwegyin Nikāya in, 11, 83, 255n33; schools in, 124
Mānitasirī, U, 84–85, 254n31
Markgraf, Walter. *See* Dhammānusārī, Ven.
Matara, 53, 55, 247n26
Mathers, Samuel Liddell MacGregor, 26, 27, 43–44, 48, 70, 201, 245n60; Ananda M's adoption by, 43, 244n59
Maung Mya, U, 153
May Oung, U, 94, 121, 259n73, 263n134
McGuire, John, 257n53
McKechnie, John, 112, 208, 260n77. *See also* Sīlācāra, Ven.
McMahan, David, 8
Mead, George Robert Stow, 29, 31, 107, 109
meditation: Ananda M's/Bennett's practice of, 1, 11, 47, 50, 55–60, 86, 96–97, 103, 125, 134, 176, 185–186, 189, 205, 249n39, 250n47, 255n38, 272n92, 275–276n29; Ananda M's/Bennett's teaching of, 75–77, 160–162, 180, 182–183, 221; *ānāpāna-sati*, 63; *borān kammaṭṭhāna*, 249n39, 250n47; *brahmavihāra*s, 75, 79; Buddhist, 47, 55, 57, 59–60, 63–64, 67, 69, 73, 75, 152, 160, 213, 224, 249n39, 253n18; in Burma, 63, 64, 73, 76, 86, 126, 253n13, 264n141; in Ceylon, 60, 76, 247n27, 249n39; by Crowley, 59–61, 79, 96, 221, 248n35; esoteric, 86; in Golden Dawn, 69–70, 77, 260n84; *kammaṭṭhāna*, 75, 86, 161, 250n47; *kasina*, 69; *mettā* or loving kindness, 63, 75, 77; on past lives, 76–77, 79–80, 184; research on, 152, 228; *samādhi* or *sammāsamādhi*, 59–60, 75, 76, 183, 191, 225, 271n84; *samatha* or tranquility, 63, 75–76, 86, 250n47, 253n12, 255n38; *sati* or *sammāsati*, 183, 191, 225, 253n14; technical terms for, 59, 253n14; in Theosophical Society, 25; *vipassanā* or insight, 63, 75, 76, 86, 126, 250n47, 253nn12–13; yogic or Hindu, 1, 11, 56–61, 86, 250n47
Mendelson, Michael E., 84, 85, 255n33
Mercury [astrological planet], 38–39, 163, 165, 243n51, 244n54
Milindapañha, 104, 275n26
Mills, Edmund, 131, 152, 154–156, 169
Mingun Sayadaw, 253n13
Minson, George Samuel, 30, 241n36
Min Yu Wai, 84–85, 203
'Miraculous Element in Buddhism, The', 191
missionaries, Buddhist, 143, 145, 151, 203. *See also* Ananda M: as missionary
missionaries, Christian, 1, 6, 11, 64, 82, 257n52, 260n91, 276n31; in Burma, 50, 74, 90–91, 123, 127–129, 143, 253n53, 257n55, 257–258n56; in Ceylon/Sri Lanka, 48, 55–56, 74, 245n2, 246n10; criticism of, 51, 91, 114; schools of, 51, 123, 257n56; SPG, 90, 91, 124,

128, 143, 158, 257n56; Temperance Societies of, 69
Monin, P., 95–96, 119, 125, 260n78
Moulton, James Hope, 138
Mullen, Kenneth, 172, 218
Müller, Max, 109, 203, 210
Muslims, 72, 88, 159
Myanmar, 7, 94, 206, 215, 252n1, 255n35, 256n50, 278n2; Buddhist sites in, 255n35; Theosophists in, 89; view of Ananda M in, 202–203. *See also* Burma
Myokyo-Ni, 210, 280n31
mythology, 24, 26, 205, 281n45

names: Ananda M/Bennett/MacGregor's, 5–6, 13, 27, 43, 73, 106–107, 134, 174–175, 198, 224, 252n5; for *bhikkhus*, 254n25, 260n78; divine, 36–37, 242n46, 260n84; in Golden Dawn, 27
Ñāṇamoli, Bhikkhu [Osbert Moore], 114
Ñāṇaponika, Bhikkhu [Siegmund Feniger], 114
Ñāṇatiloka, Ven./Thera [Anton Gueth], 93, 95, 112–114, 161, 203, 205, 262n104
Nandamālābhivaṁsa, U, 84–85, 254n31
Nandasāra, Hegoda, 208
Ñāṇissara, Mahāgoda, 66
nats, 103, 108, 127
Neumann, Karl, 100, 106
newspapers. *See* periodicals
nibbāna, 50, 68, 90, 104–105, 115, 116, 161, 176, 182, 185, 192, 260n93, 267n23, 277n3
nirvana. See *nibbāna*
non-self doctrine. See *anattā*
non-violence, 160, 161, 162, 262n109
Ñyānasirī, Sr. [Helen Wilder], 250n45, 250n49, 275n28, 277n50

Obeyesekere, Gananath, 205
occultism: Ananda M/Bennett abandons (or not), 1, 5, 10, 12, 31, 44, 46–47, 50, 60, 112, 145, 146–147, 165, 200–201, 227; Buddhism and, 3–4, 8–9, 197, 212, 227–228; definition of, 4, 231, 235n3; history of, 3–5, 200–201; principles of, 31; sleep of Siloam in, 36, 242n45
occultists: Blavatsky and, 4–5, 24–25, 231n3; Golden Dawn and, 26, 31, 200; Gunns and, 175; Hinduism and, 3–4; modern or reconstructionist, 46, 80, 200, 253n21; practical, 4, 25; view of Ananda M/Bennett of, 197, 200–201, 221, 276n37
Ohn Ghine, M. M., 117, 278n1
Olcott, Henry Steel, 3–4, 8–9, 56, 65, 122, 210; Ananda M and, 106–107, 109–111, 196; Besant-Judge conflict and, 27–29; Blavatsky's rift with, 25; obituary for, 111
Oliver, Ian, 220, 281n43
Oman, John Campbell, 143
'On the Culture of Mind', 65, 74, 75–80, 103, 160–161, 164, 176, 183–184, 192, 223; Crowley's changes to, 77–78, 164 (*see also* Crowley, Aleister: 'Training the Mind' and)
'On Religious Education in Burma', 86, 98, 124
Open Court, The, 121, 142, 156–157
Open Door, The, 202–203
oral traditions, 59, 149
ordination: of Ananda M, 5, 11, 22, 64–65, 73, 80–81, 83, 116, 141; in Burma, 11, 62, 64, 73, 80–81, 83–84; Burmese terms for, 83; in Ceylon/Sri Lanka, 64, 114, 247n15; *sāmaṇera* (novice), 11, 55, 73–74, 81, 113–114, 126, 205, 250n43, 262n105; *upasampadā* (higher), 11, 73, 80–84, 113, 116, 126, 141, 205, 250n43, 254n29, 265n147; water, 81, 83
ordination speeches, 22, 65, 73, 81–82, 86, 106

Ordo Rosae Rubeae et Aureae Crucis (R.R. et A.C.), 36, 242n44
Ordo Templi Orientis, 7
orientalism, 2, 6, 87–88, 104, 227, 235n3
orientalists, 3–4, 53, 63, 93, 104, 121, 138, 160, 247n19
Osiris, 23, 37

Pagan [Bagan], 119
Pali, 10, 54–55, 73, 74, 75, 82, 85, 86, 97, 113, 127, 185, 189, 246n7, 250n47, 251n61, 265nn147–148; *paritta* chanting in, 215; translations from, 97, 139, 211, 247n24, 252n11, 253n14, 270–271n81, 278n6
Pali Canon, 2, 73, 183, 185, 191, 276n34, 281n49; *Jātaka*, 54, 247n23; *Suttas*, 76, 77, 106, 183, 203, 276n34, 277n48; as Theravada language, 220, 246n7. *See also* Abhidhamma; Vinaya
Pali Text Society, 106, 124, 127, 131
Paññāsāra, Dehigaspe, 208
Pasi, Marco, 6
past lives, 76–80, 151, 174, 176, 184, 199, 213–214, 253n17, 268n43
Payapyu Sayadaw, 255n33
Payne, Francis, 131, 150, 153, 164, 173, 194, 207–208, 271n86, 275n20
Pearn, B. R., 88, 89, 256nn46–47
Pegu (Bago), 118, 119, 124
Peiris, William, 206
Pemberton, Jean, 170, 274n15, 276n44
Pereira, Cassius, 52–54, 57–58, 63–64, 71, 76, 87, 96, 116, 148, 157, 175, 187, 189, 193, 203, 249–250n43, 252n62; on Bax studio lectures, 178, 180; as editor, 278n6; meditation booklet by, 250n47; obituary by, 194, 223; ordination of, 204, 250n43
Pereira, Jeannie, 53, 66
Pereira, J. E. Richard, 53–54, 66, 100, 113, 153, 187, 218, 251n53

periodicals: Ananda M–U Dhammaloka conflict in, 91–92, 141–142; in Bangkok, 91–92; *bhikkhu* advertisement in, 155–156, 270n70; Buddhist, 65; in Burma/Myanmar, 73, 92, 120, 122, 135, 142, 143, 202, 254n27, 264n141; in Ceylon/Sri Lanka, 59, 115, 196, 206, 245n3; Christian, 142–143; death notices in, 196; in Great Britain, 42, 92, 95, 131–137, 142–143, 145, 147–148, 155–156, 178, 186, 196, 267n24, 275n20; in India, 91; Theosophist, 109, 110, 111, 122, 142, 151, 248n33; in United States, 21, 136, 143. *See also Buddhism* (periodical); *Buddhist Review, The*; Crowley, Aleister: *The Equinox* journal of; *Looking Glass*; *Open Court, The*; *Sarasavi Sandaresa*; *Truth, The*
Perreira, Todd LeRoy, 2, 220–221, 271n81
Phay Zaw Gyi, 203, 206, 278n4
Phelps, Myron, 57
Pike, Albert, 4
Piyadassi, Galayaye, 214, 217–219
Piyaratana, Doḍandūvē, 66
Poggendorff, Johann Christian, 22, 240n23
Po Me, Moung, 101, 103
Poussin, Louis de La Vallee, 138
Powell, Charles F., 251n54
Powell-Brown, Capt. J., 95, 166–167, 259n73
Powell-Brown, Ethel, 95, 97, 114, 152, 165–167, 168–169, 259n73, 260n82
Power, E. E., 208
prāṇāyāma, 58, 59, 63, 250n47
precepts, five, 56
'Propaganda', 129, 143, 159, 221
Protestant Buddhism, 3
Prothero, Stephen, 4, 9
Purser, William, 90–91, 127

races or racism, 2, 87, 170, 191, 255n40, 256n49

Rakkhine. *See* Arakan
Ramanathan, Ponnambalam (Sri Paránanda), 1, 10–11, 56–61, 189; speeches of, 56, 248n32; teacher of, 248n31; Theosophists and, 56–57, 248n33
Rāmañña Nikāya, 55
Ramesh, Jairam, 220
Rangoon, 11, 107, 112, 160, 170, 256nn46–48, 262n121, 271n86; Ananda M describes, 103; Ananda M in, 86–87, 95–97, 119, 120–121, 136, 141, 158, 166, 223; Ananda M travels beyond, 118–119, 228; British or Westerners in, 86, 88–90, 114, 135, 143, 159, 256n46; *Buddhasāsana Samāgama* in, 71, 86, 114, 119, 281n43; cosmopolitanism of, 86, 88–89, 256n46; Crowley in, 96; Dharmapāla in, 117–118; Ledi Sayadaw in, 126; missionaries in, 90–91, 257n54, 257n56; reformists in, 126; sponsors in, 73, 86, 93–95, 121, 123; Theosophists in, 122–123, 259n70, 264n136
Rangoon College, 82, 120, 127, 173, 263nn127–129, 265n147
Rangoon College Buddhist Association, 64, 119, 120–121, 126, 128, 158, 225
Ratnajinendra, M., 206
Reeves, Oswald, 156
Regardie, Israel, 200, 222
reincarnation, 4, 7, 79, 102. *See also* past lives
'Religion of Burma', 122, 158–159, 183, 203, 221, 223; Besant's version of, 111, 122, 162, 224, 281n50; omissions in, 159
Religion of Burma and Other Papers, The, 5, 210, 223–225
Rēvata Thera, Veragampita, 53–54
Rhys Davids, Caroline, 105, 138, 156, 203; articles by, 98, 101, 103, 105; in *Buddhasāsana Samāgama*, 100; in Buddhist Society for Great Britain and Ireland, 156, 226; letters to, 87; translations by, 87, 258n60
Rhys Davids, T. W., 3, 105, 106, 131, 138, 150, 203, 210, 226; in *Buddhasāsana Samāgama*, 100; in Buddhist Society for Great Britain and Ireland, 131–132, 226; letters to, 152
rituals: Buddhist, 74, 85, 103, 155, 215, 279n10; Egyptian elements in, 240n27; Golden Dawn, 31, 35–38, 49–50, 55, 77, 82, 200, 241n41, 242n46, 243nn48–49, 246n6, 253n18, 254n26, 272n93 (*see also* Taphthartharath)
Robertson, Alec, 57–58, 63, 66, 204, 250n43, 278n7
Rogers, John D., 69
Rosher, Charles, 39, 41
Ross, G. R. T., 82, 119, 122, 127, 263n133
Rost, Ernst Reinhold, 134, 136, 149–150, 165; on British mission, 131–132, 146; on Clapham talk, 139, 148, 157; Fisher and, 154, 280n30; interview with, 133; as sponsor, 93, 98
Rost, Reinhold, 93, 258n59

saddhā, 64
Śaivites or Śaivism, 10–11, 50, 56, 58
samādhi. See meditation: *samādhi* or *sammāsamādhi*
samatha. See meditation: *samatha* or tranquility
Sangha, 13, 63, 67, 110, 167, 185, 199, 201; Burmese, 80, 210, 264n141; Ceylonese/Sri Lankan, 55, **62**, 64, 66, 215; as refuge or jewel, 65 (see also *tiratana*); ritual culture of, 85; in West, 81–82, 153
saṅkhāra, 75, 76
Sankin Sayadaw, 84–85, 167, 254n31
Sanskrit, 97, 270n81

Sarasavi Sandaresa, 65, 66, 68, 69
Sāsana-Dhaja, U [E. H. Stevenson], 114, 153–154, 269n54, 269n64
Saunders, Kenneth, 90, 127
Sayā U Pyé, 127, 265nn147–148
schools, 17–19; in Burma/Myanmar, 84, 86, 94, 103, 119, 120–121, 123–125, 158, 203, 264n140, 270nn78–79, 278n2; in Ceylon, 51, 56, 68–69. *See also* Hollesley Bay Colonial College; Rangoon College
'Scientific Analogy', 192
Sepher Sephiroth, 46
Servants of the Buddha, 58, 204–206, 252n62, 278nn6–7
Shwe Pyar Sayadaw, 278n3
Shwedagon Pagoda, 89, 94, 95, 103; 'In the Shadow of . . .', 93, 121
Shwegyin Nikāya, 83–85, 126, 255n33
Shwekyimyin Pagoda, 85, 255n35
sīla, 64
Sīlācāra, Ven. [John McKechnie], 95, 112–114, 121–123, 162, 173, 202, 203, 210, 262n105, 275n18
Singho, Peter, 247n14
Sinhala, 7, 55, 65, 115
Sinnett, Alfred P., 8, 108
Sittwe. *See* Akyab
Siyam Nikāya, 247n15
Smith, Garnet, 178
snakes, 39, 54, 243n51
Societas Rosicruciana in Anglia (SRIA), 26
soul/self: Buddhist view of, 49, 182, 184–186, 211, 276n35 (see also *anattā*); Christian view of, 158, 257n54; Egyptian view of, 23; Theosophical view of, 49, 57, 102, 108, 111, 142, 177, 185–186, 277n47, 280n34
spiritual seekers, 8, 227
spiritualism, 141, 191, 205–206; Blavatsky's view of, 3–4; Buddhist revival in, 65; criticism of, 138, 277n47; modern, 3

Sri Lanka, 7, 10; view of Ananda M in, 202, 205–206, 214–215, 217–218. *See also* Ceylon
Sri Saddhatissa International Buddhist Centre, 12, 54, 205, 214, **216**, **217**, **218**, 219
Starr, Roland Meredith, 186, 189, 276n37
Stevenson, E. H. *See* Sāsana-Dhaja, U
Stewart, Josephine Madeleine Corbyn, 14, 15, 19, 236n4
Stewart, Katharine Alexandra, 15, 236n4
Stewart, Walter James Lionel, 15, 236n4
Story, Francis, 212
Strauss, C. T., 190
suffering (*dukkha*), 3, 49, 185, 188, 190, 192
Suffolk, 18
Sumaṅgala, Hikkaḍuvē, 66, 100, 142
Sutin, Lawrence, 222, 281n46
Suzuki, D. T., 138, 190, 210
Symonds, John, 222, 271n92

talismans, 35–36, 241n38; Bennett's consecration of, 36–39, 41, 46, 188, 200, 242n43, 243n48
Tan Hmaw Yan, 157
Taphthartharath, 38–41, 46, 48–49, 165, 200, 221, 243n49, 244n54, 244n56, 246n6, 272n92
Tejarama Thera, U, 74
temperance, 68–69, 123, 221, 251n60
temples, 24, 88, 247n12; in Akyab, 72, 252n2; Bodh Gaya, 107; in Ceylon, 10, 52, 54, 56, 61–62; classes in, 124, 203; Daḷadā Māligāva, 61; in Great Britain, 134–135, 212, 218; in Mandalay, 83; in Rangoon, 95, 103. *See also* Vajirarāma Vihāraya
Tha Do Aung, 74
Thai Buddhists, 52, 247n12, 247n15
Tha Nu, Dr., 65, 73–74, 116, 278n3
Thathanabaing, the, 119, 263n125

Theosophical Society: in America, 6, 27, 30–31; Ananda M and, 139–140, 177, 218, 220, 223–226; Bennett's membership in, 24, 223 (*see also* Bennett, Allan: as Theosophist); Besant-Judge conflict in, 27–31; Buddhism and (*see under* Buddhism); 'East' for, 4; eclecticism of, 24; in England, 7, 24–25, 106; Esoteric Section of (*see* Esoteric Section or School); founding or founders of, 3–4, 24, 27; Golden Dawn and (*see under* Golden Dawn, Hermetic Order of the); in India, 4, 25, 106, 225; influence of, 10; Masters or Mahatmas of, 4, 25, 26, 29; philosophical Brahmanism and, 75; racial views of, 87, 255n40; scandals in, 27–29; scholarship on, 9; Spiritualists and, 277n47. *See also* Burma: Theosophists in; Ceylon: Theosophists in; London: Theosophists in

Theravada Buddhism, 49, 54, 63, 203, 208–209, 214, 251n61, 278n1; Ananda M's use of term, 2, 159, 220–221, 271n81; meditation in, 249n39; *Open Door* defends, 203

Theravada Buddhists. *See* Burmese Buddhists; Ceylonese/Sri Lankan Buddhists

Thitthila, U, 126, 265n146
Thoth, 23, 38–40, 243n50
Thudhamma, 83–84, 113, 263n125
Tibet, 4, 173, 190
Tibetan Buddhism, 59, 261n90, 270n81
Tike Soe, 119
Tin Myint Moe, U, 203
tiratana, 65, 81, 160, 184
Tisdall, Rev. W. St. Clair, 143
To Mega Therion, 9. *See also* Crowley, Aleister
Trainor, Kevin, 75, 279n10
Trotman, Francis, 143, 158
Truth, The, 141–142, 163–165, 271n91

Tumlong, 173
Turner, Alicia, 65, 92, 94, 254n29, 262n103
Turner, Victor, 235n2
Tweed, Thomas, 8

U Byar Tawya Monastery, 94–95
United Kingdom, 7, 210, 214, 217, 219–220
United Kingdom Buddhist Day, 214–217
United States of America, 12, 20–21, 27, 46, 170–171
upasampadā. *See* ordination: *upasampadā*

Vâhan, The, 29–31
Vajirañāna, Paravahera, 208
Vajirañāna, Pelene, 53
Vajirarāma Vihāraya, 53, 204, 247n21, 250n43, 250n47
Vayama, U, 121
vegetarians, 25, 274n13
Vesak, 80–81, 103, 173, 207
Vicāra, Sayadaw U, 85
Vijegunawardhana, Edward Lionel, 69
Vimuttimagga, 76, 253n17
Vinaya, 83, 84, 86, 94, 147, 149, 155, 220, 253n22, 276n29
vipassanā. *See* meditation: *vipassanā* or insight
Vipassi Thera, Malandeniye, 54
Visuddharama East Monastery, 84–85, 255n34
Visuddharama West Monastery, 85, 255n34
Visuddhimagga, 69–70, 75–77, 86, 127, 183, 185, 214, 251n61, 253n17, 265n148
Vythilingam, M., 56–57, 248n32

Waite, Arthur, 175
Webb, Russell, 208–209
West Ridgeway, Joseph, 51–52
Westcott, William Wynn, 25–26

Western *bhikkhus*, 112–114, 141, 153, 171, 206, 209, 217, 254n29, 262n103; advertisement for, 156–157; in Akyab Plan, 82, 101; Burmese view of, 128; Purser and Saunders on, 127–128; residence built for, 94–95
Western Buddhists, 3, 11–12, 48, 91, 127, 141, 150, 180, 227–228, 251n54; statistics about, 131, 148, 150
Western civilisation or society, 81, 86–87, 102, 129, 161, 179, 187, 215, 227–228
'Western Education for Buddhist Bhikshus', 66–68, 125
Western Esotericism, 3, 6, 12, 221, 227; scholarship on, 9, 31, 241n37, 274n7, 274n9
Wijesekera, Anoji, 204–205
Wipulasara Mahathero, Ven. Dr. M., 225
Wisdom of the Aryas, The, 5, 186, 194, 209, 210, 211, 213, 225, 275n27; Pereira's copy of, 250n49, 275n28
Woodman, William Robert, 26

Woodward, Frank Lee, 52
World Buddhist Missionary Association, 158
World War I, 169–171, 173–174, 186, 188, 238nn16–17
Wright, Arnold, 93
Wright, Dudley, 138, 277n47

Yeats, William Butler, 4, 25, 95, 96, 259–260n77
yoga, 190, 205, 221, 248n35, 249n39; Bennett's study of, 10–11, 56–58, 61, 86, 189, 203, 227; occultism and, 60; Ramanathan's guru for, 248n31. *See also* Ananda M [Ananda Metteya]: as yogi
Youatt family, 170–172, 189
Young Men's Buddhist Association, 65

Zalewsky, Pat, 41, 243n48
Zan Aung, U Shwe, 87, 93, 121–122, 258n60, 263n132, 263n134, 265n149
Zedi Saradaw, Shwe, 73
Zen Buddhism, 210, 280n31

www.ingramcontent.com/pod-product-compliance
Lightning Source LLC
Chambersburg PA
CBHW050837230426
43667CB00012B/2037